Forfar Athletic On This Day

Forfar Athletic On This Day

David W. Potter

with a Foreword by
David McGregor

Kennedy & Boyd

Kennedy & Boyd
an imprint of
Zeticula Ltd
Unit 13
196 Rose Street
Edinburgh
EH2 4AT
Scotland

http://www.kennedyandboyd.co.uk
admin@kennedyandboyd.co.uk

First published in 2017
Copyright © David W. Potter 2017
Cover design © Zeticula Ltd 2017

Every effort has been made to trace copyright holders of images. Any omissions will be corrected in future editions.

ISBN 978-1-84921-166-6

All rights reserved. No part of this publication may be reproduced, stored in a retrieval system, or transmitted in any form or by any means, electronic, mechanical, photocopying, recording or otherwise, without the prior permission of the publishers.

Acknowledgements

I owe a great deal to a great deal of people.

First of all David McGregor – "Mr Forfar Athletic" himself – who has been kindness personified, and allowed me access to all the vast collection of programmes.

My old friends Richard Grant and Phil H Jones were also very helpful and encouraging, as was my old Primary School classmate Robert Black, son of the legend of that name in the 1930s and nephew of Willie.

David Carnegie and a few others answered my appeal on Facebook.

My distant cousin with the same name as myself, one time Treasurer of the club, and whose family were more or less built in with the bricks, was also very helpful, and Alec Hamill of Glenrothes, one-time player and captain of the club was likewise.

(Alec and I share a passion, which it is maybe not appropriate to mention here!)

I was also helped and encouraged by Duncan Carmichael, an "honest man" if ever there was one, who wrote a similar book on Ayr United.

Perhaps last, but certainly not least, to the supporters who have helped the club remain part of our lives through what sometimes have been variable fortunes.

Inevitably, I shall have missed a few people out. I apologise unreservedly.

Forfar Athletic F.C.

COMPLIMENTARY TICKET*

* THIS TICKET ENTITLES ANY CHILD UNDER 16 YEARS OF AGE FREE ENTRY TO ANY GAME, WHEN ACCOMPANIED BY A FULL PAYING ADULT, DOES NOT INCLUDE CUP GAMES.

Child's Complimentary Ticket.

Foreword

As the esteemed author of this publication stated in his introduction to one of the twenty-odd books he has penned over many a year, *Wee Troupie, the life story of Forfar and Everton legend Alec Troup*, 'Forfar Athletic are a proud wee team.'

This is indeed true, and all currently connected with the club are very proud that David W. Potter has put 'pen to paper' once again to write what is only the third book published about the 'Loons' in our 132 year history.

The first was our *Centenary History*, the second in 2009, the *Forfar Greats* which also had David as its author.

I have personally known David since our primary school days at the North School in the 'toonie' – the historic building so sadly ravaged by fire in October 2016 – and also as proud members of the 2nd Forfar Boys Brigade.

Since those far off days in the 1950s, we have shared a great love of both football and cricket. Although David has been an exile from Angus for over five decades, it has always been a pleasure to meet up and share an opinion or two on both.

It has also been of great interest to me to watch David's literary career flourish over time. He was a much more accomplished academic at both the primary and secondary school than I could ever have aspired to be, and this has certainly borne fruit in regard to the many publications on diverse subjects he has had published.

Back to Forfar Athletic and despite his first love in the game always having been a Glasgow club, his interest in the 'wee' club fae Farfar has never waned.

I am sure this book will bring many happy memories back to long standing and at times suffering Athies supporters, but also be of great interest to fans of all ages.

David McGregor
Secretary – Forfar Athletic FC
1984 –

PS – Having had a sneak preview of the January chapter, I was in fact one of the pupils who had to make their way to Mr. Gillespie's office the day after the Clyde replay!

Contents

Acknowledgements	*vii*
Foreword	*ix*
Programme Covers	*xiii*
Illustrations	*xv*
Illustration Acknowledgements	*xix*
Introduction	1
July	5
August	39
September	79
October	115
November	151
December	191
January	229
February	275
March	311
April	349
May	385
June	421
In These Years	455
Index	*521*

Programme Covers

Aberdeen home 7 January 2012	230
Alloa Athletic away 3 May 1986	386
Annan Athletic home 13 March 2010	327
Brechin City home 9 November 2013	163
Clyde away 3 November 1984	156
Clyde home 22 November 1980	180
Clydebank home 4 February 1985	276
Cowdenbeath home 1 November 2014	152
Cowdenbeath home 12 March 2002	330
Cowdenbeath home 30 August 1975	71
Cowdenbeath home 31 December 1994	225
East Fife home 8 October 1983	116
East Stirlingshire away 1 March 1975	312
East Stirlingshire home 21 April 1984	350
Edinburgh City away 6 August 2016	40
Falkirk home 12 November 1977	168
Forres Mechanics home 10 January 2009	244
Linlithgow Rose away 9 January 2016	241
Livingston away 1 March 2011	314
Livingston away 22 January 2011	261
Montrose home 28 October 1986	145
Montrose home 31 December 1983	226
Morton home 16 March 2002	330
Partick Thistle home 10 September 1988	92
Queen of the South away 1 November 1986	154
Queen of the South away 30 September 1950	113
Queen's Park away 6 March 1982	320
Rangers home 24 February 2002	302
Stenhousemuir home 17 November 2012	174
Stirling Albion away 3 December 2005	192
Stranraer home 23 December 2006	217
Stranraer home 26 September 2015	80

Illustrations

Child's Complimentary Ticket	vi
Frankie Devine	xviii
Forfar Athletic 1979	6
Chairman Sam Smith welcomes Doug Houston and Henry Hall to Station Park	15
Baxter Bridie	21
Craig Brewster	59
Forfar Athletic's first programme	71-77
Stewart Kennedy	95
Tommy Adams and Jimmy Caskie	98
Forfar Athletic v Chirnside United	107
Doug Houston	110
Gordon "Bull" Smith receives the Player of the Month award	114
James Black	121
Ken Brown and teammates celebrate	143
Alex Brash and Danny McGrain lead out the sides	148
Martyn Fotheringham	166
David Bingham scores with his head	170
Alan Rattray	171
Rab Douglas	205
Alec Troup	235
Ticket for the match on 7th January	238
Celebrations after the Forres game	243
Peter Reid's Forfar Rock	254
Ian Rodger goes up for a high ball	255
Before the infamous abandoned game against St Johnstone	259
This game v Berwick Rangers was subsequently abandoned	279
Eddie Falconer comes down during a Forfar attack	288
Jim Bett and Ray Farningham in 1982	296
Patsy Gallacher and Jimmy McColl are the two Celtic players	299
Cheery Forfar supporters in February 2002	304

Derek Parlane heads Rangers' equaliser	306
Skipper Ian McPhee leads the celebrations after promotion	346
Scottish League President David Letham hands over the Second Division Trophy to an elated Ian McPhee	355
Derek Johnstone scores for Rangers in 1982	357
Jim Liddle scores for Forfar against Stranraer on April 7 1984	358
Dundee's Scottish Cup Winning side, with Geordie Langlands	361
Team Lines for 22nd April 2017	374
Alec Troup	391
Patrick Bowes-Lyon, uncle of Queen Elizabeth II	414
The Forfar players and officials setting off for Canada in 1980	422
Tickets for the 50/50 draw.	453
Angus Athletic 1884-85	456
Forfar Athletic 1890 wwith Forfarshire Charity Cup	457
Forfar Athletics Play Up	458
Northern League Champions 1895-96	459
The men who rocked Scotland by their 2-0 win over Falkirk in the Scottish Cup of 1911	460
Forfar Athletc 1922-23.	461
Forfar Athletic 1935-36	462
Forfar Athletic 1928	463
Forfar Athletic 1928-29	464
Forfar Athletic 1932 Team	465
Forfar Athletic 1932	466
Snow on the ground indicates a very cold day	467
Forfar Athletic 1935-36	468
Forfar Athletic 1936 team	469
Presentation of portrait to James Black	470
Forfar Athletic 1948-49	471
Forfar Athletic 1949	472
Forfar Athletic 1949-50	473
Forfar Athletic players and officials. 1949-50	474
William F. Callander, Chairman 1951 - 1970	475
Forfar Athletic 1954	476
Forfar Athletic 1954-55	477
The Loons at Berwick in 1957.	478

Forfar Athletic in April 1958.	479
The Stands - 1: February 15 1958	480
The Stands - 2: January 1959.	481
The Stands - 3: The completed article	482
Forfar Athletic 1958.	483
Forfar Athletic 1960-61.	484
Forfar Athletic in civvies before a game in the early 1960s	485
Forfar Athletic in August 1967.	486
Forfar Athletic 1968-69	487
David Callander, Chairman 1970 - 1976	488
Archie Knox. Player 1965 - 1970, Manager 1976 - 1980	489
Forfar Athletic August 1976	490
Forfar Athletic, December 1977	491
Forfar Athletic 1978.	492
Alex Rae. Manager 1980-1983	493
Forfar Athletic 1981	494
The Loons of 1982 celebrate their Quarter-final success	495
Forfar Athletic Directors in 1984.	496
Centenary Season Club Directory	497
Gordon Webster, Director and Chairman, 1980s	498
Team with Division Two trophy 1984	499
Four Managers at Centenary Dance 1985	500
Forfar Athletic 1995-96	501
Neil Wilson - sometime player, Director and Chairman of the club	502
Forfar Athletic 1997-98	503
Veterans of the great days of the late 1970s	504
Forfar Athletic 1999-2000	505
Dave McGregor welcomes Neil Cooper	506
Forfar Athletic 2001-02	507
Ian Miller, Assistant Manager 2004	508
Forfar Athletic first team squad 2003-04.	509
Ray Farningham - player and Manager	510
George Shaw, Manager 2006/07	511
Forfar Athletic 2008-09	512
Dick Campbell, Manager 2008 - 2015	513

Second Division Playoff Champions 2009-10   514
Forfar Athletic 2011-12   515
Odmar Faero - Forfar's Faroese Internationalist   516
Forfarshire Cup Winners 2014-15   517
Forfar Athletic 2014-15   518
The irrepressible David McGregor   519

Illustration Acknowledgements

Most of the illustrations in this book have come from the club itself, notably the Centenary History of 1995, and the vast amount of illustrations that I found in the Aladdin's Cave of programmes lent to me by the club.

In both cases, I must acknowledge the co-operation of David McGregor and the debt that I owe to the late Jack Cowper, a man whom I met only once, and then very briefly.

I also used a few photos from the Forfar Athletic Handbook of 1949 50.

I also acknowledge the support of the various other clubs who have raised no objection to me using their programme covers.

My old friend Bob Black gave me several cartoons featuring his father.

A big thank you to all concerned.

Frankie Devine

Introduction

I have often heard it said that one can change one's job, one's sexual partner and one's mind; but two things one cannot change is one's mother and one's football club. I am in the fortunate position of not really wanting to change either of these two. I remain grateful to my parents for giving me a good start in life when other people were clearly nothing like as happy, and I am grateful for the life-long love of Forfar Athletic which started some time in about August 1954 when my father took me to the pre-season trial, although my curiosity had been kindled long before that when I used to see my father and grandfather disappear on a Saturday afternoon "up-by" to "the match".

Supporting Forfar Athletic is not easy. It is nevertheless rewarding on occasion. Sometimes, the quality of football is quite awful (and generally agreed to be such by all concerned, not least the players themselves) but there is something character building in "sticking by" someone even in adversity. Losing to Stenhousemuir and Brechin City on soulless rainy, windy, miserable days prepare you for the perils of life far more comprehensively and completely than even the most severe of Calvinistic upbringings. When one joins the Boys Brigade, one does of course flirt with Calvinism, guilt, repression and how one deserves to suffer, but Station Park on a grim November or January day teaches one what suffering is all about!

But that is only one side of the coin. The other is the (admittedly rare) triumphs. Everest was scaled for example in April 1984 – and I was there! We beat Rangers in 2013 and I cursed myself for not having gone, being one of "those of little faith" who did not think it possible and went to a cricket match instead. On the other hand, I have seen them beat St Mirren, Kilmarnock, Motherwell and Hearts, and my grandfather saw them beat Falkirk (then second in the Scottish League First Division) in the Scottish Cup of 1911, so don't anyone dare try to use the word "impossible" in my presence. The impossible does indeed happen sometimes, but one has to stress "sometimes".

Supporting Forfar is not about glamour. I have not hesitated to include in this collection dreary defeats at Dumbarton, Cowdenbeath, Stenhousemuir – to name but a few – and to note that it always seems to rain when we lose at these grim grounds. On the other hand, Station Park is a fine place to visit, and I have a friend from Yorkshire who loves to come to the ground with me for a bridie at half-time, a totally delicious experience which can soothe the most harrowing of bruisings on the football field, Yet there is the undeniable fact that the pitch is not entirely visible from the attractive, robust, yet somewhat ill-designed stand. And I was there at its first game!

Advancing years make a seat desirable, but the time was when I scorned and despised the standites. They were toffee-nosed, middle-class, bourgeois "kind o' fowk". Those were the days when I stood on the terracing and enjoyed the crack and the banter. I loved the railway, and that square half-mile of Forfar Station and Station Park was all that was beautiful in life. To walk up North Street was a pleasure and indeed my boyish excitement intensified as we went under the old railway bridge (now demolished) where stood "Blind Jock" (as he was called) playing his accordion into whose bag I was allowed to throw a coin as he squeezed out "Mary, My Scots Bluebell" or "Westering Home". And then, I paid my nine pence and in I went to see the old wooden stand, virtually blown away in a gale one night in 1958, and legendary characters like Willie Wilson.

You wouldn't have said that Willie was born with a silver spoon in his mouth. A denizen of the local "Poors House" in the Arbroath Road, he went around the town selling sticks. Shamefully mocked and tormented by those who should have known better, Willie nevertheless loved Forfar Athletic, hobbling up North Street with his club foot and his walking stick telling everyone in his high-pitched voice with a speech impediment "Ah think we'll win the day". During the game he showed approval with "That's hut" after a fine piece of play. He was always desolate when we didn't win, but simply buttoned up his threadbare, worn and shabby raincoat and headed home saying "Mebbe next week". Sadly Willie did not live long enough to see 1984.

At the other end of the social scale was the Earl of Strathmore, the grandfather of Queen Elizabeth II. Unlike so many of his class who occasionally had to give the impression of enjoying football, this chap (and the son who succeeded him) was a genuine football and Forfar Athletic supporter, and remains to this day, I think, the only fan who has ever arrived at Station Park to see a game in a chauffeur driven car. This was hardly tactful in the grim economic days of the 1920s and 1930s but the Earl was forgiven a lot for his love of Forfar.

There will be much mention in this book of a man called James Black. This is only right, for he was the man who played for, managed, organised, saved and campaigned for the club – a duty that he did selflessly and uncomplainingly, rightly claiming that he never took a penny for all he did for Forfar Athletic. After all, it was not exactly a job that was going to make him a millionaire! Such selfless devotion, even though he had an inclination to dictatorship and an uncompromising desire to get his own way, was what made Forfar Athletic. He laid down the guidelines for many people in the future – one thinks of Jim Robertson, Sam Smith and David McGregor, to name but three – to lead the club and what it means to the town and so many people – far, far more than the sometimes sparse attendance at home games would have you believe.

The writer may well be accused of concentrating too much on the old days. He accepts that charge and defends himself on two counts – one is that the distant past of Forfar Athletic is in danger of being lost and forgotten about, and the other is that recent past is well enough documented in any case, not least on *You Tube*. Sadly *You Tube* took a long time, far too long, to be invented. What one would give to be able to see "Jeck" Cable in action, the wiles of Eckie Troup, the bustlings of Davie McLean who was always encouraged to "rummle them up" (what does that mean?), a goal from Davie Kilgour (pronounced "Kilgoor" in Forfar) or even some resolute defending from that man whom I never really met but was so much of my childhood – Doug Berrie?

Unashamedly, national events of a footballing and even a non-footballing nature will be mentioned and intertwined with the fortunes of Forfar. Football must always be seen in its context. There will thus be references to the two awful world wars fought in the 20th century and minor ones like the Boer and Falklands wars, the General Strike, political leaders, Coronations, three-day weeks, unemployment, deaths of local people and other things. Football must always offer relief from the horrors of life. Karl Marx once said that religion is the opium of the masses. That is no longer true. It is football.

And football moves with the times. Forfar's first radio broadcast was against Airdrie in 1955, their first TV appearance (in highlights form) was in January 1963 at Hamilton and the programme of April 8 2000 mentions the appearance of Forfar's first ever website. But these technological innovations, incomprehensible to our founding fathers, are sideshows to the main issue, which still consists of trying to score more goals than the other team. That is what football is all about, and it is really such a simple game.

But a lifetime of supporting Forfar must always give one a sense of humour and the ability to shrug one's shoulders and utter the immortal words "That's fitba!" I was no longer living in the town when the depths were plummeted in 1974 and 1975. I tried to feign indifference and even to pretend I didn't come from Forfar when football was mentioned – but, like Peter in the New Testament, "my accent gave me away" when I called everyone "min", or used the word "some" immediately before an adjective – they were "some unlucky", it was "some sair", I was "some no weel" or that Brechin were "some jammy" to get off with a draw.

It is my earnest hope that my readers enjoy this book. It has been a pleasure (occasionally a painful pleasure when detailing a hammering from Cowdenbeath, for example) compiling it. I am grateful to the Forfar programme, *The Forfar Dispatch*, *The Dundee Courier* and other magazines and periodicals. The book is unashamedly dedicated to all who love the club. And that includes you!

David W. Potter,
July, 2017

July

Forfar Athletic 1979. With the Forfarshire Cup after their 3-1 victory over Dundee in July.

July 1 1916

It was a Saturday and it started with a whistle, but there the similarity to football sadly ended, for this was war. It was the first day of the Battle of the Somme, and many Forfarians awaited the whistle that summer's morning, the whistle that was to be the first step, they said, on the journey to take them in triumph to Berlin.

At least four Forfar players – Scott, Mitchell, Wylie and Bruce were to fail to return from that conflict, and many others would return badly maimed or suffering from the mental trauma which war brings and was often described as "shirking" or "malingering" or cowardice. While great tribute was rightly paid to those who played their part, nothing but contempt deserves to be poured on those who led them into it – and the finger has to be pointed at politicians, military leaders, Churches and the Royal Families of Europe.

Some of them were treated as demi-gods in their lifetime, but not necessarily by those who had fought for them. While Armistice Day was always well observed, and rightly still is, in November at Station Park, there were many who found it hard to stomach the sight of the name Earl Haig associated with the sale of poppies.

Forfar suffered dreadfully in this war, although not necessarily any more than any place else. How blessed is my generation and those who have come after me whose conflicts with Germany are on the football field and against men like Franz Beckenbauer, a far more agreeable "Kaiser" than the one he was named after!

July 2 1980

No-one could accuse Archie Knox of being lazy or of lacking in ambition. Hurt by the failure to grab promotion last year and stung by the jibes that his players were "not trying" for promotion – it had certainly been "let slip" for a few seasons now – Archie had all his players back for training at this early date, a good month and a bit before the season would start in earnest, and only a month after the return from Canada, a trip which, he was convinced, would benefit the club in the long run.

His general cause for concern last season was the inexplicable loss of form after the New Year, something that could only be partially explained by injuries and bad weather. In particular, goals had dried up. Station Park was not yet back in commission because of its "annual grass-growing and re-turfing" so the players used the Steele Park (always difficult to have to play football on the side of a hill!) and *The Forfar Dispatch* has pictures of them doing all their physical jerks under the shadow of the Balmashanner War Memorial.

Those who claimed that there was no "close season" at all these days had further reason for their displeasure at the sight of this – players back at training at more or less the same time as the schools were coming off for their holidays! Football was in any case having a bad Press at the moment because its image had been somewhat tarnished by the disgraceful outbreaks of hooliganism at the Scottish Cup final. Someone thought he recognised a Forfar man on the TV among all the "ba'heids" who invaded the park, but no, that couldn't be right!

July 3 1911

Valentine Lawrence, Forfar's right half who had played such a great part in the defeat of Falkirk in February was today transferred to Manchester City. Commonly known as "Tine" or "Val" or even "Lennie", Lawrence had been born in Arbroath but lived in Dundee and had only played one full season for Forfar, but this season had been enough to encourage *The Courier* to say that he was one of the best players who "ever donned a black and blue jersey".

Lawrence could play at left half as well, and of course in the 1910s, the position of wing half was crucial. Newcastle United, then the leading lights of English football had taken him down to Tyneside (where he would hardly have felt homesick, for their team was full of Scotsmen!) for a trial, but changed their mind about him and now Manchester City stepped in. Forfar fans were disappointed, but the Forfar officials would come to a satisfactory financial arrangement with the Manchester club, and everyone wished him well.

In the event, things did not work out for "Tine" at Hyde Road (then home of Manchester City) and he only stayed a year before moving to Oldham. The Great War then disrupted things badly, but he returned to play for Dundee Hibs, Morton and Dumbarton. But his best years were with Forfar. He should have stayed here!

July 4 1934

The Courier today had a report on George McLean who was back in Forfar on an extended holiday having broken his leg playing for Huddersfield Town at the end of last season.

Geordie was very happy about the progress which had been made because everything had knitted together very well and the splints had been removed, although he was still using crutches and did not really expect to be back by the start of the season. He had hopes, however, of being ready to play again pretty soon after. Geordie was of course the younger brother of Davie, and had played for Bradford Park Avenue before joining Huddersfield.

The broken leg had been caused on March 31 1934 when Manchester City defender Sam Barkas (maybe he meant Sam Cowan) had fallen on Geordie's outstretched leg as he was on the point of scoring, and in later years, in his chip shop at the East Port, Geordie would never tire of telling his customers about the incident, and, as is frequently the case, the details became more horrific and the agony became all the worse. In all truth,

Geordie did carry a great deal of justified anger about the injury, not necessarily directed at Sam Barkas, but just at the general unfairness of it all, although his claim that it deprived him of a cap for Scotland was possibly exaggerated. Geordie returned to play for Forfar in 1936, where, although he had a fierce temper and was no stranger to "the early bath", he was still a fine player and only marginally inferior to his brother, the great Davie.

July 5 1946

The AGM of the Scottish League was held in Glasgow today, and it was confirmed that for next season there would be a "C" Division (Eastern Section) consisting of 10 teams, Forfar among them.

The others would be Brechin City, Montrose, East Stirlingshire, Edinburgh City, Leith Athletic and a new team called Stirling Albion who had come into being following the collapse of King's Park, the team who had played in Stirling until their ground suffered bomb damage. Sadly, St Bernard's of Edinburgh had now lost their ground and had effectively resigned from the Scottish League. This made 7 teams and the "C" Division (Eastern Section) was to be made up to 10 with the reserve sides of Dundee, Dundee United and St Johnstone.

After considerable discussion and indeed resistance from vested interests in Division "B", it was agreed that there would be one team promoted and relegated between Division "B" and "C" providing that the winner of Division "C" was a bona fide first team and not a reserve team. The winners of the Eastern and Western sections would play each other if necessary.

All this of course was good news for Forfar and credit must be given, not for the first time, to the political abilities of Jim Black, that inveterate "button-holer" and "knocker-on-doors" on Forfar's behalf. It was also agreed that although the prices for Division "A" and "B" would be 1 shilling and 6 pence, for Division "C" it would only be 1 shilling, something that seemed only right for "C" Division games would be in competition to "A" and "B" Division ones in the same area.

July 6 1920

As the country tried to come to terms with the aftermath of the Great War which they were supposed to have won ("If that was a victory, I wouldn't have liked to see a defeat" was a common cry), it was no surprise that football was still in as much chaos as any other sphere of life.

Forfar had been refused admission to the Central League but other teams of the Eastern League had been accepted, leaving the Eastern League not very viable, and Forfar in severe danger of running out of competitive fixtures. This was the theme of the speech of James Black at Forfar's AGM at the Masonic Hall tonight.

The past season had been far from satisfactory in the general mayhem of troop demobilisation, labour unrest, unemployment and other problems. More games had been lost than won, but there was good news in the sense that the club was still solvent (just) and the Committee were re-elected to face what was to be an uncertain future.

Privately, Black had plans to apply for membership to the Scottish Alliance League in which the bigger clubs fielded their reserve teams. He also continued with unflagging energy to look for homespun local talent. There was no lack of interest in the game of football, indeed if anything the Great War had made it more popular for it had provided some welcome relief from the unrelenting horror, and of course a fair amount of football had been played by Army teams etc. There was however a distinct shortage of young men.

July 7 1885

The seasons of football and cricket were not as clearly delineated as they would become in later years, but it was generally supposed that July was not the best time for football, as football was far too energetic a game for the heat of July when the more sedate pastime of cricket was surely the order of the day. Those who argue in favour of summer football a century and more later may have a point, although most of us agree that it is not quite so simple as all that to accept the facile arguments that the weather is better. Not always so!

Nevertheless it comes as a bit of a surprise to discover that the new team of Forfar Athletic played two games against Broughty Ferry and one of them was a 2nd XI team! Forfar won 4-1 in the 1st XI game at Forfar, and 4-2 in the 2nd XI game at Broughty Ferry. No other details are given, which is a shame. What a pity it is that TV, video etc. had not yet been invented! Queen Victoria would soon be celebrating her Golden Jubilee in 1887. She was now slowly getting over the death of her husband Prince Albert (he had died 24 years ago!) having found a few counter attractions in the charming Benjamin Disraeli and the brusque but loyal Scotsman called John Brown. Forfar's main attraction, however, throughout her long reign remained Peter Reid rock.

July 8 1964

Yes, yes, I know this is meant to be a football book, but it would surely be remiss of me not to give a mention to the excellent Strathmore Cricket team of this era!

In 1964 they won everything in sight (in 1965 they DIDN'T win the Strathmore Union and everyone thought the word was coming to an end!) and tonight without a great deal of bother they won the Three Counties Cup in the final at Meigle against the Perthshire Cricket Association. Man of the Match was quite clearly George Myles who scored 57 in a total of 138 and then took 7 for 21 as the Perthshire men were dismissed for 61.

There was just no stopping this team in which great players abounded – Ian Ogilvie, Neil Prophet, Gavin McKiddie and of course the peerless Nigel Hazel. And oh yes, there was a footballing connection – for the Scorer that night was a young man called Walter Lee who in later years became the turnstile man at the Stand at Station Park!

It was often said that we at least had the summer to recuperate from the ravages of the winter of cold days at Station Park and frequent defeats. As for the cricketers they went to Montrose on the Saturday and won by 10 wickets! There were those who claimed that they were the best team in Scotland in 1964. They can't have been very far off it – and even people from Arbroath and Brechin agreed! But you couldn't really say that about the football team, could you?

Chairman Sam Smith welcomes Doug Houston and Henry Hall to Station Park

July 9 1932

Forfar Athletic made a short lived entry into the Five-A-Side tournament at the Dundee Police Sports Highland Games at Dens Park, Dundee, before an astonishing crowd of 12,000. Admittedly the weather was absolutely splendid, but the writer in *The Courier* has to admit that "rugged, heather clad mountains" are absent from this Highland gathering, and instead there are chimney stacks and slated roofs – something that was hard to reconcile with "Bonnie Dundee".

This being a Saturday afternoon, the chimneys were not belching out smoke, thankfully, but it was "these, and not the sporting gods of Olympus" which were watching this struggle in the lyrical words of the journalist not entirely unaffected by the imminent Olympic Games in Los Angeles. Apart from the football, there was cycling, wrestling and a race of bare-footed policemen in full uniform, truncheon included, to find their boots in a sack.

After all that, the Five-A-Side was a little tame, and the Forfar supporters were disappointed to see their favourites lose to Arbroath by a goal and a corner as distinct from a goal. Dundee United won the other semi-final and then beat Dundee in the final. The Forfar Five were assuaged by large quantities of beer after the game, and, in a statement which would have delighted those of us who oppose summer football, expressed delight that they did not have to play "real" football in such searing heat.

July 10 1948

In an attempt to keep football going during the summer, Forfar held a huge Five-A-Side tournament at Station Park. There was no real need for this in the sense that football did not go away anyhow in spite of the counter-attractions of the Australian cricketers – the Invincibles – in Great Britain on Bradman's last tour or the imminent Olympic Games to be held in London, not to mention the talking points involved in the beginning of the National Health Service which meant that you now got to go to the doctor for free!

But Forfar Athletic needed some money to keep them going over the summer months, so a tournament was arranged. There were in fact to be two tournaments – one was for the local junior and juvenile teams and there were fixtures like Celtic "B" v Renton "C", and there was the other for the real amateurs who have loads of enthusiasm but not necessarily any talent – we had games like Bricklayers v Academy, Vale of Lunan v Callanders and Eassie v Letham.

It cost sixpence to get in, and it was a fine money spinner for the club, although the pitch was rather too big for teams with only five players, not all of whom were necessarily in the peak of condition. And all this in the scorching heat of July. Nurses and ambulances were standing by!

July 11 1945

The country had voted in the General Election a few days ago, but because of the delays of counting the soldiers' votes, it would be another two weeks before the result could be announced. Scarcely less important issues were going on in Scottish football at the same time.

Still smarting from their failure to obtain entrance into the Scottish League a month ago, Forfar and some other clubs met in the Station Hotel, Perth to discuss the possibility of forming a Central League.

The clubs were Forfar, Brechin, Montrose, East Stirlingshire, the new Stirling club called Stirling Albion and a combined representation from Edinburgh where the situation was complicated with talks of amalgamation of Leith, St Bernard's and Edinburgh City.

As things stood, Forfar would be playing in an Eastern League but that League did not really have enough teams to make it all viable, and the League season would be over by the New Year! Several things were decided. One was to have another meeting next week with Mr George Graham of the SFA invited to attend; and the other was in the meantime to approach teams like Rangers, Celtic, St Johnstone, Dundee, Hearts and Hibs to see if they wished to enter their reserve sides for this competition.

It was also decided not to invite a combined Inverness team to join on the grounds of travel logistics. The official Scottish League response was the vague one that there might someday be a "C" Division, but this was not a possibility in the immediate future.

July 12 1932

Forfar Athletic supporters were distressed to read in today's *Courier* that Davie Kilgour had gone to Dartford. What was worse was that the club had lost £150.

This had come about for no other reason than that Dartford's Manager William Collier was back in his native Kirkcaldy on holiday. Collier was of course part of the immortal Raith Rovers half-back line of Raeburn, Morris and Collier of a decade previously and had his ear to the ground as far as the Scottish football scene was concerned. Hearing that Kilgour and a fellow called Micky McGregor, who had played for Dundee United, and other teams were available, Kilgour nipped on a train from Kirkcaldy to Dundee and signed the pair of them.

Forfar were furious because Kilgour was still registered with them, and indeed was on the open-to-transfer list with the not inconsiderable price tag of £150 on his head. But Dartford were in the Southern League of England, an unofficial League as far as transfer negotiations were concerned. "Wily Will", as he had been called in his playing days for Raith Rovers was aware of this, and signed Kilgour for nothing. Forfar protested about this, but achieved nothing. To be fair, £150 was perhaps a bit much to ask because Kilgour was past his best and recovering from a broken collar bone – two factors that perhaps explain why there had been no great rush for him from other clubs, although St Mirren had expressed interest.

July 13 2012

The impossible happened today when a team called Rangers suddenly found themselves in Division 3. That would have been totally unbelievable even a year ago, but came about because Rangers went bust on February 14, and this club was a "new" Rangers (called "newco" or "sevco") who had been removed from the Scottish Premier League and had to apply to the Scottish Football League.

They were accepted, but being a new club had to start at the bottom. It was assumed that Forfar's vote would have been for Rangers to be admitted to Division Three, although there would have been those who wanted them to join Division One. Rangers in Division Three was of course good news for Forfar, although not this year, because it would be assumed that Rangers would be promoted from Division Three in 2013 and would join Forfar for season 2013/14, as indeed happened.

Forfar therefore benefitted financially from the big crowds that Rangers brought. It was a bizarre situation, but had been brought about by "unsound finances" – to be as tactful about it as possible – with a particular belief that somehow or other, Rangers didn't need to pay income tax! HMRC disagreed, and Rangers went bust.

While it was sad to see such a famous club fold, one could see how it all happened from the days of 20 years previously when they bought players they could not afford, and who in any case failed to deliver the goods for them on the European stage. Rangers were not, of course, the first or last Scottish club to endure serious financial problems in these days, but one could look with pride at Forfar who were never a wealthy club and sometimes were very poor, but they were well run, efficient and, above all, honest.

July 14 1948

The Rotary Club's guest speaker tonight at the Royal Hotel was a Mr Yeaman who had been an SFA referee, but now recently retired. He gave his talk about the current and past state of Scottish Football. He talked well and in a very entertaining way, saying, for example, that he had always liked coming to Forfar Athletic because of their traditional hospitality including of course the famous "bridie". The difference between refereeing at Forfar and a bigger ground was that at Forfar the referee could hear every single abusive comment that was directed towards him, some of which he actually found quite funny. He had always enjoyed refereeing David McLean; he told the story about his very first game in the senior list, which was at Station Park and McLean was the captain of Forfar. At the toss of the coin, he told both captains that this was his first game and that he was rather nervous – possibly not a wise move to two seasoned professionals. Dave, however, and his opposite number just smiled and said "Leave it a tae us. We'll gie ye nae bother!" And neither he did, until halfway through the second half when McLean went down in the box, and Mr Yeaman said "No penalty". McLean turned to him and said "Gie's a shot o yer whustle, mannie, and I'll blaw it for ye. He shuvved me!"

Baxter Bridie

July 15 1938

The International situation was now causing extreme concern. The war in Spain, often described as "the dress rehearsal for the big show" was still going on with appalling ferocity and indescribable cruelty, and Hitler who had arranged his Anschluss or union with a not particularly enthusiastic Austria, was now beginning to demand parts of Czechoslovakia.

One did not need to be a pessimist to detect another war approaching with, this time, all the horrors of aerial bombardment, but in the meantime there were the holidays approaching and hard on the heels of that, the new football season.

1938 had shown several things – that Scotland could win at Wembley, that Celtic were the best team in Britain through winning the Empire Exhibition Trophy and, most importantly for Forfar and the smaller teams, East Fife of the Second Division could win the Scottish Cup!

Forfar were gearing themselves for the new season opening in a month's time by signing a player called Zander Smith, described with a touch of exaggeration by *The Courier* as an "Anglo" (a term normally used for a Scotland Internationalist who played for an English club.) He had played for Forfar East End in the past but had recently been given a free transfer from Wrexham. (Pedants could even point out that Wrexham was in Wales!) He was remembered by the East End supporters as a wing half who could play on either side of the park.

July 16 2016

The football season opened on this extraordinarily early date to allow for the new format of the Scottish League Cup, and Forfar welcomed Dumbarton to Station Park before a crowd of 428. The game finished in a 2-2 draw, but the new rules of this competition insisted on a penalty shoot-out in those circumstances. Forfar won 5-3 on penalties, thus giving them a bonus point.

In the 36th minute Josh Peters scored Forfar's earliest ever goal in a season with a right footed goal to the bottom right hand corner. After Dumbarton equalized early in the second half, Tommy O'Brien scored with a lovely goal from outside the box, but a moment's lack of concentration in the defence allowed Dumbarton to equalise.

Jamie Bain, just on the final whistle, earned the unwelcome distinction of being Forfar's first red card of the season when he was sent off for a second yellow.

The game then proceeded to penalties and for Forfar, David Cox, Lewis Milne, Jim Lister, Andy Munro and Gavin Swankie did the needful. It was not bad entertainment, but there was a general agreement among the crowd that July is possibly a better month for cricket and golf than football.

July 17 1955

One of the secrets of Forfar Athletic's comparative prosperity (in contrast to some other Second Division clubs) was the enthusiasm and commitment of the Forfar Athletic Supporters' Club.

This sunny Sunday, they organised an open-air concert at Station Park which drew a crowd of well over 1,000 (about the same size, more or less, as a Forfar home game in the mid 1950s). The entertainment consisted mainly of Scottish music, with contributions from Milne Morrison, Cathy McCabe, Mary Lynch, Doris Gilfeather, Danny Mitchell, the Gie (sic) Gordons Broadcasting Band and the Forfar Instrumental Band.

The fact that it was outside was of course a huge hostage to fortune because it would have been a disaster if it rained (as of course happened distressingly frequently with the Forfar Games) but as it is, it was a great success on a bright but slightly windy day which occasionally distorted the sound.

The fact that it was on a Sunday led to a little tut-tutting from those of a religious persuasion who also did not like cricket and golf being played on a Sunday, but the Sabbatarians had been declining in number and power for some time. In any case, the concert made a huge profit and the Supporter's Club were able to present the club with a fairly substantial cheque.

July 18 1908

Forfar suffered a bad blow today with the news that the popular David "Chappie" Gowans was leaving Forfar Athletic, where he was captain, to take up a similar role with Dundee "A", although he was to be officially described as a "Secretary". This seems to mean a sort of a Coach, as well as a "Manager-player" as *The Courier* puts it, and it was a full time job, so for "Chappie" (no-one seems to know why he was so called) it was a good move, particularly as he lived in Dundee.

For Forfar supporters it was a bitter blow but he was neither the first nor the last to hit that particular trail from Forfar to Dundee. *The Courier* tries to soothe the feelings of the Forfar supporters when it states "As a skipper and a player he has done a lot for the county town club, and although now quite a veteran at the game, he showed many a young player a lesson on how to play".

We do not know how "Chappie" got on at Dens Park, but, interestingly and revealingly, he fails to get a mention in either of Norrie Price's two excellent books on Dundee "Up Wi The Bonnets" and "They Wore the Dark Blue". For the town of Forfar it was a bad Saturday. In the cricket at Lochside before a large crowd, Brechin put on 195 for 7 and then Strathmore were dismissed for 25. "It was a regular procession to and from the verandah" as *The Courier* puts it.

July 19 2016

A trip to Balmoor in Peterhead is never a great idea on a Tuesday night, but at least the weather in July is generally good. Peterhead finished the 2015/16 season very badly, blowing up unaccountably towards the end, and then losing to Ayr United in the play-offs when promotion to the Championship looked a distinct possibility.

Forfar's end to the season had been a great deal worse, of course, but the Loons had had a good win at Balmoor on April 2, which had given some temporary hope of avoiding relegation. For a team which had just been relegated, Forfar supporters were well represented in the crowd of 508.

They saw little to cheer them up however in the game which ended up being a 2-0 win for the home side. Angus Mailer took the place of the suspended Jamie Bain, but neither he nor anyone else could prevent the first goal (an own goal by the luckless Andy Munro) nor the second goal which came via the penalty spot, after a fairly soft decision. Forfar then buckled to their task, but had little luck and Peterhead held firm for the rest of the game. It was however a fine night to watch a game of football! And not a bad night for the drive home either.

July 20 1936

Just to prove that football players lived ordinary lives as well, a presentation was made to Bob Black, Forfar's prolific forward on the occasion of his forthcoming marriage to Nellie Gray from his fellow workers at the "Haughie", more commonly known as the Haugh Works. Not only was Bob a talented footballer and loyal employee of the "Haughie", he was also an accomplished chimney sweep, a job that was much in demand in those days of coal fires. On this occasion, Bob was presented with an easy chair from his colleagues and also had a poem written to him by Angus Potter, described in *The Evening Telegraph* as "Forfar's Poet Laureate".

> Here's tae yersel and bonnie Nellie
> Aye hae butter, breid and jelly
> When ye're standin at the aisle wi Billie,
> Keep up yer back.
> Lang may ye read the *Evening Tele*
>   Bobby Black.
> May ye aye hear burdies sing
> Aye see the "blackies" on the wing
> See "Bolty" dae the Heilan Fling
> Roond opposing backs,
> And hear the praise yer antics bring
>   Fae Jeemy Black!
> Blessings on ye happy pair
> May yer hearts be never sair
> Nae sorrows, sighs of worldy care
> May ye aye laugh
> And spend some happy oors I' chair
>   Ye goat fae Haugh!

July 21 1992

It was Forfar's privilege to welcome one of the grand old names of English football to Station Park when Sheffield United came to town for a pre-season friendly. They were members of the inaugural English Premier League for the following season of 1992/93, but it was probably true to say that their best days were behind them.

But what a glorious past they had! Winners of the English League in 1898 and the English Cup in 1899, 1902, 1915 and 1925, they were a team of some pedigree, and their ground of Bramall Lane had the distinction of having hosted both an England International against Scotland and a Test Match against Australia.

It was sad that only 463 Forfarians availed themselves of the opportunity to see them, but then again it was holiday time and recently relegated Forfar were in the doldrums in any case. It was a good game to watch however with Carl Bradshaw and Brian Deane scoring for the Yorkshire side, then Ian Pryde pulling one back for Forfar who were unlucky not to equalise on several occasions near the end.

One occasionally has to wonder about what makes some people tick, however; here, at the end of an anodyne, gentlemanly pre-season friendly, Sheffield's captain Brian Gayle clashed with Forfar's Stewart Petrie and was shown the red card for what could only really be described as an assault! We recalled however that Gayle had learned his trade at Wimbledon; we nodded sagely at the folly of it all. The season had not even started!

July 22 1953

In a move that no-one really realised the implications of at the time – but they would ten years later! – Andrew "Skip" Soutar, ex-player and now Vice Chairman of the club took time off his work in the agricultural industry to sign Doug Berrie who had recently been released by Dundee United. Forfar had to act very quickly for Arbroath were also interested.

Born in Calcutta in 1927, hence perhaps his swarthy skin colour, Doug had played for Dundee United since 1946 and would now play for Forfar, until he was eventually given a free transfer in 1964 when he was not far short of his 40th birthday. He could play in either full back position, and was totally reliable.

Perhaps his best game came in 1957 when he faced Clyde's very talented Tommy Ring, a couple of weeks after Ring had played for Scotland against England at Wembley and scored a brilliant goal in the first minute. Tommy never got a kick that day at Station Park. Always immaculately turned out both on and off the pitch, and seldom in trouble with referees, Doug was a perfect ambassador for the club and an inspiration for youngsters, and although no-one would claim that he was the best football player Forfar have ever had (that would have to be Troup or McLean, perhaps), he contributed more and for longer than any other player to the stability of the club's defence.

July 23 1939

George Shepherd, the long term trainer of Forfar, indicated his desire to be relieved of his duties. He had been with the club for a total of 52 years as a player and then as a trainer.

He had been much prized and much loved by everyone and had seen more or less every single game of Forfar's history since he started playing for them in 1887 – and he probably was a boy spectator at some games before that! In those days, the word "trainer" meant all sorts of things from treating injuries to being "de facto" Manager of the club.

He was never a man to suffer fools gladly, and like most shrewd old football men, "Shup" as he was commonly known, could spot a malingerer or a chancer about a mile away!

He seemed to have the ability to get along with Jim Black (not everyone did) and although the two of them had their differences, (occasionally in public), Black was generally shrewd enough to realise that there were some things, like the fitness of the players, for example, that it was best left for "Shup" to deal with.

"Shup" was of course a part-time employee of the club, but it is hard to believe that he earned an awful lot from the club, and in any case, his main motivation was the love of the club and love of the game. He was as much a supporter as he was anything else. It was somehow appropriate that he died within a month or two of his friend Jim Black. They were always associated with each other in the running of Forfar Athletic FC.

July 24 1936

Two Forfar men and their wives were in Glasgow, it being the Forfar Holiday Week. They went into the famous Bank Restaurant in the centre of Glasgow for their lunch. The Bank Restaurant was of course owned by Willie Maley, the Manager of Celtic. Maley was there and was a genial mine host, as always. He was interested to know that they came from Forfar, and they talked about David McLean, the late Tom Hanick and other matters of interest with Maley, charming as always, saying how much he loved Forfar "my favourite wee town".

When the subject turned to James Black, the atmosphere changed a little, for one of the men did not like Mr Black and proceeded to give him a "good Forfar knifing", talking about him being a dictator who was far more interested in himself than he was in Forfar Athletic, and how he crawled and toadied to the Earl of Strathmore in the hope of somehow earning a knighthood.

Maley listened for a while then uttered the immortal words "Have I misjudged him? Surely that can't be my friend Jim?" One of the wives then chipped in with a more balanced assessment of the man, while Maley then waxed lyrical about the qualities of his friend and said that football needed men like Black, and how Forfar Athletic would have gone to the wall long ago if it had not been for Jim Black who devoted all his time unselfishly to his club, and if he was a little dictatorial at times, well, that was a fault that could be lived with.

Many people, of course, had similar criticisms of Maley himself!

July 25 1949

Historians will try to tell you that the late 1940s were an "age of austerity" with loads of shortages, poverty and deprivation. Rubbish!

The age of austerity had not reached Forfar, not today anyway. This was "Games Day", the day of the "far famed Forfar Games" as *The Forfar Dispatch* put it.

It was a tidy little earner for Forfar Athletic, with Jim Black shrewd enough to impose only a minimal charge for admission on the grounds that the beer tent would do the real money making for the club, as indeed would the teas in the "mert", although there was still the all-pervasive smell of "coo shairn" which detracted a little.

It was the first day of the Forfar Holiday Week, and with everyone in a happy holiday mood, excesses in behaviour were generally tolerated on the grounds that "It's the holidays". Everyone enjoyed the athletics, cycling, tossing the caber, Highland dancing and wrestling that went on, and of course it was a great opportunity for Forfarians to meet each other and indulge in the usual banter, bitching and gossiping that was and remains a feature of the town.

New babies were shown off, (including, one imagines, your writer – "He's ferly growin") older ones got the occasional hammering for bad behaviour and even older ones disappeared with a new boyfriend behind the stand or to Carseview for a "walk" behind the haystacks. But this year, the all pervasive question was "Foo are we gain tae dae in the "B" Division?" The season was starting soon.

July 26 2008

On the first day of the new season and the first game with Dick Campbell properly in charge, Forfar struck an early success with a good 2-1 win over Arbroath at Gayfield in the League Challenge Cup North East Section.

The League Challenge Cup was of course designed for teams other than those in the Premier League, and it has often been a source of sorrow to me at least that Forfar can't do a little better in it. Had the tournament been in existence in the times of the great days of the mid 1980s, it would have been difficult to resist the conclusion that Forfar might have won it on several occasions.

Be that as it may, it was still odd to see Forfar playing Arbroath at Gayfield at a time of year when everyone was still playing cricket at places like Lochside, Lochlands and Forthill. 563 spectators turned up to see Arbroath take a lead just before half-time, but then Forfar came more and more into the game and won two penalties. Neither decision went down all that well with the home crowd (well, they never do, do they?) but it mattered not for Kilgannon and then McLeish slotted home.

It was indeed an experience to be at Gayfield on such a day, recalling the days when Forfar often played there on New Year's Day, the gales howled, the rain came horizontally, and the sea was more than a little choppy.

July 27 1980

In a pre-season friendly which doubled as a Forfarshire Cup tie, Forfar played very well at Station Park but lost 2-3 to Premier League Dundee United. In spite of it being the "Holiday Week" (in days gone by, this match would not have been possible because of "The Games" and other things) a good crowd turned up including quite a few of the tangerine-bedecked from Dundee.

Forfar had already won a trophy this pre-season – the Scottish Brewers Trophy won in a tournament held at Keith and involving Dumbarton as well – and looked fit as they ran out, along with new signing, goalkeeper Stewart Kennedy, one time of Rangers and Scotland.

He did not have the best of starts for Forfar were three goals down at half-time and two of them were own goals! Neither of them was Kennedy's fault but they did show an as yet imperfect understanding with the defenders.

However, Forfar took those blows in the chin and fought back in the second half with Ronnie Robb scoring twice, once taking advantage of a slip by Dave Narey and the other a truly tremendous goal from a distance. Hard as they tried, Forfar could not equalise, but it was generally agreed that they deserved a draw – a point conceded, in his own gruff, ungracious and generally inimitable style, by the grumpy Jim McLean of Dundee United. Not for the first not last time, Jim was not all that happy with his own players.

July 28 1979

For the first time for nearly 50 years, Forfar lifted the Forfarshire Cup. Sadly, this venerable old trophy had been sadly neglected of late, sometimes being given up on altogether and on other times left unfinished, such were the exigencies of the modern fixture list.

This was in fact last year's competition being finished off as a sort of pre-season friendly at Station Park between Forfar and Dundee. It was one of these "typical Farfar holiday week" sort of days where it rained more or less all day, although it was warm enough.

1,600 abandoned their traditional summer pursuits to come and see Forfar win 3-1. Ken Brown scored with a penalty, then Raymond Farningham and Ian Reid scored the other two to win Forfar the Cup. Both teams had slightly weakened sides, but it was still a Cup win for Forfar, and how we delighted to see it shown off at the end to the drookit fans.

There were not many Dundee supporters there – they had fallen very badly from grace since the halcyon days of Ure and Gilzean nearly twenty years ago now – but the memory remains of the look of disbelief on the faces of a couple of them in the stand. Forfar, they seemed to be saying, so often the butt of jokes, simply are not allowed to beat Dundee!

But they had, and we celebrated, although the loudspeaker announcer seemed to have had some sort of hot line to Cassandra or Teiresias of Ancient Greece, for while the game was actually being played, he announced that the Cup would be presented to Forfar Athletic at the end of the game!

July 29 1981

The rest of the country may have been more "teen up" (as they say in Forfar) with the Royal Wedding of Charles and Diana with all its vainglorious pomp and bogus claptrap, but something more significant happened in a pre-season friendly against Dundee, when Stewart Kennedy fractured his jaw. Being the determined and loveable bloke that he was, Stewart would come back, but it meant that Ian Boardley was to be the goalkeeper for the coming season.

That was no problem, for Boardley did well, but the town was saddened to know about the injury to a man who had hardly known about Forfar before he signed for us in 1980, yet who was destined to play for us 281 times. Kennedy had of course played for Rangers, winning two Scottish League medals and two Scottish League Cup medals with the Ibrox side, and of course five caps for Scotland.

It was the last of these against England at Wembley which brought him notoriety, but as with Fred Martin in 1955 and Frank Haffey in 1961, it is always the easiest thing in the world to blame the goalkeeper, when one has to remember that there are 10 others in the team who must share the blame.

No-one in Forfar however until Stewart's retiral from the game in 1992 would have a bad word to say about the ever-consistent and reliable Stewart with his unerring ability to read situations and be in the right position to make a save. He is one of the few players ever who will be remembered more for his Forfar career than his Rangers one. Rightly he is called "Stewart Kennedy of Forfar".

July 30 2016

Forfar don't exactly do things by halves, do they? I suppose, if you are going to go out of the League Cup before August arrives, it is as well to do it in style, but losing 7-0 to Dundee at Dens Park before 2219 supporters (with a fair sprinkling of Forfarians) is going a bit far, one feels.

The kindest things that we can say is that we held them for about the first 15 minutes before "the roof fell in", "the wheels cam aff the certie" or whatever cliché you would like to use. But, there were of course now three divisions between us and our near neighbours, and given the past 30 years or so of Dundee's history, it was hard to feel jealous of them.

Funnily enough, we reckoned we were in a better state than they were since their Golden Age of Gilzean and Ure. Relegations, bankruptcies, boycotts, administrations and the fanatical desire to sell their best players had been the lot of the loyal, but now humble, Dundee supporters.

We thought about all these things as the goals rained in past Grant Adam and the beleaguered defence, and we also reflected that it was now 50 years to the day since England won the World Cup at Wembley in 1966. Aye, July 30 is not a great day for football, is it? But let's be positive. The important thing was the League and it hadn't started yet. Difficult to find much else to console ourselves with, though. We wished all the best to Paul Hartley and Dundee in their efforts to survive in the Premier League, but poor Paul wouldn't see the year out.

July 31 1999

This one was hard! Admittedly Victoria Park, Dingwall did have happy memories for us from 1995 when we won the Third Division there but it was still a long journey home with the knowledge that it is not yet August, and that we are already out of the Scottish League Cup, a competition in which we have had a reasonable amount of success over the years.

All the jokes about Scottish teams getting home from Europe before the postcards suddenly seemed not quite so funny. The season had not really started yet, and we had lost a lot of money already. Two things would make it worse – one was that Ross County, who were now a Division above us, would be drawn in the next round against Dundee United at Tannadice – (now we would have really enjoyed that!) and the other, although no-one could possibly guess this at the time was that the winner was scored three minutes from the end of extra time (it was that close!) via the penalty spot by a man called George Shaw, who was making his debut that day for the Dingwall side and who would one day be Forfar's Manager (a none too successful one, admittedly). Forfar had actually scored first through MacDonald, but Ross County had equalised before half time, and then we had held our own until near the end. But it was all so early and not really time for football yet. Time to return to the cricket!

August

OFFICIAL PROGRAMME OF EDINBURGH CITY FOOTBALL CLUB

The CITIZEN

Ladbrokes LEAGUE 2

Hutchinson NETWORKS LTD

© 2016 Kevin Illingworth

Meadowbank Stadium – Saturday 6th August 2016   Kick-off 3:00 p.m.

FORFAR ATHLETIC

Ladbrokes SPFL League Two   Issue 4   Price £2.00

August 1 2015

Where better to open the Scottish League Cup campaign than at Hampden Park?

The weather was lovely, although the occasional shower threatened and indeed arrived just about the full time whistle, but by that time 441 fans had seen Forfar deservedly beat Queen's Park and progress to the next round.

Derek Young, that man of many clubs who had of course played at Hampden in front of larger crowds than this, scored first for Forfar after a good passing move involving several players. That was after about quarter of an hour, and then about quarter of an hour after that, Forfar were awarded a penalty (by no means a clear cut one, but let's not argue!) and Martyn Fotheringham stepped up to take it. Foxy's effort was saved by the goalkeeper but in the ensuing melee Danny Denholm managed to squeeze the ball home and Forfar were 2-0 up. This often spells danger for Forfar to be two up so early in the game, but the defence, with Tom O'Brien particularly impressive, held out in what was really a rather sleepy second half in the pleasant Glasgow sunshine.

As Forfar had also won last week in the League Challenge Cup, Dick Campbell had every reason to be pleased with his men. The season was well begun. (The ending was to be not nearly so nice, but we didn't know that as we travelled home that day!)

August 2 1897

The football season had not yet started, but Forfar sports fans had every reason to be proud of their cycling hero John Killacky, mine host of the Queen's Hotel.

Today at Celtic Park, the home of Scottish Cycling in those days, John won his favourite event – the 5 mile Professional Sprint Race. He did this in 12 minutes 40 seconds. 5 miles is a long time to watch cyclists going round and round a track when they will naturally hold back and keep all their energy for the final lap.

To counteract this, the organisers had arranged that two shillings and sixpence (half-a-crown) – or about 12 pence in modern currency – should be given to the leader at the end of each lap. This certainly increased the pace on this hot day, and the last lap of the 20 saw Killacky, Silver and McFarlane all come round "almost in a line" and it stayed that way until the last hundred yards when in circumstances of great excitement, Killacky edged forward and won the race.

One of the first men to congratulate him was Willie Maley, the newly appointed Manager of Celtic and himself no mean cyclist and athlete.

News travelled quickly in 1897 with the telegraph, and news reached the town about half an hour later. A crowd assembled at the Station to see Killacky and his cycle dismount from the train that night. He soon earned the nickname "Killacky of the Trackie", and of course, he is commemorated today in the corner named after him. As Andy Murray is to Dunblane today, John Killacky was to Forfar at the end of last century.

August 3 2013

After decades of striving and much sheer bad luck, Forfar eventually beat Rangers and put them out of the Scottish League Cup thanks to a Gavin Swankie strike late in the last period of extra time with a penalty shoot-out looming!

This result, almost impossible to imagine even 10 years previously, rocked Scotland (even in Rangers' straitened circumstances) and ensured a degree of affection and admiration for Forfar at places like Celtic Park, Pittodrie and Tannadice and meant that the names of Hill, Baxter, McCulloch, Malcolm, Andrews, Fotheringham, Kader, McCabe, Malin, Templeman and Swankie with Campbell as substitute will live for ever as "the men who beat Rangers".

And yet, in some ways it was a hollow victory, because Rangers, since their entry into administration on Valentine's Day 2012, had been a shadow of what they once were with even their enemies known to express a certain pity and compassion for them in their plight, deserved and justified though it undeniably was.

To his credit, Manager Ally McCoist, no longer the cocky "cheeky chappie" so beloved of Sue Barker on "A Question of Sport", shook everyone's hand and acted like a gentlemen, although others attached to Rangers, notably a well-known comedian, didn't.

4,079 fans saw a fine game at a sunny but slightly windy Station Park in which Gavin Swankie put Forfar ahead, but then Fraser Aird equalised for Rangers and then Swankie headed the late winner. It was a fine and historic occasion, and Forfar fans, never known for their triumphalism, smiled their satisfaction, enjoying the sound of silent Huns.

August 4 1914

Even to a child in Forfar this day, it was obvious that something exciting was going on. Words like "Belgium", "ultimatum" and "mobilisation" were being thrown about, even by people who did not really understand what it was all about. And at 11.00 tonight, we would know for certain if there was going to be a war.

But it had happened so suddenly and the impending football season was still in everyone's thoughts with rumours that Geordie Langlands was soon to be on his travels again, this time to St Mirren. Contrary to the impression given by some historians, not everyone was swept away with war fever.

Churches and local politicians banged the drum about "duty" and "patriotism" but more sober and thoughtful people wondered why, for example, John Morley, one time MP for Montrose Burghs (which included Forfar) had resigned from the Cabinet along with the Labour man John Burns. And Ramsay MacDonald, the other Scotsman who represented Labour, was also against the idea. Besides, we now seemed to be Allies of the Czar of Russia! But the main mood was excitement and the possibility of getting away from those dreary jute factories.

Mind you, the football season was coming as well, and it would be nice to see how "wee Troupie" – as the diminutive Alec Troup, who had exploded on the scene in 1914, was called – would do in the new season. There was something to look forward to there as well. Surely a war was not going to disrupt all that?

August 5 2006

It was the start of the new season at Forfar and the first game for new Manager George Shaw, a man who had played for many clubs, Forfar included, but mainly Partick Thistle and Dundee. He had been Assistant to Ray Farningham, and had taken over the job, on Farningham's recommendation, in May. There had been little hiding the fact that Forfar were "cash-strapped", and the impecunious state of the club limited what Shaw could do over the summer of 2006 as we all watched the World Cup in Germany.

Today 382 turned up to watch Forfar take on Stranraer. It was not the best of games – "end of season" stuff someone with a sense of humour described it – but Forfar won 2-1 with goals from Craig Lumsden and Alan Rattray, and everyone departed reasonably happy with life.

Shaw himself pronounced himself satisfied and next week's game was a creditable 0-0 draw against Raith Rovers in Kirkcaldy. We then beat Dundee in the League Challenge Cup, but after that the rot set in big time, and we were reminded of the really bad days of the mid 1960s and mid 1970s as we won only another three games in the League that season.

Poor George Shaw, for whom nothing went right, found himself out of a job by March.

August 6 1936

War was now raging in Spain, and the Berlin Olympics had been opened a few days ago by the Fuhrer Adolf Hitler, but *The Forfar Dispatch* football writer is none too concerned about these events as he previews the season which will start at Airdrie on Saturday.

He is surprisingly optimistic considering that the team finished sixth bottom last year, and is delighted by the fact that seven of the men likely to start at Airdrie on Saturday will be "Forfar men" i.e. born and bred in the town, while the other four are not that far away either – goalkeeper McFarlane and half backs Morton, Laird and Gabriel all having strong local connections. Such an insular attitude, as it seems to modern eyes, was common at the time and indeed had a lot to commend it in that the players would have a particular loyalty to the club and the supporters.

The supporters, for their part, could all meet and talk with the players at their work and would thus have a particular emotional investment in the club. There was of course a down side to it as well in that one had to guard against exclusiveness and any impression that "incomers" were not welcome, but in any case, it would all depend on how the team were to perform. But our scribe was confident that the players would not let Forfar down.

August 7 2004

Forfar opened their League season with a good 1-0 win against Brechin City before 766 fans. It is always good to begin the season with a win over local rivals, and today was a good game, the only goal coming from Barry Sellars on the stroke of half-time. Barry of course is one of those characters who kept coming back to Forfar amidst stays at other teams like his native Arbroath for example.

In the same way as people suggest that the road between Derby and Nottingham should be called Clough Way, maybe the Forfar to Arbroath railway (if ever it were to be resurrected – we can but pray!) should be called the Sellars Line.

Forfar's team was Brown, Rattray, Lowing, Forrest, King, McClune, Sellars, Lunan, Tosh, Shields and Stein. It was indeed the middle of a purple patch for Forfar because the previous week they had defeated Morton in the League Challenge Cup, and they would go on to win every game they played in August apart from a heavy defeat at the hands of Dundee at Dens Park in the Scottish League Cup.

Forfar would also have a good run in the League Challenge Cup that autumn, but League form hit a very bad patch. It would have been hard, however, for anyone watching this game against Brechin to imagine that Brechin would go on and win the Second Division by the end of the year!

August 8 1959

Forfar, having managed to avoid the bottom six in the Second Division last year, were not starting the League Cup in the dreaded Section 9, but shared Section 7 with Brechin, East Fife and Queen of the South.

The season began with a trip to Palmerston Park, Dumfries to face Queen of the South who had been relegated from Division One last season. The Queens' supporters could comfort themselves with the text in the Book of Revelations in the Bible which assured them that "the queen of the south will rise up", but today they were held to a 1-1 draw by Forfar, something that was considered an honourable result for both teams.

On a lovely summer day with bright sunshine yet a cooling wind, Forfar in fact were the better team, and led 1-0 at half-time through a goal by Arthur McIvor. Queen of the South however came more into the game in the second half and earned an equaliser after some hesitancy in the Forfar defence.

It was a good start to the season, however, and everyone looked forward to the visit of Brechin City to Station Park on Wednesday night, which would be the first full season at the "new" Station Park with its new stand and improvements to the terracing. Forfar's team was McKay, Steen and Berrie; Brown, Ogilvie and Buchan; Scott, Newton, Craig, Brodie and McIvor.

August 9 1952

It was not the sort of weather than one associates with the start of the season as heavy rain washed out every single cricket match in the area.

Forfar's League Cup section consisted of Morton, Cowdenbeath and Hamilton – a tough, but not impossible section to qualify from in the opinion of most fans – and Forfar's first game was at Central Park, Cowdenbeath, a ground that had the advantage, like Station Park, of being close to a railway station.

The small crowd, huddled under what little shelter there was at Central Park, saw a rather one-sided game as Forfar definitely got off on the wrong foot to start the season, losing 0-2 and, frankly, it could have been a lot more. The only Forfar players that get pass marks in a somewhat scathing review in *The Courier* are inside forward George Cunningham and centre half Alec Hamilton. "Forfar are faced with many forward problems" says the scribe who clearly calls things as he sees them, and "they failed to link into a useful combination".

Cowdenbeath, on the other hand, showed real potential but were berated for easing off in the second half because "other teams may not be so kind as Forfar". Clearly, there was not a great deal for Forfar supporters to be happy about here, but the more philosophical among them who had faced their fair share of "the slings and arrows of outrageous fortune" in their time reckoned that if you are to have a bad day, the first day of the season is not the worst time to have one. You have the rest of the season to fight back!

August 10 2004

Love Street, one time home of St Mirren is sadly no longer with us. In August 2004 it was still there, albeit extremely rundown and on its last legs with one of these quaint old wooden stands which looked like as if it were a fire hazard.

This Tuesday night before a crowd of over 1,100, Love Street saw a remarkable 5-2 win for Forfar against the home side in the League Cup. St Mirren a side with a remarkable pedigree in the Scottish Cup, although less so in the League Cup, were simply swept aside by Ray Stewart's rampant Forfar team, for whom Paul Tosh scored two and Andy Millen, Barry Sellars and Eddie Forest one each, even though the Paisley side scored first and last.

This represented Forfar's best ever result against St Mirren at Love Street, and as good as any recorded by the Loons in the west of Scotland. It was a remarkable trip. En route we took a wrong turn and found ourselves driving through the infamous Ferguslie Park where we saw, among other scary things, a house on fire!

And when we got there we found ourselves sitting beside the then Joint Chief Executive of the SFA, a man called David Taylor who was proud to describe himself as a Forfar supporter. And so he should be, for both he and his late father played for East End at one time! David Taylor, an extremely able administrator, rose to even more dizzy heights with UEFA in 2007.

August 11 1984

A new era dawned for Forfar as they played their first game in the First Division. Appropriately enough it was a gloriously hot day with the pie stall selling loads of Coca Cola and orange juice instead of the more normal tea and Bovrils.

The Partick Thistle supporters enjoyed their bridies, however, but that was about all they enjoyed that day for Forfar showed that last year's glorious success was no fluke as they beat the Glasgow men 4-0.

The Thistle supporters, always a decent bunch – sociable in the Glasgow style and without any trace of religious bigotry – stood and applauded the Forfar goals scored by Jim Liddle, Gordon Scott (who "bagged a brace" as a newspaper put it, conscious perhaps the grouse season opened tomorrow on the glorious twelfth) and Ray Farningham.

The local fans, never the easiest to please, went home that day thinking that there was little wrong with the world – good weather, good football and a team that was no longer the laughing stock of Scottish football but which was going to make its mark on the game.

The contrast between 1984 and 1974 could hardly have been more pronounced, and those who had endured the horrors of ten years ago could now enjoy the pleasures. The team that day was Kennedy, Lorimer, McPhee, Morris, Brash, Weir, Liddle, Farningham, Gallacher, Scott and MacDonald with Gary Murray coming on as a substitute.

August 12 1970

Football had had a good summer in 1970, mainly because of the very successful World Cup in Mexico won in spectacular style by Brazil, and shown on TV,

TV ownership now being more or less universal in Forfar and elsewhere. It was a pity that Scotland were not there, however, and a further blow to Scotland's prestige was dealt when Celtic lost the European Cup final in May. 1969/70 had not finished well for Forfar, who were second bottom in the Second Division, but summer 1970 had seen changes at Station Park – a new Chairman David Callander as distinct from his uncle Will, a wholesale clear out of players and an intake of others, and a few ground improvements.

The season had opened on Saturday with a creditable 2-1 over old rivals Stenhousemuir and this Wednesday night, Forfar were at Hampden to play Queen's Park. A 1-1 draw was the result in the huge empty bowl that Hampden was with our goal coming from Harry Waddell, and everyone was happy with that.

Hopes were now beginning to be expressed that Forfar were about to have a good season, and optimism was in the air. There was always a groundswell of good will for Forfar in the town at the beginning of the season, and you could almost touch the atmosphere. Sadly, it didn't last all that long!

August 13 1955

A large crowd assembled in the bright sunshine to welcome the new season. Motherwell were the attractive visitors for the first game in the League Cup Section.

Motherwell were a strange unpredictable team. Winners of both the Scottish Cup and the Scottish League Cup not all that long ago, they would nevertheless have been playing in the Second Division this year again had League reconstruction not saved them from relegation. Their colours of claret and amber were attractive, and they brought a big support with them. They had fine players like McSeveney, Redpath, Aitkenhead, Humphries and a full back with the name of Willie Kilmarnock, leading to all the trick questions for youngsters like "How can Kilmarnock play for Motherwell?" etc.

Today, to the immense disappointment of the Forfar crowd, Motherwell were 3-0 up at half-time with Forfar's goalkeeper Mike Wimbury, an amiable Englishman from Coupar Angus, having a shocker. The Forfar side battled hard and Willie Dunn scored a goal in the second half, but the classy full timers of Motherwell were simply too good and Motherwell won 6-1.

The Press consoled Forfar with the reflection that they wouldn't meet a team of Motherwell's calibre every week, but it was a sad start to the season for the Loons. They were not the only team to get a thumping that day, for in Belfast a team called Great Britain lost to Europe 4-1. It would be the last time that anyone would try to arrange a serious football match for "Great Britain".

August 14 1948

Forfar opened what would be one of their best ever seasons with a 5-0 victory over Kilmarnock "A" at Station Park.

This was the first game of the season in Division "C", a division which Forfar were desperate to get out of because it involved playing too many reserve teams like those of Dundee, Kilmarnock and Aberdeen.

The writer of *The Forfar Dispatch* is delighted to confound Tommy Muirhead, one time of Rangers but now a respected journalist, who predicted in a national newspaper that Kilmarnock "A" would not only beat Forfar handsomely but would win the "C" Division at a canter.

The Forfar Instrumental Band played before the start in the fine weather, and our writer in the *Dispatch* suddenly lapses into a brilliant piece of Forfar dialect when he says that the arrival of the teams was the cue for Geordie Simpson, the conductor of the Band to "pet his stickie aneeth ees oxter, merch his leds aff, and let the referee dae the tootlin".

One wonders what Tommy Muirhead would have made of that, and indeed what he made of the 5-0 score line in which Ian Rodger scored two, Jimmy Wotherspoon scored two and Chick Robbie scored the other. Forfar fans went home in rare good humour that night, but of course notes of caution had to be sounded in that it was only Kilmarnock's reserve team, and that there was a long, long way to go.

August 15 2006

The time was when Forfar beating Dundee would have been a great moment in the life of both places, euphoria for the county town, depression and heart searching for the city men.

Not tonight however as Forfar beat Dundee 2-1 at Station Park before a miserable crowd of less than 1,000 in the Scottish League Challenge Cup. The name of the tournament gave it away because it was a tournament which excluded the Premier League clubs, and Dundee had, for the past 25 years or so, struggled to be called a Premier League club, fighting against generations of incompetent and sometimes corrupt institutional management and stewardship with a particular desire to sell their best players for money rather than build a team.

Since the early 1960s, they had also had to contend with the rise of Dundee United across the road. It was possible even to feel sorry for their woebegone supporters that night at Station Park, as Second Division Forfar scored twice through Darren Gribben (picking up a fine pass from Alan Rattray) and Frazer Coyle with a fierce drive from well outside the box. The game was more or less over and the Dundee fans sitting disconsolately in their cars and buses when our old friend Gavin Swankie pulled one back for them on the full time whistle.

Aye, aye, I thought. Yon Thomas the Rhymer got it right when he said that "Farfar will be Farfar still, when Dundee's a' dug doon".

August 16 1915

Alec Troup signed for Dundee.

Alec would have been happy to stay with Forfar, but Forfar Athletic had been compelled to close down for the duration of the war, such were the problems of getting players, war-time transport and a certain amount of moral blackmail from bodies like the Press and the Church that "22 young men should be at the Front".

But Dundee were still in existence and Mr McIntosh had been very impressed with "wee Eckie" when he saw him. He now arrived in Forfar to sign him. There were stories about how Troup was up a ladder at his job as a plasterer in East High Street at a joiner's yard and that he signed the piece of paper on a coffin (still, presumably in the course of being made and therefore untenanted). How many of these stories are true, and how much owe their existence to fertile, dramatic, rhetorical Forfar gossip we do not know, but Troup was now a part-time professional player (full time was not allowed in war time) with Dundee and would play in the First Division of the Scottish League next year.

But these were uncertain times, and how long it would be before conscription was introduced, no-one knew. Certainly the war which had been going on for over a year now showed signs of deadlock, and there had been one or two obvious disasters at the Dardanelles, for example. For the moment, though, Troup would play and star for Dundee. It was a frequent gripe from Mr Black in later years that in the circumstances of the time and with Forfar being in abeyance, Troup was a free agent, and Forfar therefore received not a penny in a transfer fee.

August 17 1949

The Forfar Dispatch gives the unlikely statistic that 4,000 attended this 2-2 draw at Station Park to see Stenhousemuir in the League Cup.

It was a Wednesday evening and sometimes Wednesday night games attracted more spectators than Saturday games because shopkeepers were available to attend, but even so 4,000 seems a bit high. Other newspapers admit there was a good crowd, and it was certainly a fine night with Forfar on the crest of a wave having begun the new season well with a win over Hamilton Accies at Douglas Park on Saturday.

1949 was also the time that saw the boom in football attendances and Forfar shared in this. Forfar's goals came from Ian Rodger who was found on his own and then, according to *The Forfar Dispatch* it was "peels". (What does this mean? Perhaps, as in bowls, it means simply the scores were level.) However Stenny fought back as they always do, and were leading 2-1 with only minutes remaining when Forfar were awarded a penalty when Rodger was downed in the penalty box. Dick Cruickshank took it and scored to give Forfar a draw.

Most of the large crowd felt that they were worth a win, but for Forfar starting the season with a win and a draw, this meant that we were indeed living in the "promised land". Forfar would indeed go on and win the League Cup section, although concern was beginning to be expressed about the form of the talented but now ageing Tommy Adams.

August 18 1984

Normally an Angus Derby between Forfar and Brechin City would be a low key Second Division affair of little interest to anyone other than the denizens of the two towns. Outbreaks of violence in the 1930s had been not unheard of in the aftermath of this fixture, but today things were different with 1,500 reasonable and well behaved fans at Glebe Park and a certain amount of national attention paid to the two teams of the county of Angus, now referred to as a "football growth area". Glebe Park, meaning in old days the "ground belonging to the Minister" is always a pleasant place to visit with its quaint little matchbox of a stand, the proximity to the cemetery and the hedge running up the side of the pitch.

Local rivalry is of course a factor whenever Forfar appear, but both communities are usually wise enough to realise that they both need each other. On this occasion, Forfar were well on top with two magical goals from Kenny MacDonald in a fine 2-0 victory. Brechin came close particularly in the second half, but Stewart Kennedy ignored all the chants of "Wembley" from the intellectually challenged of the home support and organised his defence in masterly fashion. Forfar had now won two games out of two, and there can't have been many other occasions in the past when Forfar fans left Glebe Park singing "We're top of the League, and you're no.'"

August 19 1987

Forfar didn't win but they acquitted themselves well in one of their rare trips to Celtic Park in the Scottish League Cup.

A crowd of slightly less than 20,000 saw the home side win 3-1 with two goals from Andy Walker and one from Billy Stark while Forfar's one goal came from a Kenny MacDonald penalty when MacDonald himself was pulled down by Paddy Bonner.

The scoring was all over by half time, and the second half got a little tedious until the Celtic fans realised that Forfar goalkeeper Stewart Kennedy used to play for Rangers. They shouted predictable things about Wembley, but then began to sing a song "Have you seen a handsome Hun? No".

It must be admitted that Stewart, fine goalkeeper though he might be, was no Ronald Colman or George Clooney, but he had a good game against a club which had just taken on a new lease of life with the return of Billy McNeill as Manager. At the end Stewart was given a grudging cheer from the Celtic supporters.

For Forfar and their Manager Henry Hall, this was a learning experience, not least for the very talented Craig Brewster who would make his own impact on Scottish football in a year or two. Forfar's team was Kennedy, W Bennett, Hamill, Brazil, Smith, Clark, Blackie, M Bennett, Scott, Brewster, MacDonald with substitutes Morris and Ward.

Craig Brewster

August 20 1955

Forfar suffered a bad 2-5 defeat to neighbours Dundee United in the Scottish League Cup at Station Park, a result which more or less condemned the Loons to an early exit. Yet they held them to 2-3 until the last ten minutes when defensive frailties let them down.

Dundee United in 1955 were no great shakes. They were a Second Division team and looked upon as the poor relations of Dundee FC on the other side of the road. As a very young fan that day, your writer was rather amazed to hear an old Dundonian shouting "Come Away the Hibs" when everyone knew that Hibs played in Edinburgh!

It had to be explained that until 1923, they were called the Dundee Hibernian before changing to Dundee United in perhaps a deliberate attempt to distance themselves from the Irish troubles of the 1920s.

Be that as it may, it was a depressing experience for a youngster, and possibly a lifelong antipathy to Dundee United stemmed from the sight of triumphalist Dundee United supporters in the stand in that fatal last ten minutes. Len Dick and Tommy Martin scored for Forfar, but in fact Dundee United were "a' ower us" as the disgruntled Forfarians put it. Forfar's goalkeeper Mike Wimbury was the only defender "not to blot his copybook" according to *The Courier*.

August 21 1926

Forfar's first home game of the season was a derby against Arbroath which attracted a crowd of 3,500 spectators, almost half of whom had travelled from Arbroath by train, motor car, motor bike and even push bike, although the very strong blustery west wind made it difficult for them. The Earl of Strathmore was there, cheering on his beloved Forfar but being seen to express sympathy too with the Arbroath Directors when they missed a penalty.

Forfar had of course been readmitted to the Second Division after the Third Division had collapsed last year, and made the most of their good luck in a fine 2-0 win with a goal scored by the veteran Davie McLean from a penalty, and another from "Newman" the trialist centre forward. Frank Hill at left half was quite clearly the man of the match, dominating the midfield and spraying passes. "Frankie didn't pass the ball, he stroked it and caressed it" said one admirer. It was McLean's first game back at Station Park where he received a rousing reception. Funnily enough Forfar seemed to be play best against the wind, but Arbroath would rue their penalty miss from ex-Dundee forward Johnny Bell, who was famously good at shoulder charging, causing the Arbroath fans to sing to the tune of the Red Flag (this was the year of the General Strike, remember, and socialism was very much in the air) "Oh, Johnny Bell, went through himsel, and cawed the goalie a tae Hell". Not this time however, Johnny! Forfar's Frank Bridgeford was very capable of dealing with all that Arbroath could throw at him! Johnny bounced off him!

August 22 1914

The country had been at war for about three weeks now, and the air of excitement prevailed. *The Courier* printed ridiculous stories about how the Germans were completely "enveloped" in Belgium, and the Germans were asking for an Armistice from the Russians, while in Japan the Mikado (whom everyone thought was a character in the Gilbert and Sullivan opera of that name) muscled in on the side of the Allies.

The football season had started, although many people thought it "unpatriotic" to play the game when 22 young men could have been in the Army instead. Unpatriotic or not, Forfar travelled to Dens Park to play Dundee "A" (the reserve team) in the Central League. Their departure from Forfar Station that Saturday lunch time coincided with the emotional farewell of some Forfar soldiers, kilts and kit bags and all, leaving for someplace in England for basic training.

Dens Park was a great deal less intimidating, with Forfar winning 1-0, unluckily if you read *The Courier*, deservedly if you read *The Forfar Herald*. The only goal of the game came from a fine shot by Alec Troup, while "Jummer" Petrie and both the Fergusons are also singled out for praise.

On the train home that night, some of the players openly questioned whether they should "join up". After all, everyone said that it would be "over by Christmas" and it would be a shame to miss out on such an adventure, would it not? Could you play football in the Army? The lassies would like the look of you in a kilt! And the food was good in the Army, they said.

August 23 1980

Just what on earth was that all about then? Forfar travelled to Arbroath this Saturday and played well to win 3-2 with a couple of late goals, but the team and the support were still struggling to come to terms with the astonishing events of midweek.

Archie Knox having departed to Aberdeen, Forfar had appointed Steve Murray as Manager on Tuesday. This had looked to be a good appointment for Murray had enjoyed a great playing career for Dundee, Aberdeen and Celtic. He was articulate and impressive, and the general feeling in the town was that this was a good replacement for Archie Knox and that there was no reason why Forfar couldn't continue to go from strength to strength.

Murray then took a training session on the Wednesday night, introducing himself to all the players and making a favourable impression. Then on the Friday news broke that he had resigned!

Journalists and supporters struggled to understand this, and Forfar Athletic were once again in the national spotlight, this time for the wrong reasons and earning a fair amount of undeserved ridicule.

Jock Stein, Murray's boss at Celtic Park, and now Manager of the national team, shook his head in disbelief when he heard the news. A couple of years later, Murray became Manager of Montrose – and managed to stick around for a little longer at Links Park than he did at Station Park! A Manager who never even saw a game must be something of a rarity, and that training session that he supervised must have been really bad!

August 24 1963

It was a glorious day, but that was about all that was good about it, as Forfar travelled to Shielfield Park in Berwick, a mile or two over the border, to lose 1-3 to Berwick Rangers in the Scottish League Cup, a result which confirmed that Forfar were bottom of the five-team Group Nine.

Group Nine was the punishment for ending up in the last five in the previous League campaign, so with Forfar now at the bottom of that with only one point, it was hard to resist the conclusion that Forfar were indeed the worst team in Scotland.

And yet they had put up some sort of a fight at Berwick, Ewen scoring for us in the second half after we had held the Englishmen until half-time. The fact was that quality players were simply not there, and although we tried to cheer each other up by saying that it was "only" the League Cup, and the real business of the Scottish League had not yet started, nevertheless we knew we were in for a struggle.

But we cheered each other up by singing a few Beatles songs and telling dirty jokes about Christine Keeler, the lady who had enjoyed a "friendship" with John Profumo, the Minister of War (yes, War! And this was 1963, 18 years after the last war had finished!) and had caused him to resign, because she was also simultaneously "friendly" with a Soviet attaché. She would eventually bring down the Prime Minister, Harold McMillan, as well.

August 25 1923

A good crowd of about 2,000 on a bright sunny, albeit somewhat breezy, day saw Forfar play their first home League match of the season at Station Park. They had already had an honourable draw against St Bernard's in Edinburgh, and today's opponents were Dunfermline Athletic, generally considered to be one of the weaker teams in the Division in spite of coming from a fairly large town.

They were booed as they came on to the field, possibly because they were irrationally associated with Andrew Carnegie, the so-called philanthropist but in fact a ruthless capitalist, and believed to be a war profiteer.

Forfar were well on top throughout the game and it was something of a travesty that the final score was only 1-0, the goal scored by Willie Black, and had it not been for Jim Paterson in the Dunfermline goal, the score would have been a great deal more. The team generally played very well and frequently the ground resounded to applause.

This was the beginning of Forfar's third season in the Scottish League Division Two, and although no-one could say that they had distinguished themselves, nevertheless, they had held their own, and the start to the 1923/24 season was very promising. Form would not always remain like that, however, but this was a good day and Forfarians rejoiced in the idea that football, the local obsession, was back.

August 26 1939

Station Park was a strange place this Saturday as Airdrieonians came to town. "We're still here" was the topic of conversation – in two respects.

Rumours had abounded throughout the summer of 1939 of the club being compelled to fold, but the crafty James Black had quietly encouraged these stories (while publicly denying them) to force Forfar people to realise that the club really did need their support and money.

That was, of course, secondary to the world crisis with war expected at any moment. The Germans and the Russians had signed some sort of a deal, and already some supporters appeared at Station Park with their gas masks, pointing to the big gas tank behind the ground and asking what would happen if a bomb hit that. "Aye, leddie, there wid be naebody left ee toon bar the country fowk" was the answer.

Ominously, but in tune with the general brooding heavy atmosphere, the game took place with intermittent thunderstorms and occasional torrential rain. The football was poor, but Forfar did put up some sort of a fight, having the misfortune to have their centre forward Milne carried off with a broken arm when he crashed into a wooden fence at the side of the park, but Airdrie won 3-1, their first goal coming from a horrendous goalkeeping error. Both teams were given a loud ovation as they left the field, because, for all that anyone knew, this might be the last game of football at Station Park – ever.

August 27 1986

This was a remarkable and totally unpredictable night as Forfar beat St Mirren 5-1 to reach the quarter finals of the Scottish League Cup.

Forfar were in the First Division at the time and might have fancied their chances of a victory against Premier League St Mirren, but few could have predicted the score line, which in every way reflected Forfar's more or less total command of the game.

Forfar scored first through John Clark, but then St Mirren got a lucky equaliser from a deflection. Before half time Ray Lorimer put Forfar ahead with a long range effort which beat everyone, then soon after that, Gordon Scott made it 3-1. The young and very impressive Craig Brewster scored from outside the box in the 80th minute to put the issue beyond doubt and just on full time Steve Lennox made it 5.

Forfar fans found all this very hard to believe, but the Buddies found it even more difficult. A group of them tried to invade the stand to discuss matters with their Manager, Alec Miller, while singing a song that was inviting him to go and have sexual intercourse at a place other than Love Street, before some of the Forfar Directors invited the thickos to leave the premises.

On this performance, no-one could have predicted that St Mirren, even with another Manager, would win the Scottish Cup next May. It would have been even more unlikely for anyone to predict that Forfar supporters would be cheering them on, for their opponents would be Dundee United, who had been lucky to get the better of Forfar *en route*.

August 28 1954

Forfar earned their first point of the season in a 2-2 draw against Hamilton Accies at Station Park in the Scottish League Cup.

It was a good game with Forfar's goals coming early through Neil Young and late through Tommy Martin. Both teams had been heavily beaten by St Johnstone, so were unlikely to qualify for the Quarter Finals of the League Cup. So why is this game significant? Because it was my first (as far as I can recall) visit to Station Park to see Forfar.

A day short of my 6th birthday – in fact it was probably part of my birthday treat (Treat? In later years going to see Forfar sometimes felt like a punishment!) and having managed my first overhead kick with a football that very morning at the back door, I was intrigued to see that Hamilton's right back could do that as well, in his case clearing his lines quite spectacularly. And who was Hamilton's right back? A man called Bobby Shearer who went on to play for Rangers and Scotland a few years later. He probably would not have appreciated my remark about Hamilton's horizontal stripes that "If they ahd been green, it wid ave been Celtic".

The highlight of the day however, was when the ball ran out of play at the corner where the "mert" joins the "faraway" end, and I picked it up and returned it to Tommy Martin who said the immortal words "Thanks, son!". My love affair with Forfar had begun.

August 29 2015

Somerset Park, Ayr is not a ground that has moved with the times as much as some others. It is not an all seater ground, unlike that of neighbours and rivals, Kilmarnock whose empty stands look absolutely awful on TV.

The "honest men" (and "bonny lasses") are no strangers to the Premier League but could not be called a Premier League club. They have had their good seasons and many good players. Like Newcastle, they are also a real "United", being a union of Ayr and Ayr Parkhouse in 1910, unlike other "United" teams, notably the Dundee version who were just called United for the sake of it, or to replace the name "Hibs".

Other distinctions are that they are the only team in Scottish, and possibly British, football with only three letters in their name, and the only team whose ground has the same name as an English County Cricket team.

Today, Dick Campbell's men travelled to Somerset Park on the back of three impressive League victories. Although Lewis Allan scored first, Ayr then scored twice and Forfar were indebted to Michael Travis for a late equalizer. Forfar's team was Douglas, Black, Dunlop, Travis, Campbell, Hay, Young, Hodge, Denholm, Templeman and Allan, while Smith, Fotheringham and Malin were the substitutes.

With three wins and a draw, the League campaign was well begun, and there was no indication as yet of the horrors that were to come our way later in the season.

August 30 1919

This was possibly the most poignant game in the history of Forfar Athletic Football Club, for it was the first competitive game after the Great War, which had now been over for nine months, but in some ways was still going on. Indeed in some places – Russia, Ireland and the Middle East – there was still fighting in the usual way that a large war begets a few minor ones. And for some, of course, the war would never end. Loved ones didn't always come back and if sources like "Forfar In The Great War" are to be believed, the losses in our small town were horrendous.

But there was at least a football season (Forfar had managed to play a few friendlies earlier in 1919) in what was now called the Eastern League against Cowdenbeath. As a side effect of the chaos going on in 1919, someone had managed to steal Cowdenbeath's boots on the train journey, so they had to borrow some from Forfar Celtic Junior team. But unfamiliar boots or not, the game was a hammering – 0-5 for Cowdenbeath with Forfar never really in it, but it was hardly surprising, for so many men had been lost, injured, suffering from the "Spanish flu", still not demobbed or for one reason or other no longer available. Jim Black had struggled to get 11 men on the park that day, compelled to use veterans and youngsters. *The Courier* says the Forfar need a "stiffening" – but that was obvious. It would take a long time, but the main thing was that it was far better to talk about Cowdenbeath, Dundee Hibs and Arbroath than Verdun, the Somme or Mesopotamia.

Opposite and on following pages:
Forfar Athletic's first programme

OFFICIAL PROGRAMME 5p

FORFAR ATHLETIC F.C.

FORFAR ATH. v COWDENBEATH

SCOTTISH LEAGUE — SECOND DIVISION

STATION PARK, FORFAR   SATURDAY, 30th AUGUST, 1975

ART
TAXIS
4855

TOYOTA
IN ANGUS
IAN FISKEN
KINGSMUIR GARAGE

Tel.: FORFAR 2980

AUGUST MOON
Telephone: 4105

Licensed Restaurant
(Proprietor: ALLAN IP)

114 CASTLE STREET, FORFAR

CARRY OUT SHOP
2 Canmore Street, Forfar

RAMSAY LADDERS

Aluminium Ladders : Staircases
Fire Escapes : Platforms : Landings
Walkways : Special Fabrication

61 WEST HIGH STREET, FORFAR

Depots at London, Coventry, Leeds, Newcastle, Edinburgh, Glasgow.

COLOUR
T V
AT ITS BEST
COLIN M. SMITH
9 EAST HIGH STREET, FORFAR
Also at 20 Glengate, Kirriemuir

THE BETTER SERVICE SHOP

DINITROL GML
EUROPE'S PREMIER QUALITY RUSTPROOFING

Contact:
Dundee Dinitrol Rustproofing Centre
Tel.: KELLAS 287 : 259 : 345

Used Cars may also be treated

GEORGE MILNE
ELECTRICAL CONTRACTOR

Installations of All Types

SEE OUR SHOWROOMS FOR YOUR LIGHT FITTINGS

(Spanish, European and Scandinavian)

Telephone: FORFAR 2154

ANGUS MARTS (Properties) Ltd.

invite enquiries for
**PROPERTY SALES
BUILDING SOCIETY
MORTGAGES & INVESTMENTS**

Apply:
45 EAST HIGH STREET, FORFAR

Telephone: 2655/6

EDITOR'S NOTES

Today sees the start of a new era in the history of Forfar Athletic with the production of a regular club programme to be published at all home games. I hope that this will also coincide with an upsurge in the club's fortunes on the field and I am confident that this will happen. The league cup-ties against Alloa Athletic and Brechin proved that the team has more co-ordination and shooting power than for some time and despite the setback against Meadowbank, all at Station Park are full of confidence for the hard league programme ahead.

Regarding the programme I will be very pleased to hear of any ideas you may have to improve the programme or any questions you may wish to put to either the club management, the manager or any of the players and I will endeavour to print the answers for you.

I also hope to run quizzes, etc., for our younger fans with attractive prizes and of course the programme itself could be lucky.

A number is printed on the front cover and the winning numbers will be announced at half-time.

Look forward to hearing from you. Just write to me, the Editor, c/o Station Park.

FROM THE MANAGER'S DESK

Hullo Folks,

This is my first weekly bulletin to you. In future issues I will be telling you of my hopes and plans for the future. I will try to keep you all in the picture. I will be commenting on each as it comes along. And if it is possible I will answer some of your queries.

First of all I must make my position clear. As I stated at your annual general meeting I could not do very much with the team when I was

---

MAKE

McLAREN'S

YOUR GOAL

BRIDIES are the

CENTRE of Attraction

Come inside and be RIGHT . . .

Don't stay outside and be LEFT !

If you PASS you penalise yourself.

You'll come BACK to shop at the CORNER.

J. McLAREN & SON
MARKET STREET
FORFAR

Telephone: 3315

From FUSES to
FLOODLIGHTING . . .

SWITCH ON with

IAN WATSON

Electrical Contractor

12 KEMSLEY PLACE,
FORFAR

Telephone: 3452

Estimates without obligation

NEAREST BAR to the PARK

COMMERCIAL HOTEL
(Pat & Sandy McIntyre)

78 NORTH STREET, FORFAR

Telephone: 3181

FORFAR TRAVEL BUREAU

36 WEST HIGH ST., FORFAR

Telephone: 3140

RAIL, AIR & COACH BOOKINGS
HOLIDAYS in BRITAIN and Abroad

appointed manager last year. I made that clear at the time. But I did say I would introduce new blood and try to build up gradually.

Then in the close season I would start putting a new team together — with some of the existing playing staff, of course. My main aim is to produce a side which will play entertaining and exciting football. If, at the end of the season, they can be mid-way up the League so much the better. That is the target I have set my sights on.

But please remember that team-building costs money — sometimes a lot of money — and just now I have to cut my coat according to the cloth available.

In the League Cup games I think you will agree that the forwards have been producing football which is both fast and exciting. Unfortunately the defence made four mistakes. This week I will be getting the back four together to tighten up their play.

These are just some general comments to start with. I'll be letting you know more in our next programmes.

Good luck, good watching.

Yours,

JERRY.

FUND RAISING FOR THE "LOONS"

Under the above heading we would first of all thank the advertisers who have made this programme possible and we trust that you will give them your full support.

The annual sweepstake run by the Supporters' Club is underway once again and anyone who requires a ticket, only 5p a week, contact any committee member.

Gordon Webster is trying to get a Second "200 Club" off the ground and anyone interested, please get in touch.

THIRSTY ?
TRY ONE OF

CAMPBELL'S

FIFTEEN DELICIOUS VARIETIES NOW !

BUY QUALITY — BUY CAMPBELL'S CRYSTAL CLEAR LEMONADE

CHAPEL STREET, FORFAR

GARDEN MACHINERY

For all your requirements contact the Specialists

Kenneth Garland

19 Queen Street, Forfar

Tel.: 2978

LET OUR TEAM TAKE CARE OF YOUR BUILDING PROBLEMS

WEBSTER & PATULLO LTD.

Building Contractors

KINGSMUIR - FORFAR

Telephone: FORFAR 2274 & 3998

MECHANICAL EXCAVATORS & LORRIES AVAILABLE FOR HIRE

TODAY'S LINE UP

FORFAR ATHLETIC
(Colours Today — Red with Black and White Trim)

Team From: MILINSKI, WILL, CLARK, RITCHIE, LOWE, McHUGH, BRASH, STEIN, PAYNE, TRONT, BANNON, KYLES, SPINK, BOYLE, BROGAN.

Referee:
W. J. MULLAN
(Dalkeith)

Linesmen:
C. McBETH
(Aberdeen)

A. G. MUIR
(Blairgowrie)

COWDENBEATH
(Colours — Royal Blue and White Candy Stripe)

Team From: WILSON, CALLAGHAN, JONES, SEITH, REID, SIMPSON, McHALE, HUNTER, HARROW, MURPHY, ROSS, LAING, KINNELL.

Today's Match Ball has been donated by AGRICAR of Forfar.

Next Home Game — Saturday, September 13th v. Stirling Albion. K.O. 3 p.m.

RESULTS SO FAR

League Cup —		F. A.	Scorers
Aug. 9—Queens Park	(a)	0 - 5	
Aug. 13—Alloa Athletic	(h)	2 - 1	(Payne, Brogan);
Aug. 16—Brechin City	(h)	4 - 0	(Spink, Bannon, Payne, Boyle)
Aug. 23—Meadowbank Thistle	(h)	1 - 4	(Brogan)

SNIPPETS FROM THE PAST

10 YEARS AGO

Forfar fell to their third successive defeat when they lost at home to Stenhousemuir. The only noteworthy performance of the game for the home side was the shooting ability of youngster Archie Knox, and of course he went on to prove it in higher spheres. Goalkeeper Jim Stewart was to blame for both the visitors' goals.

Forfar Athletic 0, Stenhousemuir 2. Scorers: Dakers, Howie. On 28/8/65.

Team: Stewart, Carrie, Brodie, Duthie, Young, Arnott, Barclay, Knox, Junior, Potter, Mackle.

25 YEARS AGO

Arbroath came to Station Park needing victory to clinch Section D of the League Cup, but a great victory for the "Loons" before a crowd of 4,000 meant that Alloa clinched the Section. The "Dispatch" rated the game as one of the best for a long time, classing it as hard, fast and exciting stuff. Commended for his defensive qualities was full-back Sam Smith who, of course, is now a committee member of both the parent club and Social Club.

Forfar Athletic 4 (McKenzie 3, Falconer), Arbroath 1 (Milne), on 2/9/50.

Team: Brownlee, Smith, Stevenson, Garrie, Young, Cruickshank, Adams, McKenzie, Falconer, McLean, Perrie.

TODAY'S VISITORS

Today we welcome Cowdenbeath F.C. to Station Park for the first game of the new Second Division season. Like ourselves they must be classed as outsiders for promotion but they too will be out for a good start. They have made a slightly better start to their programme than ourselves and depending on last Wednesday's result (not known at time of going to press) were in with a fair chance of winning Section 9 of the League Cup.

Their manager is the experienced Don McLindon who was a player with Dunfermline, St Johnstone and Partick Thistle before becoming manager at Alloa. It was from there that he replaced Andy Mathew as manager at Central Park.

Their team is a mixture of youth and experience, the most experienced being goalkeeper Willie Wilson and full back Willie Callaghan. Wilson, a regular with Hibs in the sixties, moved on to Berwick Rangers before arriving at Cowdenbeath. Callaghan, too, arrived via Berwick after giving yeoman service to Dunfermline for many years, winning Scottish honours. He, of course, is a brother of Celtic's Tommy.

Other experienced players are Billy Laing, ex Rangers, Billy Simpson a rugged half-back who used to perform for Hibs and latterly Alloa. Winger Davie Ross played two trials for the "Loons" in Jake Young's era but Andy Mathew pipped Jake for his signature. Full-back Mervyn Jones, a cousin of John Greig, formerly played for Hibs and Stirling Albion.

Forwards McHale, Murphy and Harrow who has been attracting the Scouts lately, are all products of junior football, while Reid and Hunter have both sampled higher things with Hearts and Hibs respectively.

Last Seasons Results

Many of you regulars will remember the controversial ending to last season's League game with our visitors today. After Peter Mulherron had given the Loons an early lead, Cowdenbeath equalised in the last minute when the ball crashed down off the crossbar and referee Tom Muirhead awarded a goal despite the fact that the stand side linesman disagreed.

Then on New Year's Day Forfar were a bit unlucky to lose by the odd goal in three. Details were :—

Forfar Athletic 1, Cowdenbeath 1, on Saturday, 7th September, 1974. Scorer : Mulherron. Team : Milne, Fraser, Aalbrecht, Taylor, Hopcroft, Lowe, Cooper, Mulherron (Harrow), Phinn, Scott, Kyles.

Cowdenbeath 2, Forfar A. 1, on Wednesday, 1st January, 1975. Scorer : Mulherron. Team : Milinski, Will, Lowe, Moore, Robertson, Brash, Cooper, McManus, Mulherron, Hopcroft, Kyles.

SOCIAL CLUB SCENE

Entertainment over the next 10 days will be provided by :—

Tonight : TIPPENS
Tomorrow : MICKEY MOUSE
Thursday : EDDIE RAFFERTY in THE LOUNGE
Friday : EDDIE & THE TRAVELLERS
Saturday : PASSPORT
Sunday : BEEF.

LUNANHEAD PRECAST

Telephone: FORFAR 2510

LOCHHEAD SAND & GRAVEL

Telephone: FORFAR 2445

PLAYER FOCUS

Every week on this page we will turn the spotlight on one of the Station Park favourites. Today we start with team skipper John McHugh.

Full name — John McHugh;
Birthplace — Glasgow;
Date of Birth — No comment;
Height — 5 ft. 10 ins.;
Weight — 12 stone;
Previous Club — Clyde;
Married — Yes;
Family — 1 boy aged 2;
Occupation — Physics Teacher;
Car — Cortina G.T.;
Biggest influence on football career — John Prentice;
Favourite other team — Q.P.R.;
Most difficult opponent — Davie Robb, Aberdeen;
Most memorable match — Glasgow Select v. Leeds United;
Favourite Food — Steak;
Favourite T.V. Show — Kojak;
Favourite Singers — Neil Diamond, Chris Kristofferson.

TODAY'S MAN IN THE MIDDLE

Today's referee is the highly experienced Bill Mullan from Dalkeith. We at Station Park can only hope that his appointment today is a lucky omen for he was the man in charge of our only League victory over Raith Rovers last season.

Mr Mullan, a P.E. teacher in everyday life, was formerly on the F.I.F.A. list before an accident on the Forfar-Brechin road brought his career to a temporary halt two seasons ago. He handled the 1971 League Cup Final as well as many semi-finals and Internationals throughout Europe. He has also controlled the latter stages of the European Nations' Cup in Belgium (1972) and the Inter-Continental Cup in South America.

We wish him well today and throughout the season.

Kings & Co. Ltd.

QUARRYING & CONTRACTING

WHINSTONE, AGGREGATES, SAND, CEMENT, etc., Supplied.

FARM ROAD REPAIRS a Speciality with us.

ROBERTS STREET - FORFAR

Telephone: **Forfar 2374**

County School of Motoring

MINISTRY OF TRANSPORT
APPROVED
DRIVING INSTRUCTORS

Inquiries and Booking Arrangements:

76 EAST HIGH STREET
FORFAR   Tel.: **2195**

ALEXANDER BAIN
JOINER & UNDERTAKER

34 WEST HIGH STREET
FORFAR

Telephone: **3285**

E. MACARI
Newsagent & Tobacconist

90 EAST HIGH ST., FORFAR

Telephone: **3364**

A SHOP FOR GOOD TOYS

CAR SERVICES

MANOR STREET, FORFAR

Tel.: **3994**

CAR SALES AND REPAIRS

IAN S. NEILL

Painting Contractor

MONTROSE ROAD
FORFAR

Telephone: **4451**

August 31 1964

One of Forfar's largest crowds for several years rolled up to Station Park this Monday night to see Forfar take on East Fife in the play-off for qualification to the League Cup quarter finals. Forfar had started the season in stunning form, winning all four games in Section Nine and winning a League Cup section for only the third time since the inception of the League Cup in 1946.

East Fife of course were League Cup specialists, having won the trophy on three occasions, and this tie was given an added dimension with the news that Celtic awaited the winners in the quarter finals.

The referee was the famous Tom "Tiny" Wharton and the crowd saw a thrilling contest which Forfar won 4-3. Forfar had twice gone ahead with goals from Hamish Watt and Kenny Dick only to be pulled back, then East Fife took the lead before Dick scored again to level the tie. That would have been enough to be going on with, we thought, but in the midst of sheer delirium, Forfar scored again near the end when East Fife's centre half Young put the ball past his own goalkeeper Kruzycki.

It was an odd way to win a game, but of course the second leg awaited at Bayview a couple of days later. There the predictable happened, and Forfar's season never really recovered after that. East Fife then went on to beat Celtic 2-0 in the First Leg at Bayview before succumbing 0-6 at Celtic Park. How would Forfar have done?

September

September 1 1888

This was the day of Forfar's highest ever score in a competitive match, when at Station Park they beat Lindertis of Kirriemuir 14-1 in the First Round of the Scottish Cup. It is, of course, easy to disparage this result on the grounds that Lindertis were a very poor team, and they made the fatal mistake of winning the toss and choosing to play uphill to the "far away" goal. As a result they were 11 down at half-time (although there was a danger of losing count) with Jeck Cable, Eck Lamont (who rejoiced in the unlikely nickname of "Wap" or "Wappie") and Jamie Dundas absolutely rampant and even described as unstoppable.

Meanwhile the rain and the wind continued to hammer down that autumn afternoon on spectators who had no shelter from the elements. In the second half, Forfar added another three and Lindertis, now playing with the wind, scored as well to a chivalrous and sporting cheer from the Forfar fans.

It was widely believed however that the referee from Dundee (his name does not seem to have been given) took compassion on all concerned and shortened the game. Although this remains Forfar's best ever score, it was by no means the best score on that day in the Scottish Cup – Lochgilphead, for example, beat Balaclava Rangers 15 -1, and Cowlairs beat a Temperance Abstainers team 18-2 , the latter result perhaps indicating that "the demon drink" so thunderously denounced from pulpits maybe was not all that bad!

September 2 1939

In one of the most surreal games of football that Forfar have ever played, the Loons travelled to Montrose for a Second Division game.

They lost 4-1, and even the goal that they got was an own goal! But the game, like all games played that afternoon, was a dreamy, irrelevant one in front of a poor crowd with everyone's thoughts elsewhere. Yesterday Hitler had invaded Poland, and today the House of Commons was in emergency session with the drafting of an ultimatum and the declaration of war now inevitable. Some soldiers and those in emergency services had already been called up, and gas masks were visible among the crowd at Links Park, for everyone believed that an air attack was imminent, even before the declaration of war. The national anthem was played before the game, and received a loud cheer when it finished, and some of the war wounded of a previous conflict were seen to weep in their wheel chairs.

Montrose v Forfar games often seemed to lack the bite of the other Angus derbies at the best of times, and today when Montrose's goals went in, there was little more than polite applause and a resigned sigh from the Forfar side. The full time whistle came, and everyone scurried off home to listen to their wireless for news of their uncertain future. Many of them believed that they had seen their last ever football match. That was not necessarily true, but many long years would pass before things returned to anything like normality as far as football was concerned.

September 3 2006

Sunday football was becoming more common by 2006, but it was still fairly unusual in Forfar to have a game on the Sunday, caused in this case by Scotland having played the day before and having beaten the Faroe Islands 6-0 at Celtic Park. (On previous occasions they had had a little more bother with that opposition!)

So Ayr United came to Forfar this Sunday, as Forfar's distinctly unimpressive start to the season continued. Already out of the League Challenge Cup and the Scottish League Cup, they had only one win to their credit in the Scottish League. The Sky Sports Yearbook states laconically that "Forfar lost touch by mid-season". There were signs by this stage in early September that they were already losing touch, their inability to score goals a particular source of frustration for the fans.

In this case Ayr (who were not, in fact, a great deal better today) scored before half time and held on to their lead throughout the second half. It was one thing to have a bad season; it was quite another to know and to have that sinking feeling as early as September 3 that a stinker of a season was imminent and indeed unavoidable. Those of us who recalled the mid 1960s and the mid 1970s shuddered at the thought – but at least Scotland were better than the Faroe Islands!

September 4 1897

Forfar opened their Northern League season with a fine win over Dundee Wanderers before a good crowd of "not all that far short of the 1,000 mark" and the crowd were particularly impressed by a spirited fight back in the second half to win 3-2 after having been 2-0 down at half-time.

As was often the case at Station Park, the wind played a disproportionate part in proceedings because the terracing at the western end of the ground had not yet been built up and therefore the ground was exposed to the prevailing west winds. The Wanderers who had brought a few supporters from Dundee with them were 2-0 up, with Forfar's defence, now lacking Scott and Janes, guilty of "erratic kicking". It was a different matter in the second half, however, because Forfar simply peppered the Wanderers goal and Bowman and Boath scored with long range shots, and McFarlane sealed the game with a penalty kick.

A feature of Station Park was the appearance of goal nets. Not everyone was in agreement with these things, which did certainly billow in the strong wind and were distracting to the players, but on the other hand, they did minimise the arguments about whether it was a goal or not, as had happened, for example, in the 1893 Scottish Cup final between Queen's Park and Celtic.

September 5 1931

This may have been the depth of the economic depression which had led to the collapse of Ramsay MacDonald's Labour Government a fortnight before and its replacement by a National Government, but 600 Forfarians went to Arbroath by train and another 200 by road to see the first derby of the season.

However, as *The Arbroath Herald* reports gleefully, they departed in silence having seen their team go down 0-2 in one of the quietest derbies of them all. It was a hot sultry day with loads of people enjoying themselves on the beach, rather than going to the football.

Forfar were compelled to play the ageing Davie McLean when outside left Duncan injured himself before the game started. Davie was not as fit as he might have been (he was now over 40) and his deft flicks to colleagues and cannonball shots were missed as Arbroath scored once in each half, and it was only in the later stages that Forfar came into the game with Arbroath's goalkeeper Kelly doing well to keep Forfar at bay. Forfar's team was Sunter; Collie and Smart; Smith, Geddes and Ogilvie; Linton, Lawie, Black, Cabrelli and McLean.

The Sporting Post that night carried the story that Scotland's goalkeeper John Thomson of Celtic had been carried off injured at Ibrox that day. It was not until the following morning that the Sunday papers carried the dreadful news that the young Fifer had died at 9.30 pm on Saturday night. It was one of Scottish football's saddest days.

September 6 1919

Dundee was certainly the place to be on the first Saturday of September 1919.

Not only was it the last day of the cricket season with Forfarshire playing a side called Joe Anderson's XI which was in fact Perthshire (there had been very little cricket in 1919 with all the manpower shortages and general chaos), but there were two football matches as well.

Curiously to our modern eyes, Dundee and Dundee Hibs were both playing at home across the road from each other. Dundee (for whom Alec Troup was one of the few successes) lost 1-2 to St Mirren in the Scottish League, but the Hibs, rather fortunately and with the help of an early penalty, managed to beat Forfar 3-1 in the Scottish Qualifying Cup.

This was hard on Forfar (and generally admitted to be so in the Dundee Press) particularly as Jim Black had the devil's own job to scrape together eleven fit men to wear the black and blue. He had negotiated the transfer of two brothers called Gilligan from Dundee, and thus the following team took the field – Scott, J Gilligan and Gibb; Johnstone, Moir and Souter; Malcolm, Langlands, S Gilligan, Ewen and Bruce. The centre forward Sam Gilligan hadbeen given the honour of kicking the first ball at the new Hampden Park, in 1903, when he took the centre for Celtic, and he subsequently played for Bristol City in the 1909 English Cup final. Considering that this was a makeshift team, Forfar had reason to be proud of what they had achieved at Tannadice, but it still, even in the aftermath of such a cataclysm as the Great War, hurt to lose to a Dundee team, particularly the downmarket Hibs!

September 7 1895

On a sunny but rather windy day at Station Park in the Northern Football League, Forfar beat the Aberdeen side Orion 4-3 in what was generally agreed to have been a sporting encounter.

Curiously, when Station Park is nowadays considered to be one of the flatter pitches, Forfar are described as kicking off "downhill" with the wind and the sun behind them, which must mean they were playing towards the "Whitehills" or "town" or "station" end of the ground.

The wind would in fact play a significant part in the game for Forfar were winning 4-1 at half time but struggled by the end to keep the Aberdonians to 4-3. Indeed had Orion not lost a player to injury, it might have been a different story. Forfar's best players were Dave McFarlane, the famous Jack or "Jeck" Cable and a man called Scrymgeour who scored two goals. With a name like that, he must have come from Dundee!

The significance of this game was profound, for Forfar, who had already inflicted an 8-1 thrashing on Montrose, began to develop a little confidence in themselves and won the League by the end of the season, a tremendous achievement by the club who had endured more than their fair share of misfortunes in the past – and would certainly continue to do so in the future.

September 8 1981

Not often in almost 100 years of Forfar v Arbroath derbies has there been such a one-side occasion as this one. Played eccentrically on a Tuesday night, the game saw the amazing spectacle of Arbroath supporters heading for their cars and buses long before the final whistle, their team humiliated 6-0 in what can only be described as a "rout".

It was a fine Forfar side with Steve Hancock scoring twice and Brian Rankin, Alec Brash, Raymond Farningham and Billy Gallacher once each. Arbroath rarely got the ball over the halfway line to mount any sort of attack, and the joke was that it was six-nil and Arbroath were very lucky even to get nil. Forfar had started this season well. Still in the League Cup and with wins over Alloa and Berwick as well, things were looking good for this young and still very enthusiastic Forfar side.

It was indeed not a bad midweek at all for Forfar fans, for the following night in the World Cup Qualifiers, not only did Scotland beat Sweden, but Norway actually beat England on the famous occasion when the hysterical Norwegian commentator told people like Winston Churchill, Lady Diana and Maggie Thatcher that "Your boys took a helluva beating".

Not half as bad as the beating Arbroath took the night before, however!

September 9 1967

Forfar beat Arbroath 1-0 at Station Park – and that was good – but there was something definitely missing from Station Park that day.

No longer would we able to run up the "far away" terracing (the west end of the ground) to wave at passengers on trains steaming into and out of the station. On the previous Monday September 4, the last passenger train had run to and from Forfar, for the line from Stanley to Kinnaber had been closed to passenger traffic. (It would still be open for goods for some time). To say that this was a blow to the town was stating the obvious, and to those of us whose family roots lay in the railway it was a vicious wound.

But it had been part of the Beeching cuts of 1963 and public protests and letters to newspapers were of no avail. The fact that in 1967 we had a Labour Government while Forfar had always voted Conservative (Why? I never understood that – do you?) meant that there was no hope of a reprieve. The eventual closure of the station itself in 1982 would lead to a bizarre situation whereby Station Park was actually further away from a station and a railway line than most, if not all grounds in Scotland!

This game was not a bad one with Dave Keddie scoring the only goal of the game in the first half, but the big topic of conversation was the death of nine miners in a fire that day in the Michael Colliery in East Wemyss in Fife.

September 10 1994

Today was Forfar's first visit to Inverness on League business.

The Scottish League had been reconstructed to allow for Ross County and a new team called Inverness Caledonian Thistle. Many Invernesians felt that it would not work, but events have proved them wrong. When Inverness Caledonian and Inverness Thistle agreed to the merger, it was also agreed that a new stadium would be built, but for the moment Caledonian's stadium at Telford Street was deployed, and it was here that Forfar appeared, having won their first four League games of the season.

Quite a few Forfar supporters made the way up the A9 wishing to see football in Inverness, a rare treat for Forfar. This was of course a Division Three game; Forfar, having failed to qualify for Division Two, found themselves in the basement, something of a comedown since the great days of ten years ago. It was a fine autumn day, and first impressions of the ground were favourable, with the general view expressed that they did not really need a new stadium – but of course staying at Telford Street would have upset supporter of Inverness Thistle!

The crowd was 1731, far more than Forfar's average attendance both at home and away, but the game was a disappointment. Although Ian Heddle scored in the first half, Caley Thistle won 3-1, a result which gave those who had supported the merger a great boost. After a bad spell, Forfar then went on to win Division Three that season, and of course Inverness Caledonian Thistle never really looked back.

September 11 1897

Odd events at Station Park today, and something that is hard to parallel, or even imagine, in the 21st Century, although it was common enough in the early days.

Forfar were due to play a team called Arbroath Wanderers today in the Scottish Qualifying Cup, but as the trains came in to Forfar Station from Arbroath that morning, no Arbroath Wanderers disembarked.

Eventually a wire was sent to the effect that the Wanderers had missed their train and were coming either on a later train or by road (which would in 1897 have been long, difficult and would have required horses). Forfar then decided to open up their pay boxes (no turnstiles as yet at Station Park) to admit the crowd.

Still no Arbroath Wanderers had appeared long after the scheduled kick-off time, and with Forfar Athletic, their supporters and the referee all beginning to get impatient, another telegram arrived saying that they could not raise a team – something that had been the case even when they sent the first telegram which was now looked upon as stalling or playing for time.

Forfar, to their credit, gave everyone either their money back or a voucher for any other game this season then asked for volunteers to play a practice game with the Forfar players. This was good public relations and everyone joined in a general cursing of anything to do with Arbroath. As for Arbroath Wanderers, they disappeared soon after this, something that was hardly surprising! And Forfar, of course, were in the next round of the Qualifying Cup.

September 10 1988

Today's Match Sponsored by **J GAS**

FORFAR ATHLETIC v PARTICK THISTLE

STATION PARK, FORFAR
SATURDAY, 10th SEPTEMBER 1988

Official Programme **40p**

September 12 1908

Forfar had started the season badly following the loss of Geordie Langlands to Dundee.

Today they travelled to Nursery Park, Brechin to play the new club Brechin City. Football had been slower to start in Brechin than in other Angus towns, although they had good reason to be proud of their cricket club. The football club, Brechin City (Forfar people always sneered at the word "City" but they did have a cathedral, so were entitled to use that term) had been formed in 1906 with the amalgamation of two Junior teams, Brechin Harp and Brechin Hearts.

Already in the few games that they had played each other, a certain amount of local rivalry had been in evidence. Today in spite of Forfar having lost two games and drawn one in the Northern League, a reasonable crowd went with them by train, and although they returned with a 2-2 draw, it was generally agreed that Brechin were the better team and should have won.

The Courier admits that Forfar had their problems with Cargill "hors de combat" for a long spell of the game, but also says that Forfar goalkeeper Orr had a splendid match, and that "the locals were weak at shooting". Forfar have been "badly out of joint" this season, but had this weekend signed a new forward called McConnell of Dundee Harp who had played for Perth Craigie the previous season. He was described as a "top class finisher" and that was something that Forfar were badly needing.

September 13 1980

Having been temporarily knocked off their perch at the top of the League in a 0-1 midweek defeat at Recreation Park, Alloa, the Loons returned to the top today with a 3-2 win over Meadowbank Thistle at Station Park.

It was a win but a far from convincing one, and *The Forfar Dispatch* writer is compelled to admit that he was happy to hear the final whistle, something that the body language of the crowd seemed to agree with, for they all edged round to the east end of the ground and stood at the top of the terracing ready to charge down the steps on their way home after several minutes of urging the man in black to "blaw yer f***in' whustle, min!".

Forfar were without Billy Gallacher and Alec Brash and with respect to those who stood in for them, they were sadly missed. Forfar's goals were scored by John Clark (one was a penalty) and the other came from Neil Watt. Forfar's best players were all defenders – Stewart Kennedy, Billy Bennett and Kenny Brown – and that was surely significant.

But on the other hand, a win was a win, and there always is merit in a team which can win even when not playing at their best. "Winning ugly" was surely better than spectacular and glorious failure, and conventional wisdom at all levels of football did say that the way one wins League Championships and earns promotions is by grinding out results. "Champagne soccer", never seen in great quantity at Station Park at the best of times, could wait for some other day. We were back at the top of the League.

September 14 1895

Seldom can a writer have got something more wrong than did the writer of *The Forfar Herald* when he says that "Football is evidently dying in Montrose as well as in Forfar".

More than 120 years later, we really must dispute that judgement, but he bases it on "the great contrast between Saturday's attendance and the crowds that used to assemble a few years ago at Links Park. A reaction might set in this season but with the perpetual draining of provincial clubs by the wealthy professional clubs of the big towns, there is little hope".

Clearly a man of melancholic temperament, our scribe would have had more cause for despondency in the score line which read Montrose 7 Forfar 3 in this Northern League game. Goalkeeper Thom had a good game and but for him, "one shudders to think what the score line might have been", and left half Mann played well while up front the veteran John Cable (the famous "Jeck") showed a lot of his old pluck and dash. Centre forward Boath scored a good goal, but the loss of seven was "rather too many".

However, this was early in the season still, and our writer was not to know that the Athletic were to recover spectacularly and at the end of the season would be champions of the now revitalised Northern League. And, the attendances would improve as well. The game did not die.

Stewart Kennedy

September 15 1951

Forfar paid their first ever visit to Celtic Park.

They had earned this right by a very successful League Cup qualifying campaign, in which they had won a section which contained difficult opposition in Kilmarnock, Dumbarton and Ayr United.

This game was the first leg of the League Cup quarter final. It was probably true to say that the sight of "Paradise" was a disappointment given its general run down condition and the hideous cow barn of a shelter which rejoiced in the not entirely inappropriate name of the "the Jungle" bestowed on it by soldiers returning from the war in the Far East. There were holes in the roof of this structure and weeds growing on the terracing.

36,000 were there to see Celtic win fairly easily 4-1. Bertie Peacock, Joe Baillie, Bobby Collins and Jimmy Walsh scored for Celtic while Forfar's only goal came from George Cunningham. But Forfar were in no way dismayed at their performance, for there was still the second leg at Station Park to come.

In any case, the large cheque and the fact that the players could now say that they had played at Celtic Park against men like Tully, Evans and Peacock (who were their heroes in some cases) sweetened the pill considerably. It was almost certainly the largest crowd that Forfar had ever played in front of, and the part-timers were given a hearty reception from the huge crowd of over 30,000, many of whom still remembered Davie McLean who had played for Celtic over forty years ago.

September 16 1950

The Korean War was now in full spate, and there was a widespread fear that with China and Russia becoming involved, it might turn into a full scale World War.

At a slightly more mundane level, Forfar had now quite clearly recovered from their poor start to the season. Having lost their first three games, they had now won five in a row and today's 1-0 win over Queen's Park at Hampden was a particularly satisfactory occasion.

They fielded two trialists from Aberdeen Sunnybank, Alec Johnstone and Eric Harper, and both made a strong impression, but it was Stewart McLean who scored the only goal of the game in the second minute, and it was a cracker from 25 yards. Forfar's star man was the veteran Tommy Adams, "now at a walking pace" in the words of *The Sunday Post* who welded the team together in a "workmanlike intelligent side", but also impressive was young Ian Duff in the centre forward position. With a bit of luck, he might had added to the Forfar score. Queen's Park on the other hand are described as "a ramstam bunch" and their shooting was wild to the major disappointment of the 5,000 crowd, a figure that says a great deal about football attendances in the post-war era. Forfar's team was Brownlee, Harper and Cruickshank; Wotherspoon, McKenzie and Falconer; Adams, Johnstone, Duff, McLean and Perrie.

September 17 1934

The town of Forfar, and Forfar Athletic FC in particular was shocked by the sudden death of Provost Tom Hanick who was among other things Chairman of Forfar Athletic.

He collapsed and died suddenly at the Sheriff Court where he was about to preside as magistrate. He was only 56. His contribution to the club had been immense. He was a great friend of Willie Maley of Celtic and used this on numerous occasions to the club's advantage, not least in securing Forfar's future when the Third Division imploded in 1926, leaving Forfar with the distinct possibility of having to apply for some Regional League.

He appears to have been a man who was genuinely loved by everyone (not all local politicians are as well liked as they pretend to be!) and his funeral was quite the biggest that the town had ever seen. He was a friend of the poor and the old folk, a practising Roman Catholic who was nevertheless quite prepared to drive a horse and cart through bigotry by being friendly with Rev WG Donaldson of the Old Kirk, and a man who also loved football and Forfar Athletic.

By birth a Forfar man, whose father had also served as Councillor, Hanick had a great antiquarian interest in the history of the town. He was a bachelor and lived with his sister in East High Street. There is of course a permanent reminder of this great and nowadays undervalued man in the naming of Hanick Terrace after him.

Tommy Adams and Jimmy Caskie

September 18 1959

This Friday saw one of Scotland's worst ever mining disasters. This was at Auchengeich in North Lanarkshire when 47 men were killed through smoke inhalation and fire.

Games were played on the Saturday (Forfar losing 1-5 to Alloa at Recreation Park) with the men still trapped underground and the mine had to be flooded to put out the fire. It was a few days later before the men could be found.

One of them was Donald Weir, aged 30, from Kilsyth, who had played for Forfar until recently. He had joined the team in 1956 but had never really starred in the inside left position. He was possibly a little too tall for an inside forward who were usually small nippy players in the 1950s, and certainly not quick enough. Prematurely bald and not really very athletic, Donald nevertheless had played a few good games.

He had appeared for Celtic a decade previously (even on one occasion scoring a goal against Rangers) but Celtic were in a bad way in the late 1940s and he did not last long with them. He was often confused in people's minds with another Weir called Jock Weir who played with Celtic at the same time and who won a Scottish Cup medal with them in 1951. Donald went on to play in Irish football for a spell, after he left Celtic, before turning up for Forfar.

September 19 1951

This was one of the best games in Forfar's history as they drew 1-1 with Celtic in the second leg of the Scottish League Cup semi-final at Station Park to lose 2-5 on aggregate.

6,900, with a large Celtic contingent from Dundee and indeed Forfar itself, saw a great game with some factories and shops bending to reality and closing early to allow fans to attend the early evening kick-off. It was a game full of incident, not least the disappearing ball which vanished into the crowd early on and failed to return!

Forfar scored first, but even before that happened, Forfar were denied a penalty kick when Sean Fallon appeared to handle inside the box, yet the decision was a free kick outside the box. However Forfar went ahead when captain McLean scored from another free kick in the 35th minute, and they might even have scored again. However, the tie was effectively killed a minute before half-time, when Bertie Peacock scored into an empty net after Forfar's defence was posted missing.

In the second half, Peacock was brought down in the box, but took the penalty kick and sent it past the post, possibly deliberately, on the suggestion of Charlie Tully, because it was an extremely soft penalty.

The teams were Forfar: Ingram, McNellis and McCluskey; McLean, McKenzie and Hamilton; Adams, Fearn, Lawrence, Cunningham, Mechan while Celtic had Devanney, Fallon and Rollo; Evans, Mallan and Baillie; Millsop, Walsh, McPhail, Peacock and Tully and the referee was Mr Anderson from Edinburgh.

The Courier which reports this game carried another two items of interest – there will be a General Election on October 25, and Forfar Town Council have decided to buy Gallowshade Fruit Farm from Mr D Allison at the cost of £20,000 with a view to building a housing scheme there. It was a decision which would permanently change the shape of the town!

September 20 1924

Season 1924/25 would see Forfar relegated into Division Three of the Scottish League, and the problems were already apparent at this early stage of the season.

Admittedly the opposition today were Clyde at Shawfield, a strong outfit, but Forfar were simply not there in the game as an attacking force and went down 4-0 which could have been a great deal worse but for some good goalkeeping, stout defending and sheer luck. *The Sunday Post* is quite scathing about the play of both Forfar full backs Braid and Grainger. "Seldom has such weak back play been seen in Second Division football as that by the Forfar pair" and in truth the rest of the team did not seem to be much better, although the half backs were "not so very bad". Forwards Thomson and Cook were given a little praise, but there was not much else to be happy about. There was simply not enough creative talent to supply the ageing Langlands.

Jim Black of course knew that the players were simply not good enough, but in the economic circumstances of the early 1920s, there was no money to spend on other players. Changes were required, though to the team of Smith, Braid and Grainger; Rae, Smart and Nichol; Miller, Jeffrey, Thomson, Langlands and Cook. In the meantime, there was considerable speculation about how long the minority Labour Government of Ramsay MacDonald was likely to last.

September 21 1895

Forfar beat Dundee "A" 3-1 at Station Park today. Two Dundee teams Our Boys and East End had now amalgamated, to call themselves Dundee, and to play in the Scottish League. There were rumours that they were hoping to move from Carolina Port to a place in the Dens area just outside the city.

The "A" team were sometimes called the "Swifts" or less flatteringly, the "stiffs" or the "ham and eggers" on the grounds that they were not paid, but they were given a meal for playing. They still played in the Northern League but today they were well beaten by a good Forfar side for whom James Cable scored twice and the other was scored by Scrymgeour, ironically enough from Dundee.

The Forfar Herald does not go into any great detail about the game but remarks "Our local team have, I notice, again erected their grandstand. Though only about one quarter of its former size, it will no doubt prove amply sufficient and a 'boon and a blessing' to all who are pleased to speculate a small sum for a comfortable seat". One would like to know more about this. What side of the ground was it on, for example? One assumes it was on the same side as the present stand. It seems to have replaced a previous structure, and may well have lasted until the early 1920s. What a pity that no-one ever, in 1895 or even a later date, thought fit to take a photograph of what the ground actually looked like, although a photograph of Celtic's visit in 1914 shows a small stand on the north side of the ground.

September 22 1984

Forfar's good start to the First Division continued with a good 3-1 win over Meadowbank at the Meadowbank Stadium in Edinburgh. It was all the more creditable for they were a goal down at half-time and Meadowbank looked the better side after a very early goal, but Forfar fought back in the second half with the benefit of an own goal and counters from Gary Murray and Bobby Cormack.

The stadium was a funny one with no atmosphere, and absolutely nothing at all on three sides of the ground. Meadowbank had a good start to the season themselves, and had reached the semi-final of the Scottish League Cup where they were due to take on Rangers.

Sadly they would not be allowed, for safety reasons, to play their leg of the semi-final at the Meadowbank Stadium, so they would have to use Tynecastle. With their Manager Terry Christie, a school headmaster in his spare time and who wore his characteristic duffle coat, they were often described as the "Cinderella" team of Edinburgh, but they brought a much needed dash of life to the capital where football triumphs were by no means common, and mediocrity was tolerated to a remarkable extent.

Glasgow obviously won a lot of trophies, and Aberdeen and Dundee United were now beginning to make their mark, not least in Europe, but Edinburgh's Hearts and Hibs would continue to struggle for some time. It was even possible that Cinderella might even get to the Ball long before the Two Ugly Sisters, but today Forfar, another Cinderella in some respects in 1984, had got the better of them.

September 23 2003

Station Park and 1,110 fans saw another Forfar giant killing, in the Scottish League Cup, when Forfar of the Second Division beat Premier League Motherwell 4-2 on penalties after a pulsating 3-3 draw in which it was difficult to distinguish which of the two teams was the Premier outfit.

Motherwell, managed by Terry Butcher and helped by Maurice Malpas, scored first with a 3rd minute toe-poke from Steven Craig, and the Fir Park side looked well on top until Darren Henderson equalised near half-time. Then in an astonishing ten minute spell Paul Tosh scored twice only to see his strikes levelled by Keith Lasley and Stephen Pearson. That seemed to be that, we thought. Forfar had had their moment of glory, but now that the Premier League team had made it 3-3, they would surely now go on to win.

But, no, backed up by an increasingly noisy support, Forfar stuck to the task and took the game to extra time. Once again the emotions of pride and apprehension took over. We had done well, but this was now extra time against full-time, and better trained, players. Yet again, Forfar competed bravely and indeed might have won when Paul Tosh charged through on his own and fired just wide.

Penalties it was – into the Whitehills End goal – and after two Motherwell players who missed, it was Paul Shields who sunk his penalty to give Ray Stewart's men victory and to allow Forfar fans their chance to sing and dance. The win earned us a trip to Ibrox to meet Rangers. It would be a fairly predictable hammering, but there would also be a fat cheque to minimise the pain.

September 24 1949

Forfar travelled to Gayfield to play the Arbroath first team in Division "B" for the first time in 15 years, for the two teams had not been in the same Division since Arbroath were promoted in 1935. Such was the interest in this game that four extra carriages were added to the train, the incentive being that the fare was reduced to two bob (10 pence).

The Forfar Dispatch writer, clearly a card player says "it not only took a trick, it was a veritable Grand Slam". The attendance was an excellent 6,000 and they saw a fine game in which Forfar were clearly the better team and deserved their 3-2 victory.

Tommy Adams, a wise old fox, realised the sun was in the eyes of the Arbroath keeper who was not wearing a cap, and tried what was called a "drooper" over his head. Sunter and Rodger then added more goals when the Maroons threatened to come back into the game, and Forfar ran out worthy winners and possessors of "bragging rights" over the Red Lichties for the foreseeable future. "The Maroons were fair wannert" in the immortal words of *The Forfar Dispatch*. The train back to Forfar was a happy one that night, and the jollity continued in the Jarman's Hotel and the Commercial Hotel when the train disgorged its delighted passengers.

September 25 1954

The weather was pleasant, but Forfar fans were far from optimistic as they trudged up North Street to see Forfar and old rivals Stenhousemuir. The performances so far had been distinctly uninspiring, and today Doug Berrie was out injured and a youngster called Doig from Forfar Celtic was being given a game.

Also, and here was my claim to fame, I actually knew and had spoken to, that very morning, Forfar's new goalkeeper! He was a policeman called Andy Rough who had played for Forfar East End, and who had lodgings with Mrs Milne, my next door neighbour!

It turned out to be a great game of football, ending up in a 2-2 draw which Forfar felt that they should have won. They played with refreshing speed and enthusiasm from the start and before half-time Willie Dunn and Ian Stewart put Forfar two goals ahead. Not only that, but Tommy Martin hit the post and then a Stenhousemuir defender headed off the line with the goalkeeper beaten. Forfar were cheered off the park at half-time for a tremendous performance, but, Forfar being Forfar, they let things slip for a few minutes in the early part of the second half and Stenhousemuir were able to draw level. But then Forfar rallied again, and with a bit of luck might just have grabbed a winner.

It would have been so important to me, for I had not yet seen them win a game. This was Forfar's first League point of the season, the other two games having been painful defeats to Angus rivals Arbroath and Brechin City. But then again when you are only 6 years old, you are allowed to burst into tears when Forfar lose. Later on in life, it is not nearly so socially acceptable, even though the emotion is just as keen!

September 25 1948

Forfar Athletic v Chirnside United. Scottish Qualifying Cup-tie, at Station Park, Forfar, 25 September, 1948.

September 26 1925

Clackmannan are one of the teams that never survived the harsh economic times of the 1920s. Today they came to Station Park for a Third Division fixture, Forfar having been relegated from the Second the previous season. There was a certain feeling (correct, as it turned out) that a Third Division of the Scottish League was not particularly viable, for no other reason than that some clubs found it difficult to travel long distances.

Today's visitors to Station Park were not destined to last long, and today's defeat to a Forfar team which was really too strong for the Third Division was a heavy one. Not deterred by a few early reverses this season, Forfar had now steadied the ship and today they put on a great performance to delight their fans as they beat Clackmannan 5-0. Jacky Connon scored late in the first half and then in the second half Eck McLean scored twice and Willie Davidson and Alec Nicoll once each.

This was a vital win for Forfar, because last year's demotion to the Third Division had not gone down well in certain quarters in the town. Rumours abounded about a plot to oust Jim Black and his committee, or even for one of the junior teams like Forfar East End or Forfar Celtic to try to join the Senior Leagues at the expense of Forfar Athletic. Such stories were of course fanciful, but must be seen against the background of the 1920s where revolutionary changes in society in general were forever threatened and the General Strike, of course, was not far away.

September 27 1958

Forfar and East Fife served up a tremendous game of football today at Station Park. It ended 4-4, (something that came close to the fabled but fictitious score line of East Fife 5 Forfar 4) and both teams deserved the utmost credit for the way they entertained the crowd of slightly over 1,000.

East Fife were ever so slightly on the decline by now from their heady days of a few years earlier when they had graced the First Division and (almost incredibly to modern ears) won the Scottish League Cup three times before Celtic even appeared in a final!

But the sustained success could not go on for ever and the good players like Charlie "Legs" Fleming, Dod Aitken, Jimmy Bonthrone and Henry Morris had all gone. Forfar's goals were scored two each by Jimmy Russell and Peter Craig, and they did well to come back from a 2-3 half-time deficit.

Station Park was a strange looking place with two stands on the north end of the ground, but neither completely serviceable. The old wooden one was, fairly obviously, falling apart and was very vulnerable to gales, whereas the new one was not yet completed. There was a very narrow bottle-neck between the two of them, which was frankly rather dangerous when the crowd was moving round at half-time.

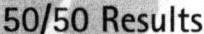

▪ ▪ ▪ ▪ 50-50 ▪ ▪ ▪ ▪

Did you buy a 50/50 ticket when you came in today? If not why not? The 50/50 is run by the Forfar Athletic Supporters Club and apart from the printing costs 50% goes to the winner and 50% goes to the club. Each ticket costs 50p so the more tickets sold the better the prize that can be won!!!

50/50 Results

Saturday 26/09/09 v Elgin;

Winner

David Potter (yes, that David Potter), Kirkcaldy won £245.50

Go on buy a ticket today and good luck.

September 28 1983

It was rewarding, and yet sad at the same time to go to East End Park, Dunfermline and see Forfar win 2-1 with goals from Jim Liddle and Ray Farningham.

Forfar were, of course, off to a flier in the Scottish League Second Division with six wins and a draw out of seven starts. Dunfermline, on the other hand were struggling, in their excellent stadium with a fine stand built (to replace a grizzly, wooden horror of a structure) from their prosperity of 20 years earlier when Jock Stein was their Manager. Tonight East End Park held only 856 people, a shocker of an attendance for a town the size of Dunfermline.

Sitting in their nice stand, one could not but notice the difference in attitude between the two teams – Forfar were slicker, more determined and faster to the ball, whereas the Pars were ill-organised and played with the attitude of "defeat is inevitable" even when they held Forfar to 1-1 for a considerable period of the game.

Some of the Pars fans, a reasonable bunch it has to be said, were full of praise for Doug Houston and his men while others were of the "no comin back" variety who inhabit Station Park as well when times are tough. Football always will have its winners and its losers. Forfar were (temporarily) in the ascendant, but the decline of Dunfermline looked to be terminal.

Doug Houston

September 29 1930

Forfar won the Forfarshire Cup for the third time in their history by beating Dundee 2-1 at Dens Park.

This time there was no parading in triumph through the streets as there had been in 1906 and 1908, but this victory was definitely one of the better results in our history, for Dundee were in the First Division at the time. The game was played on a Holiday Monday and attracted only a "moderate crowd" – something that perhaps said something about the economic recession, which was now having a considerable impact on the jute industry – although there was a fair sprinkling of Forfar supporters there.

Dundee showed respect for the competition by fielding a full strength team, and the result caused a few ripples round Scotland, although in all honesty it has to be said that Dundee had done well to avoid relegation last season, and were not enjoying the best of times. A feature of both teams was the amount of men who had played for the other in the past. Forfar's Davie McLean had played for Dundee (among many others), for example, and Eckie Troup had started his career with Forfar and was now nearing the end of his career with Dundee after his return from Everton.

Dundee scored first, but Forfar, masterminded by McLean, fought back and wee Davie Kilgour, a prolific scorer at this time scored once in each half. Forfar's star man was goalkeeper Charlie Sunter. Poor Eckie Troup was jeered at by a few idiots in the Forfar support as if to prove the Biblical adage that "a prophet is without honour in his home town." It was a great day for Forfar, and James Black was beside himself with joy, making a joke that, as President of the Forfarshire Association, he could hardly present the Cup to himself, so the Vice President Mr Oram of Brechin had to present it to Forfar's Chairman Tom Hanick.

September 30 1939

This momentous month in world history finished with Scottish football in turmoil and Forfar Athletic in crisis. The first hysterical reaction to the outbreak of war on September 3 had been to stop football altogether.

This was relaxed a few days later, and on September 26, the Scottish League had come up with a plan to have two Regional Leagues of 16 teams each – but Forfar Athletic, Brechin City, Montrose, East Stirlingshire, Edinburgh City were to be excluded while Leith Athletic and St Bernard's of Edinburgh were asked to amalgamate. No logic or thought seems to have gone into this plan and it naturally caused outrage.

Today in the Hotel Seaforth in Arbroath, all six Forfarshire clubs met and passed a resolution deploring the decision to exclude the three Angus clubs. Sadly, this did not prevent Dundee, Dundee United and Arbroath from voting FOR the proposal at the Scottish League meeting a few days later! The proposal was passed by 31 votes to 7.

All this effectively meant that Forfar Athletic were left with little option to close down "for the duration" although they did try manfully to play some Forfarshire Cup games and a few friendlies for a spell. There was a certain legacy of justifiable bitterness as well towards the three "I'm all right, Jack" clubs who had apparently changed their position, although it had been put to them that the alternative to the two Regional Leagues would have been no football at all. War-time football is regarded as unofficial, but it was certainly better than nothing.

QUEEN OF THE SOUTH F.C. LTD.
BLUE AND WHITE
OFFICIAL PROGRAMME

No. 4 (XIII. Series) 30th September, 1950 PRICE THREEPENCE

TEAMS:

QUEEN OF THE SOUTH

Right   HENDERSON   Left
1

SHARPE   JAMES
2   3

M'BAIN   WALDIE   AIRD
4   5   6

WOOTTON   PATTERSON   C. BROWN   J. BROWN   JOHNSTON
7   8   9   10   11

Kick-off 3 p.m.

Referee:
Mr SCOTT, Paisley.

PERRIE   M'LEAN   SUNTER   M'KENZIE   ADAMS
11   10   9   8   7

CRUIKSHANK   YOUNG   WOTHERSPOON
6   5   4

STEVENSON   SMITH
3   2

Left   BROWNLIE   Right
1

FORFAR ATHLETIC

The "Standard"
For NEWS and ADVERTISEMENTS.

Read "Onlooker's" Review every Saturday.

Published by the Queen of the South Supporters' Association and
Printed by Thos. Hunter, Watson & Co., Ltd., Standard Press, Dumfries

Gordon "Bull" Smith receives the Player of the Month award for September 1977

October

TODAY'S MATCH SPONSORED BY

W. WELSH
Roofing Contractor

SEASON 1983-84
OFFICIAL PROGRAMME 25p

SCOTTISH LEAGUE
DIVISION TWO

FORFAR ATHLETIC
v EAST FIFE

STATION PARK,
FORFAR

SATURDAY, 8th
OCTOBER, 1983

October 1 1938

One would not really imagine the Prime Minister Neville Chamberlain to be a natural hero of Forfar Athletic supporters.

Even those (distressingly many) who voted Conservative would have found him pompous, stiff and unlovable, always dressed in black and always carrying an umbrella as if he knew that it was going to rain soon!

But today he was the hero of the hour, for yesterday he had negotiated what posterity called the Munich Agreement, winning "peace in our time" as he said.

In fact it was peace for less than a year! But Forfar fans turned up at Station Park today singing his praises, not least the very many supporters now in wheelchairs and invalid carriages from wounds received only 20 years ago as an eloquent testimony to the folly of war. So, the National Anthem was sung with gusto and everyone was upbeat – until the game started!

Forfar were hammered 6-2 by a good Alloa side, but Forfar were terrible. "Forfar's problems were many and reconstruction an immediate task" as *The Courier* uncompromisingly put it. That annoying thing was that they had gone two goals down, then fought back to make it 2-2 with goals from Geordie McLean and Bob Samson, before collapsing in the second half as Alloa simply ran riot.

What had started off a great day had now become a nightmare, but at least the fans left the ground convinced that future problems would be on the football field rather than the battlefield.

Winston Churchill and a few others, however, demurred.

October 2 1999

Forfar delighted their paltry crowd of 397 with a marvellous display of attacking football to defeat Dumbarton 5-0.

The season had not really had much going for it so far with only two victories in the League and already out of both the Scottish League Cup and the League Challenge Cup.

Not only was to-day a great performance in itself, it was the springboard to four successive wins in the month of October. A hat-trick was scored by Steven Milne, a player on loan from Dundee.

Looked upon as something of a prodigy, this 19-year-old spent all season with Forfar, scoring 16 goals in 35 appearances, and there are those who believe that he should have stayed a little longer with Forfar. He might have done better not to return to the crazy world of Dens Park in the early years of the century where a Scottish Cup final appearance was followed by administration!

Innes MacDonald and Andrew Cargill scored the other goals in what was a really incisive and impressive Forfar performance which had the supporters cheering them and clapping them off the park – something that one would have to describe as a rare phenomenon these days.

Manager Ian McPhee pronounced himself delighted with the performance. Another loanee that day was Barry Robson, a man who went on to have a distinguished career with many clubs, notably Dundee United, Celtic and Aberdeen. Forfar's team was Garden, McCheyne, Craig, Taylor, Rattray, Donaldson, MacDonald, Cargill, Brand, Milne, Robson with McPhee, McIlravey and Morris as substitutes.

October 3 1981

Forfar continued their impressive early season form with a very competent 3-1 win over Stranraer at Station Park.

This game had followed a week of almost continuous rain leading to serious flooding in several parts of the country, but it had all stopped now and the ground was visibly drying out.

Having only lost one League game so far, to Montrose, Alex Rae's Forfar approached this game with a certain degree of confidence, the only other blot on the copybook so far being an admittedly dreadful 6-0 hammering from St Mirren. That had knocked them out of the Scottish League Cup in the quarter final second leg and was all the more disappointing because the first leg of the quarter final had been a very creditable 1-1 draw.

Today, although Stranraer scored first against the run of play, Ray Farningham equalised before half time and John Clark scored twice in the second half to allow Forfar to win the game with a degree of ease. The team was Boardley, Morris, Bennett, Brown, Brash, Allen, Gallacher, Farningham, Hancock, Clark and Leitch with Watt and Craig as substitutes. This victory put Forfar into fourth place in the Second Division, and it would, of course, be the year in which Forfar had their great Scottish Cup run.

It remains an open question whether they would have won the League this year without the Cup run. I always felt they were good enough to win the League, but sadly too many games were drawn instead of being won, and promotion was still a year or two in the distance.

October 4 1951

The death was announced of James Black at the age of 85, a legendary figure in Forfar Athletic history. He had been ill for some time, and had spent most of 1951 in a Dundee nursing home. He was in with Forfar Athletic at the very start and basically ran the club from 1884 until his death, proudly boasting that he never took a penny for doing so.

In between times he was a referee, taking charge, for example, of the first ever game at Dens Park, Dundee and running the line for Scotland on various occasions, notably the Scotland v England international of 1912. He was commonly known as "Mr Forfar" at SFA meetings and was a great friend of men like Willie Maley of Celtic.

He was never universally popular in the town – but that possibly says more about small town jealousy than it does about "Jeem" – but his contribution to town life did not stop at football, for he was a Justice of the Peace and a Parish Councillor.

In the Great War he served on the Tribunals to decide whether men should be conscripted or not, and did his best to save many a Forfar man from the carnage but was frequently outvoted by the military.

He was affable, cheerful and sociable, albeit a shade too dogmatic on occasion, and everything that Forfar Athletic was in 1951 could be put down to James Black.

His funeral in the Old Kirk and the Newmonthill Cemetery was attended by all the dignitaries of Scottish football. If Willie Maley was "the man who made Celtic", then James Black was "the man who made Forfar". He lived in North Street and was survived by his second wife Sarah.

James Black

October 5 1968

Forfar were now a respectably placed sixth in the Second Division (dizzy heights compared with two or three years ago!) following a hard fought game at Bayview against East Fife in which Forfar emerged victorious 2-1 with goals from Jim Young and Ian Wyles. Both centre halves were Forfarians John Fyfe of Forfar Athletic and Alan Guild of East Fife. They were close friends and indeed members of the same BB Company (And how do I know that? Because so was I, as indeed was the Forfar legend David McGregor!) but today there was no quarter sought or given.

Arguably, East Fife might have earned a draw, but Forfar triumphed, to the delight of the sizeable travelling support in the crowd which was not all that far short of 2,000. Indeed a feature of Forfar's revival from the awful days of 1965 and 1966 was that the support was now returning and even attending away games, proving that there always a residue of good will for the club. Not all the support, mind you, were renowned for their sensitivity or intelligence, for one of them singled out Alan Guild and shouted at him "Guild, you're just a Farfar c***"

That was bad enough, but it was aimed at the wrong guy, another East Fife defender who did not even remotely resemble the said Alan Guild. The same Alan Guild, incidentally, gave me a lift to and from the game in his car. We were both at St Andrews University at the time. We were good friends, really. He was in fact just a "Farfar – er – chap" –and a damned good football player, too!

October 6 1934

Arbroath would eventually win promotion this year from the Second Division, but they very definitely had luck on their side at Station Park today in their 3-1 victory over a plucky Forfar team who never gave up fighting.

The relentless rain failed to deter a crowd of 2,300 from attending, including the Earl of Strathmore and his son the Honourable Michael Bowes-Lyon. Some of the men who had been unemployed or on short time in the jute factories were not too impressed by Jim Black's grovelling and sycophancy, but give the Earl his due, he was a good Forfar supporter, even though he was the only fan to arrive in a chauffeur driven car!

Forfar's only goal was a penalty converted by Willie Black, and although all Forfar was outraged by both of Arbroath's goals looking as if they were offside – we would be, wouldn't we? Neutral opinion in the shape of *The Dundee Courier* agreed with us – and the other goal was brought about when goalkeeper Blackwell slipped in the mud.

Arbroath did have one excellent player in wing half Colin McNab, ex-Dundee and Scotland, who dominated proceedings and did not allow the wet conditions in any way to detract from his excellent passing. But Forfar did not enjoy the best of luck today, and the Earl was seen to shake his head in frustration sometimes. Forfar's bad luck however did not excuse the stones thrown at some of the Arbroath supporters as they left to get their train, behaviour which embarrassed and appalled some of the older Forfar supporters who averred that "kicket erses" would solve that problem!

October 7 1922

Forfar's second season in Division Two of the Scottish League had not been going too well of late, and today they travelled to Millburn Park, Alexandria in Dunbartonshire to play the once mighty Vale of Leven.

The Vale used to be one of the leading lights of Victorian Scottish football but had lately fallen on bad times. They won the Scottish Cup three times in a row between 1877 and 1879 (including the final of 1879 when Rangers failed to turn up!) and were founder members of the Scottish League in 1890, but they were basically a village team and found it difficult to cope with professionalism and the rise of the city clubs. Now they were struggling and would not see the decade out as a senior club.

Today however, they were far too good for a poor Forfar team and duly won 2-0. Forfar's goalkeeper Jock Bruce was described as the best man on the field but unable to prevent the Vale's two goals scored by Donald and described as "beauties" by *The Sunday Post*. The same newspaper talks about how Forfar's ex-players George Henderson, Davie McLean and Alec Troup are faring for Rangers and Dundee, and also tells of the tragic death at the age of 52 of music hall artiste Marie Lloyd. Forfar's team that day was Bruce, Boath and Morrison; Miller, Smart and Dear; Dawson, Drummond, Anderson, Langlands and Dall.

October 8 1983

There just seemed to be no stopping this Forfar team these days!

Today East Fife were disposed of fairly comfortably in the end, but it was a hard won battle on a fine crisp autumnal day, the sort of day which one associated with the "tattie holidays" from school. 1-1 at half time (Forfar's goal having been scored by Jim Liddle) was a fair reflection of the play, but Forfar won a penalty which Kenny MacDonald converted and then Gordon Leitch settled the issue to make the final score 3-1.

The crowd of 925 may have been slightly disappointing for those of the old school, who kept insisting (even in the face of documentary evidence) that Forfar used to play in front of crowds of 2,000 and more every week, but the crowd was certainly larger than had been the case a few years ago. In any event, those who were there found it very difficult not to become enthused about this Forfar team, for they were a very complete outfit who played for each other, and there was no-one who thought himself better than the others. The goalkeeper Stewart Kennedy was predictably superb, the full backs Bennett and McPhee reliable, the midfield creative with Ray Farningham and Billy "Seagull" Gallacher playing superbly, and Liddle and MacDonald more than prolific goal scorers. We were now at the stage where we looked forward to every Saturday, and instigated conversation about football rather than the old days where we had to hide under the table when the subject was brought up. Was this, however, all a dream, and if so, when were we going to waken up to the old days of losing to East Stirlingshire, Albion Rovers, Stenhousemuir and Brechin City?

October 9 1954

The relationship between Forfar and St Johnstone was never great, and things would come to a spectacular head eighteen months later when a game was abandoned, but today did not help matters.

St Johnstone were a team who never really fulfilled their potential. One could argue that Perth is not really a footballing city, because given the size of its population, the Saints really should have done better. Their ground, Muirton Park, reputed to be the broadest and lushest surface in the country, is no longer with us, but one pleasing feature of St Johnstone was the amount of female supporters that they always brought with them.

Today however at Station Park, although they won 2-0, they won very few friends in Forfar by what could only be described as dirty tactics with a particular targeting of Forfar's centre forward Willie Dunn, who was twice carried off but insisted on returning, even though he had head and facial injuries. Willie Dunn was always popular among the Forfar fans who did not like him being roughed up like that by the wild men from Perth.

Clearly some of the opposition players were regarded as Devils rather than Saints. Forfar's legendary supporter, Willie Wilson of the Poor House, was moved to use his famous and damning diatribe of "awa, ye durty man!". Coming from the good-natured Willie who never swore, this was strong stuff! None of this however could disguise the unpalatable fact that this was another home defeat for Forfar, who really should have won against this bunch of Fair City crunchers.

October 10 1936

While there was a certain amount of discussion about the morality and indeed the advisability of Scotland playing Germany at Ibrox the coming Wednesday, the main focus of interest was of course on Forfar v Montrose at Station Park.

Forfar had been going reasonably well, having won four of their nine games and drawn another three. Today they had little bother in defeating Montrose 4-1 and the Forfar faithful departed in a rare state of euphoria, having seen two goals from Willie Black, one from Geordie McLean and another from Geordie Preston.

Willie Black, who was hitting the net regularly, was currently the subject of some transfer speculation and two well-dressed men with soft hats had been seen in the stand. They were clearly from some English clubs, but no-one, not even *The Forfar Dispatch* was able to identify them.

Poor Montrose, however! They were clearly struggling to find any kind of form, brought very few supporters with them (unlike Brechin and Arbroath) and when they were awarded a soft penalty, their attempt caused a strange sound to echo round Station Park – that of laughter. Herbert, who had been one of Montrose's few successes, ran forward to take the kick, but miskicked and hit the ground while the ball trickled towards McFarlane in the goal. It was one of Dave McFarlane's easier penalty saves, but that did not stop him boasting about it in the dressing room afterwards.

October 11 1971

Floodlights came to Station Park tonight.

In fact they had been there for some time and used for training purposes and now and again in a game, but now this Monday night, Provost Margaret Thorpe switched on the lights officially before a friendly against Aberdeen.

To their credit, Aberdeen sent almost a full team allowing Forfar fans a chance to see men like Joey Harper, Jim Forrest, Davie Robb and Alec Willoughby. To no great surprise Aberdeen won 3-0, for Forfar were undergoing one of their periodic low points of the 1970s and Aberdeen had temporarily, at least, displaced Rangers as the second team in Scotland.

They would have done even better but for an incomprehensible decision to sell Martin Buchan to Manchester United at a time when they were going for the Scottish League the following February! Joe Harper scored two goals and Jim Hermiston the other. The floodlights were generally agreed to be adequate, and Forfar were well ahead of many teams in the old Second Division. Floodlighting had been around for the larger clubs since the mid-1950s, and were the pre-condition of European games and midweek evening fixtures.

Some cynics looked at Forfar's lowly League position and wondered where Forfar fitted in to all this, but it was at least a token of Forfar's forward thinking at a time when there was little happening on the field to cheer anyone up. In any case, there was a big crowd to see Aberdeen and the floodlights, visible from Balmashanner and Gallowshade.

October 12 1968

Everyone knew that Forfar were steadily improving, and that a really good side was beginning to assemble at Station Park under the inspiring player-manager Jake Young, but the scale of this victory took the breath away from everyone.

The victims were Stenhousemuir, traditionally tough and doughty opponents of Forfar and usually on about the same level. It was always said for example that Forfar's nightmare scenario for a Scottish Cup draw would be "Steniemair awa fae hame" because that meant a probable defeat and no money, for Stenny were even more poorly supported than Forfar.

Ironically, although both football teams were much ridiculed, their cricket equivalents were certainly not and were among the leading lights of the Scottish scene. On this day however Forfar beat Stenhousemuir 9-1 and it could have been more. Jim Young scored a hat trick, Ian Wyles had two, Ally Carrie, Ian Stewart and John May had one each and there was even an own goal as well! In serious danger of losing count, the home support chanted for double figures near the end, and were even chivalrous enough to cheer when Stenny's goal went in between Forfar's fifth and sixth.

It was not a record score for Forfar because that was when they beat Lindertis of Kirriemuir in the Scottish Cup 14-1 in 1888, but as far as could be ascertained, it was Forfar's best ever League win, and Forfar found themselves in the enviable but unusual position of grabbing a few headlines in the papers on Sunday and Monday. The only crumb of comfort for the sporting Stenhousemuir was that they had no supporters at the game. Or if they did have any, they would have scattered long before the end.

October 13 1888

Only Ned Doig (who remains to this day the only Scotland Internationalist to have been born in Letham!) in the Arbroath goal stood between Forfar and victory today in this fine Scottish Cup tie won rather fortunately 2-1 by Arbroath.

Station Park held a "goodly concourse of spectators" and Arbroath were "well represented in the crowd". This was hardly surprising for in 1888 it was probably cheaper and definitely easier to get from Arbroath to Forfar than it is today. This was thanks to the wonderful railway line which was now past its 50th birthday.

Forfar had their star men in "Jeck" Cable and Jamie Dundas, while apart from Doig, Arbroath also had John Petrie who had scored all these goals (no-one seems to know exactly how many) in the 36-0 win over Bon Accord three years ago. The game was fast and furious and possibly hinged on the bad injury to Forfar's Bowman late in the first half compelling him to hobble along hopelessly on the left wing for the rest of the game.

Even in spite of that, Forfar dominated when they were 2-1 behind but some "bad shooting" over the bar let them down, as well of course as the fine saving of Ned Doig who would in 1890 go to Sunderland and win four English League Championship medals with the Wearsiders. Defeat in the Scottish Cup is always a bad blow for it deprives a club of a great deal of money, and Forfar felt sore about this defeat for a long time afterwards.

October 14 1907

Part of the deal involving the transfer of Davie McLean to Celtic was that Celtic would come to Forfar to play a friendly, and on this Holiday Monday, "the Fast", as it was called, Celtic did indeed arrive for a Friendly to kick off at 2.30 pm. Even though it was by no means a full Celtic team and there were two trialists playing (one of them Willie Semple, who played more games for the club, although mainly as a reserve), Celtic were given a great reception by the 2,000 crowd who were thus given the chance to see Davie McLean playing in his new colours alongside the great Jimmy Quinn.

It was remarked by all who saw him that Jimmy Quinn, the most famous footballer of his day, looked remarkably like "an ordinary man" as he got off at the Station and walked to the ground, being sociable to everyone and indulging in earnest conversation with his friend Davie McLean, while Manager Maley was as genial as always, saying that Forfar was one of his "favourite little places".

Celtic won 2-1 with McLean scoring one of the goals. Forfar's goal was netted by Geordie Langlands and the teams were Forfar: Orr, Gibb and Harvey; McFarlane, Gowans and Bruce; Robertson, Docherty, Langlands, Hutcheson and Cook. Celtic: Adams, Craig and Orr; Hay, Loney and Mitchell; Trialist, Quinn, McLean, Kivlichan and Semple.

Curiously a myth grew up about this game, namely that it was a Scottish Cup tie and that Forfar won. It was always difficult to persuade people that the truth was a little more mundane, but I think that the game was confused in local oral tradition with the genuine Cup tie played between the two teams in 1914 (when Celtic won 5-0) and the Cup tie in 1911 when Forfar did indeed provide a great giant killing by beating Falkirk.

October 15 1921

In the first season of Forfar being in the Second Division of the Scottish League, they travelled the short distance to Tannadice Park (or Clepington Park as it was sometimes still called) to play Dundee Hibs (better known as Dundee United nowadays). The attendance was reasonable, with a fair contingent from Forfar. Forfar were unlucky to go down 0-1 to the "Dundee Irishmen".

After a far from impressive start to their Scottish League career with only one win so far in eight starts, Forfar today did at least give some indication that things might improve. Allan Smart and Eck Gerrard stood out in a fine defensive performance, while up front Geordie Langlands, now approaching the veteran stage but still very fit and able, "kept the kettle boiling". Sadly he did so without any success, for the Hibs scored early in the second half, and Forfar – now playing against the stiff western breeze (there was no "shed" then to keep it out) – failed to equalise, although they had some close calls.

Many Forfarians were struck by the tremendous poverty and distress in the huge slum tenement areas of Dundee, linked to the obvious problems of alcohol. It seemed clear that Lloyd George had not yet managed to deliver on his rash promise of "a land fit for heroes to live in". The heroes were now all back home from the war, but there weren't jobs for them all, nor good houses nor very much else. Some Dundonians were now listening to their indefatigable Prohibitionist campaigner Neddy Scrymgeour; others were beginning to pay attention to the man from Lossiemouth who was going to change it all – James Ramsay MacDonald.

October 16 1937

Forfar had started the season reasonably well, and Links Park, Montrose was the scene of another fine Forfar win as they defeated the home side 4-2 with a much changed team of Orchison, Lawson and McGregor; Gilbert, Laird and Nicholl; Bain, Sturrock, Smith, Campbell and Wattie.

Yet the victory was not as comprehensive as Forfar would have liked. The main difference, according to the writer of *The Forfar Dispatch*, was that Forfar took their chances when offered whereas Montrose didn't. Even so, Forfar gave every impression that they were going to throw away a three-goal lead after Laurie Campbell, Bert Smith and John Wattie had put Forfar well ahead.

Montrose fought back, scored twice and really should have scored more but Forfar, with even their forwards helping out their hard-pressed defence, held out until Bert Smith relieved the tension by making it 4-2 at the end.

The writer of *The Forfar Dispatch* seems to have enjoyed sailing on the Loch, or perhaps he was in the Royal Navy in the Great War, or maybe he just enjoys being beside the seaside in Montrose – which does indeed have a lovely beach – for he loves naval metaphors, talking about how this was "a stormy trip" after some "clear skies" and "plain sailing" but when Bert Smith scored the fourth goal which finally "drowned" Montrose, Forfar had reached their "haven".

October 17 1914

The war had been raging for over two months now, and already the casualties were significant, but Forfar gave their supporters something to cheer about by travelling to Gayfield, Arbroath and beating the local side 3-1.

Forfar's team was Scott, E Ferguson and D Ferguson; Nicholl, Chapman and Leighton; Mitchell, Walker, Langlands, Troup and Petrie, and with this win they consolidated their position at the top of the Central League.

The Arbroath Herald sings the praises of Alec Troup "In Troup they have a little marvel. When he fastens on the ball it is difficult to know whether he intends turning round altogether or making a clear road for goal. It was that sort of play that tells its tale".

But Forfar had unearthed another dynamic talent in right winger Jack Cable junior, the son of the legendary "Jeck" Cable of the last century, and with Geordie Langlands in the centre leading the line brilliantly, Arbroath "could not hold a candle to Forfar". Troup scored twice, one of them a penalty and Langlands added the other, while Milne scored for Arbroath. The game was watched by Arbroath's largest crowd of the season and the receipts were £27.

A special train was run by the Caledonian Railway Company from Forfar to Arbroath, but "less than 200" travelled on it. It is interesting that this attendance was considered a disappointment! About 300 had travelled on the February special.

But overshadowing all was the Great War. British propaganda could not quite hide the fact that, although France had been saved, Belgium had in fact been more or less lost with the fall of Antwerp a week ago, and that the war would definitely not be over by Christmas. *The Courier* has the headline "Germans Driven Back". An old Forfar lady said "Driven! Driven! I would have made the buggers walk!"

October 18 1994

The funeral was held of Sam Smith, one time Chairman of the club.

He had died a few days previously after a short illness. It would have been hard to dispute the contention that he was the man who had resurrected Forfar. He had played for Forfar in the late 1940s and early 1950s when his job as an auctioneer brought him to the town, but it was when he took over as Chairman of the club in 1976 that things really began to happen. Frankly, in 1976, Forfar were on their knees, well past all the gallows humour, and it really was difficult to see any sort of future for them.

By 1984 they had won the Scottish League Second Division, but that was only half the story. They came close to beating Rangers on numerous occasions, and Forfar was identified as a growth area in a sport which had seemed to be in almost terminal decline. All this was due to Sam Smith and his vigorous leadership of the club with his encouragement of men like Archie Knox, Alec Rae and Doug Houston on the playing side of things, not to mention the equally important administrative skills of men like David McGregor and Gordon Webster.

Yet he was also a very humble man who would take time to speak to supporters and listen to their views. He was not a native Forfarian, but by the time of his death there was no man better known or better loved in the town. If Jim Black was the man who made Forfar, Sam Smith was the man who brought them back after decades of gross underachievement.

October 19 2013

Forfar had an impressive 2-0 victory before 579 fans at the Excelsior Stadium over the team called Airdrieonians.

This team has had a strange history. They were originally called Airdrieonians and in the 1920s were one of the best teams in Scotland with players like Bob McPhail and the irrepressible but self-destructive Hughie Gallacher. They won the Scottish Cup in 1924 and reached the Scottish Cup final as recently as 1975 and 1992.

Because to poor crowds and worse stewardship, they went bust and for a few weeks earlier this century were actually out of the League and replaced by Gretna.

Then Clydebank also went bankrupt and Airdrie were allowed back into the League as Airdrie United. After a few years, they reverted to the name Airdrieonians!

Confusing, but today at the Excelsior they were themselves confused by a good Forfar side who won 2-0 thanks to a goal from a trialist called Jamie McCluskey after some good work by Dale Hilson, and then Ross Campbell, son of the Manager Dick Campbell, scored with a late penalty kick. It was a feisty encounter and only Forfar's third victory of the season. Forfar's supporters have been mystified so far by form this season. There have been victories over Rangers (in the Scottish League Cup) and Dunfermline but there was also last week a miserable defeat at home from Stranraer.

It is never easy to be a Forfar supporter. You don't know where you are sometimes!

October 20 1900

The song in the air was "Goodbye Dolly Gray", a music hall hit in the times of the Boer War, which was being fought with such ferocity in South Africa. This very morning a couple of Forfar young men had departed to join the Army, enticed by the promise of good regular food, a uniform which included a kilt and a new exciting life which would be far better than the grim monotony of the Mull or the Haughie.

The afternoon however, a fine crisp autumn day, saw Forfar convincingly beat Dundee Wanderers 3-0 at Station Park in the Scottish Qualifying Cup. In truth the score should have been a lot more than 3-0 for Forfar had another three goals chalked off for offside, and Don in the Dundee Wanderers goal had such a fine game that he even earned a cheer from the chivalrous Forfar supporters at the end. Forfar's best man was full back Dickie Gibb, but also singled out were Janes, Edward, Neave and Cowie. It was always gratifying to defeat a Dundee team, but no-one could have said that the Wanderers were one of Dundee's better teams.

Then again this was far from a vintage Forfar team either, for they had lost four and only won two games in the Northern League, but they were now the only Forfarshire team left in the Scottish Qualifying Cup, and indeed they would win through to the Scottish Cup itself this year only to collapse woefully to Leith Athletic after the New Year.

October 21 1922

Logie Green in Edinburgh still retains the distinction of being the only ground outside Glasgow to have hosted the Scottish Cup final. It did this in 1896 when the contestants were Hearts and Hibs. Sadly it has now been built over by houses, but in 1922 it was the home of St Bernard's, an Edinburgh team which failed to emerge from World War Two.

Today Forfar travelled there, and could consider themselves unlucky not to come back with a point, for they put up a brave show and when Anderson reduced the leeway from 2-0 to 2-1 near the end, the Stockbridge side had to defend stoutly for the last five minutes.

Forfar were described in complimentary terms by *The Sunday Post* as being "a big strapping team, all gluttons for work" but they had a weakness near goal, and the Edinburgh side's defence had been in the past described as being "as impregnable as the Edinburgh Castle".

This was Forfar's second season in the Second Division of the Scottish League, and they were determined to stay there. Money was hardly in copious supply, but attendances remained high and there was a great deal of interest in the town in the fortune of the local club, as witnessed by the crowd who waited outside the Post Office in Castle Street at 5.00 pm for the arrival of the telegram with the score. Today's team was Bruce, Braid and Binnie; Boath, Smart and Dear; Dawson, Drummond, Anderson, Langlands and Gray.

October 22 1955

Stranraer, that most distant of clubs, had been admitted along with some others to the Second Division of the Scottish League for season 1955/56.

Supporters noted with despair that Forfar would have to travel there on January 3 – something that hinted at clear, logical thinking in Scottish League headquarters! – but now, as luck would have it, Stranraer were drawn to come to Forfar in the Scottish Cup at the strangely early date of October 22.

There was thus a certain novelty in the sight of the men from the south, a team which, for all its geographical remoteness, would nevertheless develop a certain affinity with Forfar over the years. Today the men whose ground is closer to many grounds in Ireland than it is to Station Park, scored two early goals, and as *The Courier* pawkily put it, "with recent displays in mind, Forfar supporters began to lose interest in the next round".

But this Forfar team fought back with goals from Tommy Martin and then Albert Craig before Willie Dunn scored a second half hat-trick thriving on great service from Sandy Elder and Wilf Allsop. Rarely had the faithful seen such a game and it was "a grand 1s 9d worth for the fans". "One and nine" coincidentally was the basic adult price for admission to the Gaffie and the Regal, the two local cinemas.

It was maybe a sign of the times that we saw a Stranraer-supporting family (father, mother and two sons) getting into an Austin car to drive home. They were friendly and told us they had left home at about 6.00 am this morning, and hoped "with a bit of luck" to be back by midnight. Such dedication! Since then, I have to admit to a soft spot for Stranraer, who, founded in 1870, are the third oldest team in Scotland behind Queen's Park and Kilmarnock.

October 23 1954

Forfar had failed to register a win so far in the 1954/5 season, but they gained some creditable draws, and today they came good with an emphatic 3-1 win over Dundee United in the Scottish Cup at Tannadice to the delight of their supporters (about a hundred) who had travelled through on the bus or car to Dundee.

The journey was in many cases financed by the wages from the "tattie Holidays" (the two weeks off school to work for the potato harvest. Some said, not without cause, that it was slave labour, but the money was handy) and was conditional on a visit to DM Brown's or Draffen's for a new pair of trousers or a raincoat. On the same day Hearts beat Motherwell 4-2 to win their first ever Scottish League Cup (and, incredibly, their first national trophy since 1906) but the talk in Forfar was all about how they had put Dundee United in their place.

The secret was simply good team work, and surprise was expressed that this was their first win of the season. The fast running inside forwards Albert Craig and Wilf Allsop were singled out for praise, with Craig in particular having a great game and scoring the first goal himself instead of passing to Willie Dunn who had strayed offside. Some of Forfar's team lived in Dundee, and in particular it is easy to imagine the pleasure of Doug Berrie who had been described as surplus to requirements by Dundee United several years previously. Doug was far too nice a man to gloat – but I wasn't!

October 24 1964

Boghead, the home of Dumbarton, and crisp autumn sunshine do not always go together, but this was a fine day for the few Forfar supporters, celebrating perhaps the end of their "tattie" holidays, who travelled west to see their team. At this stage, Forfar were neither bad nor good, but today they definitely swung to the good with an excellent 3-1 win over the home side.

The game was a great day for that ever-loveable Forfar warhorse Kenny Dick. Sometimes confused with an earlier player called Len Dick and certainly confused in a magazine called *Soccer Star* which called him Kenny Kick (no kidding!), the whole hearted Kenny today silenced his critics by scoring a great hat-trick before half-time. They were all good goals too, the last one in particular when he rounded two defenders to score, but that it is not to diminish the other two – the first one being simply the striker's knack of being in the right place at the right time and the second a header from a Tommy Mackle cross.

It was a pity that the game wasn't at Station Park so that more Forfar supporters could see this hat-trick, for although Kenny was generally popular, there were a few (aren't there always?) who persecuted him shamefully when he was having a bad day. Today also marked the closing ceremony of the Tokyo Olympic Games and the Scottish League Cup final won narrowly 2-1 by Rangers over Celtic.

October 25 1958

Tommy Cormie and Jimmy Russell scored the goals which gave Forfar a narrow but deserved 2-1 victory over Cowdenbeath at Central Park.

A visit to Central Park is always interesting. Never the most scenically attractive of Scottish grounds, Central Park however sparkles with character and certainly is redolent of the way that football used to be. But change was slowly coming to the Fife minefields as well as every place else, and facilities were improving. 1958 was also a year of full employment, and everyone needed coal.

Prime Minister Harold McMillan would say "we've never had it so good" and of course he was right, even in the Fife coalfield where no-one would have a good word to say about the Conservatives! Cowdenbeath still had their stock car racing but at the moment they had a very poor team and were, by some distance, clearly bottom of the Second Division.

Having said that, they put up a good fight and a Forfar team which was not without experience or talent struggled to beat them. Impressive for Forfar was inside forward Eric Brodie and the young trialist goalkeeper Donald McKay. On the larger scene, today at Hampden Park, Hearts won the Scottish League Cup for the second time in five years when they beat Partick Thistle rather easily 5-1.

October 26 1977

Forfar make them all sit up and take notice by giant killing Premier League Ayr United to reach the quarter finals of the Scottish League Cup.

Ayr had won the first leg 2-1, but Forfar's 3-1 victory at Station Park was enough to win them the tie 4-3. Things did not look at all good for Forfar when Ayr United first missed a penalty then went ahead to make it 1-3 on aggregate.

Then came that electrifying burst of 3 goals in 10 minutes. First Gavine delightfully flicked on a Knox free kick for Rae to hammer home. Payne equalized the tie with a shot which hit a post them ran along the line before, almost reluctantly, deciding to go in. Then Henry Hall cut in himself from the left to slip the ball past the goalkeeper.

The scenes of pitch invasions etc. (although deplorable in some ways) were nevertheless an indication of the enthusiasm that the new management of the past two years had achieved. Those who had seen 1974 and 1975 could not believe the transformation of the club. The fact that 2,020 appeared on a Wednesday night to see a game under floodlights with a BBC News crew there as well was more or less uncharted territory for the club, and quite unbelievable for those who remembered the bad old days. The team was Nicol, Smith, Boath, Brown, Brash and Rae, Knox, Payne, Gavine, Rankin, Hall with substitutes Graham and Clark. Queen of the South would be the opponents in the next round, and we could hardly wait!

Ken Brown and teammates celebrate

October 27 1956

Second from the bottom Forfar Athletic boarded the train to Stirling in the morning with a certain feeling of International tension and crisis in the air. There were two apparently unrelated areas of world concern. Hungary, then regarded as having the best football team in Europe, were rebelling against the Soviet Union and would soon be brutally crushed causing, among others, the great Ferenc Puskás to flee to Real Madrid.

Not all the baddies however lived on the eastern side of the Iron Curtain, for Great Britain's Prime Minister Sir Anthony Eden was picking an absurd and potentially dangerous fight with Egypt over the Suez Canal.

A Third World War seemed to be a distinct possibility, and Forfar's players and officials saw at Perth Station the chilling sight of reservists in uniform with kitbags. Less chilling but more noisy were supporters in green and white favours en route to Hampden to see Celtic v Partick Thistle in the Scottish League Cup final. (It ended in a 0-0 draw.)

Fortunately, things did not get all that bad for Great Britain, but they did for Forfar who went down 1-4 to the slick Stirling Albion at Annfield (as distinct from Anfield, the home of Liverpool). Willie Dunn scored first for Forfar against the run of play early in the first half, but then the roof fell in, and Forfar were lucky to get off with losing only four, with only Doug Berrie getting anything like praise, and questions now beginning to be asked about the hitherto very impressive goalkeeper from Arbroath, Jimmy Mowat.

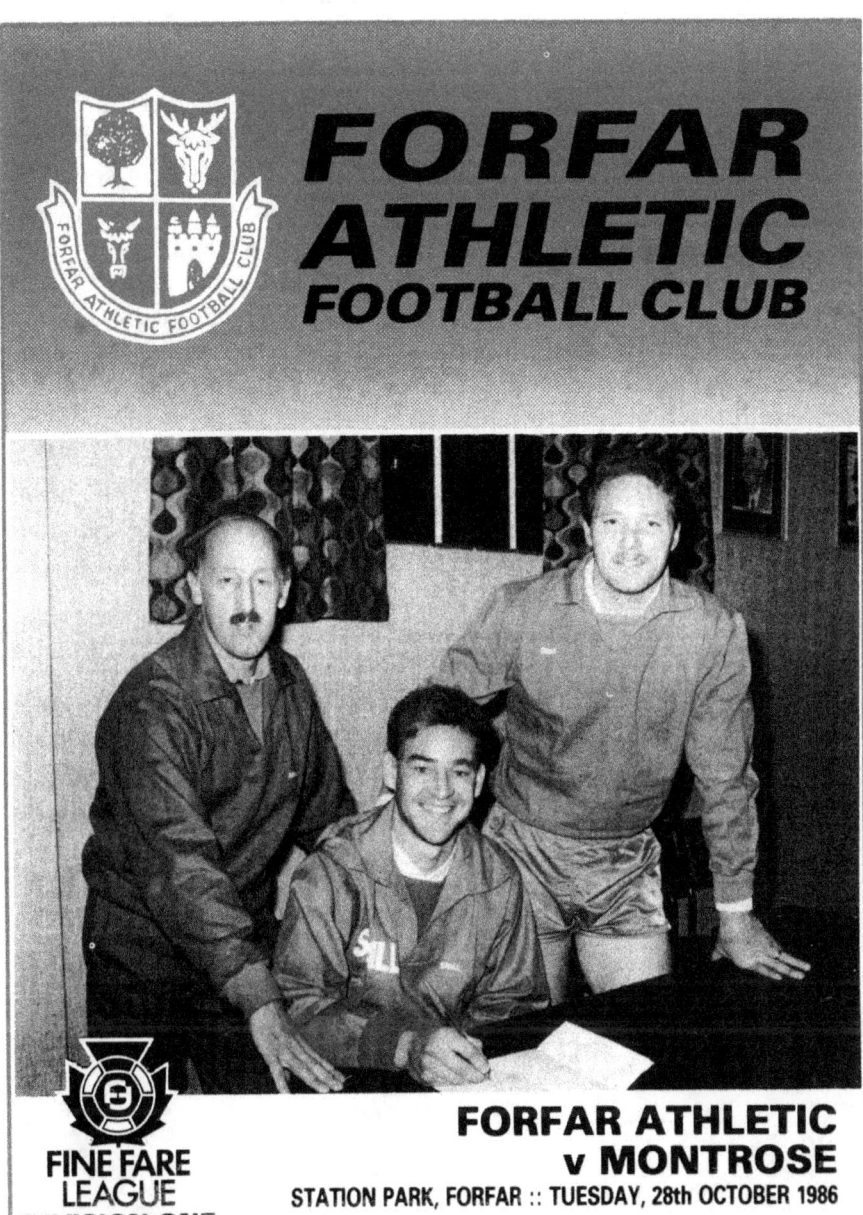

October 28 2003

A visit to Ibrox is always a memorable experience, even though, as on this occasion, we came away on the wrong end of a 6-0 thumping.

This was a Scottish League Cup last 16 game, and the pill was considerably sweetened by the cheque which the 26,327 spectators provided, even though Rangers were going through a very bad spell and were even at this early stage of the season struggling to keep up with Celtic.

The game itself does not remain to any large extent in the mind other than the numbing feeling of hopelessness against what was a crack outfit, but I do recall the two guys playing the trumpet to entertain their fans. Nothing outright sectarian about guarding walls or garments that daddy used to wear, but more a selection of stirring, muscular, Victorian, patriotic songs like "God Save The Queen" and "Rule Britannia" and even "Will Your Anchor Hold In the Storms of Life" – something that brought a tear to the eye of ex-BB boys like myself.

Less welcome was the sight of the fifth-columnist Forfar Quislings who flaunted a flag with "Forfar True Blues" on it at half-time. And in spite of all Rangers' undeniable quality, were not the seeds of their destruction already there in the shape of their foreign players with no loyalty and no commitment? Rangers could not really afford them, yet kept paying with money that they did not have, being too arrogant to understand that they too, like everyone else, had to pay Income Tax? Forfar, on the other hand, with their share of the "gate" for this game had solved their financial problems for many years.

October 29 1966

Few of the paltry crowd at Station Park today would have realised that this would be the last time that the grand old Glasgow team Third Lanark would visit Station Park.

Winners of the Scottish Cup in 1889 and 1905, the Scottish League in 1904 and only seven years previously the beaten finalists in the Scottish League Cup final, the name Third Lanark seemed to be more or less engraved on the fabric of Scottish football.

Producers of great players like Jimmy Carrabine, Jimmy Mason and Ally MacLeod, it was now no secret that Thirds were in dire financial straits, partly because of living in Glasgow beside the giants, but also because of blatant internal corruption and theft on a grand scale.

Yet they came here with their now faded red jerseys and their gallant but dwindling band of supporters cheering on the Hi-Hi-Hi's or the Warriors or the Redcoats or the Sodgers, for they had originally been an army regiment called the 3rd Lanark Rifle Volunteers.

Today, although the form of both teams had been poor hitherto, they served up a good game which Forfar won 5-3 thanks to a hat-trick scored by Jackie Thoms. As the second half developed, it was seen that some of the crowd gathered round transistor radios – very annoying crackling things if you weren't interested in what they were saying – listening to the progress of the Scottish League Cup final won 1-0 by Celtic against Rangers.

It was a shame that so many of the crowd had divided loyalties, for the Forfar game was in doubt right up till the final whistle and Thirds were given a great reception. They then travelled home to Glasgow via Forfar Station – and that wasn't going to last very much longer either!

October 30 1978

Forfar do not, as a rule, very often grant testimonials to players but an exception was made in this case to Alec Brash. "Brasher" had been a fine centre half for the side, and was much loved for his whole hearted commitment to the cause. Celtic were invited to send a reserve team and, aware of the long standing friendship between the teams, they duly did so. Naturally, Billy McNeill, the newly appointed Manager and still struggling with a poor side who had still not yet recovered from the transfer of Kenny Dalglish in 1977 and the consequent parting of the ways with Jock Stein, did not send a full team but Danny McGrain, slowly recovering from a dreadful injury, was captain and reasonably familiar faces like Johnny Doyle appeared as well.

A large crowd of about 2,000 on a fine evening turned up to see the Celtic XI win 3-0 with a hat-trick from George McCluskey. Playing on the left wing that night was a young man called Ian McPhee, who never really made good at Celtic Park, but soon found his *métier* in a different position at Station Park, and became one of the real legends of the club. The 3-0 score line was possibly a little hard on Forfar, and many of the Celtic supporters from Dundee and elsewhere were heard to express surprise that Forfar were a Second Division team with some fine players, a trim, little ground and clear organisation. Danny McGrain, diabetic or not, was also reputed to have enjoyed his bridie at full time!

Alex Brash and Danny McGrain lead out the sides.

October 31 1964

This Forfar side was by no means the best in our long history – in fact glances at League tables etc of that era are depressing and would tend to make one think that it was one of the worst, but this Hallowe'en Forfar gave evidence that they did have the ability to fight back, even when a long way from home and without any supporters other than their own officials.

Stair Park, Stranraer is far away and the team so far this season had done little – they had won four games but lost seven – to persuade any of their supporters to forsake their "dooking for apples" and "guising" (the traditional pastimes of Hallowe'en) in favour of the long trip to the south-west.

Stranraer scored first, but then Moss Barclay put Forfar back on level terms with a fine lob. However, when the team went in 3-1 down at half-time and then 4-2 twenty minutes later, it was a fair assumption that a tanking was about to be unleashed.

But not a bit of it. Kenny Dick, Tommy Mackle, Ally Carrie and Gordon Harris rallied the team and supplied Jim Gray for a fine hat-trick which maybe did not take a single yard off the long journey home, but nevertheless made it a great deal more bearable that it might have been. It was a shame that we did not see this sort of performance a little oftener this season.

November

OFFICIAL MATCHDAY PROGRAMME £2

FORFAR ATHLETIC V
COWDENBEATH

Scottish Cup 3rd Round
Saturday 1st November 2014
3pm Kick-Off

November 1 1986

It was an almost perfect day for my first ever visit to Palmerston Park, Dumfries, home of Queen of the South.

A lovely autumn day for the drive down, the roads not crowded at all, a visit to Robert Burns' house and his mausoleum in St Michael's Churchyard, a lovely lunch, a good keenly fought game of football between two well matched teams before a large crowd of 1750 spectators and the score a deserved 1-1 draw ... as it seemed.

Forfar had done well and John Clark's goal had been a good one. A draw at Palmerston was a good result, we reckoned. But then with the last kick of the ball (literally, for the referee signalled for full time immediately after), a fellow called Cloy scored in off the post for Queen of the South.

"Oh dash it!" "Oh confound it" "A thousand curses" I said, but a Queen of the South supporter (who had been around for a long time) put his hand on my shoulder, wished me a safe journey home and uttered the immortal but hardly original words "That's fitba!"

And so the visit to the Burns house became the highlight of my day – the tea outside Glasgow wasn't all that bad either – as I struggled to recall the words about how the mouse was settling down in its house against the "craunreech cauld" when "crash, the cruel coulter" ruined it all for him. Oh, Mr Cloy, you will never know how much you ruined my day and soured my impressions of the fine town that is Dumfries!

Queen of the South

Official Programme
30p

FINEFARE LEAGUE — DIVISION ONE

FORFAR ATHLETIC

Saturday, 1st November, 1986. Kick-off 3 p.m.

FINE FARE LEAGUE

November 2 1935

A sensational incident at Tannadice Park saw George McLean sent off.

It was late in the game, and Forfar were being well defeated by Dundee United when McLean was seen to be "involved" with two Dundee United men, Kay and Collington. Geordie, recently freed from Huddersfield Town, seemed to be the victim rather than the aggressor, but while this was going on and everyone was paying attention to the "clash", no-one realised that the ball was still in play, and Donaldson scored for Forfar.

The goal was given, to the astonishment of everyone, then George McLean was called over by the referee Mr Finlay of Freuchie and sent to the pavilion. Nobody seemed to be aware of what was going on, but in any case it mattered little for a very poor Forfar side went down 1-4 to Dundee United, triggering (not for the first nor last time) the refrain of Dundee Delighted and Forfar Pathetic.

Such defeats hurt Forfar supporters in these days, for this was before the rise of Dundee United. They were still a very poor side with a desperately awful stadium, whose stand even as early as 1935 was showing signs of dry rot and general decay, and whose supporters that day became even happier when the tannoy crackled into life and told them that Celtic had beaten Dundee at Parkhead.

Forfar were struggling that season however. Their team was McFarlane, Collie and Ramsay; Morton, Laird and Gabriel; R Black, W Black, Donaldson, McLean and Cameron.

No. 8

CLYDE

v FORFAR ATHLETIC

SCOTTISH FIRST DIVISION
Saturday, 3rd November, 1984

VIEW

30p

November 3 1984

Shawfield, the home of Glasgow Greyhound Racing and Clyde Football Club, was falling apart.

Both the dogs and Clyde had seen better days, and it was hard to imagine that, only a generation ago, Clyde with stars like Harry Haddock, Tommy Ring and Archie Robertson, were leading lights in the Scottish game, winning the Scottish Cup twice.

O tempora! O mores!

Here, in the teeming, unrelenting Glasgow rain, before a minuscule crowd huddled together under the Shawfield shelter, Forfar, in their first season in Division One and respectably placed, were taking on the Bully Wee.

The game was punctuated by the noise of doors banging at the back of one of the shelters. These are the booths normally occupied by the bookmakers!

As often happens in such circumstances, both sides served up an excellent game of football, and although Forfar came off second best, they had nothing to reproach themselves for. After the loss of an early goal as both teams tried to come to terms with the muddy conditions, Forfar hit back and after two John Clark goals, returned to the sanctuary of the dressing room 2-1 up.

As we stood for the hot Bovril served by a hard faced but welcoming Glasgow lady, the half-time loudspeaker told of several other games which were off; we wondered about whether this game would be completed, but there were no puddles on the pitch and the game proceeded.

Alas for Forfar, Clyde now took control and ran out 4-2 winners, in spite of outstanding performances by Stewart Kennedy in the goal and Alec Brash in the centre of the defence. So it was back to the car in the incessant downpour. Not yet 5.00 pm but already dark as we swished through the Glasgow streets.

"From scenes like these, old Scotia's grandeur springs..."

November 4 1961

The Bully Wee Clyde were at the top of the League, and going well.

Harry Haddock (with a name like that, he should have been playing for Arbroath) was still playing for them and they really should have been in the First Division. But they had become a yo-yo team, like Stirling Albion, going up and down the Divisions.

They attracted a crowd of about 2,500 this pleasant autumn day. Such was the hold that football had over Scotland, Glasgow in particular in 1961, that 40,000 were attracted to Cathkin (not all that far away from Shawfield) that day to see Third Lanark take on Rangers while another 10,000 were at Firhill to see Kilmarnock.

Forfar's performances this year had been reasonable – they had won four games out of 14 and drawn another four, and that was considered acceptable for a support that was never too demanding in its expectations. Today it was another draw, a goalless one. It was a good result for the Forfar side of McKay, Berrie and Knox; Robertson, Sweeney and Adams; Bonthrone, Milne, Coburn, Legge and Thomson, but it did not always make for good watching.

Most Clyde supporters however agreed that in goalkeeper Donald McKay, Forfar had something special. It seemed too that something might be happening in Dundee this year. They beat Celtic 2-1 at Dens Park that day. Was this to be a challenge for the Scottish League Championship?

November 5 1994

This is the first season of the Third Division.

Those who felt that Forfar really should be a Division above that, had a certain amount of evidence to back them up. Forfar, give or take the odd hiccup, had been doing fairly well. On the back of an excellent home victory over Arbroath last week, they travelled today to Recreation Park to play Alloa, a team with whom they have had many jousts in the past.

Those who expected fireworks on Guy Fawkes Day, however, were slightly disappointed but it was a regulation 1-0 win with a McCormick goal in the second half. There was a certain solidity about the team with veteran Ian McPhee starring in defence, and David Bingham continuing to attract attention with his fine forward play.

The crowd was given as 525, although there were at least two more than that, for I saw them climb over the wall at the Main Road side of the stadium in full view of passing cars!

I arrived late and the game was already 10 minutes gone when I saw this outrageous deed. But it was also a feat of some agility, not to mention courage, and for that reason I decided not to "shop" them. Now too old to attempt the same, and never the best of athletes even in my prime, I walked up to the turnstile and paid for my entrance.

November 6 1897

Forfar had no game today in the Northern League, so they arranged a friendly at Station Park with a team that they had never played before called Vale of Atholl.

They were last year's Perthshire Cup winners, and attracted a reasonable crowd even though the first signs of winter, in particular early darkness, were beginning to make themselves felt.

The visitors were a little overwhelmed in both senses today – by the hospitality of the club and by the strength of the Forfar team to whom they lost 5-2, although they did have the consolation of having one of their goals described as a "raker" by *The Forfar Herald*.

It was by no means a full Forfar team for they took the opportunity to blood a few youngsters including a fellow called Milne whom the scribe of *The Forfar Herald* damns with faint praise in a decidedly back-handed compliment – "Possessed of an abundance of weight and speed, he should, with those qualifications, make up for what he lacks in the finer points of the game".

The big game in the locality today was the visit of Celtic to play Dundee at Carolina Port, and quite a few Forfarians had availed themselves of the opportunity of going to that game to see Celtic win 2-1.

November 7 1914

The war had been going on for three months now, and it was by this time painfully obvious that the war would certainly not be "over by Christmas".

James Black, who had always encouraged recruiting officers to talk to young men at half-time in games, was now beginning to think that football would have to stop. There were certainly severe logistic problems with transport.

Today, for example, Forfar did not find it easy to get 11 men to Bayview to take on East Fife in the Scottish Qualifying Cup. This game was itself a replay and the 1-1 draw would necessitate yet another game, as no-one had as yet thought of penalty shoot-outs. *The Courier* says that this was an excellent game, and that Forfar really should have won.

Yet it was East Fife who scored first through Hunter before Geordie Langlands equalized. "Dyken" Nicholl and "Jummer" Petrie had chances for Forfar, but the best save of the game was from Scott in the Forfar goal who injured himself in doing so.

So a draw it was, and the chivalrous Methil crowd gave both sides a rousing reception at the end before Forfar set out for their battle with war time transport to get home again. The general feeling was that it was only a matter of time before football was to be stopped – in fact Forfar struggled through to the end of the season – and players were compelled to join up.

There was already considerable emotional blackmail to do so, but already casualty lists were beginning to appear in *The Forfar Herald* and *The Courier*. Another four years of hell awaited humanity.

November 8 1930

The "unemployed" gate was in evidence at Station Park today.

Many men were too proud to be seen going in that way and stayed away, but the half price gate for old people, young lads and "not in work" still did well, as unemployment seemed to be getting totally out of control. Not without cause did many supporters believe that the depression was a worldwide plot to discredit the Labour Government of Ramsay MacDonald, but the effects of being out of work were devastating to a man and his family.

Nevertheless, some solace was found at Station Park today in a 4-1 defeat of East Stirlingshire, Forfar's first win for over a month. For Forfar, not for the first nor the last time it was the two Davies, McLean and Kilgour who did the needful. Kilgour scoring two from a distance, and McLean orchestrating it all and scoring another. The supremely talented inside right Charlie Lawie scored the fourth goal.

The game had been a bit of a non-event in the first half, although goalkeeper Charlie Sunter was given a lot of credit for a few fine saves, and deserved the nickname given to him of "Charlie Shaw" after Celtic's great custodian of a decade previously. Forfar used the breeze to advantage in the second half with the wily old McLean, now 40 and still superbly fit, leading the line brilliantly and distributing balls to both wingers with "verve and aplomb".

The crowd departed in good spirits but not without some apprehension for the future, for rumours abounded of possible factory closures before the New Year.

November 9 1901

The war in South Africa may have taken a turn for the better as far as Great Britain was concerned, but there were still too many casualties.

Those who did manage to make it home to Forfar were of course feted like heroes, but if injuries made it impossible for a man to work, then there was little that the Government seemed to want to do for him. The country was settling down under the new King Edward VII who would be crowned next summer, but all these things were as nothing compared with the disaster that befell Forfar today.

They went to Arbroath in the Northern League and lost 0-8, one of the biggest hammerings in their history. *The Courier* does say that the pitch was in a deplorable condition because of heavy rain, while *The Arbroath Herald* talks about "Gayfield Loch", praises the Forfar support who came in large numbers to stand in the rain and watch the cataclysm but condemns the Forfar players for rough play in the second half, although admitting that they had many reasons to "gnash their teeth".

As this game followed a 4-0 beating by the same opponents the previous week, Forfar fans were all too aware who the best team in the County was. The train home was a miserable experience, although maybe the drink provided an anaesthetic.

"Loads of beer but ate nothing" (Eight-nothing? Get it?) was the gallows humour of the following week, mixed up, presumably with a certain amount of teeth-gnashing. Newspapers are coy about mentioning the names of Forfar players involved in this game. In this respect, the Editors are surely being very tactful indeed. I will be likewise.

November 10 2007

Forfar, rock bottom of the Scottish League, badly in need of a win – and generally struggling without, frankly, having the money to do very much about it – travelled to Borough Briggs to play Elgin City.

Their last win, indeed their only win of the season, had been against Elgin at Station Park at the end of August, and since then it had been doom and gloom.

Now out of all three Cup competitions, a grim winter lay ahead and a severe challenge for Manager Jim Moffat, an amiable PE teacher from Fife who had of course played in the goal in the past with distinction. His squad could best be described as mediocre, but they did not lack spirit or determination.

Elgin City had been an ambitious Highland League club with a tendency to do well in the Scottish Cup until they were admitted to the Scottish League at the turn of the century, since when, without ever setting the heather on fire, they had at least held their own.

It was of course a long way away for Forfar with very few fans to support them, but the 472 crowd did at least see a fair game of football which resulted in a 2-2 draw, Forfar's goals coming from Martyn Fotheringham and Sean Kilgannon. In the context of what had gone before (last week they had lost 0-2 to East Stirlingshire at home and gone out of the Scottish Cup to Dumbarton) this was considered to be a fair result which indicated that there might just be some hope for the future.

Martyn Fotheringham

November 11 1961

Armistice Day at Station Park saw the usual minute's silence, poppies on sale and boys going round the ground at half time with a sheet into which the crowd were invited to throw money for the Earl Haig fund.

A surprising amount of Great War veterans were still around in 1961 including a few with obvious facial disfigurements or damage to one limb or other. The minute's silence was treated with appropriate respect and today's game against Berwick Rangers was a good one, ending up 2-2 although everyone seemed to think that Forfar should have won.

Ross scored first for the Loons, but then a penalty was conceded when left-back Knox handled on the line.

Nowadays that would have involved a red card, but in 1961 a penalty sufficed. Berwick scored from it, then scored from open play to put them 2-1 ahead. Legge then equalised ("Legge has jist scored wi' his fut" said a less than totally gifted fan, who thought he was funny) and the game continued in its intensity, but no further goals came.

Forfar thus consolidated their middle of the League position, but the big news came when we got home. Grandstand, the BBC sports programme told us that Dundee had beaten Rangers 5-1 at Ibrox in a game which was nearly fogged off.

Many supporters had heard a false rumour that the game was off (both Celtic's game at Parkhead and Queen's Park's at Hampden were indeed postponed) and turned back, thus missing one of the more remarkable days of the season.

November 12 1949

An astonishing crowd of nearly 10,000, including a train load from Forfar, (these were the post-war boom years) saw Forfar pull off a fine victory over Dundee United at the primitive Tannadice Park.

This was Forfar's first year in the "B" Division, having won "C" Division last year, and although they were not yet setting dominating the League, they did not seem likely to be relegated either.

Dundee United, on the other hand, who had removed Celtic from last year's Scottish Cup, were second from the top and a good tip for promotion. Not today, however, for Forfar played delightful football, impressing everyone with their fine blend of youth and experience and stayed on top throughout the game.

The only surprise was that it took Forfar so long to break down the United defence, but they did so in the 75th and 76th minute through Cruickshank and McLaren. Forfar's star however was ex-Rangers, Hibs and Everton's Jimmy Caskie who was now perhaps at the age of 35 not as quick as he once was, but had lost none of his craft. But this was a fine Forfar performance, and it was always great for Forfarians to put one over Dundee United.

The buzz word of the late 1940s was "austerity", something that seems to mean that middle-class people were having to pay more taxes, while for the working class, things were clearly improving! There was nothing austere about Forfar that night. Some things may still have been on the ration, but joy was unconfined. And there did not seem to be any problem laying hands on alcohol!

November 13 1993

It was hard to resist the conclusion as one looked at Station Park today that the good days had gone, and might never return.

The heady days of the a decade ago seemed remote as 427 brave souls turned up on this dreich, archetypal November day to see East Stirlingshire score first and Forfar looking woebegone and ragged until David Bingham, one of the few rays of light in the club, equalised.

Yet Forfar were not without their good points either. Stuart Petrie had now gone to Dunfermline Athletic, up two Divisions, and was doing well for them, but Forfar still had some very good players in Alec Hamill, the veteran Ian McPhee and Ian Heddle, for example, and on paper at least, they seemed difficult to beat.

Yet there had been a horrible run of four defeats in October and that seemed to have put paid to any chance of promotion that there might have been. The trouble with the Forfar support was that, having had a taste of being up the Leagues, they found it difficult to accept less, and they were not slow in letting their players and management know about their feelings.

In the old days, when one had never experienced the good life, poor performances were simply what one accepted, unless it got too bad! But thing were different now, and today when the referee's full time whistle went, the moaners and complainers were out in force.

David Bingham scores with his head against East Stirlingshire

November 14 2006

Forfar honoured one of their best and certainly longest serving players in Alan Rattray when they organised a Testimonial game this Tuesday night for him against Aberdeen.

It was a part of other activities that had been arranged for him. It was not the strongest Aberdeen side by any means but there were a few recognised first team players among them, and Forfar did well to beat them 1-0.

Born in 1979, "Ratts" had now been 10 years with the club, although he had been farmed out to Dundee Violet for a spell. For Forfar, he had been a first team regular since 1998 and of course he was not finished yet. He had been captain for several years as well. He was a defender who give his all and tackled ferociously on occasion. This inevitably meant that he was no stranger to the yellow card!

He was a Dundonian, and fan of Dundee United when he was young. He went to Rockwell Secondary School, and his PE teacher was no less a man that Henry Hall, who of course had played for and managed Forfar. His first Manager was Tommy Campbell and at the time of his Testimonial he had played for no fewer than 7 Managers, all of whom bore eloquent testimony to his enthusiasm and commitment. One of them summed him up by saying that he was just a "genuine nice guy".

"Ratts" himself rated his leading of Forfar out to play Rangers in a televised Scottish Cup quarter final in 2002 as the highlight of his career.

Alan Rattray at his testimonial.

November 15 2008

Forfar's form this season had been a bit of a mystery to their fans, as the players tried to settle down to play for the new Manager, the much-travelled, very experienced and decidedly voluble Dick Campbell.

Last week's game against East Stirlingshire had been a shocker and it was no accident that the attendance for today's game against Berwick Rangers dipped by exactly 100 from 427 to 327.

Goalkeeper Ally Brown became an immediate hero by saving an early penalty kick and today we saw a much improved performance. Forfar had gone ahead through a penalty kick scored by Derek Lilley, then conceded the lead immediately after. It required a late long distance clincher by Kevin McLeish to settle the result.

There was however a certain steel in this performance with Andy Tod making a difference to the defence, and discerning spectators in the stand had to share a certain admiration for the body language of our new Manager. He certainly involved himself in the game, even to the extent of the occasional bad word reaching our delicate ears (I'm sure we were mistaken and he was talking about all the "muck" in this damp November weather!) and he was clearly making an attempt to identify with the supporters.

The jury was still out on the performances of the team and would remain so for a while, but we were prepared to give him a chance.

November 16 1977

Forfar Athletic reached the semi-final of the Scottish League Cup to join Celtic, Rangers and Hearts.

This astonishing feat, almost unbelievable in the context of where Forfar had been a few years previously, came about when Forfar beat Queen of the South at Station Park before a crowd of 6,000.

Old timers and even youngsters simply could not believe what they were seeing – the stand packed full, long queues to get in at the turnstiles and the game having to be delayed because Queen of the South's bus got stuck in a traffic jam in the Dundee Road! You simply had to pinch yourself. You were still pinching yourself the day after when newspapers like *The Glasgow Herald* stated "The jokes about Forfar Athletic are over."

There had indeed been many jokes about Forfar – doing a lap of honour when they won a throw-in etc. – but now everyone sat up and took notice. The first leg at Palmerston had been a thrilling 3-3 draw, but here it was Billy Gavine who took the honours with a fine individual goal about 10 minutes before half-time.

Forfar did not then make the mistake of lying back and waiting for it to happen – Queen of the South had ex-Celtic man Harry Hood in their ranks and England Test cricketer Chris Balderstone on the bench – but kept up the pressure all through the second half, and when the full time whistle came, Forfar were as likely to add a second as Queens were to equalize.

Forfar's team on that most epic of Wednesday nights was Nicol, Smith, Brash, Brown, Clark, Rae, Knox, Rankin, Hall, Gavine and Payne with Gallacher and Graham as the substitutes. Rangers awaited in the semi-final, but that is another story.

November 17 1989

"Ye cannae tak the breeks aff a Hieland man" was the general stunned reaction to the news that Forfar were being docked two points by the Scottish League when they only had eight in the first place!

This was because some pettifogging bureaucrats had noticed that on October 28, Forfar had fielded a player called Vince Mennie in a game against Airdrieonians when he was still registered with Falkirk. The irony was that the game had been dreadful (typical of Forfar in these awful days of 1989) and Forfar had lost 1-4. Mennie had not starred either! So no benefit had accrued to Forfar because of their technically illegal action.

Feelings of outrage permeated the town, and there was a certain justified belief that had Celtic or Rangers perhaps committed such a heinous oversight as all this, a warning might have been issued instead. But then again the big clubs would have paid for a lawyer to make sure that it didn't happen, or the eagle-eyed members of the Press would have drawn someone's attention to it in the first place.

To be fair, there were precedents and certainly in later years, the authorities did not hesitate to deduct points or even to remove clubs from the Scottish Cup for such a breach or rules, but this miserable November when everything was going wrong for the club, it seemed like another nail in the coffin. It was clear that the fight to avoid relegation was going to be a major one. And yet, it was only a few years ago that things had seemed so lovely for Forfar.

November 18 1967

This was another bad result for Forfar.

They had started the season reasonably well, but had slipped a bit recently, suffering from injuries and a "loss of form" – a quaint euphemism for what is more commonly described on the terracings in the vernacular as "playin' a load o' p***" – and today they were totally outclassed at Palmerston Park.

The team was Ritchie, Carrie and Dick; Fyfe, Walker and Potter; Newman, Knox, Junior, Stewart and Malcolm, and the fact that there was a "Newman" and a "Junior" in the forward line tells its own story. Today the slick Queen of the South side demolished us from the start, their star man being an excellent player called Mike Jackson who, had he been around at Celtic when Jock Stein was there, might just have made it for the Lisbon Lions. As it was he was discarded at Parkhead and Queen of the South picked him up.

The 0-3 thumping told its own story for Forfar, but yet this would become one of Forfar's better seasons, finishing 7th in the League. Local boy, John Fyfe, recently back from a dreadful broken leg sustained in January, was a hard-working and strong defender . At right back Ally Carrie (sometimes called "Kalihari") was a fine player as well, while up front Archie Knox would surely have done better today with more support.

Today was a bad result and a long depressing drive home in the dark, but things would take a turn for the better after the New Year.

November 19 1983

All good things have to come to an end sometime, and Forfar's run of 14 unbeaten League games came to an end today at Ochilview the home of Stenhousemuir.

Perhaps in tune with the occasion, it was a dull, damp, dark-by-halftime, somehow archetypal November day, redolent of what Scottish football in the lower reaches is meant to be all about.

Ochilview can be a lovely ground on a fine day with, as its name suggests, a lovely view of the Ochil hills. Not today though, they were totally invisible, and not a soul could be seen on the open terracings.

I watched the game from the small match box of a stand, my day slightly spoiled by the result (1-2 against) and the behaviour of a small group of local louts whose knowledge of football was about as impressive as their social skills and their general IQ.

I was all set to argue with them until I realised the truth of the old adage that there is no point in arguing with someone unless he is intelligent.

I then thought of complaining until I realised the absurdity of getting annoyed at someone connected with Stenhousemuir who, frankly, do not have a great deal going for them in anything.

I eventually shrugged my shoulders and sighed about the deficiencies of the Scottish educational system. I was sorry for those who teach at Larbert High School, however! Forfar's goal was scored by Raymond Lorimer, and it would be true to say that Forfar deserved a draw.

November 20 1954

What a thrilling game this was!

Forfar, who had only a couple of weeks ago recorded their first League win of the season, delighted the Station Park faithful on this dull, bleak November day with a 5-3 win over promotion chasing Greenock Morton, replete with famous names like Willie Hinshelwood and Alec Linwood, both of whom had won representative honours for Scotland.

The crowd was a little over 1,000 and contained quite a few supporters from the west boasting about "the Ton". They were a friendly lot but made a few patronising remarks about what they saw as the rather primitive condition of Station Park (not that Cappielow was a great deal better!)

As the game wore on, Morton began to look comfortable with their 2-1 lead, but this Forfar team, playing with a great deal of verve and courage, fought back and inside the last 10 minutes in the gathering gloom of a dreich November day – many years before Forfar contemplated floodlights – a total of five goals were scored. It was difficult to make out who did the scoring – and it all happened so quickly in any case – but Forfar scored two to make it 3-2, then Morton equalized, but then Forfar scored and scored again to make the final score 5-3! It was astonishing stuff, but it was games like this that made your writer (just turned six) love football and love Forfar Athletic! The team was Rough, Berrie and Blyth; Stewart, Crawford and Elder; Currie, Craig, Dunn, Allsop and Martin.

November 21 1908

Forfar had been having a wretched time in the Northern League, but today they registered a rare victory in the competition with a win over Dundee Wanderers at Clepington Park – or at least they would have done if the referee had not been compelled to abandon the game eight minutes short of full time because of darkness.

This sort of thing tended to happen a great deal in Edwardian times, and one wonders why the kick-off couldn't have been brought forward to 2.00 p.m rather than the accustomed 2.30 p.m or sometimes even later.

The reason of course was that jute factories in Dundee and Forfar did not close until lunch time on a Saturday morning, and no-one would miss their Saturday morning shift because that was when they were paid!

Dundee Wanderers would not last long after this. They would be taken over by Dundee Hibs the following year and their ground would become Tannadice Park. Forfar's goal was scored by McInally, but the star performer seems to have been Whitton in the goal for when the Forfar "uprights and crossbar were peppered" he was up to the task.

It was a shame that darkness prevented the game from being completed. It does seem to have been a particularly dark day, however, because Montrose v Lochgelly United and East Fife v Dunfermline similarly ended prematurely today. In the case of the Montrose game there was an additional complication in that the Lochgelly United hamper containing all their equipment had mysteriously disappeared!

FORFAR ATHLETIC FOOTBALL CLUB 1980-81

SCOTTISH LEAGUE DIVISION TWO

FORFAR ATHLETIC v CLYDE

STATION PARK, FORFAR
SATURDAY, 22nd NOVEMBER, 1980

OFFICIAL PROGRAMME 20p

EDITOR'S COMMENTS

One win and two draws from our last three games can't be all that bad and certainly I felt there was a distinct improvement last week at Dumfries. Let's hope it continues today. There is certainly plenty of action on the Station Park front these days. On the playing front it's a welcome today to new signing Rab Morris signed after our last home game and he certainly seems to have fitted in very well to the scheme of things. Off the field work has begun on the re-construction of the West Terracing while planning continues with regards to the up grading of flood-light system which will I believe rank it along side the best.
The big news too on Tuesday was that the club are to be allowed to build a new Social Club on the site of the now closed Troup's Garage on the Dundee Road. I believe work will start shortly and it will certainly be interesting to watch developments here.
Finally a word of best wishes to-day to Chairman Mr. Smith, who entered Bridge of Earn on Thursday for a Cartilage operation. I trust it will not be long before he is back at his desk.

DAVID McGREGOR

VIEWPOINT

Most times I enjoy reading the sports Writers and if their material is controversial why not? Argument and debate on soccer is better than apathy. As Mae West remarked "Better to be looked over than overlooked".
So it is that I have been so interested in Ian Archer's (Daily Express) remedies for our game.
Small minded Directors of small town clubs should surrender their perks etc., etc., should look for more capital locally. What perks does he mean? What perks are there with Forfar Athletic other than the satisfaction of seeing your team trying to do well and the pleasure, at times, of the community being behind everyone in their efforts.
He says the S.F.A. should insist that no one runs a football team without a coaching certificate backed up with visits abroad. Some of us have had a footballers lifetime of learning the game and abroad. By the same token shouldn't the S.F.A. insist that soccer scribes who would have you believe that they know it all, prove it by passing the same certificate.
There is much more, but your Ediotr wouldn't wish me to use too much space, however, if you are wondering what brought all this on, the same newspaper writer wrote a few weeks ago of the 'Cottage Industry' of teams like Forfar Athletic. I ask, what does one know of Forfar's aspirations, finances, administration, cottages or castles if one has never left the asthmatic atmosphere of the big time, big town rat race.
Let's have your views, you want a live programme.

SAM SMITH, CHAIRMAN.

FORTHCOMING MATCHES

HOME v Stenhousemuir, Saturday, 6th December k.o. 3 p.m.
       v Arbroath, Thursday, 1st January, 1981, k.o. 3 p.m.
       v Brechin City or Keith, Scottish Cup 2nd Round, Saturday, 3rd January, 1981, k.o. 3 p.m.
AWAY v Cowdenbeath, Saturday 29th November, k.o. 3 p.m.
AWAY v Montrose, Saturday, 20th December, k.o. 3 p.m.
       v East Fife, Saturday, 27th December, k.o. 3 p.m.

TAYSIDE RESERVE LEAGUE
Week commencing 24th November — Arbroath Away
Week commencing 1st December — Aberdeen Home
(Further details will be announced to-day)

MEET THE REF.

Thirty three year old Man in the Middle David Murdoch is today making his first visit to Station Park since March 1979, when he handled a match with East Fife. However only four weeks ago he was in charge of our league game at Meadowbank. A married man Mr. Murdoch lists Music, Public Speaking and Dining Out as his hobbies.
He has been refereeing for 16 years and holds the unique distinction of having refereed two Scottish Junior Cup Finals, the first when he was only 26 years of age. Promoted to the Grade 1 list in 1976 he now takes charge of many top Premier League clashes and has also had a handful of trips abroad.

November 22 1919

The Great War (as it was now called) had been over for a year now, but in some ways it was as if it was still going on.

Demobilisation had not yet been totally completed, and for some men returning, there were problems finding a job or certainly getting their own job back.

Lloyd George's boast about "a land fit for heroes to live in" had already been seen as a hollow boast and had been thrown back at him by political opponents as labour troubles abounded.

Forfar were struggling in the Eastern League. Like everyone else they had lost players in the War and the Spanish flu epidemic (which was now mercifully subsiding), and three Forfar players had been poached by Dundee, namely Alec Troup, Dyken Nichol and George Henderson.

A win over Dundee, therefore, even if it is just Dundee "A" (or their reserve side) brought more than a little satisfaction. In truth it was a poor game watched by less than 1,000 spectators in weather than one always associates with November – dark, dreich and damp.

But Forfar's 2-1 win was confirmed in the last few minutes when Johnstone, Forfar's centre-half, sent in a weak shot which goalkeeper Capper allowed to drift into the net. Earlier, Soutar had equalised for Forfar but the star man was Scott in the Forfar goal.

November 23 1963

Bottom of the table Forfar Athletic travelled to Somerset Park, Ayr to lose 2-1 in a game in which they fought hard and didn't enjoy the best of luck.

It was a day however on which football took second place to International events, for the previous day, President John F Kennedy had been shot dead in Dallas, Texas.

This was of course one of the "life-defining" events of the 20th century when everyone recalls where they were when they heard the news, and the subsequent few days including the live televising of the alleged assassin being himself assassinated.

Forfar's team at Somerset Park that day was Henderson, Delaney and Dick; Arnott, Anderson and Kennedy; Ewen, Gray, McMurdo, Queen and Reid.

After due deference was paid to the dead President, (a minute's silence was held at most Scottish grounds that day) the game kicked off with Ayr United fielding Johnny Hubbard the South African ex-Rangers player, now clearly past his best but still a tricky player. Ayr scored in the first half, and then when they scored again in the last 15 minutes, the game seemed dead, but this Forfar team, although short of talent and basic skill, did not lack fight and Queen pulled one back. It was simply one of those many days in the dark years of the mid-1960s when Forfar quite simply did not get the breaks.

Ayr United were not a great deal better than Forfar, it must be said.

November 24 1934

As long as the team does reasonably well at home to keep its own supporters happy, anything that happens away from home is probably considered to be a bonus.

Today, on a dull, dreich but not desperately cold November day (aren't all November days always like that?) Forfar travelled to Boghead to play Dumbarton in a town which, like Forfar, was suffering from the ravages of the economic depression under a none too sympathetic Government.

Forfar did well, with Gabriel scoring in the 10th minute and then McGregor seeing his penalty kick saved. Forfar might well have won, but Dumbarton equalised for a draw which brought credit to both teams.

This game was not, however, the main talking point in the town on Monday, for in the Sunday evening service at the Old Kirk, the Rev WG Donaldson, who had been in post since 1908, suddenly collapsed and died in the pulpit. Ironically the hymn being played was "The Sands of Time Are Sinking".

Called "Knockie" for his tendency to thump the front of his pulpit when make a fine rhetorical point in a sermon, Rev Donaldson was generally well liked and respected in the town. He certainly would have to be described as a warmonger in the days of the Great War when he kept urging people to do their patriotic duty and enlist. Occasionally a bit pompous, he nevertheless had a common touch, and although not a great football fan, he was occasionally seen at Station Park and kept an interest in the fortunes of the local club.

November 25 2000

The new millennium had not brought any great difference to Forfar.

We had started off in Division Two (ie the third tier – confusing, isn't it, and they keep changing it!) and that was where we were toddling along as winter approached. We were in the not entirely unfamiliar spot of being 10th in the 10 team League. We had achieved two wins against Queen of the South and Arbroath, but there had been a disturbing amount of defeats, not least when Berwick Rangers had visited Station Park at the beginning of October to win by the unusual score of 5-3. And this was the return fixture to Shielfield Park just over the Border, a place made famous in the eyes of the world in 1967 when Rangers beat Rangers (Berwick beat Glasgow) and infamous to Forfar eyes a year earlier when Forfar were given a dreadful hiding on Christmas Day.

430 were here this raw November day to see an honourable draw, Forfar's goal coming from a likeable character called Willie Stewart, a good player but with a major character flaw, some would say, of being a Rangers fan.

"Willie the Hun" was his affectionate nickname on the terracings, and maybe it was because of Shielfield Park and all its memories of 1967 but he did look particularly pleased with himself when he scored his first half goal. 1-1 at half-time and in spite of many chances missed at both ends, that was how it remained.

No-one should under-estimate that point, for Forfar escaped relegation at the end of the season on goal difference!

November 26 1977

On a bitterly cold November day, on which quite a few other Scottish games were postponed or abandoned, Forfar beat Albion Rovers 3-1 in a tough and feisty encounter in the Second Division.

Forfar enjoyed a certain amount of media attention in view of their imminent League Cup semi-final encounter with Rangers on Monday night. (In the event, it would be postponed because of frost).

League form had been inconsistent at the start of the season, but Forfar were now mounting a credible challenge for the Second Division title and had delighted their fans by brilliant performances against Ayr United and Queen of the South in the League Cup.

Today's referee, Mr Cuthill from Edinburgh, had earned himself a little notoriety at the start of the season by being knocked out when hit in the face with the ball, then sending off Johnny Doyle of Celtic who had certainly kicked the ball – but accidentally hit the referee with it!

Mr Cuthill was clearly stunned at the time and apologies were later tendered and accepted, and today he had a good game as Forfar, with goals from Rae, Gavine and Gallacher, won 3-1.

The game is remembered for an incident in the north-east corner of the ground, when some of the locals were having a go at one of the Albion Rovers defenders who had been guilty of a few misdemeanours and had been having "words" with the referee and a few Forfar players.

The player suddenly put his hand in his mouth, took out his false teeth, smiled at the Forfarians and put them back again. He earned a good laugh for that!

November 27 1937

Depression in every sense was the order of the day this grim dark November occasion at the rundown Tannadice Park.

The Courier is upbeat about it, but then again it would be, because it is a Dundee paper and United won 2-0, but there is something particularly upsetting about having a lot of the game and not being able to score, then blowing up at the end and allowing the other team to win.

This is precisely what happened here. Clarkson had scored for the home side in the first minute, but then Forfar, inspired by half backs Nicoll and McGregor, pressed forward and simply lacked the necessary confidence and conviction to score. As the daylight faded, and the defending of the Tannadice side became ever more desperate, United were awarded a free kick outside the box. Forfar's goalkeeper McFarlane left his goal to place a defender in a better position, the referee's whistle went, McFarlane was still not back in his goal, so the Dundee United player took the free kick and hit the ball into an empty net.

Forfar protested, naturally, but to a certain extent it was Forfar's own fault. That, and the clearly worsening international situation made it a miserable walk down to Dundee East Station in the darkness of a raw November evening to get the train home!

November 28 1953

Forfar moved off the bottom of Division "B" with a hard-worked win over Queen's Park at a cold and windy Station Park today.

Forfar had just signed a young man from Dundee called Wilf Allsop and there was also a trialist from Coupar Angus called Albert Craig playing, as Forfar were compelled to ring the changes after some desperately awful results.

Queen's Park were playing with the strong wind in the first half, and for a while looked as if they were going to overwhelm Forfar. But the wind was capricious and unpredictable and Queen's Park were prone to shoot at every opportunity. Their shooting was wild and greeted with derision by the Forfar faithful, with the ball ending up out of the ground on several occasions.

Forfar, however, used the wind a little better in the second half, kept the ball more on the ground and eventually, Tommy Martin sneaked one in about half way through the second half. The Spiders were then just too tired to get back into the game, and young referee Mr Phillips of Wishaw (who would become one of the best) finished the game with Forfar 1-0 to the good.

Forfar fans went home happy (a rare emotion that season) and their joy was complete when the wireless told them that Alloa had lost, and that Forfar were therefore only second bottom! Hardly a cause for celebration, mind you, but a good day nevertheless.

November 29 1930

Raith Rovers had seen better days.

A few years ago under the tutelage of James Logan and with men like "Tokey" Duncan, Dave Morris, Will Collier and the incomparable Alec James, they had been a force to reckon with and could on their day beat anyone.

But financial circumstances had compelled them to sell their stars, and things had imploded rather badly on them. Like everyone else (this was 1930, remember) money was a problem. Today the Kirkcaldy men appeared, each man wearing stockings which were not necessarily the same as other members of the team, and most of these stockings looked as if they had been "around for a while", let us say.

The pitch at Station Park was hard, for there had been a frost overnight, but the sun was now out and shone brightly, particularly on Forfar who really should have won by a lot more than the 1-0 score line.

The wonder was that it was late in the second half before Davie McLean scored the only goal of the game. Charlie Lawie then hit the woodwork in the dying minutes as both teams struggled to cope with the low sun coming from the west end of the ground. Raith Rovers only real chance had come early in the second half when a man with the unlikely name of Fred Panther was through and ballooned the ball over the bar.

Forfar's forward play was sometimes "dazzling" according to the *Fife Free Press,* a newspaper which was far from uncritical about its own team. It was one of Forfar's better days, but they were still depressingly in the lower half of the table.

November 30 1963

Forfar fans are famously very patient with their team.

They will not forgive any perceived shirking of tackles or lack of effort, but they have a tremendous tolerance of basic lack of skill, of which, it has to be said, there can be a rather a lot at Station Park.

Demonstrations and protests are, therefore, rare. They moan a lot and "I'm no comin back!" is a frequent refrain after a defeat, but that is usually as far as it goes – and they do come back next week!

Today however an 8-2 home defeat by Montrose was too much. Against local rivals, it had been a truly woeful performance, which might easily have reached double figures. Angry voices were heard at the end of the game as a crowd gathered in front of the main stand, and later round the back, to vent their displeasure at the way the club was being run.

There was a distinct and pleasing lack of foul language, but the attacks were venomous on the Callander family for their perceived lack of investment in the club, and in particular their failure to appoint a competent and dedicated Manager for the footballing side of the club. The general perception was that Will Callander, whatever else he had done for the town, was simply "no a futba' man".

There would be a recovery of sorts later in the season, but for the moment Forfar, with dwindling crowds and anchored at the foot of the League, were at rock bottom – and, not for the first or last time, the sick jokes and the gallows humour took over local conversation. The two fictitious Chinese players were introduced yet again – Wi Wan Eence and Fu Lang Since.

December

FORTHBANK NEWS

*Official Programme of
Stirling Albion Football Club*

**BELLS SCOTTISH FOOTBALL LEAGUE
DIVISION TWO SEASON 2005/06**

OFFICIAL CLUB SPONSOR   PRUDENTIAL

Saturday 3rd December 2005
Kick Off 3.00pm

Bells League Division Two

Stirling Albion v Forfar Athletic

Volume 25
Number 14

December 1 1979

Forfar brightened up this dull December day with a sparkling 3-0 win at Recreation Park. Alloa, a local side, had clearly hit a bad patch and would in fact end up rock bottom at the end of the season – a situation with which Forfar's fairly large travelling support were able to sympathise and identify!

The low attendance of about 400 was an indication of how highly the locals rated their team. A goal by John Mitchell before half-time, then a penalty by Alex Rae followed by a third from Ray Farningham set Forfar on the way to victory with the defence comfortably mopping up any attack from the Alloa men.

Forfar's form had been mediocre up to now, it would have to be said, and had included, for example, a defeat at East Stirlingshire the previous week, but this win turned the corner for Forfar. What delighted the fans more than anything else was the way that Forfar played.

One could detect a will to win that had not been so obvious early in the season, and as we started our cars in the bleak early dark December atmosphere of central Scotland, we had reason to be optimistic. Early December is never really anyone's favourite time of the year, but a good football match does help to dispel the midwinter blues.

But then Christmas was approaching, and everyone was already going berserk about it! "Don't know who they are playing next week, but I'm going to watch them", said a fan who hated Christmas, but loved Forfar.

December 2 1989

Things were not going very well at all for Bobby Glennie and his Forfar team these days.

There had only been one win all season, and that was against Albion Rovers in October, and the cause was not helped by the deduction of two points for playing an illegal player.

November thus yielded a total of minus 1 point. A draw against Clyde managed to prevent a run of seven defeats in a row, and today at a cold Station Park before a crowd of 552 spectators brought another defeat, this time at the hands of Greenock Morton. The Cappielow men were now managed by their old favourite Allan McGraw, and this season had tended to draw games rather than win or lose them.

Today, as is often the case, when you are down and you need a break, that is precisely when you don't get a smile from Lady Luck. New signing Charlie Adam tried hard, and Craig Brewster and John Clark both had desperately bad luck, but no goal came, and then in the second half, Tommy Turner scored for Morton and that was curtains for Forfar. They battled courageously however, with Brewster particularly impressive.

Forfar thus entered winter embroiled in a grim battle against relegation with last season's two promoted clubs Albion Rovers and Alloa. By sheer chance, however, they just happened to be the next two opponents.

December 3 1904

"Is there to be no end to Forfar's misery?" wails *The Forfar Herald* following a 2-1 home defeat to Cowdenbeath in the Northern League.

The only crumb of comfort seemed to be that the referee, Mr McArthur, stopped the game nine minutes early on the grounds that he could not see the play, darkness having descended even earlier than expected that grim December day.

Forfar "may well ask for a reprise", although it was not at this stage clear whether the Northern League would allow this or whether the result would have to stand. In any case the "miserable Forfar outfit" were at the bottom, and their supporters were not slow to vent their displeasure at this turn of events.

Forfar's crumb of comfort came late in the game when Blyth defeated goalkeeper Thomson with "a low swinging cross", (whatever that meant). Shortly afterwards, the referee decided enough was enough, presumably because the goalkeepers, like himself, could not make out the flight of the ball.

So the crowd trudged home, some perhaps wondering how the other teams in the town, the juniors like Forfar Celtic, North End and East End had done, for there was little other than football to excite the minds of the male population. But there was always drink, that tempting but totally deleterious blandishment which could make one forget the all-encompassing poverty and the thought that there was a mind-numbingly boring job to go to in the factory on Monday morning.

Certainly Station Park was providing very little comfort these days.

December 4 1948

Forfar had a good win today at Hampden against Queen's Park reserves, commonly referred to as Queen's Park Strollers.

Victorian football clubs seemed to have an obsession with walking, for there were loads of teams called Rovers and Wanderers, for example, but Strollers seems to have been unique to Queen's Park's reserves. A posh middle class Glasgow gentleman would take his lady friend for a "stroll" round Kelvingrove Park rather than a more vulgar "walk"!

The reserves of professional teams were often called the "ham and eggers" on the grounds that they wouldn't be paid, but they would nevertheless be given their tea, usually ham and egg. Be that as it may, Forfar had a good day today at Hampden, beating the Strollers 4-2 with two goals from Ian Rodger, and one each from Dick Cruickshank and Eck Gerrard. The game was played on a raw, early dark December day in front of a very sparse crowd, but there was as yet no sign of any bad weather.

Forfar were now handily placed with 15 games played and 21 points won in Division "C". They were still two points behind Brechin City but there were seven games left; Forfar's trump card was that so many of their games had to be played at home and the team of Brownlee, Anderson and Wilson; Robbie, Shaw and Cruickshank; Gerrard, Morrice, Rodger, Wotherspoon and Sunter looked to be capable of taking on most teams in the Division.

December 5 1936

Forfar had a really terrible game today at Central Park, Cowdenbeath.

Several other games were off because of the snow, and this one had been in some doubt for a while until a telegram arrived confirming that the game was on, and that Forfar should travel.

They must have wished that the weather had been a lot worse, for in one of Forfar's many dark days, they managed to lose 7-1 to an ordinary Cowdenbeath side, the only excuse being the injury to right back Gordon Rutherford, commonly referred to as Mr Rutherford, because he was a teacher at Forfar Academy! Willie Black scored with a penalty kick near the end, but that was the only crumb of comfort.

Cowdenbeath being at the centre of the Fife coalfield, leaflets were issued to the crowd inviting young men to join in the fight against Fascism, with a particular invitation to consider joining the war in Spain where the Republican Government was struggling against Franco's Army, reportedly aided by the dangerous Adolf Hitler.

But there was more to that this weekend, apart from Forfar's heavy defeat and the snow which blocked the road from Forfar to Brechin.

A constitutional crisis had developed over King Edward VIII's desire to marry his disreputable lady friend Mrs Wallis Simpson who was American, not of royal blood and had been twice divorced.

Oh, dear! What was the world coming to? What on earth was going to happen? As a general rule, men said "Good for you, Eddie" with a wink, smile and leer, but women disapproved of "that Yankee trollop". More importantly, so did the Church of England, so Edward VIII, who had only become King in January, was compelled to abdicate in December. And all that in a week when Forfar had suffered a severe hammering in Cowdenbeath!

December 6 1890

Forfar Athletic had no game today, but that was because there was a County game with Forfarshire playing Lanarkshire in Wishaw, and two Forfar players in Alec "Wappie" Lamont and Jamie Dundas were playing for the county side.

Some Forfar supporters travelled to Wishaw to watch the game and cheer on the Forfar men with cries of "Well played, Wappie" heard quite a lot in the sparse crowd. Dundas played in the centre and Lamont on the left wing. The weather was desperately cold, and although the weather had its effect on the crowd, the question was now being asked "Has County football had its day?"

These games were looked upon as games in which players who were aspiring to International honours or indeed a transfer to an English team where professionalism was now legal (as distinct from surreptitious but nevertheless widely practised in Scotland). This game was described as "pleasant" which is not perhaps a compliment, because football in the 1890s was usually hard and uncompromising.

Lanarkshire won 3-2 but Dundas had hard luck when he ran almost the length of the park and was on the point of shooting when he was robbed by a defender. Both teams enjoyed a dinner at the end of the game, and the game at Wishaw at least finished better than did the game at Larkhall on the same day which had to be abandoned because of rioting when Celtic were leading Larkhall Royal Albert 4-0!

December 7 2002

For the first time ever (as far as anyone could ascertain) Forfar played Huntly today at Station Park.

This was in the First Round of the Scottish Cup, and Forfar, with a fair amount of recent history of falling at the first or second hurdle of the Cup approached this game warily, knowing that it was a potential banana skin.

Huntly is a town not entirely dissimilar to Forfar in that it is a market town and services a fairly large agricultural area. Their team, however, had no great record of success in the Highland League until the 1990s. Benefitting from the defection of the two Inverness sides and Ross County to the Scottish League, they won the Highland League five years in a row.

Thus, before 544 fans the well-warned Forfar side did not take them lightly and duly won 3-1 with two goals from Martin Bavidge and one from Kevin Byers. The Highland League team fought well, and with a little luck might have earned a closer result or even a replay, something that would have horrified the Forfar Directors and management on the grounds that the last thing they needed was a trip to Huntly on a Tuesday night in December!

This victory dispelled the gloom caused by last week's 5-1 thrashing at Raith Rovers, hard on the heels of another defeat at Berwick the week before. Form this year had blown hot and cold with runs of victories and runs of defeats, but the important thing tonight was that Forfar had got through to the next round.

December 8 1951

It is not often that the regular attendance at Station Park doubles (or even, as in this case, almost trebles) because of an opposition player, but the attendance on this day rocketed to 2,500.

This was to see the great Jimmy Delaney making his debut for Falkirk. Jimmy Delaney was still the hero of Scotland because of the two goals that he scored for Scotland against Nazi Germany in 1936 at Ibrox (causing, it was said, the Fuhrer to be very upset) and then the winning goal he scored for Scotland against England in the Victory International of 1946, bringing great cheer to those who had suffered so much in recent years. He had already won a Scottish Cup medal with Celtic in 1937 and an English Cup medal with Manchester United in 1948, and in 1954 he would complete a remarkable and unique treble when he won an Irish Cup medal with Derry City! Now past his prime, "old twinkle toes" played on the right wing, and today at Station Park, there was the remarkable phenomenon of the crowd assembling on the "Delaney wing" side of the park, then moving round at half time to the other "Delaney wing".

It was a fine game today with Forfar fighting back to earn a 2-2 draw, and the close marking of the defenders, McCluskey and McKenzie in particular, nullifying the Delaney menace. Willie Brown in the centre for Forfar scored a remarkable goal. He was unmarked when the ball came to him. He swung with his right foot, missed altogether, but then recovered his equilibrium and prodded it with his left!

John Lawrence scored the other. The team was Ingram, Harper and McCluskey; McLean, McKenzie and Cunningham; McNellis, Lawrence, Brown, Hamilton and Newman.

December 9 1905

Seldom does politics take precedence over football in Forfar circles. The country had been plunged into uncertainty by the resignation earlier this week of Arthur Balfour.

This led to the sudden ascension to power, on the invitation of King Edward VII, of Henry Campbell-Bannerman, the leader of the Liberal Party, a Glaswegian, who now lived at Belmont near Meigle, and who had been seen now and again in Forfar.

There would of course have to be a General Election early in the New Year to confirm this, but this was exciting for Forfar people attracted by the promise of cheaper food from the Liberal policy of Free Trade.

Forfar Athletic celebrated this turn of events by beating Dundee Wanderers 3-1 at Station Park in what was called the Carrie Cup. It was a local competition, as the Northern League did not have enough clubs to keep them playing all season.

The weather was mild enough, but very dull and dark with the referee cutting the half-time interval short so that the game could be guaranteed to be completed on time. Forfar's star man was goalkeeper Rodger, while the half back line of Melvin, Murray and Fairweather are given honourable mentions as well, particularly in the first "moiety", a word very common in the Edwardian Press for "half".

Forfar's form up to now had been variously described as "nondescript" "mediocre" or simply "poor" but today's result gave them a boost, even though it was generally agreed that Dundee Wanderers were no great shakes.

December 10 1983

Those who had studied Classics under the late Dr Jack McKenzie at Forfar Academy were particularly delighted to see this fine victory in the Scottish Cup against an Edinburgh team called the Spartans.

The Spartans were of course famous in Ancient Greece for being tough, and 300 of them had saved Greece at Thermopylae in 480 BC, but today their modern equivalents, formed in 1951 as a team of Edinburgh University graduates and now playing in the East of Scotland League were simply swept aside by this superbly competent Forfar side.

Forfar had played them at a similar stage a few years before and it had been tight, but Forfar made no mistake today with two goals each from Kenny MacDonald and Jim Liddle.

Forfar's League form had been superb so far this season, losing only one game so far. This was three weeks ago at Stenhousemuir, and many had thought that they were unlucky to go out of the League Cup by a single goal to St Mirren.

Stewart Kennedy had one of his very rare absences today, and PE Teacher Jim Moffat was in the goal. The crowd was 942 and it contained quite a few from Edinburgh supporting the Spartans. Forfar would now go on to big things this season in the Scottish League Division Two, but they would not last much longer in the Scottish Cup losing 0-1 to Dunfermline on a miserable Monday night in early January.

December 11 1993

Perhaps "indifferent" was too kind a word to describe Forfar's form this season so far, although there had been a certain improvement of late.

But today was Scottish Cup day, and Queen of the South came to town. Queen of the South, I always feel, are the great underachievers of Scottish football, for with a large and rich area to draw on, they really should be doing better. Queen's had already defeated Forfar in the League. Not today, however.

Forfar, aware of the presence of BBC TV cameras for the Highlights programme, really turned it on and defeated the Doonhamers 8-3 with some marvellous goals, aided and abetted by some woeful Queen of the South defending. The Doonhamers seemed to be employing an offside trap, but if you are to do this, you really have to be very efficient at it, and this the Dumfries men certainly were not. The baby-faced David Bingham scored a hat-trick (one was a penalty), Ian Heddle and Ian Downie scored two each and Scott Kopel scored the other.

The goals and the game are still mercifully available on You Tube and commentator Jock Brown rightly goes into ecstasy about some of the Forfar goals. It was one of Forfar's best performances for a very long time indeed, and was much celebrated.

We were able to look forward to a Scottish Cup run in the New Year, and were cheered up by the news that we had another home tie against Ross County (who were not yet in the Scottish League but would be admitted next season).

Unfortunately, it did not turn out well.

December 12 2015

Forfar's miserable 0-1 home defeat to Cowdenbeath triggered a minor sensation in Scottish football circles and a major shock in Forfar ones when Manager Dick Campbell was sacked.

This had followed a dreadful run of form, but many had thought that Dick had done enough to earn a stay of execution in getting Forfar into the next round of the Scottish Cup by beating Queen's Park the previous Saturday.

It is probably fair to say that opinion in the support was divided on the issue. Everyone agreed that the form of the team was dreadful, but a sizeable majority felt that Dick still had it in him to ward off relegation, for he was still a well-loved and respected character. He was in many ways a Manager from a bygone age with loads of couthy, (shall we say?), expressions frequently heard from the terracing and stand, but there was a fundamental goodness and decency in him.

He had done a great deal for Forfar since 2008, taking them from the Second Division and in May of 2015 coming tantalisingly close to earning promotion to the Championship, while struggling with cancer for a part of this time in charge. He was Scotland's longest serving Manager at the time, and he said that he was "humbled" by the letters of support he received from Forfar sympathisers.

Goalkeeper Rab Douglas resigned from the club in protest, and it remains an open question whether Forfar did the right thing in sacking him, particularly as they were relegated from the First Division in any case, at the end of the season.

Rab Douglas

December 13 2003

Forfar were today involved in a thrilling game of football at the Shyberry Excelsior Stadium against this team called Airdrie United.

This team had sprung Phoenix like from the ashes of Airdrieonians, a club who had been one of the leading lights of Scotland in the 1920s but had fallen on bad times in the early years of the 21st century and had been liquidated.

But what was left of this club had clearly "knocked on a few doors" and Forfar had, last season, the honour of being the first club to play against the new team Airdrie United, or as the learned would have it, Airdrie Redivivus (restored to life).

Today however was a great game of end to end stuff. Airdrie at one point were awarded a penalty kick, which was not agreed with 100% by the Forfar contingent (or indeed the neutral members of the Press), but Forfar's goals were scored by Barry Sellars, Hugh Davidson and Paul Tosh.

The crowd was a reasonably healthy 1072 and the stadium certainly looked very nice, but one could not help wondering just how long the new Airdrie United were going to last. Their basic problem was that they were simply just too close to Glasgow. Forfar were doing reasonably well this season, undefeated since September 13, although their Scottish Cup defeat to East Fife on a penalty shoot-out a fortnight ago had been a sore blow.

December 14 1968

You cannot very often say that Forfar have been "giant killed" but this was precisely what happened here at Station Park on a cold day on a hard but playable pitch when Nairn County came to town.

It seems to have been the first time that these teams ever met, and it was widely believed that Forfar would win easily, for Forfar were going well that season and would eventually finish up sixth in the old Second Division.

But whether it was the hard pitch or sheer complacency, the Highlanders won 2-1 to record what was undeniably the best ever result in their history. Yet it was a pleasant experience too, for their supporters arrived in large numbers and were very friendly. Their Chairman wore a kilt (on a very cold day!) and although some of our less well educated supporters sang to him "You can stick your Nairn County up yer kilt", he was cheerful and pleasant.

Their supporters made a real day of it by staying in Forfar until midnight, most of them stunned by the unexpectedness of their victory as well as the amount of drink consumed. I recall drinking with a few of them in a pub at the Cross called "The Strangers Inn" (remember that one?) and thinking what a nice bunch of people with that lovely Highland accent talking about "Nern Coonty".

I was even jealous of them. Today's result was a bitter one, for we did feel that in season 1968/69 we might have had a reasonable run in the Scottish Cup. Nairn County, as it happened, departed anonymously to Berwick Rangers on the first Saturday of the New Year.

December 15 1935

In one of Forfar Athletic's saddest ever days, the death was announced of Jimmy Cameron at the age of 29.

He had played for Forfar a week previously against Edinburgh City on a freezing cold day at the somewhat primitive East Pilton, which of course had no modern facilities like showers or even a hot bath.

Left winger Jimmy scored the equalizing goal for Forfar in a respectable 2-2 draw, but then he had to stand all the way from Edinburgh to Dundee, where he came from, in the corridor of a draughty train while the temperature outside plummeted. (The rest of the team travelled home on another train which went round by Perth rather than Dundee.)

As the train stopped at Kirkcaldy, Jimmy apparently dabbled with the idea of breaking his journey and having a hot meal at the Station Hotel, but he decided against it. That decision cost him his life.

Hardly surprisingly, he contracted pneumonia and in the pre-National Health Service days, that was a very serious illness, and eight days after his last game for Forfar he died in his Dundee home.

He was a popular and much loved player who had played for Dundee United, Celtic and Arbroath, but his best football was played for Forfar whom he had joined the previous year in 1934. The club were well represented at his funeral.

December 16 1978

Last year's impressive season had seen Forfar propel themselves to unprecedented heights in competitions. But it had been flawed slightly by an unexpected defeat in the Scottish Cup at the hands of East of Scotland League side Vale of Leithen.

Excuses like "too many other commitments" and "poor pitch" simply did not wash. Forfar had taken them too lightly and had, most unusually for a team like Forfar, been "giant killed". Now sheer chance and the luck of the draw gave them a chance, less than 12 months later, to right matters for they were drawn once again at Victoria Park, Inverleithen.

This time, there was no mistake. A bus load of supporters went this year as well and saw Forfar reverse the score line of 4-1 with goals scored by Billy Gallacher, Henry Hall, Archie Knox and Ian Reid.

It was a beautiful ground in a beautiful part of the country, or rather it would have been at a different time of year, but this was December in the Southern Uplands, where you get a lot of snow, and Forfar were just glad to get away home again before the weather turned nasty.

And this time they returned to sighs of relief and the knowledge that they could spend the New Year looking forward to a possible run in the Scottish Cup.

December 17 1983

It is always a pleasure to welcome Dunfermline Athletic to Station Park.

A team of great tradition who had risen from nowhere to win the Scottish Cup in 1961 and 1968 and to make an impact on Europe were a lesson to everyone. Sadly it did not last, and the 1970s were all about decline and 1983 found them in the same Division as Forfar for the first time in a long while.

They brought a reasonable and civilised support, but foul wet weather restricted the attendance to little more than 700 when on a better day, Forfar might reasonably have expected about 2,000.

Those who did attend saw a great game however with Forfar scoring in the first half through Ray Farningham and the score stayed that way with chances at both ends, and Forfar perhaps more likely to score another than the Pars to equalise.

After the game, Dunfermline's genial Manager, the ever-loveable Jim Leishman said that he wouldn't be at all surprised if Forfar won the Second Division Championship that season. Many people smiled politely and thought that Jim was just being polite to his hosts as he tucked into his post-match bridie, but then again, Jim did know a thing or two about football.

The happy pre-Christmas atmosphere was ruined that day, however, by the news of a bomb attack in Harrod's in London which killed six people and injured many more.

December 18 1897

There is a myth that Christmas was not celebrated in Victorian Scotland.

Not so! Certainly, it was a bigger occasion in England, it was less important than the New Year and did not become a public holiday until 1958, as the grip of Presbyterian repression slowly relaxed. It was nothing like the hysterical over-indulgence that it is now, but a glance at *The Forfar Herald* for December 1897 will show advertisements for Christmas Cakes and Christmas Gifts "for the very special one in your life" such as a hand bag or an umbrella.

The same newspaper also tells us that Forfar had a narrow and not really very impressive win over Lochee United at Station Park today in the Northern League. The weather was good for the time of year, and the turnout was encouraging, for Forfar had been playing well recently, but today the game was rather dull with the only goal of the game coming when Shepherd passed to Couttie to score. Hitherto, the shooting had been "poor and wayward" and neither team had shown themselves to their true potential.

Still, the Forfar crowd reckoned as they made their way home in the midwinter darkness illuminated only partly by gaslight that a win is a win, and defeating any Dundee team is always good.

December 19 1936

It was a windy day in Edinburgh as Forfar travelled to Meadowbank (not the present stadium of that name) to play Leith Athletic.

Leith, called "the zebras" because of their black and white striped shirts had recently moved from Marine Gardens to Meadowbank. In some ways this was a shame because the dressing room accommodation at Marine Gardens was actually the interior of a ballroom.

Meadowbank, however, was little more than a wooden shed! Leith Athletic had enjoyed some great days, but were slowly losing their support to neighbours Hibs, who although hardly setting the heather on fire, were at least a First Division team.

The weather was not cold in spite of the wind and the time of year, but there were the occasional squally showers and it was far from pleasant. Danger signals were up for Forfar when half-time was reached with Forfar having played with the wind, and the score was still 0-0. Soon after the restart, Jimmy Carver, Forfar's hard working inside left, was badly injured and compelled to play on the wing as a virtual passenger.

This, and the fact that Leith now had the wind behind them, turned the game and the zebras scored twice through Murphy and a trialist without reply from Forfar. Forfar then finished the game with only nine fit men when Geordie McLean (as was his wont) "clashed" with Harrison of Leith and they "were invited to depart" as the newspaper reporter put it.

On this occasion, it seemed that Geordie was rather hard done by, and there was nothing really in it anyway, but it was another defeat for Forfar who had started the season reasonably well, but now seemed to have lost their way.

December 20 2008

Forfar earned a rather fortuitous 1-0 win over old rivals Stenhousemuir at Station Park today.

A last minute penalty, scored by Sean Kilgannon, was after a rather unfortunate incident, in which Shirra of Stenhousemuir had been sent off for using his hand to stop a goal. I have always felt that the law is just a little too draconian on this point, for I feel that a penalty kick is sufficient punishment without the mandatory red card.

Be that as it may, Kilgannon, who had come on as a substitute only a few minutes earlier, converted the penalty; we even felt a little sympathy for Stenhousemuir.

The referee was George Salmond from Arbroath, who had of course captained Arbroath and Scotland at cricket, and was generally regarded as one of the better referees. The game had not exactly been a thriller, although both teams had hit the woodwork early on.

Forfar had seemed destined for mid-table respectability at best this season, but this result was a blow to Stenhousemuir, who had started their campaign at the speed of an express train; although they had faltered a little, were still top of Division Three at this point, but would need the benefit of play-offs before they could slip into Division Two at the end of the season.

468 braved the cold and the darkness of this midwinter day to see an encounter which was tough and competitive but lacking in any real skill – and how often have we said that about Forfar?

December 21 1967

David Prophet McLean, arguably Forfar's best ever player, was found dead in his bed in the Craig O Loch road this morning by his faithful and beloved wife. He was 77, and still frequently seen at Station Park, Dens Park and Celtic Park, the grounds that he had graced.

His lengthy career saw him play for Forfar, Celtic, Preston North End, Sheffield Wednesday, Third Lanark, Rangers and Dundee before he ended up back at Forfar. His distinctions are numerous.

Until recently, he was the youngest ever player to score for Celtic. He actually scored more goals in Scottish football than Jimmy McGrory – except that many were either in war time football or for Forfar in the Second Division. He remained a cult hero in the town until his death, having also played cricket with distinction for Strathmore Cricket Club.

Always willing to talk about the game, he averred that, although he played at a time where few players made a lot of money, money was never as important to him as the companionship of the game and the opportunity to play alongside and against the greatest, singling out the saintly Jesse Pennington of West Bromwich Albion and England as his most chivalrous opponent.

He was a great friend of Jimmy Quinn (whom he was not able to dislodge from the centre forward spot at Celtic) and of Jimmy "Napoleon" McMenemy. When Celtic beat Rangers in the Scottish League Cup final of 1957, he and McMenemy were the only people allowed into the dressing room after the game to congratulate them.

A few days after his death, there was a very impressive one minute's silence at Station Park before the game against St Mirren. Davie's ghost would have been upset at the score line however – a total tanking for the Loons who lost 0-5 to the Buddies.

December 22 1934

Raith Rovers had fallen from grace from their great days of ten years ago when Dave Morris and Alec James played for them.

They were now struggling, but today in the gathering gloom, the two teams played out a very entertaining game with Forfar coming from behind to snatch a victory.

The Rovers were leading 1-0 with a goal from Fulton, but the few Kirkcaldy supporters claimed that they should have been 2-0 up. The same player had "scored" just on the half time whistle but the referee, Mr Rees of Aberdeen, had disallowed it on the grounds that the 45 minutes had been reached seconds before.

The game was slowly beginning to "dwindle in intensity" until the last 10 minutes when Forfar suddenly turned the tables and scored three times. A fine move involving Davie Ramsay and then Jimmy Cameron opened the defence and placed the ball at the feet of Bob Black to put Forfar level. Then Bob Laird found himself unmarked in the penalty area and made no mistake, and with Station Park now in an uproar, Cameron once again showed his class and placed the ball in front of Willie Wann, a trialist from Perth. 0-1 had suddenly become 3-1, and the referee was so excited by it all that he brought things to a close some three minutes early, thereby denying the Forfar crowd even more goals!

Forfar had enjoyed a good December, and were now 7th from the bottom of the League, something that made for a better Christmas than might have been the case. And there were signs that unemployment was now slowly beginning to subside with the factories almost back to working a full week.

December 23 1961

Forfar delivered a much deserved Christmas present to their fans in the shape of a 5-1 home win over Albion Rovers at Station Park.

League form had been indifferent, to put it mildly, and we were already out of the Scottish Cup, hammered mercilessly 5-1 by Jock Stein's Dunfermline at a miserable East End Park ten days ago.

Today however the Forfar team of McKay, Berrie and Knox; Robertson, Sweeney and Adam; Smith, Bonthrone, Coburn, Scott and Reid turned it on to defeat an Albion Rovers side in even more desperate straits than Forfar were. Yet Albion Rovers scored first, a shot from McQuarrie from long distance getting the better of Donald McKay, who seemed to slip when going for it. But Forfar fought back through Jackie Coburn, before in a purple spell before half time Bruce Reid, Ashy Scott and Hugh Smith (with a brilliant individual goal) put Forfar well ahead. The second half was a little duller, but with veteran Doug Berrie playing out of his skin, Forfar remained well on top, earning a penalty late on which Hugh Adam converted.

It was nice, as always, to see Forfar supporters leave the ground with smiles on their faces, particularly as they walked down North Street passing all the windows with well-lit Christmas trees. Much of the conversation centred on the sudden upturn in Forfar's form, but also on when and if the Dundee bubble would burst. Dundee were top of the First Division, having beaten both Celtic and Rangers in November. Could it possibly last? And how hysterical would *The Courier* become if they did?

FORFAR ATHLETIC
.v.
STRANRAER

SFL Division 2
Station Park - Saturday
December 23, 2006

sponsored by:
orchard timber products ltd.
timber sheets doors floors windows

newford park, orchardbank ind.est., forfar dd8 1td

tel. no. 01307 474800   fax. no. 01307 469026

Match-Ball Sponsor
- J. P. WHYTE

programme £1.50

December 24 2005

For many reasons this was one of the most astonishing Christmases that Forfar have ever spent.

First of all let us consider Gretna. They rose and fell with breathtaking suddenness in the early years of the 21st century, reaching the Scottish Cup final in 2006 (and losing unluckily to Hearts on a penalty shoot-out) and the Scottish Premier League and even Europe (although they had to play their home games in Motherwell!) before suddenly collapsing and disappearing in 2008.

It was scarcely believable, but Christmas Eve 2005 was Forfar's best day against them. Few games were played that day – a combination of bad weather and the perceived undesirability of playing games on Christmas Eve. (As a lukewarm fan of Christmas, I disagree with that!)

Forfar who had lost (deservedly, because they were awful!) five games in a row travelled to Raydale Park to meet the still undefeated Gretna.

Gretna is, as we know, very close to England, a long way away and nobody really wanted to see the famous anvil or get married on a wet sleety Christmas Eve. So the Forfar Army was hardly there in strength, but those who weren't there, missed seeing Darren Gribben's two goals in the 2-1 victory, which would have raised more eyebrows if Santa Claus hadn't been hogging all the highlights.

You see, one of the great things about Forfar Athletic is that the unusual comes at no extra price – even on this bizarre occasion in the far south-west of Scotland.

December 25 1965

A phenomenon of the 1960s was the way in which Christmas gradually took over from New Year as the main midwinter festival in Scotland, but if Christmas Day was a Saturday, games were still played on that day.

In 1965, in what must be Forfar's most miserable Christmas of all time, the Loons travelled to Berwick (bad enough at any time) and lost 8-1 at Shielfield Park, leaving Forfar absolutely bottom of the League with only four points to their credit.

It was perhaps a mercy that it was Christmas Day and that very few supporters (if any at all) travelled with the team who even suffered the indignity of finding the Berwick supporters cheering them on near the end, for they were so totally outclassed.

Forfar's support had now turned from anger at a few bad performances in the autumn to something that was a great deal worse – sheer indifference, with the subject of conversation being changed in the direction of Jock Stein's new Celtic or England's ridiculous hopes of winning the 1966 World Cup whenever anyone tried to talk about Forfar Athletic.

The nomenclature of the forward line said it all – Newman, Potter, Newman, Newlands and Mackle. The defence read Stewart, Carrie and Duncan; Marr, McNeill and Knox. Archie Knox would of course go on to better things both as a player and a Manager, and it is often said that a result like this one is "character-forming".

Right enough, when you are at rock bottom, the only way you can look is upwards. Forfar would improve gradually throughout 1966, but the memory of this Christmas Day remains. It would have made Ebenezer Scrooge look merry and jolly in comparison!

December 26 2016

Forfar showed that they were, perhaps, capable of winning the Second Division Championship by coming from behind to beat Clyde 4-3 in a very exciting match at Station Park.

689 spectators were there on a coldish but pleasant enough day, and they were well rewarded for their attendance.

Clyde, managed by ex-Rangers Barry Ferguson, belied their lowly League position by putting up a performance which would have delighted the ghosts of Christmas past like Harry Haddock and Tommy Ring. After Gavin Swankie opened the scoring for Forfar with a lovely goal at the far end, within 10 minutes Clyde were 2-1 up at half time, but Martyn Fotheringham equalised with a fine left foot shot from just outside the penalty box. But then Forfar conceded a needless penalty half way through the second half and when McDonald converted for Clyde, it looked as if Forfar were going to lose. But this Forfar team, made up in endeavour and heart what they lacked in basic skill and football brain, and in the 80th minute Jim Lister scored with a header. A draw would have been a fair result, we agreed, for both teams had played well in energy-sapping conditions until just on the 90th minute when David Cox rose above them all to head home a glorious winner after a good cross from Jamie Bain.

Five long minutes of added-on time remained but the win was a real bonus to the Christmas celebration, but most of us had enough compassion in our heart to feel a little for Clyde and their wholehearted, if somewhat ungrammatical manager, Barry Ferguson.

December 27 1976

No-one will ever say that 1976 was one of the vintage years of Forfar Athletic's history, but it did at least finish on a high note this Holiday Monday as Forfar beat East Stirlingshire 4-1 in front of a crowd of about 300, it seemed.

Several games were off, but Forfar did try hard to get the game on as they had suffered a few lost to the weather recently. Given that this was only Forfar's second win of the season, and only their second of the calendar year at Station Park, no-one could accuse that gallant band of supporters of being glory hunters or Johnny-come-latelies who only follow success. Today they enjoyed themselves in the cold as Mark Law, Sandy White and Charlie Guthrie (none of these three being exactly world beaters, but they were honest triers) and an own goal put Forfar on the road to a rare triumph.

There was even at this dark hour of our history a certain belief that now that Sam Smith and Archie Knox were in charge of the team, that there might just be some light at the end of the tunnel. It was however still a very long tunnel and only a small chink of light, but the enthusiastic round of applause at the end of the game (much appreciated by the players) showed that there remained a residue of good will towards the club in the town.

There was almost a feeling that the next few years were going to be a great deal better. We even sympathised with the East Stirlingshire officials and players. They could appreciate just exactly what all this was about!

December 28 1929

The decade of the 1920s wasn't always "roaring" but it had seen vast social changes with wirelesses, "talkies" at the cinema, Labour Governments, General Strikes, women getting to vote etc. but thankfully no more wars.

Forfar had gained entrance to the Scottish League and had stayed there, although there had been a narrow squeak in 1926. Today they closed the decade with a very creditable draw at Palmerston Park, Dumfries against Queen of the South, a team which had only been born after the Great War. The game was 2-2, and Forfar's hero was the diminutive Davie Kilgour who scored two lovely goals. One was a snap shot from a distance; the other came immediately after, when he ran through, himself, and scored from well outside the box. "Even the ranks of Tuscany could scarce forbear to cheer" at that one, for several Queen of the South supporters were seen to rise up in the stand and to cheer such brilliance. A late goal from Queen of the South earned them a draw, but Forfar travelled north with every reason to be pleased with themselves, for this was a fine performance.

Kilgour himself "a little wee led" as he was described by those who saw him, sat in the corner of the compartment of the train quietly playing cards with his friends while James Black, eye ever on the chance of making money for his beloved Forfar, wondered just how much he could earn for him on a transfer, if this form continued.

But for the moment, Kilgour was staying with Forfar and Forfar were highly placed in the League table as the 1930s approached. Now what would they bring for Forfar and the world?

December 29 1951

The 2-5 scoreline against Forfar at Cliftonhill, Coatbridge disguised the truth. This was, in fact, an excellent Forfar performance in which the team showed spirit to fight back against several really bad breaks of the ball, and had luck been on their side, it would have been a totally different story.

Coatbridge in midwinter does not sound like anyone's idea of enjoying themselves, but Forfar always got on well with the tough men from the Lanarkshire coalfield, and today, a cold but crisp December day, a reasonable crowd turned out.

It was goalkeeper John Ingram who had cause to feel particularly ill-done by the Goddess Fortuna. He mis-kicked an attempted clearance and the ball ran into his own goal. Another goal went in just on the stroke of half-time, then another soon after to make it 0-3. But this Forfar team could fight, and duly did so and Willie Brown, described unflatteringly in the *Forfar Athletic Centenary History* as "a most unlikely looking centre forward" nevertheless scored a good goal . Then Johnny Lawrence netted a penalty. 2-3 and Forfar looked as if they could get an equaliser. Sadly Albion Rovers got another two near the end with poor John Ingram looking at fault for both of them.

Thus ended the bitter-sweet year of 1951. On the one hand Division "B" status had been consolidated and the two League Cup games against Celtic had strengthened the financial position, but the club had suffered the bad loss of James Black in October. But the grand old man was still with us in spirit, and would from his own corner of heaven be looking forward to the visit of Arbroath on New Year's Day.

December 30 1933

Forfar had no reason to love Forthbank, the home of King's Park in Stirling.

Not only had they suffered their record 12-2 defeat at New Year 1930 there, but today they went there and lost 6-1 with words like "rock bottom" being freely used to describe how badly they played.

In mitigation Forfar's half backs Morton and Soutar were both out injured, and the substitutes from the Junior ranks were out of their depth, especially after King's Park scored in the first minute. In the second half, inside forward Whitelaw was taken off injured, as well. The only real crumb of comfort was a goal scored by Bob Black.

Forfar's form had not been all that poor up to this point, nor had King's Park's been all that good, but today there was simply no comparison between the teams, as Forfar finished the none-too-inspiring year of 1933 on a very low note.

Monday, New Year's Day, saw a dismal 0-3 surrender to Arbroath, so it would be fair to say that the prospects for 1934 did not look very bright.

Forthbank shares the name of the current Stirling Albion ground, but, although in the same area of town, it is not the same site. The original Forthbank was badly damaged by a bomb in World War II, and as a result King's Park folded, but resurfaced in the shape of Stirling Albion who played at Annfield until moving to Forthbank in 1993.

Steve McCormick salutes the fans as he celebrates his first goal of three in our last home game v East Stirling (Photo – Jack Cowper)

DIVISION THREE

FORFAR ATHLETIC v COWDENBEATH
STATION PARK, FORFAR
SATURDAY, 31st DECEMBER 1994

OFFICIAL PROGRAMME – 70p

SEASON 1983-84
OFFICIAL PROGRAMME 25p

TODAY'S MATCH SPONSORED BY

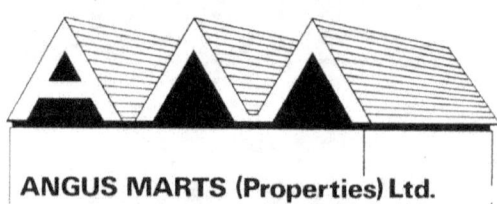

ANGUS MARTS (Properties) Ltd.

ESTATE AGENTS AND DEVELOPERS

22 WEST HIGH STREET, FORFAR, ANGUS. Telephone Forfar 62655/6
5 ST JAMES PLACE, BRECHIN, ANGUS. Telephone Brechin 2148 – 3834

SCOTTISH LEAGUE
SECOND DIVISION

FORFAR ATHLETIC v MONTROSE

STATION PARK, FORFAR

SATURDAY, 31st DECEMBER, 1983

December 31 1977

Forfar finished the somewhat momentous year of 1977 at Stark's Park, Kirkcaldy. The crowd of about 2,000 contained a sizable minority of Forfar fans who sang and cheered their team on to an impressive 2-1 victory.

Who would have thought it? Forfar in the semi-final of the Scottish League Cup (they had been all set to play Rangers at Hampden in late November until a sudden frost caused a postponement until the spring)? Forfar challenging for promotion? Forfar beating Raith Rovers, a much larger and better supported club, 2-1? Many Kirkcaldy supporters agreed that Forfar were the best team in the League.

The Fife Free Press stated categorically that "There were no excuses – Raith were well beaten by a better side". Stark's Park with its strange little stand that turned a corner, and a shelter on the other side which resembled a coal depot and which shook alarmingly when a train passed, was a trim, compact little ground with loads of chronically moaning supporters who kept talking about Willie Penman, Willie McNaught and Bobby Evans. comparing them with what was in front of them today.

The first half was even and scoreless, although Forfar were the better passing team, but then Forfar scored through substitute John Clark in a scramble in the 52nd minute, then Alec Brash with a header five minutes later. Duncan pulled one back for Raith, but Forfar did not make the mistake of falling back, and really should have had a few more by the end.

Hogmanay at the Cross and elsewhere was a pleasant experience that night, for at long last Forfar had a team to be proud of.

January

January 1 1914

No-one in the crowd of well over 3,000 could possibly have guessed what 1914 was going to bring. As it was, loads of Arbroath supporters arrived, many of them having celebrated the arrival of the New Year "not wisely but well" for this Central League game.

The pitch was heavy with both goalmouths more or less a pool of mud, but conditions were playable, and Forfar certainly showed just exactly how playable they were. Much interest centred on the diminutive inside left of Forfar. He played for Forfar North End juniors and was making his senior debut for Forfar Athletic. His brother had played for Forfar a few years before, and this wee man was called Alec Troup. His jersey looked too big and he looked like "a sheep in the Cairngorms" according to one source, but he had a brilliant game as Forfar beat their local rivals by the astonishing score of 6-1. Arbroath scored first, but then Forfar took control with Troup totally in command. He himself scored twice, Mitchell, C Scott, Chapman and Langlands the others.

Geordie "Purkie" Langlands in particular enjoyed himself against Arbroath's goalkeeper Jim Crumley, with whom he had won the Scottish Cup for Dundee in 1910. Troup's performance won universal admiration and the career of Forfar's best ever player was launched.

Everyone, even the desolate Arbroath supporters, wished each other a Happy New Year, for 1914 would surely bring prosperity and peace…

January 2 1956

New Year's Day having fallen on a Sunday in 1956 (and no-one ever played any kind of football on a Sunday in 1956) Forfar had to wait until the 2nd before they travelled to Gayfield for the New Year derby. New Year's Day traditionally had all the derbies – Celtic played Rangers, Hearts played Hibs, Dundee played Aberdeen.

In Angus, Montrose played Brechin, whereas in Forfar the only real topic of conversation was whether they could beat Arbroath, with whom there existed a keen rivalry, but not so keen that it prevented supporters offering each other a drink out of the traditional "bottle"! (Alcohol in football grounds was still legal in 1956) Sadly it was the first time that it was not possible to travel by train, for the line between Forfar and Arbroath (opened for passengers in 1839) was now closed.

In spite of this, and in spite of Forfar's "indifferent" (some said "terrible") form, a goodly crowd of Forfarians made the journey by road and enjoyed a surprise 4-0 victory, goals being scored by Craig, Dunn, Dick and Crowe. The team was Mowatt, Berrie and Elder; Telford, Muirhead and Stewart; Crowe, Craig, Dunn, Allsop and Dick.

It was a triumph as total as it was unexpected. Years later, I heard a story about Willie Dunn, one of the Forfar goal scorers, who was living then in the infant town of Glenrothes. He had been celebrating the New Year with more enthusiasm than restraint and needed the assistance of a neighbour to drive him to Arbroath. He then played the best game of his career, and it makes us wonder what sort of condition some of the Arbroath players had been in!

January 3 1927

It was a really happy New Year at Forfar!

The victory over Arbroath at Gayfield on New Year's Day was good enough, but now at Station Park on the Holiday Monday, a 1-0 win over Albion Rovers confirmed that Forfar were beginning 1927 with a bang. There had been a few deficiencies in 1926, it would have to be admitted, with form being inconsistent and unreliable rather than downright bad, but now Forfar, who had only been allowed into Division 2 by "knocking on a few doors" in summer 1926, were enjoying mid-table respectability.

Today's game brought 2,000 fans, who gave Forfar a great welcome for their win at Arbroath, and Albion Rovers did not lack support either. The Rovers, a fine team in the 1920s, had reached the Scottish Cup final of 1920 where they had been unlucky to lose to Kilmarnock.

Today they were clearly the inferiors of an industrious Forfar team, watched (as often) by one of their supporters, the Earl of Strathmore, whose daughter was now the Duchess of York and would in 10 years' time become the Queen of the British Empire. But Forfar had one of those days where they simply could not score, no matter how hard they tried. The ball simply would not run for them, and the Coatbridge goalkeeper Mason denied Davie McLean time and time again. It was only in the last minute of the game that Frank Hill managed to score from the corner of the penalty box. *The Evening Telegraph,* in a report clearly written as the game was progressing, says that Hill scored "getting the het" when he actually means, "hitting the net", one supposes.

January 4 1936

1936 would be a momentous year in world history with the United Kingdom having three kings, and war breaking out in Spain, but it could hardly have begun with more excitement, anger and violence than it did at Station Park on January 4 when Brechin came to town.

The game ended 1-1, but that was almost an irrelevance to the fact that both sides finished the game severely depleted, two on each side having been sent off, and two Forfar men off injured, leaving the Loons with only 7 men!

The first hour or so of the game had been low key, but then came the incidents deemed to be so severe that *The Courier* considered them worthy of being written about on a page other than the football page!

Geordie McLean, brother of Davie, and in later years the owner of a fish and chip shop at the East Port was the main villain. He and McDonald of Brechin "clashed". Fists flew and the referee Mr Robertson on Glasgow sent the pair of them off.

As Geordie was going off, someone in the stand made an audible remark to him (something to do with his wife, it was said) and Geordie, with the red mist now truly descending, dived into the crowd to "have a word" with the gentleman before being pulled out.

Then Forfar's Adamson was badly fouled by Keith of Brechin. Bateman of Forfar visited vengeance on Keith, and Bateman and Keith joined the queue for the early bath.

The less well educated from both towns in the 1400 crowd carried on the feud in the Market Muir after the game until the constables using their "cudgels of office" dispersed them, while serious apologising was necessary in the Boardroom to and from both sets of Directors.

Suspensions were duly dished out to the miscreants, and ironically, the general feeling was that the referee Mr Robertson of Glasgow had enjoyed a good game!

January 5 1952

Alec Troup - Wee Troupie - Forfar's Greatest Ever Player

January 5 1952

The flag was at half-mast and a minute's silence was held to mark the passing of the great Alec Troup who had died just after the New Year. Those who stood bare-headed in the rain to think about Alec Troup included quite a few who had seen him play, and they were aware of what a genius he had been in his career with Forfar, Dundee, Everton and Scotland.

This game was lucky to go ahead, but fortunately the snow had turned to rain and although other grounds in Scotland were not quite so lucky, Station Park was actually in good trim for the visit of Stenhousemuir.

Forfar had also signed a new goalkeeper called Adam Good from Darvel Juniors. He had played a game or two as a trialist, and today he was given his first official game.

The general opinion was that Good was indeed good, but he did not have a lot to do today for Forfar, (who had also won on New Year's Day against Arbroath) turned it on to win comfortably 4-1. Lawrence, Robertson and Currie scored for the home side, and there was also a deflection which was given as an own goal. *The Courier* sang the praises of the three inside men, all about 5 foot 6 inches, who interchanged at will and foxed the Stenny defence, but the star was right winger Bill Currie who, unfortunately for Forfar but typical of the early 1950s, was doing his National Service near Manchester and was only available once a month.

January 6 1923

The visit of the Stirling team King's Park to Station Park was in doubt for some time owing to the frosty weather, but to the relief of all concerned, the game went ahead after a pitch inspection. The 1,000 crowd who appeared contained some supporters from Stirling, because Stirling was on the direct railway line from Forfar. The crowd were fortunate to see a good game, with Forfar much improved on recent displays and winning 4-2. King's Park opened the scoring and after Forfar equalised, went ahead again before half-time. Forfar then equalised and went on to take complete control with the half-back line of Willie Horsburgh, Allan Smart and John Wyllie (all local lads) attracting rave reviews for their control of the game. The half back line could of course all be adapted by the local dialect to end with "ie" and were commonly referred to as "Horsie, Smertie and Wyllie". James Heron scored twice for Forfar, Anderson another and the other came from "Newman" who was in fact Willie Black of Lochee United. He was deemed to have done well enough to be signed at the end of the game. Up front, Geordie Langlands had been struggling of late – in fact he had not really starred since the War – and it was reckoned that he might be dropped to make way for newcomer Black.

January 7 2012

William Hill Scottish Cup
Forfar Athletic v Aberdeen
07/01/2012

Row C
Seat 49

~~Conc £10~~

4th Round

Forfar Athletic v Aberdeen

Station Park, Forfar

Saturday 7th January 2012, Kick Off 3pm

HOME SUPPORT - Stand Ticket, enter East Turnstiles

Adult £16
~~Concession £10~~

Row Main Stand
Seat C
49

The text missing from the right-hand end of each line of the Conditions of Issue was printed on the perforated stub, removed at the entrance to the match.

Ticket for the match on 7th January

January 7 2012

Given that Forfar and Aberdeen are only 50 miles away from each other, it is remarkable how seldom they play each other. The reason of course is that Aberdeen, who have their bad seasons admittedly, have never been relegated from the top tier and, very sadly, Forfar have never made it to the top tier.

They did play each other in the Scottish Cup in 1911 and 1923, but since then have managed to avoid each other in both the Scottish Cup and the Scottish League Cup – unlike Rangers to whom Forfar have been drawn like bees to honey or, as it us put a little more earthily in Forfar, like "blue-ersed flees to shit".

Aberdeen, chronic under-performers given the size of their support had not won the Cup since 1990, and only seven times overall, but on this occasion, they simply swept the Loons aside, after we had held them for 30 minutes. Goals came from Vernon (twice) Chalali and Megginson. Forfar, while acquitting themselves honourably against distinguished opposition (who had old Station Park favourite Archie Knox in their managerial ranks) were outplayed.

One-time Scotland Manager Craig Brown, now in charge of Aberdeen, was very impressed with Forfar hospitality. Incredibly, however, I heard a none too intelligent Aberdonian singing a song about us having a preference for sheep in our private lives. Was that not what Rangers and Celtic fans said about them? In any case, everyone knows we prefer goats! It was a big day for Forfar though and the reasonable crowd eased some financial worries.

January 8 1966

Goodness knows, there had been very little to be happy about as 1965 gave way to 1966 with a spectacular thumping at Gayfield on New Year's Day and a slightly more creditable but no less painful defeat by Brechin at Station Park on January 3.

There was some comfort when Forfar actually beat Arbroath (although they looked more like Arbroath Reserves if truth be told) in a Forfarshire Cup game on January 4, but now as luck would have it, we had to play Brechin again at Station Park in the Scottish Cup!

The day was dull, but the game considerably less so. No goals in an action-packed first half but the excitement was high, proving the old adage "the worse the teams, the better the game". An added edge to proceedings was supplied by the animosity in the crowd, who made remarks about "bridies causing Aberdeen's typhoid epidemic of 1964" (a new and bizarre one which had taken the one man with a brain in Brechin 18 months to think up!). We retaliated by talking about "Brechin Village" and how they had advertised for a "village Idiot" and were swamped by applications and so on.

All good natured stuff, you understand, but how we rejoiced when Moss Barclay scored for Forfar half way through the second half! Were we on the way to a rare victory? No, this was 1966 and Forfar had to obey the rule that they must break their supporters' hearts. They did so by conceding a late equalizer in the crepuscular gloom at the far end of the ground, as we were about to head home! "Oh, dash it all!", "Blast!", "Goodness Gracious" and "How disappointing!" were some of our comments as we reflected on the ways of the world that night.

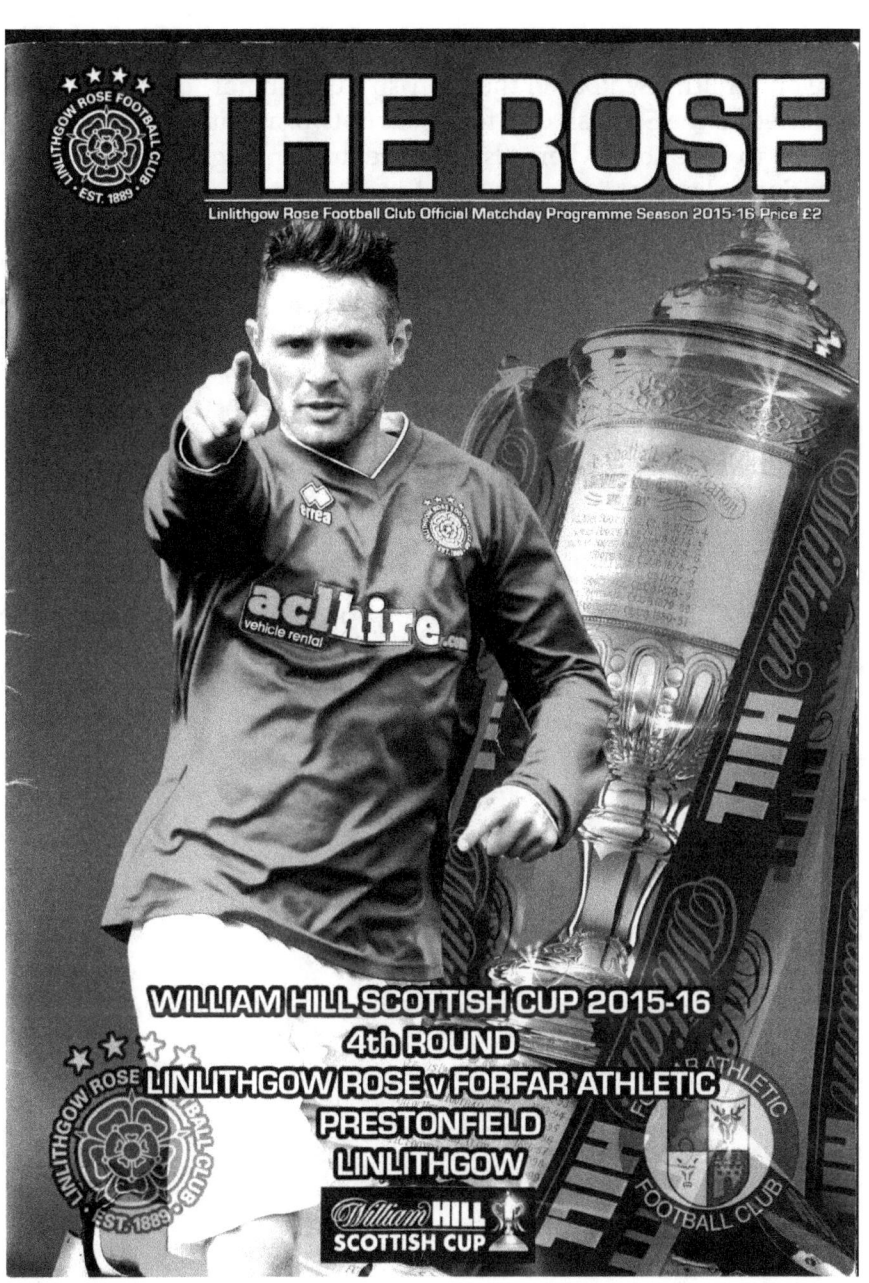

January 9 2016

For the first time ever, Forfar visited Prestonfield in Linlithgow to take on Linlithgow Rose in the Scottish Cup. "Junior" clubs had been admitted to the Scottish Cup for a year or two, and it was a refreshing change to have somewhere else to travel to. Linlithgow played in the East Super League, as it was called in the "Junior" set-up. It was as well that the Rose won through their previous tie, for otherwise Forfar might have been travelling to Wick Academy instead, a trip that would have been slightly more problematic!

The ground was trim and impressive as indeed were the team who fought back well to earn a replay at Station Park. 1-1 at half-time with Forfar's goal coming from a Michael Travis header, things then took a turn in Forfar's direction with a penalty kick and a harsh sending off. The kick was converted by Ross Campbell; when Gavin Swankie scored again to make it 3-1 things looked all over. But in what was a fine advert for Scottish Junior Football, the Rose came back and scored twice in quick succession halfway through the second half. The rest of the game was good end-to-end Scottish stuff on a heavy pitch with both leg-weary teams happy to hear the final whistle.

It was a fine experience for Forfar to travel to a new venue and to meet a team with an obviously enthusiastic bunch of Directors and an equally enthusiastic support.

January 10 2009

Celebrations after the Forres game.

FORFAR ATHLETIC
football club

FORFAR ATHLETIC V FORRES MECHANICS

sponsored by:

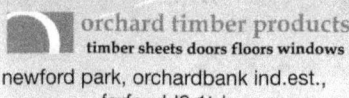
orchard timber products
timber sheets doors floors windows

newford park, orchardbank ind.est.,
forfar dd8 1td

tel. no. 01307 474800
fax. no. 01307 469026

STATION PARK, FORFAR

SATURDAY 10TH January 2009
HOMECOMING SCOTTISH CUP 4th round
MATCH BALL SPONSOR: - Donald Stewart

programme £1.50

January 10 1948

The reporter of *The Forfar Dispatch* was shocked at the sight of East Pilton Park today when he arrived for the game against Edinburgh City in the Scottish League Division "C". He had obviously been watching cowboy movies at the "Gaffie" or the Regal as well, for he said that the crowd of 100 made him and his Press colleagues feel like "lone rangers on the prairie".

The pitch comes in for particular criticism, for although the wings were grassy, the centre of the park was one sea of mud. He predicted (correctly) an early demise for Edinburgh City, for how could they keep going with crowds of 100? (The Edinburgh City who are with us today are, of course, a different team.)

The reporter, however, then enjoyed the game which ended up in a 4-3 win for Forfar. Forfar's goals came from Gordon Massie who netted two, Jimmy Morrice and a penalty from Jimmy Henderson. Forfar also missed a penalty through Bert Crockatt, who was just recovering from an injury, and who would in later years become a referee.

Hardly any Forfar supporters were at the game, and those who stayed at home must have winced and expected the worst when the scores were given out on the radio when they heard "Edinburgh City 3 Forfar Athletic… but then the announcer's voice raised a little and he said "4"!

January 11 1937

ANDY MAC SAYS THERE SEEMS TO BE NO END TO THOSE FOOTBALLING **BLACKS OF FORFAR** THERE'S BOB AND WILL, AND NOW YOUNG JOE APPEARS IN THE FORFAR TEAM.

ANDY MAC' BELIEVES THAT MR JAMES BLACK, WHEN SEEKING FRESH TALENT FOR HIS TEAM, SIMPLY LOOKS UP THE BLACKS' FAMILY ALBUM.

SEE? NOTHING UP MY SLEEVE!

— AND BOOKS A CONJUROR & ILLUSIONIST. ANYWAY, HE FEELS SURE THAT IS HOW HE GOT McFARLANE, WHO WAS CLEVER ENOUGH TO MYSTIFY SUCH A TRICKY EXPONENT OF BALL MANIPULATION AS YOUNG GLEN. THE MANNER IN WHICH HE COULD PLUCK BALLS OUT OF THE AIR WAS TANTALISINGLY EASY.

John R. Mason '37

January 11 1937

January 11 1913

There was not the slightest chance of today's game between Forfar Athletic and Dundee Wanderers being played. They were due to meet in what was called the Consolation Cup, for teams who had been knocked out of the Scottish Qualifying Cup, but today Forfar saw the worst single day of weather for over a century, according to some reports. The problem was snow, but that was exacerbated by heavy winds which caused the snow to block the roads and the railway, so that Forfar was at one point totally cut off, with even the telephone and telegraph lines blown down in the strong wind.

This meant that Mr Black could not send a wire to tell Dundee Wanderers that the game was off, but they might have guessed and couldn't have got to Forfar anyway!

A Dutch schooner was run aground at Carnoustie with loss of life, and although some sort of communication with the outside world was re-established by Sunday, it would be several days before any kind of normality returned.

Incredibly, some games were actually played in Scotland today, but there were reports of abandonments and serious injuries to players who slipped on the wet turf. As they said in Forfar at the time "It's no a day for a tree tae be oot in!" and when serious concerns were expressed about the steeple falling down, "Is there nae place we can keep it tul the stoarm blaws through?"

January 12 1963

Season 1962/63 was a grim one for Forfar, as they finished second bottom, with little comfort to be gained by the fact that absolute bottom were near neighbours Brechin.

January and February 1963 were the months of the big freeze, which knocked football for six and led for the first (but by no means the last) time to the question being asked whether summer football might be not a bad idea.

But before the big freeze actually started, Forfar managed to get knocked out of the Scottish Cup in a high profile match against Hearts, currently holders of the Scottish League Cup and generally regarded as one of the better teams of the time. The weather was freezing, the pitch was heavily sanded and only just managed to pass muster.

After the game Hearts would complain about the state of the pitch, but they won anyway by 3 goals to 1, Forfar having put up a brave show. One of the Hearts goals was scored by future Lisbon Lion Willie Wallace from the penalty spot, and Forfar's goal also came from the spot, being converted by Jim Milne. . Forfar's team was Henderson, Berrie and Delaney; Smith, Milne and Kennedy; Dick, Duthie, Kichenbrand, Kelly and Reid. Don Kichenbrand was a South African who had once played for Rangers (until they discovered that he and his girl-friend were Roman Catholics!) and was at that point "mine host" of the Queen's Hotel. In other circumstances, he might have been a good catch for Forfar, but early 1963 was definitely a very low ebb in the history of the club.

It was as well that the game was played that day, for the weather immediately got worse, and Forfar did not play another game that season until March 9.

January 13 1923

The Aberdeen Press and Journal was damning with faint praise in its assessment of the black and golds' rather lucky and narrow win over Forfar at Pittodrie in the Scottish Cup.

It said it was a "game of few thrills". The crowd was 13,000 and included quite a few Forfarians taking advantage of the railway link to pay a rare visit to Pittodrie, the teams not having met since before the War in 1911. Forfar were certainly not overawed by the large crowd, who, as often happened with Aberdeen supporters, turned on their team when things were not going to their liking.

The Dons went in 1-0 up at half-time, but a particular clap and cheer was given to Forfar's goalkeeper Jock Bruce who had saved several "certainties". And then in the second half with nothing to lose and sensing, perhaps, that Aberdeen were struggling even with the massive bulk of Jock Hutton (who would earn his first cap for Scotland in a few weeks' time) in their defence, Forfar decided to throw everything into the attack. Heron and Anderson both came close, Anderson in particular, and although Aberdeen regained some control nearer the end, there was always the chance of Forfar grabbing an equaliser which would have meant a replay at Station Park. Aberdeen were glad to hear Mr Weir's full time whistle, and Forfar returned home disappointed but able to feel good about themselves.

Mr Black was delighted with his share of the large receipts of £470, the best of the day, and enough to keep Forfar going for some time! A replay would have been nice, though.

January 14 2006

This was football at its grimmest.

Two clubs, both of whom had seen better days, in a dreadful run of form, and already under the shadow of relegation from Division Two, battling it out on a raw January day. This was Recreation Park, Alloa where 575 hardy souls (whom no-one could accuse of being glory hunters) saw Charlie Connelly score a late winner to give Forfar a victory which was possibly just deserved on the run of play. Yet no-one would really have grudged Alloa a point, either. The standard of passing was low, it would have to be said, but there was at least a certain amount of effort and passion – and supporters will always appreciate that.

Forfar and Alloa had engaged in some rare old tussles in the past, and today it was like wakening up in a hospital bad and seeing an old enemy in the next one, for they were both in a dire condition. Forfar had beaten Alloa at Station Park at the end of October, and since then had won only one game – amazingly at Gretna on Christmas Eve. This was Alloa's eleventh straight defeat in a row, with not even a draw to provide any kind of light relief.

At moments like this, one wonders what keeps clubs like this going – but the answer is there as well, in the shape of sheer determination from the Directors, the supporters and the players, who are a little short of the mega-rich footballers that we hear all about on TV!

January 15 1966

On the somewhat late date of January 15, Forfar recorded their first League win of the season when they beat East Stirlingshire 4-2.

The weather was cold and frosty, but the pitch was playable, and Forfar rewarded their 600 loyal supporters with a good game, which showed that things need not have been as bad as they had been of late.

Going behind to an early goal led to the usual groans and the "I'm no' comin' back" statements from those who had said precisely the same thing last week, but then Tommy Mackle scored direct from a corner kick – a rare occurrence, and brilliant, if it was meant – and the quixotic Tommy then started to play some tremendous football down his left wing, crossing for first Newlands and then Park to put Forfar 3-1 ahead at half-time, a score line which caused editors in newspaper offices to wonder whether there had been a mistake. Another goal was scored in the second half, and the closing stages saw Station Park resound to the rare sound of cheers as Forfar passed the ball around effortlessly.

We were even sorry for the East Stirlingshire supporters who not only had a poor team (so did we, of course!) but also suffered from a crisis of identity in that they had been in the First Division in 1963/4, then in 1964/5 had been forcibly amalgamated with Clydebank and played their "home" games at Kilbowie Park, (which was not exactly close to home), before in 1965/6 re-assuming their own identity after court cases! This was however a rare good day for Forfar in a dismal season.

January 16 1897

The town of Forfar suffered a dreadful blow early this Saturday morning with the news of the death of Peter Reid, famous confectioner and maker of the "Peter Reid rock" which sold all over the world. He had been Provost of the town and a genuine benefactor and philanthropist with his gifts of the Reid Hall and the Reid Park to the people of his beloved Forfar. He was 94. A Town Councillor said "What Burns was to Scotland, Reid was to Forfar."

Aware of this sad loss, Forfar Athletic travelled today to Carolina Part, Dundee to play Arbroath in the final of the Forfarshire Cup or the County Cup as it was sometimes known. The game started at 2.45 with Forfar playing towards the east goal, and by half-time they were 2-0 up, the first goal coming from a long through ball from "Jeck" Cable to McFarlane, and the second goal from a goalmouth scrimmage. "Centre-Half" of *The Forfar Herald* was disappointed however when Forfar allowed a 2-0 lead to slip, and thus Forfar were deprived of what would have been their first ever Forfarshire Cup.

He was also disappointed that there were no excursion trains from Forfar, and thus there were not as many Forfarians as he would have liked. The crowd however was about 1,000 and the receipts were £60. Forfar's team was Easton, Janes and Scott; Cable, Black and Mann; Thomson, McFarlane, Beat, Boath and Shepherd.

Confections of the Best Quality.

The Best Makers' Goods Stocked.

Chocolate Novelties and Fancy Boxes.

Sweets for Table Decorations.

January 17 1948

Forfar had no official game to-day because the "C" Division had more or less finished, and the Supplementary League had not yet started.

But money was still required and a friendly was arranged at Gayfield against Arbroath "A" to "keep the auld mannie's mill turnin", as *The Forfar Dispatch* quaintly puts it. Friendly or no friendly, three bus-loads of supporters travelled as well, in absolutely foul weather which was snow in Forfar, but more like sleet in Arbroath because of its proximity to the sea. The pitch was "slithery" and hot drinks were brought out to the players at half-time on the pitch.

The reporter however fancied himself as a poet and states
>"The North Wind will blow, and we will have snow
>And what will Forfar supporters do then? (Poor things!)
>They'll hie to the stand, travelling rugs in their hand
>And stamp their feet hard on the floor" (Poor things!)

As well as inspired poetry and the stamping of feet, Forfar supporters were further warmed up with a fine 5-0 victory with goals from Jimmy Morrice, Jimmy Henderson and a hat-trick from Ian Rodger.

Ian Rodger goes up for a high ball while Falconer (extreme right) looks on, in a game against Hamilton in 1948.

January 18 1930

This was a great day for Forfar supporters as they beat Brechin City 7-2 in the Scottish Cup before 3,000 at Station Park. Brechin City were not yet a Scottish League team, hard though Jim Black campaigned on their behalf, but today they arrived festooned in light blue hats and umbrellas, the colour of their team.

Forfar had been dreadfully inconsistent of late and had suffered two dreadful hammerings from King's Park and Third Lanark in the Scottish League, but today they really turned it on with the two Davies, McLean and Kilgour well to the fore. Ironically, the diminutive but superbly gifted Kilgour, the top scorer at the end of the year, did not score today but was in absolute top form, creating all sorts of opportunities. McLean, playing with a determination and a drive that hadn't been seen for a while, and clearly revelling in the large crowd, scored a hat-trick. David Forbes, Andy Wilson, Bob Geekie and Bob Black scored the others in what was a total rout. As for the Brechin supporters, they departed in silence.

But Forfar fans knew that they would be a little less subdued when they came back in the summer to see the cricket, which was the really big game in Brechin in those days with Davie Chapman, Bob Laing and Willie Eddie all in their prime. These three gentlemen incidentally were all seen and recognised among the blue-rosetted hordes who poured off the train, and then slunk back on to it.

January 19 2016

This Scottish Cup replay between Forfar and Linlithgow Rose at Station Park was a fiasco. Both teams had to tender apologies to the media and to their supporters, with even the following morning's BBC Breakfast programme carrying the story. The teams had drawn 3-3 in Linlithgow ten days previously, and an eager crowd arrived, anticipating a keen contest. Quite a few fans from Linlithgow were there, and they actually looked a reasonable bunch.

There was no violence or anything like that but some cretin threw a flare. It engulfed the park, caused a little damage to the artificial pitch, and delayed the kick-off. That was bad enough, and the Linlithgow officials were full of apologies and promising to root out the ba'heids. OK, the game got started, but it wasn't exactly Forfar's finest hour either, for the floodlights failed. After it became clear that they were not going to repair very easily, referee Mr Finnie abandoned the game.

A few jokes were made about how the flares might have created enough light for the game to go ahead, or that Forfar must remember to pay their electric bill, but the predominant mood was one of disappointment and indeed a little anger, for it had been a dreadful waste of time and money.

The game was rearranged for the following week, and the result was even more disappointing for Forfar fans, but at least it came after a game of football and Linlithgow Rose deserved their moment in the metaphorical sunshine (after the dark of a January evening in Forfar!)

January 20 1990

Forfar had really bad luck in this Cup tie against Celtic at Station Park.

It was far from a vintage Celtic side, who were in those days paralysed – like a rabbit in front of a car's headlights – by the spending power and arrogance of Rangers. Their only real world class players were Pat Bonner, the goalkeeper, and the occasionally disappointing Paul McStay, and they certainly needed him today to earn their rather lucky victory. The game was characterised by two magnificent goals, one from each side, scored by Craig Brewster and Dariusz Dziekanowski, Celtic's Polish import who had hitherto failed to impress.

It was wonderful to be part of a crowd of 8338 for Celtic's first visit to Forfar since 1951 and their first visit in the Scottish Cup since 1914, and for a long time, it felt as if there might be a shock. In retrospect this would have been no bad thing for Celtic in that it would certainly have precipitated the "regime change" so necessary for Celtic's future.

It would also have been deserved. Craig Brewster opened the scoring early with a free-kick from outside the penalty box, but it was too early in the game, for Celtic equalized soon after with a penalty converted by Chris Morris when Alec Hamill brought down Steve Fulton. It was then a very even game with chances at both ends, the best one being when John Clark headed straight at the goalkeeper. But then Dziekanowski scored with a wonder goal near the end, and the Premier League side were able to hold on to win.

The teams were Forfar; Allan, Brazil, Hamill, Smith, Hutton, Clark, Whyte, McCafferty, Clinging, Brewster and Winter with Lorimer and Leslie the substitutes while Celtic were represented by Bonner, Morris, Wdowczyk, Galloway, McCahill, Whyte, Mathie, McStay, Dziekanowski, Fulton, Miller. Grant and Walker were the substitutes.

January 21 1956

This picture was taken before the infamous abandoned game against St Johnstone on January 21 1956

January 21 1956

This was the game that the newspapers of the time correctly predicted would still be talked about in 60 years' time. It was a local derby against St Johnstone, who, crucially, were going for promotion.

Managed by Johnny Pattillo who had enjoyed a distinguished career with Dundee, the Muirton Park side were going well and brought a large crowd of supporters with them on the train.

The referee, a late replacement, was the well-respected Willie Brittle of Glasgow. He was sometimes called "brutal Brittle" for his perceived inability to put up with any nonsense. The game started well for Forfar. They survived St Johnstone's early onslaught; half way through the second half they were 3-0 up with goals from Gilbert Crowe, Ian Stewart and Willie Dunn.

Not only that, but the snow had stopped, and a watery, winter sun had appeared. The blizzard in the first half had been considerable, but the pitch had been re-lined at half-time. With 12 minutes remaining and most St Johnstone supporters heading across the road for an early train home, everything looked hunky-dorey for a shock victory for Forfar.

Then, Mr Brittle, unaccountably but apparently influenced by Johnny Pattillo prancing about on the touchline, stopped the game and led the players off. The first reaction was sheer disbelief.

The snow had stopped, there was not even an awful lot of it on the pitch, but Mr Brittle said "Sorry, gentlemen, I could not see the lines".

Forfar supporters were not slow to make allegations of bribery, and one Forfar Director claimed to have been assaulted by a St Johnstone Director in the aftermath.

The Scottish League, with its dismal propensity to side with the strong against the weak, ruled that the game had to be replayed and yes, you've guessed it, St Johnstone won!

January 22 2011

January 22 1955

January 22 1955

January 22 1955

For the first time ever, a match was broadcast live on the BBC Home Service from Station Park. This was when Airdrieonians came to town.

The BBC had a policy of broadcasting Division "A" games one week and Division "B" games the next, so when high flying Airdrie came to town, the BBC decided to come to Forfar.

They also had a policy of not disclosing where they were going, but the appearance of a jeep with a large box in it with BBC written on it gave the game away to the hundreds of fans who had spent most of the morning working to get the pitch playable now that the snow was slowly melting.

Fortunately they succeeded, and thus Peter Thomson took his place in the stand to broadcast the last half hour or so of the game. Peter Thomson was well known as a radio commentator with a rich, throaty voice although he found it hard to hide his Rangers sympathies, and soon earned the nickname "Blue Peter".

It was a good game as well with scouts in attendance to watch Forfar's Albert Craig who was having a good season. But the man of the match in the 4-2 win for Airdrieonians was Ian McMillan who would one day be transferred to Rangers. He revelled in the tricky conditions, but Forfar scored goals from Tommy Martin and a fine header from Ian Stewart. The result was in doubt until the very end when Airdrie scored in the last minute.

Peter Thomson described the game as a "tremendous game of football" but alarmed my mother (who washed the strips in those days before washing machines were commonplace) by saying that the players were getting "wetter and wetter" in those slippery conditions.

January 23 1971

Forfar paid a rare visit to Easter Road, Edinburgh on Scottish Cup business, (they had not been there since well before the Second World War) and received a fairly predictable thrashing to the tune of 8-1.

Forfar were hardly distinguishing themselves in the League but had beaten Gala Fairydean in the Scottish Cup to reach the stage where the big boys entered. Hibs were of course in 1971 a very good team indeed with men like Brownlie, Blackley, Black and Stanton. Forfar's pain was slightly eased by the cheque from their share in the 10,000 crowd.

Substitute Jim McNicoll scored Forfar's goal late in the game, and the cry from the Forfar supporters was that "they couldna mak it nine!" What was unacceptable however was the hooliganism of some of Hibs' less well-educated supporters and the damage to some of the Forfar buses. Fortunately no-one was injured, and one suspects that some of the Forfar fans weren't totally without blame either, but it was sad to hear of Hibs fans, who normally had quite a good record, being involved in this sort of behaviour.

But then again, anyone who took a walk late at night through places like Leith, Granton, Muirhouse or worst of all, Pilton might not have been surprised. It was also very sadly the time when football hooliganism was beginning to become a fashion.

I was training to become a teacher at that time, and I certainly knew what I would have done with them ... and my opinion was shared universally, except by those politicians who did not like the idea of castration.

Hibernian FC themselves strongly denounced the actions of their so called supporters and promised strict action.

January 24 1925

An eclipse of the sun affected quite a few of the games in Scotland to the extent of some teams altering their kick-off times, and others supplying candles for the gentlemen of the Press. It was only a partial eclipse, but the weather was good and the disappearance of part of the sun caused a welcome diversion when the football got boring!

Forfar however had a great deal more to bother them than a natural phenomenon for they travelled to Dykehead (near Shotts, not Glen Clova!) to play a Scottish Cup tie against the Third Division side. Forfar were of course in the middle of a dreadful season and really could have done with a Scottish Cup run to generate some cash. One of the things about a bad run is that you never get a break when you really need one, and Forfar were decidedly unlucky today at Parkside Park, Dykehead. The only goal of the game came from a soft penalty which Forfar disputed. Then Forfar missed several chances, particularly a sitter which Matt Cornock blasted over the bar when it seemed easier to score.

A replay at Station Park would have been welcome but Forfar continued their melancholy tradition of early exits from the Scottish Cup. There were a few pluses – one was the reliable form of Jock Bruce in the goal, the other was young Frankie Hill at right half alongside the experienced Dyken Nichol, but the rest was all doom and gloom – even when the sun returned from its eclipse.

January 25 1902

Rabbie Burns' birthday.

There certainly was a "blast o' January wind" for what was Forfar's biggest day up to now, for the great Queen's Park came to town on Scottish Cup business. In fact almost all of Glasgow came to Angus that day for Celtic were at Arbroath as well. Queen's Park were, of course, the founders of the game in Scotland. Looked upon with a certain amount of mystique, they were Amateurs and Gentlemen, although they had yielded to professionalism by joining the Scottish League, which they had always despised.

They were 10 times winners of the Scottish Cup – more than anyone else by some distance – and a huge crowd, probably about 3,000, assembled at Station Park to see them. Queen's Park were seen to come out of the First Class compartments of the train when it arrived at the station! But they were affable and pleasant and had in their company a group of well-clad and nice looking ladies, unusual for football teams in those days!

Queen's Park crucially won the toss and chose to play with the wind as a blizzard seemed imminent. Indeed it was, and the first half saw the Spiders 3-0 up as Forfar could not cope with the snow blowing into their faces. As luck would have it, in the second half, the blizzard stopped, Queen's Park were able to control the ball better than Forfar had done, and the game finished 4-1 for the Glasgow men. Celtic won at Arbroath is similar weather conditions, although we must treat with caution and allow for a little rhetorical exaggeration when we read the description of the "snow falling like pancakes".

January 26 1991

The First Gulf War was raging in the middle-east when Celtic came to Forfar in the Scottish Cup for the second year in a row.

Like last year, Forfar fought bravely; with a little luck, things might have been different for the home side, but in the event, Celtic ran out 2-0 winners thanks to a couple of goals from Tommy Coyne and Darek Wdowczyk.

It would be fair to say that Forfar were not on a rich vein of form – they had not won since the middle of November and it would take a major, but welcome, effort at the end of the season to avoid relegation from the First Division. However, Celtic were also disappointing their fans with several players clearly unworthy of filling a green and white jersey. In spite of all this, both teams served up a good Cup tie for the 8359 fans on a cold day at Station Park. Forfar had their moments in the first half, but, unlike last year, failed to rise to the challenge in the second half.

The heartbreak was eased somewhat by the fairly substantial cheque which filled the coffers. Forfar's team was Allan, Brazil, Hamill, Morris, Hegarty, Holt, Paton, Lorimer, Whyte, Brewster and Petrie – substitutes Winter and Clark while Celtic had Bonner, Morris, Wdowczyk, McNally, Baillie, Whyte, Miller, McStay, Coyne, Dziekanowski, Collins – substitute Fulton

January 27 1965

It was one of Forfar's strangest ever Scottish Cup ties.

It was on a Wednesday afternoon at a ground called Craiglockhart in Edinburgh, which is normally a cricket pitch. Edinburgh University would normally play at Peffermill, but the SFA had a rule that any ground used for the Scottish Cup had to be enclosed, and it was difficult to do that at the wide open spaces of Peffermill.

The game on Saturday had been snowed off, but the pitch today looked scarcely any better, – the weather had certainly not improved – and Edinburgh University, never the best supported footballing team in the world, managed to persuade few more than about 100 to turn up. They were almost all of them dressed in the 1960's student style of long scarves wrapped round their necks, a lot of them female who looked like admirers of the students rather than genuine football fans.

There were virtually no supporters from Forfar at all. (It was a Wednesday, the game was far away, the game looked likely to be off and it was the opinion of many Forfar supporters in early 1965 that Forfar were not worth watching in any case!)

Sir Winston Churchill had died the previous Sunday, and a minute's silence was observed for the great man, but the game was played in virtual silence anyway with so few people there. A luckless Edinburgh student was carried off with a broken leg, which said something about the suitability of the pitch, and the students fought hard but in the end Forfar, who were after all professionals (part-time admittedly) won 4-1 with goals from Jim Gray, Eddie McMurdo and then two near the end from Doug Soutar.

January 28 2017

Forfar maintained their challenge for the Second Division title with a 3-1 win over Cowdenbeath at Station Park.

The weather was foul, and the latter stages were played in heavy sleet which mercifully did not turn into more serious snow. Cowdenbeath scored first and were leading 1-0 at half-time but Forfar turned it round very well in the second half with goals scored by Josh Peters, Tommy O'Brien and Lewis Milne, which were much appreciated by the chilled and meagre crowd.

The game was characterised by a change of official at half time. Referee Colin Steven picked up an injury, the stand-side linesman took over and Forfarian Willie Ferguson was summoned post haste from Kirriemuir where he had been officiating at Kirrie Thistle to run the line on the "mert" side of the field.

The half-time interval was prolonged to allow for this to happen – something that the frozen crowd could have done without. But the Bovril and the pies helped things somewhat!

Willie got a cheer when he ran out, and didn't give any traitorous decisions against Forfar. Forfar's team was also cheered at the end, but it was not, in truth, a great performance over bottom side Cowdenbeath, whose nickname remains the Blue Brazil.

January 29 1964

This was a remarkable Wednesday afternoon in Forfar. It was a fine, crisp winter's day, and although there was snow on the hills, the frost was minimal and the replay duly went ahead.

The replay was between Clyde and Forfar in the Scottish Cup, the under-performing Forfar side having amazed even their own supporters by earning a draw at Shawfield on the Saturday. Forfar were bottom of the League, Clyde were second top, and everyone put it down to a piece of luck. Even in the Station Park replay, Forfar had no real chance, it was felt, although a little spice was added to the proceedings with the news that the winners would go to Dens Park to play Dundee in the next round.

Forfar Academy being in East High Street in those days, some pupils in their lunch break were astonished to see the Dundee service bus arrive and Alec Hamilton, Alan Gilzean and a few others get off the bus to go to the game. Some pupils had already decided they were going to play "hookey" that afternoon to go the Station Park, while the wiser (or more cowardly) of us reckoned that if we ran up North Street at 4.00pm we could see the final stages – for free!

We did indeed see the final few desperate minutes when Forfar, having led 3-0 at one time (goals from Eddie McMurdo, Jim Young and Kenny Dick) and having (typically!) conceded two were hanging on desperately. But Mr Stewart of Paisley blew his whistle, and Forfar had once again got the better of Clyde, a team they often did well against. A trip to Dundee now beckoned, but all those who had absented themselves from school in the afternoon had, the following morning, to pay a painful visit to Mr Alex Gillespie, the august and scholarly Rector of Forfar Academy. But it was worth it, they said!

January 30 1971

Forfar, who had not won a game since November and whose form had been particularly poor since the New Year, travelled to Boghead to play Dumbarton, more in hope than in any kind of expectation.

Dumbarton, of course, had been one of the pioneers of Scottish football, having won the Scottish Cup in 1883 and the Scottish League in 1891 and 1892.

More recently in October 1970, they had taken Celtic to a replay before losing narrowly in the semi-final of the Scottish League Cup. The weather was dull, but the pitch was playable and Forfar surprised their few supporters in the crowd of about 1,000 by holding their hosts to 0-0 at half-time. Indeed if Tommy Ward had taken an early chance, Forfar would have been ahead.

But the second half was a totally different story. Dumbarton had two ex-Old Firm players in Davie Wilson of Rangers and Charlie Gallagher of Celtic, and it was the opinion of many supporters of both teams that they had been discarded too early. However that may be, the pair of them simply took charge of this game with Davie Wilson scoring twice and Charlie Gallagher orchestrating everything.

Dumbarton were to challenge strongly for promotion this year (they would fail narrowly in 1971, but succeed in 1972) but Forfar finished fifth from the bottom in what was really a rather dismal season. Last week they had lost 8-1 to Hibs in the Scottish Cup, now 5-1 this week.

There is little doubt about it. It takes guts to be a Forfar supporter sometimes!

January 31 1959

The new stand was just about complete for the visit of Rangers in the Scottish Cup.

Frankly, it was built in rather too much of a rush and, for that reason, does not always provide spectators with the best view of the pitch, but in 1959 it looked good. All the facilities of showers in the dressing rooms were not always common in the Second Division of the 1950s.

It was a cold day, and the pitch was heavily sanded, but the game was on. The huge Rangers support were by no means uncritical of their team, and were appalled to discover that Forfar played in green jerseys (they should have remembered that from last year, but a year is a long time for the thick!). Forfar earned an own goal from Eric Caldow and left the field at half-time with the score at 1-1 and distinctly unlucky not to be ahead. Full time training in the second half told, however. Rangers won 3-1 with goals from Maxie Murray, Alex Scott and Jimmy Millar.

My mother was distinctly upset when I came home and told her that I was a "wee Fenian b*******", in the opinion of a Rangers supporter! I didn't know what a Fenian was, although I had heard the other word now and again at Station Park!

The teams were Forfar: McKay, Steen and Berrie; Brown, Ogilvie and Buchan; Rodger, Cormie, Craig, Brodie and Dick. Rangers: Niven, Shearer and Caldow: Davis, Telfer and Stevenson; Scott, McMillan, Murray, Millar and Matthew.

February

FORFAR ATHLETIC FOOTBALL CLUB

DIVISION TWO CHAMPIONS 1983-84

Today's Match Sponsored by
THE YOUNG SKY BLUES

SCOTTISH CUP
ROUND THREE

FORFAR ATHLETIC v CLYDEBANK

STATION PARK, FORFAR
MONDAY, 4th FEBRUARY 1985

Official Programme 30p

CENTENARY SEASON 1984-85

100th SCOTTISH CUP Sponsored by the Scottish Health Education Group.

February 1 1936

The weather was fine for the first day in February. Although there were still a few signs of mourning for the late King, George V, who had been buried the previous Wednesday, the hope was expressed that as symbolically the weather was improving, so too would everything else.

The worst phase of the economic depression seemed to have passed, and with a new King, Edward VIII, on the throne, things looked good. Would he ever marry, one asked?

Forfar headed to Montrose, feeling a little upset about their Cup exit at Shawfield last week, and today they played well, winning far more comfortably than the 2-1 score line would have suggested. Montrose were 1-0 up at half time, but Forfar made the key change at half time – and the name Black was well involved. Jim Black suggested to right winger Willie Black that he should change places with his brother Bob at centre forward, and this change seemed to confuse the Montrose men, for Willie scored an equaliser half way through the second half, and then later on in the game headed the winner from a Laing corner.

Forfar's travelling support (in the 1930s more and more were beginning to travel by road rather than rail, although cars were very expensive things!) were delighted at all this, some enjoying a lovely fish supper with fish reputedly caught "that very afternoon" in the North Sea before heading home.

That fellow Hitler in Germany was still a bit of a worry, though, was he not?

February 2 1889

The weather was bad enough to render the Scottish Cup final between Celtic and Third Lanark a friendly, for the pitch was totally unplayable "and the ball did not run". They did not however tell the 20,000 crowd until after the game was played for fear of a riot!

But the further east one went, the better the weather became, and although the conditions at Station Park were "cold and stormy" the pitch was definitely playable for the game against Lochee. The attendance was "meagre" however, for Forfar stars Cable, Lamont and Christie were away playing for Forfarshire at Brockville Park, Falkirk, against Stirlingshire, and Jeck Cable was prominent among the goal scorers in Forfarshire's 7-4 victory.

At Station Park, Forfar beat Lochee, one of the many Dundee teams with Irish connections, 4-0 with two goals scored in each half to the delight of the die-hards.

One wonders how much shelter there was at the primitive Station Park. The answer was probably nil, apart from the small stand. The solution was perhaps to stand with your back to the wind, and after all, fresh air in even the vilest of weather conditions was preferable to the choking atmosphere of the factories.

Across the railway, at the Market Muir in even more exposed conditions, East End went down to a team with the unlikely (but appropriate for today's conditions) name of Perseverance who did indeed persevere in the bad weather to win 3-2.

February 3 2001

Scottish football is no place for softies, is it? This game v Berwick Rangers was subsequently abandoned

February 3 1951

On a day when quite a few games were postponed because of bad weather, Forfar managed to play, taking on St Johnstone at Station Park.

St Johnstone were a chronically underperforming side and, like Forfar, languishing in the "B" Division. Their size and catchment area might have suggested that they were more likely to be expected to be playing in the "A" Division. They had experienced a few moments of greatness – they put Celtic out of the Scottish Cup in 1936 – but Perth is, quite simply, not really a footballing city, being more proficient in sports like skating, curling, horse racing and cricket.

However on this occasion, they were far too good for Forfar and won 3-1. Their star man was Paddy Buckley, a man who in later years would star with Aberdeen and lead them to the Scottish League Championship in 1955. Forfar's goal was scored by Derek McKenzie when he netted a rebound after Tommy Adams had hit the post, but St Johnstone remained the better team throughout.

Dundee's game against Partick Thistle at Firhill was off that day, and several Dundee players were spotted in the stand, for they were due to play against St Johnstone at Muirton Park in the Scottish Cup the following week. Their spying stood them in good stead, for Dundee won that game 3-1. But this game at Forfar taught Dundee not to under-estimate the Perth Saints who, on today's performance, looked like candidates for promotion. A form slump however in the spring prevented that from happening for the Saints.

February 4 1985

It was a Monday night before this much postponed Scottish Cup tie could be played against Clydebank, a team sadly no longer with us.

It was, of course, Forfar's first year in the First Division and they were delighting their fans and impressing a few others by getting a few good results against teams like Partick Thistle, St Johnstone and Kilmarnock. Forfar were holding their own, whereas Clydebank, on the other hand, were going for promotion to the Premier League. They had some good players and their physiotherapist was a Forfar man called John Jolly.

The weather had been dreadful of late with much frost but things had suddenly turned milder, and the game was on at Station Park before a crowd of 830 fans. Billy Gallacher scored the only goal of the game. He rejoiced in the unlikely name of "Seagull" (no-one seemed to know why, but one presumes, it was because of his ability to be the target for seagulls landing their "deposits" on him) and he very soon became a great local hero.

Forfar's other hero that night was goalkeeper Jim Moffat, a PE teacher from Fife, who defied Clydebank several times in that last frantic quarter of an hour, as the Bankies tried to force a replay. But Forfar held out, and Moffat, Lorimer, McPhee, Morris, Brash, Scott (replaced by Bennett), Liddle, Farningham, Cormack, Gallacher and MacDonald added to their hero status in the town as other results that night on the car radio told us that Falkirk would be visiting Station Park in the next round.

February 5 1949

Forfar travelled to Tannadice Park to play Dundee United "A" in the Supplementary League competition.

Both teams had reason to feel proud of themselves for recent performances – Forfar because they had last week won Division "C" of the Scottish League and could look forward to playing in Division "B" next year. Dundee United had, the week before that, in a result that rocked Scotland, defeated Celtic, admittedly a very weak Celtic who last season had almost been relegated, in the Scottish Cup.

Jim Black and his Committee were still basking in their triumph (if one can ever hope to "bask" on a chilly day in Dundee) and enjoyed receiving the congratulations of the Dundee United Directors, leading a Forfar observer to remark drily "Aye, Blackie can tak an awfa lot o' that athoot getting wearied".

Dundee United were playing in the Scottish Cup today at Dumbarton, so naturally all ears would be listening to the tannoy or looking at the half-time scoreboard for the score in that game while their reserves were taking on Forfar.

Forfar's supporters travelled in reasonable numbers and saw their team (who could do little wrong these days) win 3-2 against a spirited but none too talented Dundee United side. Two of the goals came from the free-scoring Ian Rodger and there was an own goal. Across the road at Dens Park, Dundee were drawing 0-0 against St Mirren – a dreadful game by all accounts – while at Boghead, Dundee United drew 1-1 with Dumbarton.

February 6 1965

Great excitement prevailed in the town with near neighbours Dundee United drawn in the Scottish Cup at Station Park.

It would be the first time that Dundee United played Forfar in a national competition since the Tannadice men won promotion in 1960. Since then, they had never looked back, establishing themselves as a credible First Division side who were notoriously difficult to beat at their home ground of Tannadice Park, where they had given several fine performances against the bigger clubs.

Financed by a very successful lottery company called Taypools, they had been able to bring in Scandinavian imports like Finn Dossing, Orjan Persson, Lennart Wing and Mogens Berg – and of course their goalkeeper was ex-Forfar man Donald McKay.

This game possibly should have been made all-ticket, for 5,000 turned up to Station Park, and one recalls long queues and much congestion on this damp February day. In the event, the game was an anti-climax for referee Mr Barclay of Kirkcaldy awarded a penalty for Dundee United within the first five minutes and their veteran full back Jimmy Briggs converted. After that, there was only really ever going to be one winner, and the game fizzled out after Dossing and Neilson added another two for United.

Yet in spite of the disappointment of the result, it was good for the club and the town to have a big day like this and to renew our rivalry with Dundee United, a club whom many of us recall as the poor club of Dundee, with an old wooden stand which creaked when you sat down and which looked as if it might collapse with dry rot at any moment. Changed days for United! Would they ever change for Forfar? Forfar's team that day was Henderson, Carrie and Smith; Duthie, Hughes and Arnott; Barclay, Potter, Soutar, McMurdo and Mackle.

February 7 1970

Forfar's record home attendance of 10,780 was set up this day when Rangers came to town in the Scottish Cup.

The game was all-ticket, with long queues the previous Sunday at the Cross for tickets that were being sold in a building at the bottom of West High Street. Rangers were not enjoying the best period of their history, clearly suffering from the major psychological problem of not being able to live with Jock Stein's Celtic. The desperation of their fans for success was obvious, as they arrived that cold but reasonably dry Saturday.

Rangers had taken the precaution of bringing their players through in midweek to allow them to see the ground and to test conditions, and John Greig, a far more pleasant character off the pitch than he ever was on it, was seen talking to and joking with veteran Forfar players like the now ageing and ailing "Skip" Souter.

Forfar were having a desperately awful season but they had recently appointed Ian Campbell to be their Manager, after the departure of Jake Young. Forfar's team was Philip, McKenzie and Sime; Knox, Milne and Fyfe; Wyles, May, Waddell, Mackle and Stewart. Excitement prevailed, strict security precautions were taken, policeman were drafted in from Dundee and elsewhere, media coverage was obvious as the large and basically good-humoured crowd arrived.

Sadly, but perhaps predictably, the game turned out to be a dreadful anti-climax as Rangers scored early and won 7-0 in what was little more than a training exercise for them with even some of their own supporters seen to depart soon after half-time.

February 8 1958

Not a ball was kicked in Scotland today, in one of the very few times that the whole football card was entirely wiped out. It was the heaviest fall of snow and the worst blizzard for at least a decade since the big freeze-up of 1947.

Forfar were due to be playing Dunfermline Athletic at Station Park today but there was no hope of play and the Pars were told well in advance to prevent a needless journey. They would have struggled to get out of Dunfermline anyway, for the snow was at least a foot deep all over Scotland with Forfar particularly badly affected. I struggled, at the tender age of 9, to get through to the "Gaffie", whose proper name was the Pavilion, to see Peter Finch at the Saturday matinee.

Football however remained the obsession with the town, with two topics discussed in between snowball fights. One was the tragedy of Manchester United whose plane had crashed in the snow at Munich on Thursday killing so many of their fine players and leaving manager Matt Busby and his star man Duncan Edwards fighting for their lives.

The other, much happier, topic was the imminent arrival next week of Rangers to Station Park for the first time ever on official business. Who would be playing for Rangers? Would Forfar put up any kind of a fight? Have you got your ticket yet? And most importantly, would the snow clear up in time to allow the game to go ahead?

February 9 1982

A terrible tragedy rocked Forfar Athletic and Scottish football tonight in a road accident just south of the town.

John Mitchell, who had joined the club from Arbroath in 1979, was badly injured when the car in which he was travelling collided with a lorry. The Muiryfaulds strait was traditionally deceptive, a dangerous stretch of the road to Dundee, on which a young Forfar man had been killed a few years previously.

The car was being driven by Alex Carswell the coach. Fortunately his life was saved but John would never play football again. This happened a few days before the famous Cup tie at Tynecastle when Forfar beat Hearts; John was visited by some of his team mates before and after this event. John had played 65 times for the club, his best performance being a hat-trick against Stenhousemuir in January 1980. He was a good goal scorer, but had suffered a few problems with injuries. He was very popular with the support who were devastated by the news. He would probably have played in the game against Hearts, for he had played in the two previous Cup ties that season. The club naturally expressed their best wishes to John and his family, and he was a regular visitor to see the team play for many years after his accident.

February 10 1894

The weather was mild for the time of year, and quite a few Forfar fans were seen in the crowd at Links Park, Montrose for this Northern League fixture won by Forfar by the astonishing score of 6-2.

Forfar won the toss and chose to play with the westerly breeze behind them. It turned out to be a very wise move, for Forfar were 4-1 up at half time, and although they did not find it quite so easy in the second half when they were against the wind, they still managed by "fine sustained play" to stay ahead and consolidate their position near the top of the Northern League. Cable scored twice, Shepherd scored twice, Anderson once and the other goal was simply put down to a "scrimmage".

Much praise was however given in both *The Forfar Herald* and *The Dundee Courier* to Muckersie in the Forfar goal for keeping the "Montrosian tally to twain" particularly when facing the wind in the second half. It was a good result for Forfar but on the broader scene, eyebrows were raised about Rangers beating Queen's Park in the Scottish Cup semi-final replay.

Thus next week's Scottish Cup final would be Celtic v Rangers. Did the legalisation of professionalism the previous summer mean that the days of Queen's Park's control and domination of Scottish football were now numbered? Was their refusal to join the Scottish League on the grounds that it smacked of professionalism going to haunt them?

February 11 1911

This was the result that rocked Scotland, as Forfar beat Falkirk 2-0 in the Scottish Cup.

Falkirk were looked upon as one of the better First Division teams in that era, finishing second in the League in 1909 and 1910, and in 1913 they would win the Scottish Cup. They were not quite as good as Celtic but managed by a man called Willie Nichol who rejoiced in the unlikely nickname of "Daddy" and with players like Willie Agnew, Tommy Logan and Jimmy Croall, the Bairns were more than a match for Rangers, Dundee and Hearts.

A huge crowd of 3,000 assembled at Station Park to see this game, and a small temporary stand was erected in the north east corner of the ground to allow more people a seat. The weather was cold but dry and the pitch was good. Forfar surprised their visitors by going ahead through "Jummer" Petrie and then before half time Dave Easson scored another with his knee. It was scarcely credible stuff from a team who were not yet even in the Scottish League, and Falkirk launched a barrage on Forfar's goal in the second half. But Bill Paterson in Forfar's goal was in inspired form, and towards the end, Forfar launched a counter-attack and gained a penalty kick, unfortunately missed by Geordie Low. Not that it mattered, for Forfar had already "staggered humanity". Forfar's team that day was Paterson, Gibb and Hannan; Lawrence, Chapman and Bruce; Lavery, Low, Bowman, Easson and Petrie.

Eddie Falconer comes down during a Forfar attack in a game played at Station Park against Hamilton in 1948

February 12 1952

For reasons best known to themselves, the Scottish League compelled Forfar, in those pre-floodlight days, to travel to Shawfield to play Clyde this Tuesday afternoon in a game postponed because Clyde were playing in a Scottish Cup tie on Saturday.

More surprising was the fact that 3,000 turned up to watch the game at a time when one would have thought that everyone would have been working. Perhaps it was Rutherglen's half day! Some of the crowd were still wearing black armbands in respect for King George VI who had died the previous Wednesday and was to be buried on the Friday coming. Less surprising was the score line which was 5-1 for the Bully Wee, Forfar's poor performance being due to the fact that several of their players were unavailable because of work commitments.

Forfar played very well and the score line was an unfair reflection on the run of play with the first goal coming from a shoulder charge, which would now undeniably be called a foul. Goalkeeper Good had the ball in his hands and was bundled into the net by the inrushing Billy McPhail (whose brother John played for Celtic and who would himself in 1957 score a hat-trick in the famous 7-1 Scottish League Cup final for Celtic over Rangers).

This legalised thuggery of shoulder charging was retained in the game for a good few years after that, until it died out under the influence of European competitions. In what was a familiar pattern for Forfar, they played well in the second half, scored through Falconer, might have scored again but then collapsed late in the game. Clyde's best player was their young left winger called Tommy Ring.

February 13 1982

For any team to win at Tynecastle is no mean achievement; for Forfar to do so in a Scottish Cup game would have been looked upon as more or less fantasy by those of us brought up in the late 1950s when Hearts had a superb team.

By 1982, Hearts had fallen on hard times, and were no longer a Premier League team – with the spectres of bankruptcy and administration never far away. Yet even so, they were expected to dispose of Forfar who were having a good season under Alex Rae, but were still often described patronisingly in the Press as "lowly Forfar" usually followed by a couthy remark about bridies.

5,671 were at Tynecastle that dull February day to see what was an equally dull game until Steve Hancock put the fat in the fire by scoring for Forfar. The longer the game went on, the more desperate were the Hearts attacks on the field and the angrier and more frustrated became their fans in the main stand. Forfar played it sensibly, kept possession of the ball as much as they could, but increasingly found that they had to rely on the goalkeeping heroics of Stewart Kennedy who revealed all his experience by the simple art of knowing where to be at any given point.

In front were two full backs, Bennett and McPhee, who played superbly, and when the full time whistle came, "there was naebudy left in the grund, bar the Farfar fowk" as it was eloquently put by one fan. You had to be sorry for the Hearts supporters and their once great side, but Forfar was the capital of Scotland that night for the first time since the days of Malcolm Canmore! The teams were Forfar: Kennedy, Bennett, McPhee, Morris, Brash, Allan, Brown, Farningham, Hancock, Leitch and Clark while Hearts had (and some famous names here!) Smith, Kidd, Shield, Byrne, MacDonald, MacLaren, Bowman, Pettigrew, McCoy, Addison and Marinello with Robertson and MacKay as substitutes.

February 14 1925

This may have been St Valentine's Day but there was very little romance associated with Forfar today.

The club was probably at its lowest ebb since its foundation 40 years ago. The team were dire, and as always happens when you are down, luck deserts you as well.

On Thursday, for example, the half-holiday when Forfar played Alloa in a re-arranged fixture, Forfar had the humiliation of recording the lowest ever gate receipts in the Scottish Second Division with only £16 raised whereas they had to pay Alloa a guarantee of £50.

This could clearly not be sustained for long and today fewer than 1,000 came to Station Park to see Armadale (who were themselves in deep financial trouble and would not survive the next ten years) comfortably win 3-1 to the accompaniment of first boos, then (which was much worse) resigned silence and even a little laughter at the ineptitude of Forfar. "Newman" scored Forfar's only goal, and that really says it all.

With the exception of Frank Hill and Jacky Connon, Forfar had what can only be described as a collective bad day in the constant rain of the miserable February weather. The trouble was that there were now too many of such bad days and although the *Sunday Post* is a little premature to talk of "nails in the relegation coffin", it was nevertheless hard to imagine any other outcome than an uncertain future in the Third Division next year.

February 15 1958

Only 9 days after one of football's saddest ever days, namely the Manchester United air crash at Munich, Forfar had one of its biggest ever days when the Loons were drawn to play against Rangers in the Scottish Cup.

It was the first time that the two clubs had ever faced each other in a competition, and great was the excitement in the town as the snow of the previous weekend melted and dwindled to nothing to allow the game to proceed.

Tickets were at a premium with all 8,000 sold out, with a huge crowd of Rangers supporters, now slowly recovering from their 7-1 beating from Celtic in last October's Scottish League Cup final.

Forfar had spent a lot of money to bring Doug Muirhead up from England, where he was doing his National Service, and hopes were high for an upset. Donald Weir, who had played for Celtic, was singled out for special treatment by the Rangers fans – who were already struggling to cope with the fact that Forfar were wearing green jerseys. As a contest the game lasted about nine minutes before Johnny Hubbard scored for Rangers. By half time Ralph Brand, Maxie Murray and Billy Simpson had all scored. The dismal procession continued in the second half with Murray scoring another two and Ian McColl, Ralph Brand and Billy Simpson making the tally 9 before, as was admitted afterwards, they eased off and allowed Albert Craig to score a header for the Loons.

Yet it was still a memorable day for Forfar, even though it revealed, if there was any doubt about it, the gulf in class between rich and poor in Scottish football and for Mowatt, Steen and Berrie; Dudman, Muirhead and Miller; Cord, Weir, Craig, Harrow and Dick, it was a day they would never forget.

February 16 1985

Forfar confirmed their credentials as one of the better teams in Scotland by beating Falkirk 2-1 to reach the quarter finals of the Scottish Cup on a cold but pleasantly sunny day at Station Park.

There had been a certain amount of doubt about the game going ahead, and indeed on the "mert" side of the ground there was as strip of snow/ice where the sun hadn't reached, but the pitch was perfectly playable and the crowd of about 1600 enjoyed a thrilling Cup tie from which Forfar emerged victorious.

Falkirk had a large support with them, some of them not always very pleasant youths who sang a song about what we could do with our Forfar bridies to which we replied that that would be a waste as another part of the body was far more suitable for the local delicacy.

As the game wore on, and Forfar took more and more control, the Falkirk youths became even more obnoxious with one or two of them being threatened by the Constabulary with a visit to the local Police Station.

However, Forfar fans were content to let their team do the talking on the pitch. Murray and Cormack were Forfar's scorers on what turned out to be a very successful day for the county of Angus in that Dundee beat Rangers, Dundee United beat Queen of the South and Brechin City earned a draw with Hearts. Forfar's team was Moffat, Bell, McPhee, Brown, Brash, Morris, Liddle, Farningham, Gallacher, Cormack, Murray with substitutes MacDonald and Smith.

February 17 1962

This was a day of many exciting Scottish Cup ties, with Celtic earning a late winner at Tynecastle and Aberdeen scoring a late equaliser against Rangers at Pittodrie.

Sadly Forfar had exited the Scottish Cup before Christmas that season, but as good a game as any that day was served up at Station Park when Forfar and Dumbarton played out a 4-4 draw with loads of controversy, late goals and missed chances in front of a disappointing crowd on a dull and cold February day. The players frankly deserved a bigger audience to watch them.

Forfar were 3-1 up at half-time with goals scored by Newman, Scott and Smith, and looking very comfortable but Dumbarton pulled it back to 3-3. Then, after Jackie Coburn had scored to give Forfar what looked like a victory, and with the crowd beginning to head for the exits, Dumbarton equalised just at the death to earn a deserved point in what was, for them, a desperately awful season.

Forfar's team was Ellacott, Berrie and Knox; Ross, Sweeney and Adams; Smith, Newman, Coburn, Scott and Reid while Dumbarton had McDonald, Alexander and Jardine; Kilgannon, Glidden and McIntyre; Neeson, McMillan, Stewart, McEwan and McCorquodale.

It was not a bad performance from Forfar, who would finish up fourth from the bottom, a place ahead of Dumbarton, but it is always disappointing to be ahead and then concede.

February 18 2006

Forfar's relegation worries were temporarily relieved by a 1-0 win over Ayr United at Station Park before an attendance of 477.

Today Michele Lombardi scored the only goal of the game to the great relief of the crowd. David Lowing had been transferred to Ayr United during the January window, and he was – not unnaturally – the target of the crowd, who do not like players who opt not to play for Forfar.

Ayr's form was not a great deal better, although both Forfar and Ayr United managed to avoid relegation at the end of the year. Ray Farningham, Forfar's Manager at the time pronounced himself happy with the result. There were not many days in that season that brought smiles to the supporters' faces, and there was no secret that there was a cash crisis at Station Park, hence the departure during the transfer window of David Lowing.

Mind you, looking at Ayr United the phrase "out of the frying pan into the fire" came to mind. And yet, at a time when bankruptcies did happen oftener than people would have liked, it had to be said that Forfar and Ayr were probably in a stronger position than most in that, although they had no strong fan base, nevertheless they did represent a community, and at the end of the day (not literally, of course!) the community would support them. And as an Ayr United supporter said to me that day "I love comin tae Forfar to get the [sic] bridie". He then went on to display a little Ayrshire prejudice by saying what one could do with one's Killie pies!

Jim Bett and Ray Farningham in the first semi-final in the Scottish Cup in 1982

February 19 1983

Forfar paid their first visit to Ibrox for a Scottish Cup tie, since the stadium had been rebuilt, and even Rangers' enemies had to admit that it was looking good.

Their fans however were a great deal less impressed with the team and the joke was that the stands had been built the wrong way round. It would have been so much more interesting watching the cars coming into the car park than the football on the field!

Forfar had of course done so well against Rangers last year and a crowd of 13,311 turned up to see the game, a game for which the Loons had been a little under-prepared because of bad weather.

However, Kenny MacDonald scored in a goalmouth scramble just before half-time and Rangers thoroughly deserved the boos that they got from their fans as they left the field. But then full time training told and it was the other McDonald, John of Rangers, who scored twice in the second half, and hard though Forfar tried to earn a Station Park replay, 2-1 was the final score.

I was sitting beside a well-educated and honest Rangers fan in the unsegregated Broomloan Road Stand, and he said that "it was a bad scene" for Rangers and also, for the life of him, he could not understand how Forfar were still in Division 2, saying that they were better than half a dozen Premier League teams. The Press the following day agreed with most of what my friend had said, and remarked how Rangers "had their usual trouble" in beating Forfar!

February 20 1897

Forfar disappointed their large travelling support by losing in the replay of the final of the Forfarshire Cup to Arbroath at Carolina Port, the home of Dundee FC.

The first game a month ago was a draw, and Forfar had fancied themselves to win this one. One of the main criticisms of Carolina Port as a ground was that it was not well served by public transport and it was a long walk from Dundee East Station to the ground for the Forfar and Arbroath supporters.

In spite of its inaccessibility, it had staged an International match against Wales last year, and today it saw a large crowd, but it was the Arbroath "faction" which departed the happier. Forfar, having been 2-1 up at half-time, simply collapsed against an Arbroath onslaught, helped by the wind, and conceded 4 goals to lose 5-2. Had it not been for a great display by Allan Easton in the Forfar goal it would have been a lot more, and "Criticus" of *The Forfar Herald* was compelled to admit that Arbroath were the better team as he shook hands with his Arbroath counterpart at the end. Forfar's goals came from "a capital shot" from Couttie and then McFarlane. Forfar's only excuse was that they had been compelled to play a newcomer from Kirriemuir called Couttie (who had however shown his mettle by scoring that goal) when Shepherd had to call off. As was the custom in those days, both teams went off for a meal together and then held what was called a "smoker" with loads of drink and singing.

Oh, but it must have been hard for the Forfar players whose supporters deserted in large numbers after the 5th goal went in!

Opposite: Patsy Gallacher and Jimmy McColl are the two Celtic players in the picture. Observe the small stand.
This is one of the very few early pictures of Station Park

February 21 1914

It was Forfar's greatest day to date in their 30 year history as the mighty Celtic came to town.

It was an opportunity to see the two most gifted ball players of the day in Patsy Gallacher of Celtic and Alec Troup of Forfar on the same football field. From very early in the morning the crowds rolled up, with the station being a busy place, and more or less the whole town was there. The Celtic team arrived with the great Jimmy Quinn, now more or less retired, carrying the Celtic hamper, smoking a clay pipe and talking amiably to the locals.

Celtic then set off in a charabanc to the Baths in Chapel Street to change, the accommodation at Station Park being deemed too primitive whereas the Baths, donated to the town by the millionaire Andrew Carnegie a few years previously, were the last word in luxury.

The game was a predictable 0-5 victory for the Glasgow men, but much interest was taken in the way that young Troup got the better of Celtic's veteran wing half and captain Sunny Jim Young, who on occasion resorted to foul tactics and was spoken to by the referee Mr Mitchell of Falkirk. Not only that but he was accosted by Troup's mother who made at him with her umbrella as he came off the park!

Forfar's team was J. Scott, Ferguson and C. Scott; Bruce, Chapman and Leighton; Easson, Walker, Langlands, Troup and Petrie while Celtic were represented by Shaw, McGregor and Dodds; Young, Johnstone and Davidson; McAtee, Gallacher, McColl, McMenemy and Browning.

February 22 1958

Atrocious conditions were in evidence at Cappielow when Forfar took on Greenock Morton.

Normally one associates Greenock with rain, but this was more like sleet which threatened to turn into outright snow. The game started with no-one really confident that the game was going to last the 90 minutes and with the brave souls of Greenock who attended this game (along with a very few from Forfar) huddled under what little cover there was at Cappielow, the ground with the sometimes incongruous sight of cranes and other evidence of ship-building on the one hand, and then a few snow-capped mountains in the distance. It almost seemed to be a different world.

Today the weather conditions kept closing in, but as often happens, the two well-matched teams served up a very good game. Len Dick scored in the early stages for Forfar, and then after Morton had equalised and gone ahead (against the run of play) Albert Craig headed an equaliser from an Ian Stewart cross. That was it at half-time, and after the ground staff manfully cleared the lines, the game proceeded.

The Forfar trainer, the venerable Davie Ogg – who had seen quite a few football games in his time – described the conditions as "the worst he had ever seen". My mother, who washed the strips in those days, agreed. But the snow relented a little, and there was even a little sunshine when the game finished as a highly creditable 2-2 draw.

Both teams got a round of applause from the fans. It would have been equally appropriate the other way round.

February 23 1929

Forfar today played one of the teams who once graced Scottish football, but are sadly no longer with us.

Bo'ness had their heyday a decade earlier when, because of their location on the Forth, the town was a vibrant centre for the munitions industry. In particular it was the place where horses were shod and trained for the war. Now, they were beginning to feel the chill winds of the depression, and although they had spent the previous season in Division One, their inevitable relegation was a blow from which they never recovered and they left the Scottish League in 1933.

Their demise, like that of so many teams in the 1920s and 1930s is an indirect compliment to the good stewardship and running of Forfar Athletic. Jim Black was never, perhaps, the most loved of men in the town, but then again the best administrators and leaders are not always the most popular!

Before a crowd of about 1,000, Forfar today won comfortably 5-1 at Station Park. Three Forfar men stood out – Davie McLean and Davie Kilgour, Forfar's terrible twins who shared the goal scoring between them, and a fine display from a goalkeeper from Kirriemuir called Orchison who was only playing because Forfar's regular goalkeeper Bruce had a family bereavement. It was a fine performance from Forfar who had shown some good form of late. Today was a remarkable day in the broader context of Scottish football for Scotland beat Ireland 7-3 in Belfast and Hughie Gallacher scored 5 of them! Not only that, but Scotland beat Ireland that day at rugby as well, winning 16-7 in Dublin!

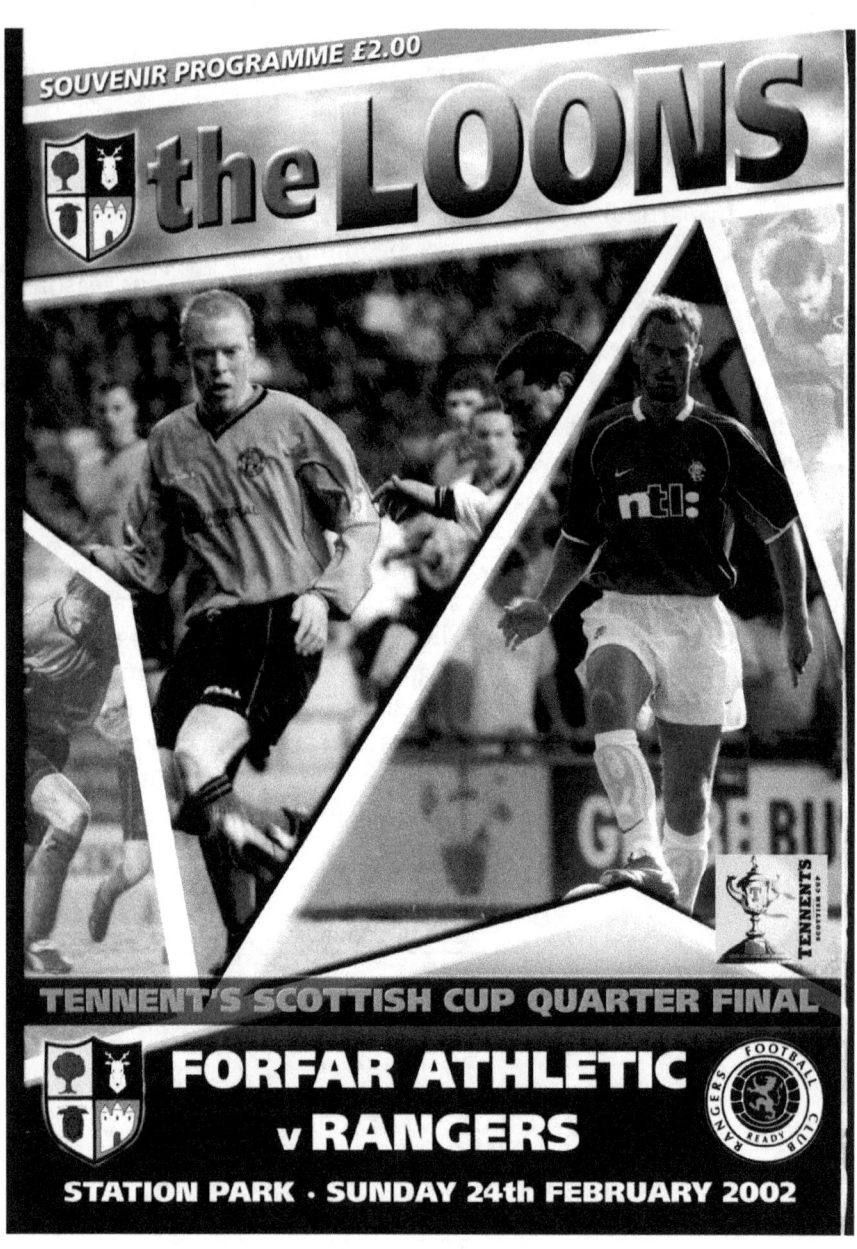

February 24 2002

FORFAR ATHLETIC FOOTBALL CLUB LIMITED

Ground: STATION PARK, FORFAR
Tel: 01307 463576

Registered in Edinburgh No. 75805
VAT Reg. No. 270 9051 67

Secretary: DAVID McGREGOR
6 Westfield Crescent, Forfar DD8 1EG
Tel. 01307 464924 (Home)
Tel. 01307 475519 (Business)
Fax. 01307 466956 (Business)

TENNENT'S SCOTTISH CUP QUARTER FINAL

FORFAR ATHLETIC -v- RANGERS
AT STATION PARK, FORFAR ON SUNDAY 24TH FEBRUARY 2002

#	Forfar	Rangers	#
1	Michael Brown	Stefan Klos	1
2	Alan Rattray	Fernando Ricksen	2
3	Kevin Milne	Lorenzo Amoruso	4
4	Robbie Horn	Tony Vidmar	25
5	Iain Good	Arthur Numan	5
6	Paul Lunan	Andrei Kanchelskis	17
7	Calum Bett	Stephen Hughes	27
8	Barry Sellars	Barry Ferguson	6
9	Paul Tosh	Neil McCann	11
10	Willie Stewart	Shota Arveladze	24
11	Kevin Byers	Billy Dodds	16
12	Barrie Moffat	Maurice Ross	21
14	Sean Christie	Russell Latapy	20
15	Roberto Morris	Peter Loverkrands	26
16	Jim Henry	Scott Wilson	19
Sub G/K	Neal Ferrie	Alan McGregor	33

REFEREE: **Stuart Dougal**

ASSISTANT REFEREES: **Wilson Irvine / Brian McDuffie** : 4TH OFFICIAL: **George Clyde**

BALL DONOR: **Gils' Motor Factors**

Chairman: David McGregor   Vice-Chairman: Neill Wilson   Treasurer: Gordon Menmuir
Directors: Ron Blair, Michael McEwan, Alastair Nicoll

Main Sponsor: UNIVERSAL TELECOM

February 24 2002

Having defeated Threave Rovers, Gala Fairydean and then Clyde in the Scottish Cup, Forfar found themselves in the quarter final against somewhat stronger opposition – 29 time winners Rangers.

The day was crisp and bright, a touch cold perhaps, but Forfar renewed their battle against the Ibrox side, regular Scottish Cup opponents since 1958. This game was on a Sunday and was televised live on BBC.

The anticipation was great, but there was a complete and immediate anti-climax when Billy Dodds scored for the opposition in 40 seconds. What caused more than a little hilarity in houses throughout the country was that the loudspeaker announcer was still giving out the teams when Rangers scored! The announcer then shut up!

In truth, it was no contest, but those who had wished to see Forfar put up a better effort and score at least one goal were to be disappointed, for the score finished 0-6. Long before the full time whistle (it was 0-4 at half time) the game was finished as a contest.

It was, however, interesting to see the difference between Rangers and Forfar – the main one being that Rangers, playing in white so as not to clash with Forfar's light blue, could pick out a man and send an inch perfect pass to him, whereas Forfar's passes were more of the "hopeful" variety. But no-one criticised Forfar, and the cheque from the large crowd and the TV money was enough to ward off financial troubles for the time being.

Cheery Forfar supporters when Rangers come to town in February 2002

February 25 1911

Forfar, the surprise packet of the Scottish Cup when they beat Falkirk two weeks previously, were given the reward of a trip to Pittodrie to take on Aberdeen in the quarter final.

The game attracted a fair amount of national attention and fully 10,000 (probably the biggest crowd that Forfar had played in front of up to this point) turned up to see the game on a bright afternoon. The crowd included about 1,000 from Forfar who were taking advantage of the good rail link, and for many of them it would have been the first time that they had been to the Granite City.

Forfar had of course played a team called "Aberdeen" before, but this was the new Aberdeen FC which had been formed out of several amalgamations in 1903 and was now holding its own in the First Division.

On this occasion, they were too good for Forfar and duly won 6-0, as one would have expected from full time professionals, but *The Aberdeen Press and Journal* has nothing but praise for Forfar and their supporters using words like "gallant" and "plucky" and "till the finish played a good losing game".

"Jummer" Petrie was singled out as playing well for the Loons, and they all got a sporting cheer at the end. On the same day, Rangers – who would win the League – were put out of the Scottish Cup by Dundee at Dens Park, and Aberdeen would find themselves drawn at home against Celtic in the semi-final. Celtic would duly win through but crowd disturbances that day would compel the SFA to play semi-finals at neutral venues from next season onwards.

Everyone behaved themselves when Forfar were at Pittodrie, though.

February 26 1927

Forfar travelled to Mill Park, Bathgate for a Scottish League Second Division game and were involved in a remarkable game in which they simply ran out of time.

4-0 down at one point, they then rallied and pulled it back to 4-3, looking as if they could equalize and then go on to win before the referee blew for full time. Allan Smart, Bob Husband (with a penalty) and Frank Hill scored for Forfar. Much attention was paid to Forfar's centre forward Frank Hill, who combined speed and aggression with an eye for goal. He was already the object of attention from several clubs in England and Scotland (he would eventually go to Aberdeen), and today he took a fine goal.

It was however a disappointing day for Forfar against Bathgate, who were already showing signs of the poverty which would lead to their being compelled to leave the Scottish League a couple of seasons later.

The local industry of shale oil was in serious decline and the town of Bathgate was slowly becoming depopulated in very difficult economic times as West Lothian struggled to come to terms with the aftermath of the General Strike.

Forfar's team that day was Bridgeford, Husband and Osborne; Godfrey, Smart and Fox: Black, Connon, Hill, McLean and Menzies.

Jim Black, Forfar's supremo, was not there that day. He was in Belfast watching Scotland play Northern Ireland. They won 2-0 with two goals from Alan Morton of Rangers at the end of each half, but it was a poor Scottish performance. The best man on the field was Patsy Gallacher, recently of Celtic but now completing his career with Falkirk.

Derek Parlane heads Rangers' equaliser

February 27 1978

Forfar earned loads of praise and glory from the media this Monday night, but were ultimately unsuccessful in their Scottish League Cup semi-final against Rangers at Hampden Park.

This was a very unlucky game for Forfar. It went to extra-time, meaning that the full time trained Rangers players were bound to have a considerable advantage. It did not help that this game came at the end of an absolutely awful spell of weather which meant that Forfar had hardly played since the turn of the year. As it was, although the frost had relented to allow this game to be played, it was still a cold night.

Forfar played in white and Rangers in red for strange reasons, and even stranger was the fact that inside the last ten minutes, Forfar with goals from Ken Brown and Brian Rankin, were leading Rangers 2-1, and the cries of the Rangers support in the 12,799 crowd were becoming ever more desperate. But Rangers did get a late equalizer, and the inevitable happened in extra-time.

Rangers, as it turned out, won the treble in 1978 but they never came closer to defeat than they did that cold night at Hampden in which Forfar emerged with all the credit, a point conceded by Rangers supporters themselves.

Forfar's team that night was Nicoll, Smith, Rankin, Brown, Knox, Rae, Payne, Clark, Hall, Gallacher and Gavine with substitutes Graham and Vannart while Rangers had Kennedy (later to become a Forfar legend), Miller, Greig, Forsyth, Jackson, MacDonald, McLean, Russell, Johnstone, Smith and Cooper with Dawson and Parlane on the substitutes' bench.

February 28 1953

It was a fine day for football at Station Park. This was just as well, for recent storms, particularly the one at the end of January had done a fair amount of damage to the roof of both the stand and the shelter.

The game was a good one, and indeed the fans saw nine goals, but sadly six were against Forfar. When the newspapers all said unanimously that Forfar's goalkeeper John Smith was the man of the match, well, that says something about how poor the rest of the Forfar team were, does it not?

1953 was not a great year for Forfar, and today's visitors were high-flying Queen's Park, that anachronism of Scottish football who refused to lie down and die in the face of professionalism. 1953 was dominated by the imminent Coronation and the town of Forfar, like everywhere else, had plans to mark the event. Today jokes were made that this was the Queen's year, so no wonder the Glasgow Queens' were doing well.

For Forfar, the only real success was Frances Joyner, one time of Raith Rovers and Dundee and now in the twilight of a glorious career. Although he was by this time visibly slowing down, he scored two and Billy Gibson scored the other one, but the local supporters were compelled to admire the play of the Spiders.

Forfar would finish second bottom that year, and just avoided relegation to Division "C".

February 29 1964

Not many games have been played by Forfar on Leap Year's Day throughout the ages, and going by this one, it's maybe just as well, for Forfar lost 1-6 to Greenock Morton at Cappielow.

It was however highly significant for the home team. They had dominated the Second Division that year, had lost only once, had reached the final of the Scottish League Cup and this victory clinched them promotion on the early date of February 29.

Forfar were doing less well.

In fact, they were rock bottom, although they had one moment of glory with a Scottish Cup win a month previously against Clyde. A trip to Dens Park followed, where they played well at the start, until the roof fell in after a dodgy refereeing decision or two.

On this occasion at Cappielow in the rain (no surprise there!) however, Forfar actually scored first through Dickie Ewen, who had played at one time for Aberdeen. Not many Forfar supporters were there that day, but the Forfar Directors were heard to cheer in the Stand. It was of course too good to last, and before half time Strachan equalised. *The Evening Times*, however, is very happy to describe Forfar's defenders as "heroes" in the half-time report. The second half was different as Wilson and McGraw scored twice each before Henderson finished it off.

The triumphant Morton support in the 10,000 crowd, however, were magnanimous to the gallant Forfar side of Henderson, Kennedy and Delaney; Young, Anderson and Arnott; Barclay, Gray, McMurdo, Junior and Ewen.

March

Programme No: 161   Price 3P

SCOTTISH LEAGUE DIVISION TWO

The Shire

EST. 1881

Firs Park, Falkirk

v

FORFAR ATHLETIC

1st March, 1975

Official Programme of East Stirlingshire F.C.

March 1 1975

The year 1975 must be mentioned in hushed tones when Forfar Athletic supporters get together and to-day was no exception, as Forfar travelled to Firs Park, Falkirk to take on East Stirlingshire.

Forfar had a total of 8 points from 27 games, their last point having been a draw at Berwick on January 11. Their last two games had been 0-5 defeats to both Stenhousemuir and Albion Rovers.

Firs Park is no longer with us, and that is a shame for it was one of the "character" grounds of Scottish football. Only 11 years previously it had housed First Division football when 'Shire had reached the upper echelons, and it retains the distinction of being the only ground where Billy McNeill was sent off! Backing on to the ground was an old ramshackle warehouse with holes in the wall through which one could look when the football got boring. Inside was a collection of rusting railway locomotives! It was bizarre.

Forfar were managed by Jerry Kerr, while East Stirlingshire's Manager was the unmistakable figure of Ian Ure, who had been Dundee's centre half when they won the Scottish League in 1962.

He had cause to be pleased with his team that day for they beat Forfar 4-0 with two goals in each half. Forfar were in the middle of a run of six games in which they did not even score a goal! But they had not lost their sense of humour, for goalkeeper Jim Milne waved to one of the 250 spectators when he went behind the goal to collect the ball!

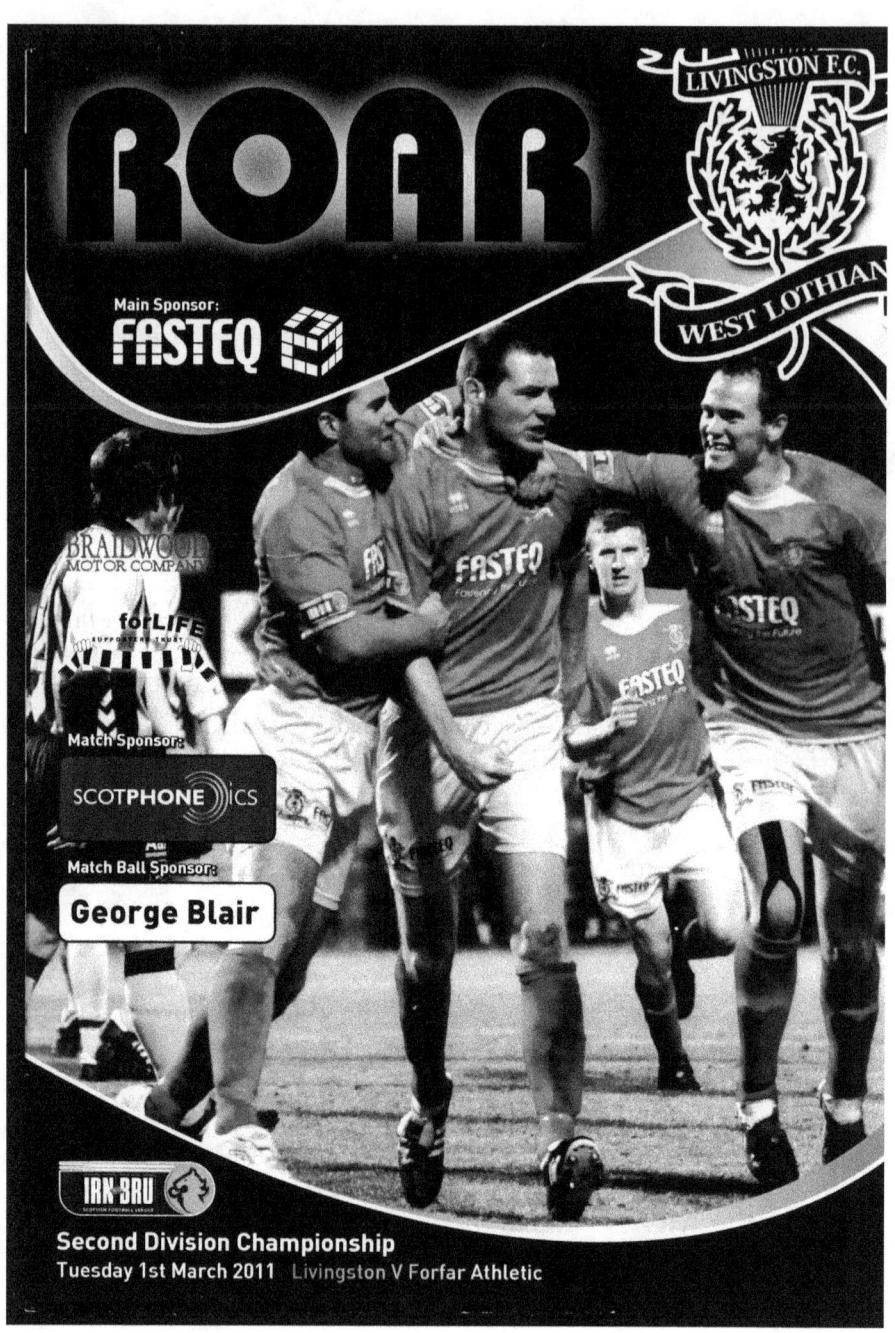

March 2 1935

Forfar were denied victory today at Station Park when Cowdenbeath's Hamill scored just at the very end of the game after Forfar had been well on top.

Being early spring, the weather was just a little unpredictable but a degree of optimism was in the air. Forfar's performances had not been great and they were a middle of the table Second Division club, as indeed were Cowdenbeath.

Hamill had scored first for Cowdenbeath but then George Preston and Willie Black put Forfar ahead and it looked as if it were going to be a home win until Cowdenbeath's late winner.

This was 1935 and Cowdenbeath were looked upon as one of the poorer teams of Scotland, even although they had enjoyed moments of glory in the old First Division. But that had been before the General Strike and its vicious aftermath, which soured the miners – who took great delight in voting Communist on occasion. A visit to Cowdenbeath would explain why.

They were also proud of their young radical activist, a girl by the name of Jennie Lee who, born in nearby Lochgelly but based in Cowdenbeath until her recent marriage to the Welsh radical Aneurin Bevan. She had shown the world that she was not going to turn the other cheek. And this was in spite of a considerable amount of ingrained anti-woman prejudice in society and even within her own Labour Party!

March 3 1962

Forfar had a habit of beating Clyde when they visited Station Park, especially when the Glasgow side were doing well.

Clyde, like Stirling Albion, tended to be one of Scotland's "yo-yo" teams, alternating between Division One and Division Two, and in 1962 they were at the top of Division Two.

On this cold day, the table toppers who arrived with a large support, found themselves two up before half time with goals from McLaughlin and Steel, and they were really looking comfortably on top of a somewhat disjointed Forfar side whose season up to this point had been far from impressive. Forfar did however give their supporters a crumb of comfort by scoring just on half-time from Hugh Smith, a fine winger from Aberdeen.

Then, Forfar decided to turn on a rare star performance in the second half. They won a penalty kick and Bill Knox, the left back, took it to score and to level the game. A few minutes later, another penalty was awarded, but this time Bill Knox was less successful, and Forfar now faced a prolonged Clyde barrage. "Junior" however played well in the goal, and veteran Doug Berrie was his normal immaculate self, and Forfar appeared to have ridden the storm. The game was heading for a very respectable draw, when Bruce Reid notched the winner for Forfar to produce one of the day's upsets.

Forfar's team that day was Junior, Berrie and Knox; Robertson, Sweeney and Dougan; Smith, Thomson, Coburn, Scott and Reid.

March 4 2017

Forfar maintained their challenge for the Second Division Championship with a hard-earned point at Broadwood against Clyde.

Broadwood was a funny stadium with stands on three sides and a building of some sort on the fourth. Only one stand was used, it being correctly deemed adequate to house the small crowd, with the away support allocated one corner of it.

Clyde had recently lost the services of their Manager, Barry Ferguson, and had appointed a couple of joint interim Managers to see them through until the end of the season.

It was a remarkable game. Forfar took the lead through a brilliant Danny Denholm goal from well outside the penalty box, and that was how it stayed until half time. Forfar's concentration lapsed and two goals were conceded in quick succession. Then Jim Lister put us back on level terms. Unfortunately, in the aftermath of this goal, our goalkeeper, Grant Adam, saw fit to make a few basic gestures at the less well-educated of the Clyde support.

There had been a little "previous" here, but even so, it seemed that a red card to Adam for being stupid was a little too draconian on the part of referee Mr Millar. Manager Gary Bollan was none too pleased, but it meant that 10-man Forfar had to put Martyn Fotheringham into the goal for the last 15 minutes. Fortunately common sense now reigned in the Forfar ranks and the game finished 2-2.

March 5 1921

On a dreadful day of rain which occasionally turned to snow, Forfar travelled to Glasgow to play Partick Thistle reserves at Firhill in what was called the Scottish Alliance League, made up mainly of the reserve sides of Scottish League First Division clubs.

In 1921 this was the only place that Forfar could play, for the Second Division of the Scottish League had not yet restarted in the somewhat chaotic conditions of the post-war world, and Forfar were too far to the North or the East to earn a place in the post-war Central League.

On this day, Forfar, whose performances this season so far had not been any too good, won 4-2, clearly revelling in the Glasgow rain. Davie McLean was now playing in England, but Forfar had unearthed his younger brother Geordie, a man who in later years would run a fish and chip shop near the East Port. Geordie, who unaccountably had the nickname "Tooks" scored twice that day, while George Miller and Bill "Carr" Boath scored the other two.

It was a rare triumph in Glasgow for Forfar, and as they waited for their train at Buchanan Street station, they heard that Celtic had been knocked out of the Scottish Cup by Hearts. They little guessed that the Scottish Cup would be won that year by Partick Thistle, who included a couple of men in the team that Forfar had just beaten!

March 6 1982

Forfar once again amazed the world by beating Queen's Park at Hampden and thus, for the first time in their history, reaching the semi-final of the Scottish Cup.

Forfar supporters were prominent in the 2,643 crowd, housed mainly in that venerable old main stand which had watched so much great football over the years. It was a miserable Glasgow day, and at half-time there was no scoring, and no apparent prospect of anyone scoring.

Then Queen's Park delighted their small, loyal and distinctly middle-class support by scoring early in the second half. But Forfar fought hard, and Steve Hancock, the hero of the previous round against Hearts, scored to level matters. Our minds were turning to the prospect of a Station Park replay next Wednesday when Gordon Leitch earned his deserved niche in Forfar history by scoring from the edge of the box.

It was often said that Forfar people speak louder than other people in Scotland (so that they could be heard above the noise of the jute looms in the factories!) so this Hampden Roar – although not as loud as 134,000 cheering a goal against England in bygone days – was an impressive one, as the realisation grew that Forfar would join Rangers, Aberdeen and St Mirren in the semi-finals.

Those who were prone to small minded local spite and hatred (not that there are very many people in Forfar like that, of course!) noted with satisfaction that both Dundee teams had been defeated. Not a bad day at all, and had Thomas the Rhymer got it right?

> Bonnie Munross will be a' moss
> Brechin a bra' burgh toon
> But Farfar will be Farfar still
> When Dundee's a dug doon!

the spider

Official Match Magazine of
The Queen's Park Football Club

PRICE 30p

March 7 1959

Forfar seem to have turned over a new leaf!

Following a few poor results, they won handsomely at Montrose the previous week, and today at Station Park, a fine second half performance saw them beat Queen's Park 4-2 with goals from Eric Brodie, Peter Craig and two from Frank McGrory. McGrory's goals in particular were well taken, and although he was no relation to Celtic's current Manager, the great Jimmy, he was quite impressive today – an impression that would sadly turn out to be illusory.

Pride of Station Park, however, was the new stand. Possibly a few imperfections still existed, notably the awful angle which to this day prevents a good view of the near side of the pitch, but nevertheless Forfar officials were in their element showing off the new facilities to the Queen's Park officials – an important group of people to impress, for Queen's Park, although their days of glory had long gone, were still regarded as part of the Scottish football establishment.

However, conventional Forfar wisdom was that spectators might come once to admire the new stand, but what was really required was a good team on the park. Was there now a chance of this being delivered? It was becoming important that Forfar kept hold of their support, for the increasing prosperity of the late 1950s meant that football no longer had the stranglehold over their supporters that they once had, and that they would have to fight for their fans.

Perhaps Forfar's new stand meant that they were a step ahead of some other grounds where the facilities were a great deal more basic.

March 8 1902

Season 1901/02 had been far from a vintage one in the Northern League, but now the weather was turning better. Excitement was beginning to build in the town about the King's Coronation in June (hardly anyone recalled the previous one in 1838).

Forfar Athletic gave their fans something to cheer about with a fine 5-2 victory over neighbours Montrose at Station Park. It was a "striking contrast" to the game against Cowdenbeath last week, which had been a bruising contest but was "lacking in skill" and ended 0-0.

The crowd was described as "goodly" and they enjoyed a good first half and a better second half as the Loons simply ran Montrose into the ground "rattling on three goals" in the last 15 minutes after it had appeared that Montrose were happy to settle for a 2-2 draw.

The Courier makes an interesting comment about Forfar's goalkeeper Mitchell who "was frequently seen in the middle of the field" as a "spectator" which seems to be saying that he got a little bored and took a walk up field. He would, of course, have worn in 1902 the same colour of jersey as the rest of the team had.

The goal scorers are not always mentioned in newspapers but Cowie is singled out in the "attacking quintette", for his shooting was always dangerous. Forfar now had played 15 games and had won 5, lost 5 and drawn 5. They were a long way short of leaders Aberdeen, but ahead of Wanderers, Cowdenbeath, Montrose, Victoria United and Lochee United.

March 9 1985

Forfar made a fairly rare trip (for this era) to Fir Park, Motherwell for a Scottish Cup quarter final to play Tommy McLean's men from the steel town.

Frankly, although Forfar had nothing really to reproach themselves for, the Premier League team were far too strong and two early first half goals (although one of them looked like a hand ball) saw Forfar off, although Billy Gallacher pulled one back in the second half in the 4-1 defeat.

Motherwell thus joined Celtic, Aberdeen and Dundee United in the semi-finals. A bizarre note was struck at half time when the 6,000 crowd (with at least 500 Forfar supporters among them) were "entertained" by a demonstration from the Army which seemed to consist of little more than arm wrestling and mutual kicks to the testicles. All this seemed to be in the interests of recruitment! It did not attract me to a military career however. Appallingly, the crowd seemed to think that this was funny and enjoyable. It was a sad comment on Thatcher's Britain and the atmosphere made me wonder if the Roman Colosseum had been like this.

Thank heavens, society had evolved football for our entertainment instead, even though this particular day was a far from enjoyable one. Forfar's team that day was Moffat, Bennett, McPhee, Brown, Brash, Lorimer, Liddle, Farningham, Cormack, Scott and Clark with Gallacher and Smith the substitutes.

March 10 1906

This night there was dancing in the streets of Forfar!

We are told that the team arrived at the station, were ushered into a series of brakes and driven through the streets of the town preceded by the Forfar Instrumental Band as crowds lined North Street, East High Street and Castle Street before the team was taken to a hostelry for a meal and a celebration with Chairman Mr Cruickshanks and Vice Chairman Mr Grant!

This was because for the first time in their history, Forfar had won the Forfarshire Cup, beating Arbroath at the neutral venue of Links Park, Montrose after a draw the previous week at Dens Park.

Particular glory was bestowed on Geordie "Purkie" Langlands who had scored the first goal and had a hand in the second in the 2-1 victory. It was generally agreed that Arbroath had the better players – indeed they should have won the first game at Dens Park – but Forfar showed more determination.

It was said to be the "biggest crowd ever seen at Links Park" with train loads of supporters from both Forfar and Arbroath, and the Montrose "neutrals" siding with the "black and navy" of Forfar. The receipts were £54, exclusive of the stand. They saw a great game with the result in doubt right up to the end.

Forfar's team on that historic day was Roger, R Murray and Shand; Melvin, A Murray and A Fairweather; Blyth, Langlands, W Fairweather, Petrie and Ritchie.

After the game, and before Forfar's triumphant return to the town, both teams had been well wined and dined at the Commercial Hotel in Montrose, with players of both sides singing songs to entertain the company. It was a night that would not be forgotten for a very long time.

March 11 2017

On a dry and reasonably pleasant spring day, Forfar's hopes of winning Division two took a serious blow in a lacklustre display against Edinburgh City.

This was City's first season in the Scottish League in their current incarnation, for they had taken the place of East Stirlingshire, who were now playing in the Lowland League. There had been an Edinburgh City in the 1930s and 1940s, but this was a different team altogether.

Forfar had looked comfortable after a fine headed goal by Jim Lister just before half time but after a few missed chances to add to the lead, complacency in the defence allowed City to grab two late goals, one by ex-Hibs striker Derek Riordan, and then at the very end a good run and strike by substitute Lewis Allan (on loan from Hibs; he had played a few games for Forfar last year) sealed Forfar's fate to the disappointment of the fans in the crowd of 446.

Thus Forfar's poor form against Edinburgh City continued. They were clearly a new team who had not yet been "sussed out" by Forfar, but the main cause for concern was that Forfar's lead over Arbroath had been further whittled. The general feeling among the fans was that Manager Gary Bollan had not deployed substitutes until it was too late.

March 12 1927

Frank Hill once again proved his worth to Forfar with an excellent performance and a great goal, but this was a good all-round Forfar performance to register a 3-1 victory over Dumbarton. Boghead was once called by everyone "fatal Boghead" because of Dumbarton's ability to beat the best on their own ground.

Boghead lived up to its name and provided, as always, a heavy pitch but Forfar, who were enjoying a good season, were the better team throughout, and won well. *The Sunday Post* says "there was little for the spectators to enthuse over".

One assumes that he means Dumbarton spectators, for there was a great deal for the Forfar men to be happy about as John Fox, Jackie Connon and then Frank Hill all scored fine goals before the Sons of the Rock managed to pull one back in the final stages.

The only bad thing about this game was the sending off by referee Mr H McLaughlan of Leith of Bob Duncan along with Davin of Dumbarton for what was described as a "clash".

On the other hand Tom Godfrey and Willie Menzies are singled out for "fine performances". Great praise is also given to goalkeeper Frank Bridgeford for some great saves. *The Sunday Post* intones "It is clear that Forfar, following their unfortunate experience in the now defunct Third Division have decided that this is never again to be their lot" and the team were destined to finish a respectably placed 10th this year.

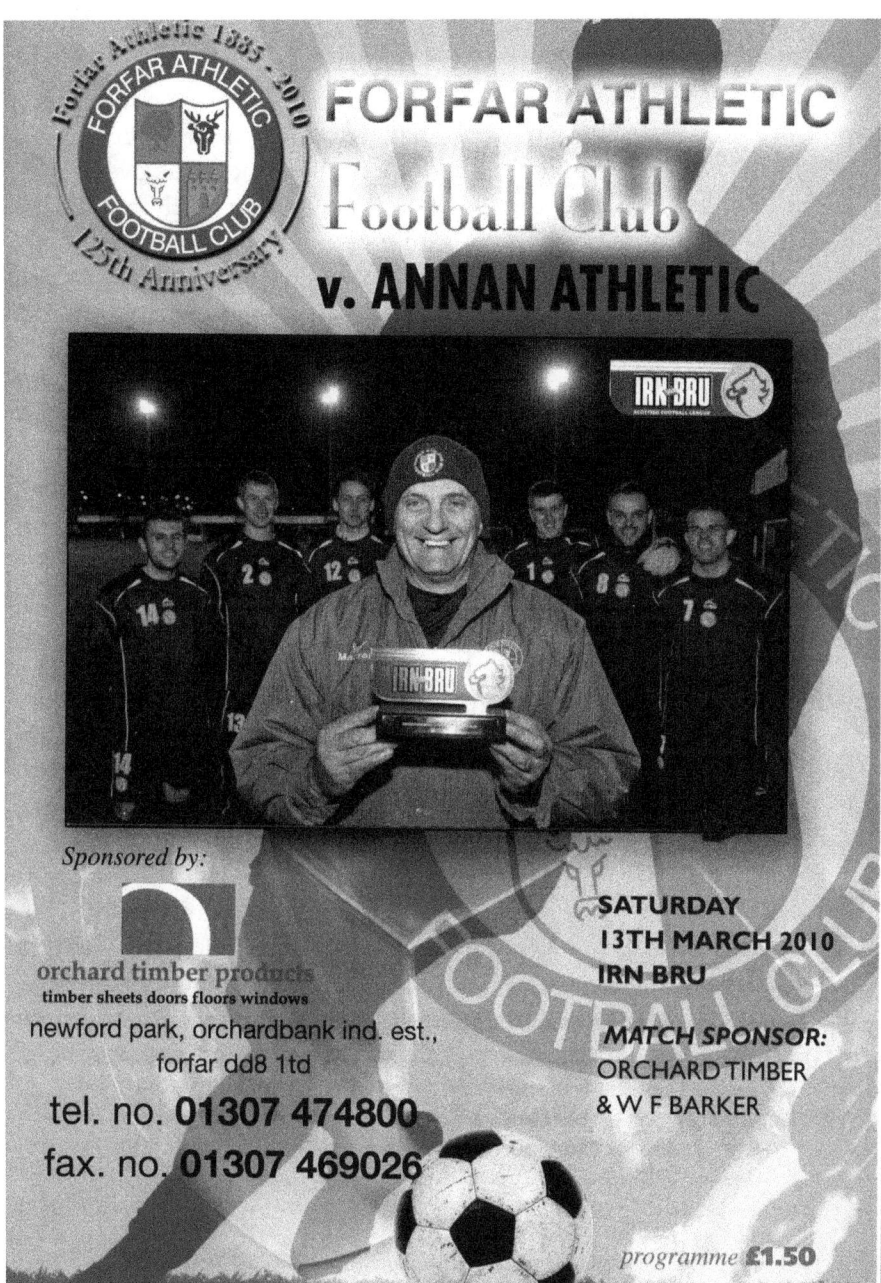

March 13 1909

There was no game for Forfar this Saturday ("Thank Goodness" said some of their fans, for recent performances had been dire) but that did not lessen the interest in football, for football politics took over.

The problem was that the Northern League (currently containing 12 teams, which was possibly not quite enough) was under pressure, for a new Central League was being formed, and for obvious reasons of travelling, the Fife teams – Lochgelly United, Kirkcaldy United, Dunfermline and East Fife – were interested, and so too were St Johnstone and Arbroath. If this were to happen, the Northern League would be in danger of disappearing because of lack of numbers.

James Black (Forfar's Lloyd George, as he was sometimes called, for there was a certain physical resemblance and indeed obsession for a cause) was of course well to the fore but failed to get a commitment from Arbroath (although he held the meeting in Arbroath to get them onside) and St Johnstone to stay with the Northern League.

This was a disappointment to the hard-working Black, who possibly now realised that Forfar's own future lay in the Central League. For the moment though, he was committed to the diminishing Northern League. The meeting dissolved, and although there was disharmony, there was no animosity and all the representatives went together to see Arbroath beat Broxburn in the Scottish Consolation Cup for teams who had been knocked out of the Scottish Cup in an earlier round.

Black was himself in need of some consolation, but he reckoned that two things were now vital for the future of football in Forfar – one was that all the local teams must stick together and the other was that Forfar Athletic must have a good team on the park. Neither of these objectives would be easy, however.

March 14 1987

Forfar were robbed at Tannadice Park in the quarter final of the Scottish Cup when, for reasons best known to himself, referee Mr Duncan of Gorebridge gave Dundee United an injury time penalty when the ball seemed to strike a Forfar Athletic player on the goal line.

Predictably, Iain Ferguson slotted home the penalty which gave the Tannadice men an ill-deserved replay at Station Park. Maurice Malpas had put United ahead, then John Clark equalized and Kenny MacDonald put Forfar ahead, a lead that they looked like holding on to, until the referee had his brainstorm.

It would have been one of Forfar's best ever results. The replay was delayed until the following midweek because Dundee United were involved in beating Barcelona on the Wednesday immediately after this game. Predictably, Dundee United won the replay (Forfar managed to miss two penalties) at Station Park. Equally predictably (given their apparent phobia of Glasgow and indeed playing at anywhere other than Tannadice), they blew up in the finals of both the Scottish and the UEFA Cup finals, a turn of events which did not exactly plunge the town of Forfar into paroxysms of grief, following the events of March.

The teams that day were Dundee United; Thomson, Kirkwood, Malpas, McInally, Hegarty, Narey, Ferguson, Gallacher, Bannon, Sturrock, Redford (subs Clark, Kinnaird). Forfar; Kennedy, Lorimer, Hamill, Morris, Smith, McPhee, Ward, Brewster, Clark, Cormack, MacDonald (subs W Bennett, M Bennett)

FORFAR ATHLETIC FOOTBALL CLUB

BELL'S SCOTTISH FOOTBALL LEAGUE DIVISION TWO

FORFAR ATHLETIC v COWDENBEATH
STATION PARK · TUESDAY, 12th MARCH 2002
Match sponsored by UNIVERSAL TELECOM

FORFAR ATHLETIC v MORTON
STATION PARK · SATURDAY, 16th MARCH 2002
Match sponsored by ANGUS COUNTY PRESS

OFFICIAL PROGRAMME - £1.00

March 15 1986

Julius Caesar in Ancient Rome was told to beware the Ides of March, and Forfar similarly came a cropper on this day.

Falling to a 2-1 defeat at home to Montrose in the First Division, is something that would have to be described as a "sair dunt" to Forfar's hopes of making it to the Premier League. Montrose were also having a respectable season, although they would struggle after this and were lucky in the end to avoid relegation, but the two points lost here was looked back upon by Forfar as a game they could have won, and things would have been so different if they had.

Mark Bennett (who would later join Forfar) scored the first goal for Montrose with a header. *The Evening Times* of Glasgow remarks acidly "the home defence did not distinguish itself in this attack". Nor did it bring itself much glory later in the first half when goalkeeper Moffat failed to hold a ball and no-one stopped McManus scoring Montrose's second. Gary Murray had scored for Forfar in the meantime, but 2-1 it was at half-time. The second half saw loads of Forfar pressure and one or two near things, but it was not to be.

It was a poor result for Forfar and did nothing to silence the "no' wanting promotion" and "Farfar in the Preemier League is jist ridiculous" brigade of the Forfar support, trudging disconsolately down the road. It remains however a painful memory.

March 16 1907

Forfar were having an awful time in the Northern League, and were second from bottom with only Hearts of Beath below them.

Today however they had real bad luck in a 3-2 defeat at Pittodrie against Aberdeen "A" with the *Aberdeen Press and Journal* quite prepared to admit that one of Aberdeen's goals did not cross the line when it came down off the bar. But Mr Winter of Dundee gave a goal.

The large crowd which yielded a gate of £40 indicated the love of football that there was in the Granite City, and they gave a sporting reception to Forfar.

A feature of the game was that there were three Robertsons playing in the game, and the Forfar right winger of that name was the best of the three. Also playing was David Troup, elder brother of Alec whose moment was yet to come, and another youngster in the centre forward position called David McLean who was the star although "as a whole, the van showed great understanding".

It was McLean who scored both goals, but after the decision about the disputed goal was given against them, Forfar seemed to lose heart, and goalkeeper Mills earned a great deal of plaudits for keeping the score down.

Forfar, as always, were well entertained at Pittodrie by the ambitious Aberdeen management, who were clearly trying to belie the general and erroneous Scottish perception that Aberdonians were mean. Forfar however boarded the train that night a little depressed about their bad luck. There were however a few optimistic signs about the future, one of them being young McLean.

March 17 1906

After a wretched winter with both the weather and results, things had suddenly turned brighter with last week's capture of the Forfarshire Cup.

Forfar treated themselves to a 4-2 victory over Lochgelly United at Station Park in the Northern League. Today was at least dry, but any attempt at good football was negated by the very strong wind which meant that, as *The Courier* tactfully put it, "the finer touches were lacking".

Forfar had suffered the indignity of having to seek re-election to the Northern League in 1904 and 1905, but this season was a comparatively better one, the reason to a large extent being the emergence of a reliable centre forward in George Langlands, a tall bustling hard-working player who rejoiced in the rather unlikely nickname of "Purkie".

The Courier also singles out goalkeeper Mitchell (who "kept a splendid goal"), defenders Shand and Ogg, midfielders Fairweather and Melvin while Ritchie was of great assistance to the prodigious Langlands.

Langlands would move to Dundee in 1909 and play an important part in their capturing of the Scottish Cup in 1910, something that he would talk about "not without cause but without end" for many years after that.

But optimism was now in the air in Forfar, not least because of the arrival a month previously of a Liberal Government pledged to do something to end the appalling poverty that prevailed. And the "feel good" factor was enhanced by the presence in the town of the Forfarshire Cup!

March 18 1961

A Jackie Coburn penalty kick was required to separate Forfar Athletic and East Stirlingshire today.

The teams were in their customary lowly spot in the Second Division, the crowd was disappointing and the standard of football was dire. No-one could dispute the commitment of both teams, but there was little in the way of skill on show. As one veteran supporter put it philosophically, "Let's face it, if they were guid futba' players, they widnae be here. They would be playin for a bigger team or even an English team!"

But Forfar did in fact have a couple of players who would move on to Dundee United in goalkeeper Donald McKay and inside left Eric Brodie, and this was a strong argument for the need for there to be games like Forfar v East Stirling.

Today's referee was Hugh Phillips, one of the best around. There was at this point in Scottish football a great deal of navel gazing and moaning about poor attendances, but the fact was that the prosperity of the 1950s had given people more options. Most houses now had a TV which showed on a Saturday afternoon horse racing, athletics, rugby league, and, heaven help us, wrestling had recently been introduced on ITV!

It was a blessing, perhaps, that in Forfar, ITV reception (until Grampian TV arrived later in the year) wasn't very good. Football was still better than a lot of the other possibilities!

March 19 1983

No-one can really call himself a Scottish football fan unless he has at some point paid a visit to Cliftonhill, the home of Albion Rovers, arguably the team which has fought the hardest and for the longest time against adversity.

Coatbridge, a child of the industrial revolution of the 19th century, lies in the shadow of Glasgow and also too close to places like Airdrie, Hamilton, Motherwell and Wishaw. On the face of it, Albion Rovers do not have much going for them – but they have had the priceless asset of men like Tom Fagan who have been willing to work for them.

They reached the Scottish Cup final of 1920 and have nurtured men like Tony Green, not to mention the great Jock Stein himself. The ground today, a sunny but blustery day, could have been used to film sandstorms in the desert, and the pitch was bone hard – something that went a certain way to explain Forfar's sub-standard performance in a 0-1 defeat.

As for myself, I took my dog in with me and offered to pay for it (after all, who with any kind of conscience can grudge money to Albion Rovers?) and a lovely Albion Rovers supporter took him for a walk at half-time while his friend warmed my heart by telling me how much he loved his trips to Forfar, revelling in the beer in Jarman's and the bridies in Saddler's.

It brought a tear to my eye, but that might have been the sandstorm or my feelings about Forfar's dire (and uncharacteristic for 1983) performance, which more or less killed off any chances of promotion in 1983, the League being won by Brechin that year. Grr! Grr!

March 20 1954

It is always a strange experience when Forfar go to Hampden Park, possibly more so in the days before Hampden was covered and made all-seated.

The huge empty bowl with the very noticeable Hampden swirl was all the more pronounced when the attendance is small, in this case little more than 1,000.

Yet in a few weeks' time, the same ground would be staging Scottish Cup semi-finals, a Scotland v England International and the Scottish Cup final, the last two of which occasions would see six-figure crowds pack into Hampden.

But the Forfar side of 1954, although their final finishing position in Division B was disappointing, were no mean performers and today at Hampden Park, the Loons showed their mettle by twice going ahead with a goal in the first half from the doughty Albert Craig, then after Queen's equalised, Willie Dunn scored again after a cross from Jimmy Blyth had been missed by everyone and even Dunn needed two bites at the cherry! Queen's Park then scored almost immediately, and the last half hour was frantic and frenetic but with no further additions to the score line, and Forfar indebted to red-haired centre half George Crawford and goalkeeper John Smith for saving the day on several occasions.

With a touch of hyperbole, one feels, a Queen's Park official said that it was one of the best games ever seen at Hampden. If that were so, it was a pity that there were so few to see it, but Forfar went home happy.

March 21 1914

Forfar, with a sparkling display of attacking football, beat Stenhousemuir 4-1 at Ochilview in the Central League and impressed the home support to such an extent that Forfar were clapped off the park in a rare tribute to an away team.

It was the forward line of Mitchell, Walker, Langlands, Troup and Petrie which really impressed the reporter of *The Dundee Courier* but the rest of the team deserved praise as well. It was the left wing in particular of Eckie Troup and Jummer Petrie which really got the team going, supplying Langlands and Walker for the first two goals. Petrie then ran down the wing himself, following an excellent through ball from Troup to score the third goal and finally Chapman came up to head home a fourth from a corner kick.

This team certainly had the makings of Central League Champions but had not had the best of starts to the season and were prone to inconsistency towards the end of the season. The trickery of Troup was already beginning to attract attention – he had played well against Celtic a month ago and word got round after that – there were several well-dressed gentlemen wearing bowler hats in the Stenhousemuir stand looking as if they were representing top English clubs, Newcastle and Sunderland among them.

The consensus however at this stage was that the teenager Troup, though an absolute magician with the ball, was still a bit small and a bit young to cope with the rough tactics of some defenders.

March 22 1924

So what was this one all about then, Forfar?

East Fife, who would finish only two places ahead of Forfar in the League table, managed to beat Forfar 8-0 with a man called Andrew Cant scoring six and Davie Edgar the other two.

The game was at Bayview and Forfar had travelled with a reasonable record in the League. There was no indication that this was going to happen. Naturally, Forfar being Forfar, rumours and mutterings began about deals with bookies etc. One hopes that there was no truth in such allegations, but certainly the score line took a lot of living with.

"Forfar can't cope with Cant" appeared a lot in the Press, as did the joke about Forfar having had a lot to drink but "ate nothing" (eight – nothing, get it?). It was one of those times when Forfarians not living in the "toonie" had to change the subject and perhaps talk about Ramsay MacDonald, the new Labour Prime Minister, rather than football!

Forfar had the humiliation of being cheered by the East Fife crowd every time they strung together a pass or two, and the *Sunday Post* uses words like "listless" "not capable" and "outplayed" in what was one of the club's darker days.

Goalkeeper Bruce, in spite of losing eight goals, was Forfar's best man – something that does not say very much for the rest whose names I will refrain from mentioning. It was a record victory for the incredulous East Fife, though.

Curiously, *The Breedon Book of Scottish Football Records* gives the score as only 7-0. The Editor must be a Forfar sympathiser trying to limit the damage!

March 23 1912

Forfar Athletic had no game today but two Forfar men featured in the Scotland v England International at Hampden Park.

Ex-Forfar Athletic player David McLean, now with Sheffield Wednesday played in the centre while Jim Black, Forfar's supremo, was Scotland's linesman. (In 1912, even in Internationals, each team was expected to supply a linesman).

The crowd was a world record 127,307 (all the more remarkable when one considers that there was a rail strike in various parts of Scotland at the time!) and they saw a 1-1 draw with Andy Wilson scoring for Scotland and George Holley for England. Press reports praised the contribution of Davie McLean who "led his line well". Davie was the first Forfar man to earn a cap for Scotland, and, but for the Great War, he would surely have won a great deal more.

Jim Black, of course, in addition to his other attributes, was a qualified and experienced referee, and he also was reported to have had a good game.

The teams were Scotland – Brownlie, McNair and J Walker; Gordon, Thomson and Hay; Templeton, R Walker, McLean, Wilson and Quinn, England – Williamson, Crompton and Pennington; Brittleton, Wedlock and Makepeace; Simpson, Jefferis, Freeman, Holley and Wall.

Rail strike or no rail strike, quite a few Forfar people were in the crowd to cheer on their hero.

March 24 1987

In all the painful memories that one has acquired in supporting Forfar over the years, this one is a collector's item of frustration, agony and anger.

The Forfar word "chawin" would seem to sum it up. This was the quarter final replay, delayed because Dundee United were playing another famous team called Barcelona the week before, and Forfar had to yield. (Why?) We thus had 10 days to "nurse our wrath and keep it warm" over the injustice of March 14. The good news for the club was that a crowd of 8,139 turned up, and there was also a BBC radio broadcast of the game with the ever loveable, albeit somewhat ungrammatical, John Greig doing the summarising.

John, apparently, told the locals before the game that he loved Forfar and even admitted he wanted us to win. But then at the far end in the first half came the two minutes which would haunt Kenny MacDonald and John Clark (not to mention the Forfar support) all their lives when first Kenny missed a penalty – hitting the post – then when, in the immediate aftermath Jim McInally handled, John (Kenny presumably still being upset at his miss) blasted his penalty yards wide! In the second half, we just knew that Dundee United would score, and Ferguson and Holt duly did that.

It was like the denouement of a Greek tragedy where the Gods decide that the victim must be punished again and again for some perceived transgression. Dundee United, who had beaten Barcelona with a great deal more ease than they had Forfar, were through to meet city rivals Dundee in the Scottish Cup semi-final. Painful!

March 25 1995

Forfar took a massive step towards promotion and the winning of the Second Division title with a 2-1 win over Montrose, one of their closest rivals, at Links Park.

Usually, Angus derbies between Forfar and Montrose tend to lack the passion and commitment that one finds when Brechin and Arbroath provide the opposition. Montrose tends to be looked upon by Forfarians as a charming but non-threatening sea resort where much golf is played, and Montrose's football team is possibly one of the less interesting ones in terms of history with very few big moments to boast about.

This was emphatically not the case today with a crowd of 1,240 in attendance at Links Park, and an element of both sets of supporters providing yet more depressing evidence of the failure of the Scottish educational system to cope with the basic lack of brain cells. There were no Scottish Premier League games today because of International commitments, so the smaller teams enjoyed a little more of the limelight than they normally would have expected.

Forfar scored a goal in each half through McCormick and the ever reliable McPhee, and the result confirmed Forfar's position at the top of the League where they had been since Hogmanay. Manager Tommy Campbell expressed his delight at the team's performances, and it now began to look as if nothing short of a miracle could deprive the Loons of a return to the First Division which was now looked upon increasingly as their natural habitat.

March 26 2016

It was probably this day more than any other in that dreadful spring of 2016 that made us think that Forfar were indeed going to go down into Division Two, and that the ploy of sacking Dick Campbell earlier in the season had not worked.

It is always depressing to go down to Stenhousemuir, but doubly so after last week had brought a victory over Ayr United and had kindled a few hopes of a resurrection. Today at Ochilview, the team battled hard, but simply lacked the ability to produce a win at that most desolate of grounds before a crowd of 429. Mark Gilhaney had scored for Stenhousemuir early in the second half, but spirited Forfar defending had prevented any further damage. The longer the game went on, the more Forfar came into it, and as the game entered its closing stages Steven Craig managed to equalise for Forfar. Forfar stayed marginally on top and even a win seemed possible, but Forfar's death wish took over. When the decisive goal came it was at the other end, as Colin McMenamin scored with a header to put Forfar into the relegation zone.

There was an air of despondency over the Loons as they trudged off the field that afternoon, and there was from now on the all-pervasive air of the inevitability of relegation. Gary Bollan was clearly struggling to find some sort of an answer to what was going on.

March 27 1897

This was a very windy day at Station Park when Montrose came to play a Northern League game.

It was also a windy and unpleasant day at Ibrox where Scotland beat Ireland 5-1, a telegram coming to Station Park to confirm this at full time.

Fair haired right back John Janes got a special cheer as he ran out from the "hoosie" behind the goal, for he had today turned down an invitation to play for the Forfarshire county side in favour of playing for Forfar.

On a day like today, the winning of the toss was a key factor, and Forfar played towards the Whitehills or east goal in the first half with the benefit of the strong wind, and also "downhill". (Station Park seemed to have a more pronounced slope in those days from west to east). It was however a good half hour before Forfar went ahead through Crichton. He then scored again with a header, and just on half time completed his hat trick after a fine through ball from Thomson. Was this to be enough in the second half when the conditions were in favour of Montrose? Thomson answered that question with a goal against the wind early in the second half, and the disjointed Montrose could not get back into the game.

It was a good win for Forfar and the crowd of about 1,000 departed happily to discuss how Scotland were to get on against England next week, or what the town of Forfar was going to do for Queen Victoria's Diamond Jubilee in the summer.

March 28 1936

At Firs Park, Forfar had an easier win against East Stirlingshire than the 2-1 score line would have suggested.

Willie Black scored twice and the defence only conceded a goal late on when concentration evaporated. *The Courier* nominated centre half Bob Laird as the best player on the field.

It was one of Forfar's better performances in a season which rarely rose above the mediocre and in which they finished sixth from the bottom. In the meantime it began to appear that the worst of the economic recession was passing, and short time working in the local factories was beginning to disappear. But there was a sinister reason for this, and people were getting more and more anxious about the international situation.

Italy had seized Abyssinia, Japan was doing the same to bits of China, Spain was on the verge of eruption and Hitler was forever making bellicose statements about the Treaty of Versailles.

Not everyone was worried, however. Hitler's decision to send forces into the demilitarised Rhineland was ludicrously likened by a Cabinet Minister to "you and I deciding to move our furniture into another room in our house"!

Forfar's team that day was McFarlane, McGregor and Ramsay; Morton, Laird and Gabriel; R Black, McLean, W Black, Preston and Laing. In the Scottish Cup semi-finals played that day, Rangers beat Clyde and Third Lanark beat Falkirk.

March 29 1969

There are few things worse in football than a narrow defeat and the gnawing feeling that with a bit of luck, a refereeing decision or two going in your favour, and if only our forwards had converted one of the chances....

It is all the worse when you have the long bus journey home from Stranraer to think about all these things. Forfar travelled to the extreme south-west (Stranraer is a lot closer to most grounds in Northern Ireland than it is to Forfar!) to lose 0-1.

This in fact was a very good Forfar side, under player-manager Jake Young, who would finish 6th in the Second Division; the team of Philip, McKenzie and Hamilton; Knox, Milne and Jake Young; May, Wyles, Jim Young, Dick and Mackle deserved more out of this game. The only goal of the game came when referee Bill Anderson of East Kilbride awarded a penalty for hand ball against Jake Young in the first half, but Forfar felt that they deserved a penalty as well in the second half. In addition Archie Knox brought a good save out of the goalkeeper and both Jake Young and Jim Young had shots cleared off the line.

But it was not to be for Forfar, and the long bus journey home meant that they probably missed Lulu singing in the Eurovision Song Contest. Mind you, it was a horrible song called "Boom-Bang-A-Bang", so maybe that was just as well!

March 30 1963

Forfar travelled to Links Park almost as if they were expecting a beating – and they got one to the tune of 0-3, one goal before half-time and two after, and a recovery never looking vaguely likely.

The old excuse that they were short of match practice because of the big freeze-up of 1963 would simply not do any longer, because they had played all the month of March, but they were still second bottom of the League, the only crumb of comfort being that Brechin were a great deal worse!

The big freeze, which had virtually killed football for about six weeks in January and February, had not helped team building nor indeed any raising of interest in the town. It had been a total financial disaster into the bargain. A man called Andy Irvine was the trainer/coach and in charge of the team, and it was obvious that he was struggling. Today, for example, hardly a soul went to Montrose from Forfar to support the team, not least because there was a great counter-attraction nearby at Dens Park where Dundee and Rangers fought out a passionate and fiery 1-1 draw in the quarter finals of the Scottish Cup with reports of crowd trouble and indeed some overcrowding.

In the meantime at Montrose, there was plenty of room! There were also another 10 games remaining to be played! Oh, no!

Skipper Ian McPhee leads the celebrations after promotion becomes a reality

March 31 1984

On this astonishingly early date, Forfar Athletic caused eyebrows to rise throughout the United Kingdom by clinching promotion to the First Division.

The venue was the rather unlikely one of Stenhousemuir with whom, it was often (unfairly) claimed, Forfar had jousted, throughout the years, for the title of the worst team in Scotland.

The weather was more than a little inhospitable was it often was at that ground with the normally empty terracings (today's crowd was given 350 – and that was good for Stenny!) and the tiny match box of a stand.

As was often the case as well, the fare was poor, at least in the first half. Forfar's large support, however, had cause to celebrate when John Clark scored with a great header. It was as if someone had pressed a switch, for the roof suddenly fell in on the Warriors of Stenhousemuir, and Jim Liddle scored a hat-trick late in the game to send the Forfar supporters into ecstacy at their 4-0 win.

There cannot have been many triumphant pitch invasions at the trim but normally desolate Ochilview over the years, but there was one today, and Stenhousemuir's players, officials and supporters, to their credit, were unstinting in their congratulations to Forfar. Forfar's team was Kennedy, Lorimer, McPhee, Brown, Brash, Weir, Liddle, Farningham, Gallacher, Bell and Clark.

April

FORFAR ATHLETIC FOOTBALL CLUB

SEASON 1983-84

SPECIAL CHAMPIONSHIP
WINNING SOUVENIR EDITION
OF THE OFFICIAL PROGRAMME

Price 45p

TODAY'S MATCH SPONSOR

BISON

BISON CONCRETE (Scotland) Ltd.

SCOTTISH LEAGUE
DIVISION TWO

**FORFAR ATHLETIC v
EAST STIRLINGSHIRE**

STATION PARK, FORFAR
SATURDAY, 21st APRIL 1984

April 1 1950

Forfar finished their first League season in Division B with a fine 3-0 win over Queen's Park at a very windy Station Park. They ended up respectably placed, although there were a few dodgy spells during the season – indeed this was their first win since January 21.

Today however Queen's Park played with the wind in the first half and failed to score. After half-time, however, Forfar took command and Sam Smith scored with a penalty kick, then Jimmy Wotherspoon scored twice as the amateurs tired.

But the man of the match was "the elusive Mr Adams" as *The Sunday Post* describes the veteran Tommy, for he gave a marvellous display of trickery on the right wing to the delight of the faithful. The crowd was given as 1,000 and many of them were worried about the way that the old stand creaked in the wind.

A Queen's Park player R Paterson (for that was how amateurs were described) seemed to fall awkwardly and broke his arm. He was taken to Forfar Infirmary and later the DRI.

After the game the Queen's Park players and officials were well entertained by the now ageing but still genial Jim Black who took great pride in the hospitality offered by Forfar Athletic, discussing at length with the Glasgow men the prospects for Scotland's success in the forthcoming International against England, and what sort of a pitch there would be at Hampden for the big occasion, while also being solicitous about the welfare of Mr Paterson and phoning to enquire of his condition.

April 2 1910

Forfar today suffered what was called a "sair dunt" as they went down 3-0 to Brechin City in the Carrie Cup at Nursery Park, Brechin.

It was a severe disappointment for the many supporters who had gone with the team, taking advantage of cheap rail fares on a fine spring day.

Yet at the start, it was all Forfar who were "a ower them", but in spite of numerous chance, they just could not score and after Brechin scored from a lovely piece of play, Forfar were simply "outclassed". *The Courier* reporter does not mince his words "while Brechin kept going all the time, Forfar were often very slow and their forwards worked without real method". For Forfar, Skene, Gibb and Fenton were given honourable mentions, but towards the end of the game Referee Johnston had occasion to send "Jummer" Petrie to the pavilion for "language".

Not a great day for Forfar, but there was more than a little consolation by news elsewhere. At Brechin Station as they waited for the train for the homeward journey, an excited railwayman dashed out of his office, brandishing a telegram with the news that Scotland had beaten England 2-0 at Hampden before a crowd of over 100,000.

So, although there was little to be happy about in Forfar's performance – in truth it had not been the greatest of seasons – the toast of Forfar's hostelries that night were the Scottish team, in particular the two goal scorers, Jimmy Quinn and Jimmy McMenemy.

April 3 1982

15,876 spectators were at Hampden to see Forfar play their first ever Scottish Cup semi-final.

Their opponents were Rangers, a team recently in the doldrums and not enjoying the best of seasons in the Scottish League. Forfar fought hard and were totally worthy of their 0-0 draw. The game finished with neither team really looking like scoring, but Forfar had a reasonable penalty shout turned down by referee Kenny Hope when Stewart Porter appeared to be tripped in the box late in the game. It would have been interesting to see what would have happened if this had been for the other side!

Sadly however this game, momentous as it was for Forfar fans who seemed to number about 3,000 in the crowd, was not the main talking point of the day, for the House of Commons was meeting in emergency session on a Saturday – a very rare occurrence indeed, for it had only happened once since the day before the declaration of war in 1939 – and this was because a couple of days previously, the Argentinians had invaded the Falkland Islands.

Much was the talk of war in the South Atlantic, but Forfar fans were also very concerned about the replay on Tuesday night. It was generally agreed that Alex Rae and his men had done very well at Hampden, or as the local vernacular would put it "they gaen the Rengers a fleg".

April 4 1925

This was a bitter sweet day for Forfar supporters. On the one hand, they would have been very happy at the news from Hampden Park that Scotland had beaten England 2-0, a result announced on the loudspeaker system as soon as the telegram arrived from the GPO.

At the same time Forfar's failure to beat Arthurlie when they had most of the pressure augured ill for their prospects of saving themselves from relegation to Division Three.

Arthurlie played at Dunterlie Park, Barrhead where they had earned themselves immortality by their beating of Celtic in the Scottish Cup of 1897. In 1925 they were a few points ahead of Forfar.

Forfar however were really struggling to avoid the drop to Division Three, where so many teams were going out of business because of poor gates and the cost of travel to distant places like Solway Star, Mid Annadale and Helensburgh.

An example of how Forfar were in the plight that they were came in the second half when George Miller scored with a fine header to put Forfar ahead – but then Forfar committed the cardinal sin of losing concentration and allowing Arthurlie to run up the field and score with a carbon copy of a header. The game then finished 1-1 with Forfar still bottom and only three games in which to save themselves.

This was extremely worrying for Forfar folk, but they could at least enjoy the triumph of Scotland who had now won the British Championship with a team of Scotsmen who all played for Scottish clubs and were captained by Dave Morris of Raith Rovers.

April 7 1984

Scottish League President David Letham hands over the Second Division Trophy to an elated Ian McPhee

April 5 1969

Forfar's excellent season continued this bright Easter Saturday with a 1-0 win over strong-going Queen of the South at Station Park today in front of a crowd of about 1,100.

The weather was good, a little windy perhaps, but the pitch, because of a fairly severe winter with lots of frost and a heavy fall of snow as recently as a fortnight ago, was a little bumpy and uneven.

Perhaps it was for this reason that the shooting is described as "hasty and inaccurate" in the first half. The teams were well balanced, but it was Forfar who went ahead just before half time when Kenny Dick was brought down in the penalty box, and Archie Knox did the needful. Those who hoped for some sort of goal feast in the second half were disappointed, for both defences remained on top until the end, with Forfar's rear guard doing their job in a thoroughly professional fashion.

It was a performance typical of the new Forfar since Jake Young had taken charge of the team. Previously, one used to worry about Forfar going ahead because we knew, in our heart of hearts, that they would probably throw it away! Indeed there was a lot to admire about this Forfar team and Archie Knox in particular was beginning to be very impressive, so much so that some of us began to wonder how long it would be before Forfar got an offer that they could not refuse for him. The team were now 7th in the League – a position that we could scarcely have dreamed of a few years previously.

April 6 1982

This Tuesday night, the "task force" was already on its way to the South Atlantic to win back the Falkland Islands from the Argentinians.

Forfar's own "task force" was on its way to Hampden to see their team take on Rangers in the Scottish Cup semi-final replay at Hampden Park. The attendance on Saturday was poor for a semi-final, but this one was worse with only 11,864 turning up – a comment on Rangers fans disgust at their team's poor performances throughout the season rather than any lack of enthusiasm from Forfar fans who were once again there in full strength.

Once again, Forfar did well, but sheer pace, full-time training and a generally better performance from Rangers did for them. Rangers scored twice before half time, with goals from Derek Johnstone and Jim Bett, but Forfar earned a penalty and Alec Brash brought Forfar back into the game. In the second half Dave Cooper added a third for Rangers while Forfar suffered another blow when Ken Brown was sent off for deliberate hand ball.

Forfar however earned a lot of credit in indirect ways when the Rangers supporters sang "There's nae bridies left!" which perhaps indicated how relieved Rangers were, and then there was the famous picture of graffiti written on an exit gate at Celtic Park which extolled the virtues of the Pope, the IRA – and Forfar!

Derek Johnstone scores for Rangers in the Scottish Cup semi final replay of 1982

April 7 1984

This was pay-back day!

All the years of hurt and pain which we had spent standing on cold terracings watching dreadful Forfar teams were suddenly wiped out when Forfar at last won a national honour in the shape of the Scottish League Second Division.

They did this at the early date of April 7 (weeks before anyone else won anything in Great Britain) by beating Stranraer 5-3, even though Stranraer scored first with a fine strike described by the man standing beside me as "a some rekker, that een" – a phrase incomprehensible to someone who doesn't come from Forfar.

But this Forfar team were not winners of the Scottish League for nothing, and Jim Liddle scored twice and John Clark, Billy Gallacher and Ronnie Scott once each to release delirium for Doug Houston's men and their supporters. It was hard not to feel emotional on this day as captain Ian McPhee picked up the trophy from the President of the Scottish League. Chairman Sam Smith, the man who had done so much to bring all this about, was in his element on the loud speaker, telling everyone of the 2,142 crowd to go to Jarman's and buy themselves a drink which he would pay for. (One assumes he was only kidding!)

It was a day that we had been waiting for a long time, for we could now throw our shoulders back and hold our heads high. It was also a time for sadness and reminiscing about the supporters no longer with us, but with us in spirit.

One thought for example, of the famous Willie Wilson, inhabitant of the "Poors House" with his club foot, speech impediment and, frankly, not very much going for him. He was the pioneer of the "That's hut" phrase when something pleased him. I'm sure I heard a ghostly voice saying it that day as Ian McPhee showed the trophy.

April 8 1995

This was tense! Forfar for so long "champions elect" of the Third Division -and recently having won 7 games in a row – had slipped up against Montrose on the previous Wednesday night before a big crowd of over 1,000.

There now therefore existed the possibility that they might "blow up" altogether. A glance at the points lead in the League table and an analysis of their current form would have made it rather unlikely, but then again there is nothing rational about supporting Forfar! It was in any case a strange world in 1995 – last night, for example, there had been a Scottish Cup semi-final (yes, on a Friday night!) for no other reason than making money on Sky TV.

It was a new greedy age of football, but at Station Park today 623 spectators saw David Bingham score in the first half and hold on, sometimes a little luckily, other times playing as if they did believe in themselves, throughout the second half. East Stirlingshire with their few but noisy supporters singing "Shirie, Pirie" were not a bad side, but eventually the referee's whistle went, and a quick listening to the other scores on the car radio confirmed that a win at Ross County next week would do the trick.

I think the main emotion was relief rather than euphoria as we drove home that night, although at the back of my mind lurked the image of Jim Peters at the Commonwealth Games of Vancouver 1954 who was miles (literally) ahead of everyone, but couldn't quite cross the line.

Jim Liddle scores for Forfar against Stranraer on April 7 1984 (opposite)

April 9 1910

Forfar had no game today, so many of their players and supporters treated themselves to a day in Glasgow to watch Geordie Langlands play for Dundee in the Scottish Cup final against Clyde at Ibrox.

It was Dundee's first ever Scottish Cup final, and the interest in the game in all of Angus was great. Langlands, a Forfarian, had played for Forfar for a few seasons before his transfer to Dundee in 1908. With Dundee, he had almost won the Scottish League in 1909 – indeed he would have done so if fellow Forfarian Davie McLean had not inspired Celtic in their famous fortnight in which they played eight games in twelve days to deprive Dundee – but now he had a chance for the Scottish Cup, considered in 1910 to be of infinitely more value than the League.

Ten minutes remained at Ibrox and Clyde were 2-0 up and well worth their lead, so much so that thousands of Dundee supporters were seen to leave the ground "crestfallen and depressed". But then Dundee got a break when John "Sailor" Hunter pulled one back in a goalmouth scramble with five minutes left. Still the minutes slipped away and with the referee, Mr Dougray of Bellshill, looking at his watch, Dundee earned a last gap corner. Englishman Jimmy Bellamy took it, and Forfar's Geordie Langlands (commonly called "Purkie") rose like a bird to connect and headed home to earn Dundee a replay. Dundee would eventually win the Scottish Cup after a second replay, but the man who undeniably made it all possible was Forfar's "Purkie".

In years to come, apparently, Geordie would never be afraid to regale an audience in a local pub like Jarman's or Fenton's about how he scored his epic goal, and there was always an extra defender that he had to knock out of the way and another foot that he had to jump in order to reach the ball!

April 9 1910

Dundee's Scottish Cup Winning side - with Geordie Langlands second from left In middle row

April 10 1920

Forfar beat Raith Rovers "A" 2-1 in a poor game at Stark's Park in the Eastern League with goals from Geordie Langlands and Sandy Thomson. At one point in the first half a mistimed clearance from a Raith Rovers defender shattered the window of the Press Box, but fortunately both the Press and the public were so ill-represented that no-one was close enough to be injured!

However, attention was really focussed on Hillsborough, Sheffield where Eckie Troup was playing in the first England v Scotland game since the end of the War. The pitch was an absolute quagmire, but both teams served up a goal feast which ended up 5-4 for England. "Wee Troupie" (now playing for Dundee, but still a Forfar loon) played brilliantly, hitting the post in the dying seconds with a shot that would have earned Scotland a 5-5 draw.

It was generally reckoned to have been the best International of them all. *The Dundee Courier* has this to see about Troup. "Alec amazed everybody by the neat, fast way he scampered through the Hillsborough mud, also by his accurate crossing and shooting abilities, to say nothing of the dance he led Ducat and clean heels he showed Longworth."

Not many Forfar people were in either Sheffield or Kirkcaldy that day, so a large crowd gathered at the Post Office in Castle Street to hear news of the game, and a groan was heard when the telegram arrived to say that Scotland had lost. Another one soon after, however, sent by the ever conscientious Jim Black, contained the snippet "Troup Good".

April 11 1908

For the second time in three years, Forfar Athletic were welcomed back to Forfar Station and then paraded in brakes through the streets as winners of the Forfarshire Cup.

They had done this by beating Montrose 4-1 at Dens Park in a game distinguished by its sporting play, even though Forfar had opened the scoring with a soft penalty. "See The Conquering Hero Comes" was played by Forfar Instrumental Band under the guidance of Baillie Lamb, and crowds of women and children, not all of them knowing very much about football, assembled to cheer the heroes like captain "Chappie" Gowans, Dickie Gibb, Davie Troup (elder brother of wee Eckie whose hour was yet to come) Geordie Langlands. Little Bobbie Robertson, on the left wing, who was showing great potential in spite of his lack of inches, had scored a goal in spite of an injury.

The game had been watched by a crowd of 3,000, about 200 of whom had travelled in a special train from Forfar, and the receipts were a huge £86. *The Courier* reports a remark made by an eminent Forfarian to the effect that this was "a great deal better than Andrew Carnegie's gift", a sly reference to the local Baths which were being built in Chapel Street.

While everyone was delighted to see Baths appearing in the interests of health and hygiene, quite a few socialists and even Liberals suspected the motives of the Dunfermline millionaire whose "gift" might have strings attached! But this night saw dancing at the Cross and at the East Port with all the urchins joining in.

Those who were there, either at the game itself or simply at the celebrations that night would not forget it for a very long time.

April 12 1986

A remarkable day at Station Park when Kilmarnock came to town.

Kilmarnock, whose supporters felt that they were by nature a Premier League club (they had been Scottish League champions little more than 20 years before) arrived in great numbers to find their promotion hopes dented by a 1-0 defeat to Forfar.

Gary Murray scored for the Loons in the second half, but the real drama came at the very end when Kilmarnock were awarded a penalty, but missed it and its retake! Stewart Kennedy once again proved his value to the club, silencing the raucous Ayrshire voices who called him the "Wembley wizard" and made offensive comments about his Rangers past.

This game raised more and more the possibility of Forfar themselves being promoted to the Premier League next year, although Manager Doug Houston did not like the word "Premier" being used. Five games remained, and although Hamilton looked certain to be top, Forfar were only two points behind Falkirk, Dumbarton and Kilmarnock. Kilmarnock's starting Eleven that day, incidentally may have created some sort of a record because there were eight Macs in it – McCulloch, McQueen, MacLeod, McCafferty, McConville, McGivern, McNab and McGuire and even one of their substitutes was called McKenna! Forfar's team was Kennedy; Lorimer, McPhee, Morris, McKillop, Clark, Lyons, Farningham, Scott, Gallacher, Murray with Smith and Ward as substitutes.

April 13 1960

A few days previously more than 130,000 had been at Hampden to see a dismal International between Scotland and England.

There were a lot fewer there this Wednesday night, but arguably they saw a better game. Forfar were distinctly unlucky not to get a win and had to be content with a 2-2 draw.

There was a strong wind (isn't there always at Hampden?) and it swirled up and down the high empty terracings making a sort of a whistle or a howl. Forfar's man of the match was Eric Brodie who scored one of the goals and made another for Roy Ewen. Queen's Park had dominated the first half when they had the wind behind them, and they scored early but they also actually managed to miss two penalties! One was well wide and the other was saved by the consistently impressive Donald McKay. Then Forfar took command in the second half and Queen's Park's late equaliser was very much against the run of play.

Nevertheless, although the game was of no real relevance to promotion from the Second Division, it was a satisfactory result for Manager Cyril Mutch, the Directors and the very few Forfar supporters there.

It was a less happy night for Rangers who managed to lose 6-1 in Germany in the first leg of the semi-final of the European Cup to Eintracht Frankfurt, a team who would soon be coming to Hampden to play Real Madrid in the final of that tournament.

April 14 2001

It is hard to feel any sort of antipathy to Partick Thistle, with their usually pleasant supporters (all right, there are a few heid-bangers amongst them as well, but then again I haven't always been proud of Forfar supporters either!) and their refreshing non-sectarian approach to Glasgow football.

Today their supporters came to town, and left deliriously happy, their team (already guaranteed promotion from the old Second Division) now Champions after earning a late draw at Station Park and hearing from the obliging Station Park tannoy that their rivals had failed to keep up with them.

Much was their rejoicing, and they deserved it, for they had endured some awful times as well; they had also joined in the respectful silence for the Forfar great, Doug Berrie, who had died earlier in the week, even though very few of them would have heard of the venerable Dundonian who had, more or less, dedicated his footballing career to Forfar.

The game itself was a good one. Partick scored first but then Andy Cargill and Ian Ferguson scored for Forfar. Then Thistle Manager John Lambie brought on Paul McGrillen (one time of Motherwell) who scored an equaliser with his first kick of the ball. Great was the triumph of the men from Maryhill – and it was not a bad result for Forfar either on this bright spring day.

I talked to a venerable Thistle supporter at the end. He recalled Jackie Husband (look him up if you don't know who he was!) and claimed to remember Doug Berrie. Clearly in his cups, the Glaswegian expressed his total love for Forfar (even though the bridies ran out at half-time) and said he wanted to come and live here.

It's the sort of thing that brings a tear to the eye of even the hardest-bitten of all old teachers...but I never saw him again.

April 15 1995

Forfar today became the first ever winners of the Scottish League Division 3.

They did this on the distant field of Victoria Park, Dingwall in front of a crowd of 2,496 which must have contained close on 500 Forfar sympathisers.

It was no surprise for Forfar had been head and shoulders above everyone else in the Third Division with only six defeats all season, and they clinched the title with four games to spare. It was a great triumph for Manager Tommy Campbell and his Assistant Brian McLaughlin, both of whom confessed openly that this was the best day of their lives.

Playing in a most unfamiliar red strip (a colour that looks alien to Forfar somehow!), the Loons scored the only goal of the game in the aftermath of a free kick from well outside the box through the excellent Bobby Mann. This was late in the first half. The second half was hardly the best game of flowing football that anyone had ever seen, (the pitch was far too hard and fiery for that after a remarkably dry Highland winter), but it passed, even though four Forfar players managed to pick up yellow cards. Referee McGillivray's final whistle came to a tremendous cheer from the Forfar faithful whose celebrations went on for a long time after that.

Ross County, whose first season in the Scottish League this was, were sporting in their congratulations. Their day would come, but this was undeniably Forfar's and the Loons were represented that day by Arthur, Glennie, McPhee, Mann, McKillop, McVicar, Morgan, Craig, Ross, Hannigan (substituted by McCormick) and Bingham.

April 16 1938

It was a very cold blustery day at Forfar for the visit of St Bernard's, the Edinburgh side from Stockbridge.

Once upon a time the club insisted that all their players had to live inside the boundaries of Stockbridge village, even though Stockbridge itself had long been swallowed up the expanding city of Edinburgh.

They were a remarkable club. They had won the Scottish Cup in 1895, and only three days previously, they had lost in the semi-final second replay of the Scottish Cup to East Fife. They still felt that had an outside chance of promotion, although today they were distinctly lucky to get the better of Forfar at Station Park.

Forfar scored first when an attempted clearance hit Ralphie Nicoll and went into the net for a somewhat fortuitous goal. St Bernard's equaliser was one of those where the Forfar defence stood still and watched the opponents score in the erroneous belief that the man, in this case a man with the unlikely and unfortunate name of Flucker, was offside. "The Flucker has scored" (or something like that) was the cry. The same Flucker made the goal in the second half, beating several Forfar defenders for Grant to score. Forfar were then denied a penalty and the game finished 2-1 in favour of the Edinburgh side.

No-one knew it at the time, but Forfar would not see very much more of St Bernard's, who failed to reappear after the Second World War. Like Leith Athletic and the original Edinburgh City, St Bernard's found it difficult to keep going in opposition to Hibs and Hearts in Edinburgh, which is not really a great football city.

April 17 1982

Still basking in the afterglow of their Scottish Cup campaign which earned them so many plaudits in the Press and on TV, Forfar travelled to the Meadowbank Stadium in Edinburgh to play Meadowbank Thistle. This team has now disappeared but, by a somewhat tortuous process became Livingston. Forfar still had an outside chance of promotion and did their chances no harm at all in a fine 5-2 win on a pleasant spring day, punctuated by the occasional heavy shower. It was a curious stadium with the stand on one side and nothing on the other three sides. Sounds and expletives were heard to echo round the ground. The team was Kennedy, Bennett, McPhee, Brown, Brash, Hancock, Gallacher, Farningham, Allen, Leitch, Clark with Porter and Craig as the substitutes.

It was in fact the only game in Edinburgh that day for the game between Hearts and East Stirlingshire in the First Division had been postponed because of an injury crisis at Firs Park – a rare but not unprecedented decision by the Scottish League. Forfar fans noticed also with wry amusement and a few caustic comments that Montrose had appointed as their Manager, Steve Murray, one time Forfar Manager who failed to qualify for a long-service medal in that he lasted only 72 hours!

The news was still dominated by the imminence of war in the South Atlantic as the British task force neared the Falkland Islands. The American Secretary of State, Al Haig, by no means the best diplomat or negotiator in the world, was at least trying to broker a peace deal, but the Argentinian junta would not budge.

April 18 1964

Just occasionally in this awful season of 1963/64 Forfar turned it on and showed the world what they could have done.

Today they went to Stark's Park, Kirkcaldy, to play Raith Rovers – who hadn't in all truth had the best of seasons themselves, but who were still a good few notches above Forfar.

Maybe Raith had given up for the season, and they certainly had a few youngsters being given a run out, but Forfar held them to 1-1 at half time, then ran amok in the second half to win 4-1. Kenny Dick and Eddie McMurdo scored two each to the delight of the small Forfar party who were there.

Forfar would now finish second bottom, the "honour" of being last going to Stirling Albion on goal average. It was a shame that Forfar had antagonised so many of their supporters with some dire performances earlier in the season.

The stay-at-home supporters had a game to watch at Station Park when Forfar Academy drew 1-1 with the John Neilson Institution, a school in Paisley. This match had been arranged by Mr Fred Thomson, Head of History at the school, specifically to give his youngsters the opportunity to play on a senior pitch. At least two, Alan Guild and John Fyfe went on to play senior football, while your author acted as linesman.

It was a great success and was rewarded by a large crowd on a bright but breezy sunny day. The news of Forfar's success in Kirkcaldy was greeted with a little incredulity, however.

April 19 1980

The Forfar Dispatch echoed the mood of the supporters when it said that with this game "the last remaining vestige of promotion hopes disappeared".

It was indeed a dreadful game of football as Meadowbank, who had been defeated 5-0 and 5-0 in their last two games, and whom Forfar had defeated 5-3 the last time the clubs met earlier in the season, managed to confound Forfar and to hold out for a 0-0 draw.

Player-manager Archie Knox, who had seen a red card the previous week, was suspended and his absence certainly had an effect on this insipid Forfar team, for whom only Ken Brown, Alex Brash, Ray Farningham and Ian McPhee showed anything like their true form. John Clark came close in the first half when he hit the side net, but *The Forfar Dispatch* reporter is compelled to conclude that "Forfar are a pale shadow of the team who were scoring freely before the turn of the year".

There were a few other factors – a very strong wind, a hard bumpy pitch and a determined Meadowbank performance – but this did not cheer anyone up, nor did it do anything to silence those who said that Forfar were not wanting to go up to a higher division.

It would take another four years to silence that particular piece of nonsense.

April 20 1957

1957 had been a far from glorious year for Forfar, but today brought a rare glimpse of what could have been.

The Scottish Cup final between Falkirk and Kilmarnock was on TV, but that was not the only reason for the poor attendance of Forfar fans, many of whom had given up for the season. Clyde on the other hand were unbeaten in the Scottish League, and had Scotland Internationalists Harry Haddock and Tommy Ring in their side. They brought a sizeable contingent from Glasgow to see if they could go all season undefeated.

Things looked good for them when Tommy Ring, who had scored for Scotland at Wembley a fortnight previously, added Station Park to the list of stadia in which he had scored. But Forfar fought back and Donald Weir equalised a few minutes later before Albert Craig delighted the small crowd by scoring before half time. Then half way through the second half after Tommy Ring had gone close, it was another Tommy – Tommy Martin of Forfar who bore a certain resemblance to Tommy Ring both in looks and style of play – who scored a great individual goal. Late in the game, Donald Weir threw himself at a cross ball to head home a fourth and to put the small band of the faithful into dream land.

This 4-1 result helped ensure that Forfar would finish fourth bottom (for a while absolute bottom had looked a distinct possibility) but it did not really matter for Clyde, who had won the League anyway. Those Forfarians who attended and resisted the blandishments of TV that afternoon made the right decision for the Scottish Cup final was an ordinary game resulting in a 1-1 draw.

Forfar's team was Mowatt, Berrie and Muirhead; Stewart, Ogilvie and Elder; Haimes, Craig, Dunn, Weir and Martin.

April 21 1956

This was a day in Scottish football on which things happened which should have happened years previously.

At Hampden, Hearts won the Scottish Cup for the first time in 50 years thanks to a 3-1 victory over an understrength Celtic side which lacked Bobby Collins and Jock Stein.

While all this was going on, the owners of Hampden Park, Queen's Park, a hundred miles away in Forfar, got the win which meant that they were returning to the First Division for the first time since 1948.

It meant that Forfar would no longer have their trips to Hampden, and that Queen's Park's supporters would be throwing their bowler hats into the air, according to the *Evening Times,* although I must admit I saw none of that on that bright but blustery day at Station Park.

They beat Forfar 4-2 with Watt Newton and Albert Craig scoring Forfar's goals, and Forfar earning praise for their hard working performance. Queen's Park were given a great sporting reception from the chivalrous Forfar supporters at the end.

But Forfar people were "all agog", the papers told us, about the imminent visit of the Queen Mother to receive the Freedom of the Burgh, something that happened on a very cold and unpleasant day next midweek – and all you really got was a wave from a well-dressed lady who claimed, unconvincingly, to come from Forfar.

No-one could ever remember her in the factories, though.

April 22 2017

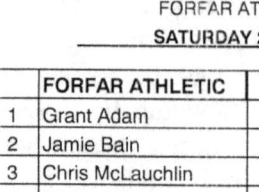

FORFAR ATHLETIC FOOTBALL CLUB
TEAM LINES 2016/17
LADBROKES LEAGUE 2
FORFAR ATHLETIC v CLYDE
SATURDAY 22nd APRIL 2017

	FORFAR ATHLETIC		CLYDE
1	Grant Adam	1	Kyle Gourlay
2	Jamie Bain	4	Martin McNiff
3	Chris McLauchlin	23	Ross Perry
4	Michael Travis	13	Jordan McMillan
5	Thomas O'Brien	5	Kerr Waddell
6	Eddie Malone	2	Ewan McNeil
7	David Cox	6	Scott McLaughlin
8	Lewis Milne	8	Matthew Flynn
9	Jim Lister	24	Jon Paul McGovern
10	Gavin Swankie	9	David Gormley
11	Danny Denholm	28	David Goodwillie
12	Stuart Malcolm	11	Sean Higgins
14	Josh Peters	12	Ryan Finnie
15	Martyn Fotheringham	10	Marc McKenzie
16	Aiden Malone	17	Scott Ferguson
17	Michael Kennedy	18	Peter MacDonald
18	Marc Scott	20	Aaron Miller
21	Jason King	21	John Gibson

Referee — Steven Reid
Assistant Referees — Mark McLean & David Watt

Main Club Sponsor — Orchard Timber Products Ltd.

Match Sponsor — Graham Environmental Services Ltd.

Hospitality Guests — Gordon Lowson & Friends
Barry Smeaton & Friends
Lesley Shepherd & Friends

Match Ball Sponsor — MCG Heating & Plumbing

April 22 1957

On this Holiday Monday – the "Fast" as it was generally known – Heart of Midlothian won themselves many friends in Forfar.

They appeared for a friendly match in aid of Forfar's project to build a new stand, as the old one was now clearly unusable following storm damage. Indeed, it should have been demolished long ago.

Hearts, who had met Forfar the previous year at Tynecastle in the Scottish Cup, refused any share of the 3,000 gate. Not only that, but a sponsor of the club offered a substantial bonus for either team if they scored loads of goals. In these circumstances, it was hardly surprising that the game ended 9-4!

Hearts' good play and general chivalrous demeanour that day possibly even explains why, to this day, a disproportionate amount of Forfarians, now in their sixties and older, have a soft spot for Hearts. This was long before they suffered from their financial problems, crazy Directors and a nasty support who seem to have a penchant for imitating Rangers – things which hardly endear them to the general public.

Hearts had a fine side in 1957 – they had won the Scottish Cup in 1956 and would win the Scottish League in 1958 – and the particular star of the side was fair haired right winger Alec Young. Funnily enough, the only Hearts forward *not* to score that day was their legendary centre forward Willie Bauld.

Forfar's goals were scored by Willie Dunn and Tommy Martin with a couple from Albert Craig, on what was a thoroughly pleasant occasion with the game well refereed by Bert Crockatt of Dundee who had played for Forfar a decade earlier.

The fans sang in his honour the current song made famous in film "Davy, Davy Crockett, King of the Wild Frontier!"

April 23 1932

Forfar lost unluckily 2-3 to Stenhousemuir this Saturday.

Davie Kilgour was taken off early with what looked like a broken collar bone, but attention was focussed on Wembley where David Davidson became the first (and to date only) Forfar player to win an FA Cup medal.

He did this when he played centre half for Newcastle against Arsenal and Newcastle won 2-1 with goals from Jack Allen. It is a shame that this Cup final is dominated by the "over the line" incident where newsreel pictures (as early as 1932) clearly showed the ball over the line as the player crossed immediately before one of the Newcastle goals, but this must not detract from the solid play of Davidson. *The Courier* states that "he played a great part against a mercurial and much changed attack".

Davidson came from Aberdeen, and joined Forfar in 1927 when the half-back line (a vital part of the team in those days) of Cameron, Davidson and Hill made a huge impact on the Scottish game. He and Hill were transferred in 1928, a sad comment perhaps on the economic problems of the 1920s when teams like Bathgate and Armadale disappeared altogether and Forfar only survived by the prudent stewardship of the great Jim Black. Davidson went to Liverpool in the first instance, then later to Newcastle where he had his great moment of glory.

He stayed on Tyneside in later life and surprised a newspaper reporter in an interview for a Newcastle evening paper when he said that the first result he looked for on a Saturday night was that of Forfar Athletic!

April 24 1937

"Fat wis wrang wi the referee?" asked *The Forfar Dispatch* of this game against Cowdenbeath. The question was asked about Mr Stewart of Blairgowrie.

The game seems to have been characterised by a great deal of handling of the ball, as the ball kept rising from the hard, bumpy pitch to hit players on the arms or hands!

This must not disguise the fact that it was a good game of football. Forfar won 4-2, with a hat-trick from Willie Black and a penalty kick from Alf Lawson – and this was after Cowdenbeath had scored first!

Forfar folk left the ground in a rare good mood, for the team had now finished 7th bottom, which was not all that bad!

The Celtic sympathisers were particularly happy when the loudspeaker told them that their team had won the Scottish Cup beating Aberdeen 2-1 in the final at Hampden.

A man, clearly a Cowdenbeath miner, had been seen standing at Jarman's Hotel before the game distributing leaflets and urging young men to go to Spain to join in the struggle against Fascism. He was politely ignored, but he was still there at the end of the game with the same message, this time telling folk that they would have to fight Franco and Hitler sooner or later. He was told, not very politely in some cases, what he could do with his Communist propaganda, but one wonders what people thought a couple of days later when Hitler's bombers annihilated an inoffensive Basque town called Guernica, just to show the world that they could do it.

April 25 1914

A beaten Forfar side nevertheless impressed all spectators at Volunteer Park, Armadale.

That day Armadale won the Central League thanks to a very narrow and scarcely deserved 2-1 victory. Forfar started off kicking against the sun and uphill, and played well with the passing movements of their forwards, particularly inside left Alec Troup, making a good impression. Many journalists were there to report Armadale's seemingly inevitable winning of the Central League.

Armadale scored first through a "gift" goal from a slack back pass. Almost immediately after that, they were awarded a penalty kick, generally described in the Press as "soft".

Forfar kept pressing against a strong defence, and just before half time Dave Easson pulled one back. The second half was a titanic struggle but Armadale held out to win both the game and the Central League, for which they were well congratulated by Jim Black and the Forfar party.

In return, Armadale replied that they had met fewer doughty opponents than Forfar all season. It was widely believed that Forfar were going to lose the services of Ernie Ferguson and Alec Troup for next season, but no offer came for Ferguson and Black was able to persuade "Troupie" that although his moment for a big transfer would come, he would be better to stay for another year to learn his trade (both as footballer and a plasterer) in Forfar.

Forfar had made a profit this year ("in the black" as was said with deliberate ambiguity) and had finished well up the Central League. What could go wrong in the summer of 1914 to spoil everything?

April 26 1975

This was the last day of Forfar's worst ever season – although there might be one or two others in contention for that award!.

Considerably fewer than 200, it would appear, turned up at Station Park to see Forfar go down 0-3 to Alloa Athletic.

Season 1974/75 had long passed the stage of jokes about the two Chinese players "Wi Wan Eence" and "Foo Lang Since", for this was a desperately awful time to support the club.

There had been one win all season, as far back as September 25 when Raith Rovers must have had an off day. And yet, one looked round the ground and saw the spectators. They were the ones who deserved the name "supporters". In their eyes burned love of the club, a certain defiance and a definite feeling that once you hit the bottom the only way you can look is up. This day was also the last day of the old Second Division with its 20 teams and 38 games. Next season there would be a new set-up. Perhaps with the new set-up would come a better Forfar team. Indeed that would happen, and surprisingly quickly, but it did not look like it that awful day in 1975.

In 1975 I was a teacher in Glenrothes. On that very day, Glenrothes won the Scottish Junior Cup. It was often put to me that the Glens should take Forfar's place. It was hard to disagree, but I did!

Forfar's team on that historic (in a funny sort of way) day was Milne, Will, McManus, Lowe, Hopcroft, Brash, Cooper, Junior, Kyles, Grimmond and Boyle. Substitutes were Stewart and Carnegie. I think when Alloa's third goal went it, I realised that I now knew the meaning of the word "nadir".

April 27 1959

Forfar used the "Fast" holiday Monday to play off a postponed game against Alloa Athletic, thereby bringing down the curtain on an eventful season.

The 4-1 victory was especially rewarding in view of the hammering that we had sustained at Recreation Park earlier in the season, but tonight Forfar were well on top with two goals from Eric Brodie, one from Frank McGrory and a penalty from Bill "Pearl" Ogilvie.

Forfar thus finished 8th from the bottom, and although no-one was getting carried away, it was felt that things were at least satisfactory, and the new stand, erected in haste over the winter, was looking well and very modern, even though it did not exactly offer the best view of the park because of its angle!

That same night, Ayr United beat Dumbarton which meant that Arbroath were promoted to the First Division. Apart from causing feelings of petty-minded local jealousy (No, that's not true! Every Forfarian rushed to offer his congratulations! Of course!) and the loss of a couple of local derby fixtures, particularly at the New Year, it did of course raise the question of why Forfar could not do likewise.

We all knew that Arbroath would not last there forever (indeed it was widely believed that they had "avoided" promotion in the past) but it would be nice, (would it not?) to have at least one season in the sun. Especially with the new stand, and prosperity in the air?

April 28 1962

Forfar brought down the curtain on a fairly miserable season with a 1-2 defeat from East Fife at Station Park before a paltry crowd of considerably less than 500.

Jackie Coburn had put Forfar one up before half-time but the black and golds of East Fife scored in the second half through Orphant and Stewart. In what is perhaps a comment on a dreadful season, both teams had two men playing for them rejoicing in the names of "Newman" or "Junior". East Fife finished half way up the League and Forfar were fourth from the bottom.

It was no surprise that this game did not attract a great deal of attention in *The Courier*, for this was the day that Dundee won the Scottish League for the first time ever. They did this by beating St Johnstone 3-0 at Muirton Park, Perth and this result had the side-effect of relegating St Johnstone.

Those of us who recalled the events on January 21 1956 (only six years previously) may well have allowed ourselves a wry smile at the discomfiture of the Perth Saints, but there was a general satisfaction expressed at the triumph of Dundee, even though we realised we would now face a daily barrage every day throughout the summer in *The Courier* about how good Dundee were.

The following 50 years or so would teach us, however, that there was little need for jealousy as far as Dundee were concerned, as folly and incompetence soon dismantled their fine side. But no-one realised that as the strains of "Bonnie Dundee" were heard at Perth Station that night.

April 29 1967

Forfar's 3-1 win over Montrose at Links Park ensured that they would finish fifth bottom with Montrose a little higher up but not all that much.

Oddly enough Forfar felt that this was a reasonable season – certainly far better than last year's performance, and probably better than what it looked like at one point during the season. Today's game was a 3-1 victory with goals from Archie Knox, Ian Matthews and Jim Young on a dry and pleasant day in front of a very disappointing crowd which clearly fell far short of 1,000.

The game did not have very much going for it. It was indeed a nothing-at-stake, end-of season fixture, of which we got rather too many in the large Second Division of 19 clubs where "seeking re-election" was only a theoretical possibility. ("Thank Heavens!" did I hear someone say?)

The crowd gradually went off to various other pursuits in the second half or became more interested vis the crackling transistor radios which were ubiquitous these days, in what was happening at Hampden in the Scottish Cup final between Celtic and Aberdeen and to a lesser extent the game at Dens between Dundee and Rangers, not to mention the English Cup semi-finals.

1967 had been a good year – the country was still basking in the glory of the victory of Scotland over England a fortnight earlier, and at this stage three Scottish teams were still in eager contention for European glory – Celtic, Rangers and Kilmarnock. Forfar had not brought any glory to their fans this season, but they hadn't broken their hearts either

April 30 1966

It was like a funeral wake as we assembled at Station Park that bright breezy Saturday for the last game of the season against Berwick Rangers.

Since Forfar's promotion to the Second Division in 1949, there had been some hairy seasons, but this was the first time that we had actually finished rock bottom. Usually there had been someone worse than us – East Stirlingshire or Brechin City perhaps – but this was the absolute pits. There had been a revival of sorts towards the end of the season and one or two respectable results – seven wins for example, but we were bottom because out of 36 starts we had lost 26 times.

We had gone out of the Scottish Cup on the distant field of Dingwall, home of Ross County, then an insignificant, miserable Highland League outfit. Today at half-time, Forfar were 0-2 down and we began to talk about girls and cricket, a clear sign that the football was awful. But then, almost as if to prove what we could do, Forfar came out for the second half, rolled up their sleeves and John Park, Moss Barclay and Tommy Mackle scored to the delight of the diminished faithful.

Although it was clear that Berwick Rangers were not really bothering because it was a mid-table friendly for them, it meant such a great deal for Forfar. It was like after the fall and destruction of Ancient Troy when the survivors gathered together to set out to look for a new home, as dawn began, symbolically, to break in the east.

We had now reached rock bottom, we had hit the gutter. The only way we could look now was upwards.

May

WASPS NEWS

v

FORFAR ATHLETIC

SCOTTISH
FINE FARE
LEAGUE
DIVISION 1

Saturday
May 3
1986

Kick-off
3pm

ALLOA ATHLETIC

1985-86
No. 21

Official Programme: **40p**

May 1 1982

The time was when the football season finished at the end of April. These days have now gone, for there were another two weeks of the League season to run.

Today as this eventful season began to wind down, Montrose came to Station Park to play a 0-0 draw. The game was not without its good points, but the big problem was actually the weather. Those who argued for summer football ought to have been at Station Park (or any other ground) that day where there was a high wind bringing showers of what could be called either hailstones or sleet, depending on one's viewpoint, and in between them there was some bright sunshine!

There had been many better days in December and January! The bizarre weather conditions and the fact that little was at stake did not deter both teams from trying their best, but no-one was too upset when the full time whistle went.

The international situation was causing a little concern as well, for we were all awaiting anxiously for news from the South Atlantic where Great Britain was about to launch its offensive to take back the Falkland Islands. Indeed that very night, the BBC Sportscene programme was interrupted for a war bulletin.

For football fans, there was of course the added threat to the World Cup to be played in Spain that year where Scotland were about to take on New Zealand, Brazil and the USSR. All this of course, did nothing to detract from the fact that Forfar were coming to the end of a memorable season. They would not get promoted, but their Scottish Cup exploits would be well remembered.

May 2 1935

James Black and Provost Tom Hanick were always "well in" with Willie Maley of Celtic, so they were able to persuade Celtic to come to Forfar this Thursday half-day afternoon to play a Charity match to raise funds for the Old Folks Treat in the shape of a summer outing. It spoke volumes for both clubs that they contributed generously at a time when the country was only just beginning to recover from the depression. Black also took his distinguished guests on a bus tour to the Spittal of Glenshee before the game.

A crowd of 1,500 came to see this game and left wondering why this Celtic team were not League champions (they would win it next year) for they gave an absolutely magical display of football which left a lasting impression on all who saw it. Celtic won 7-1. Jimmy Cameron scored with a penalty kick for Forfar, and the Celtic goals came from Jimmy McGrory who scored two (one a trademark header), Jimmy Delaney, Willie Buchan and a hat-trick from the sometimes underperforming Hugh O'Donnell.

What amazed Forfar supporters was the humility of these great men. The great Jimmy "Napoleon" McMenemy was now the trainer for Celtic, and in lulls of the game stood and discussed football with the locals, saying, for example, of Hugh O'Donnell that he wished he could score a hat-trick every Saturday, asking about how things were in this area which he admitted he did not know too well, and embracing his old friend Davie McLean.

Forfar's team was McFarlane, Collie and Ramsay; Morton, McGregor and Gabriel; Wann, W Black, R Black, Newman and Cameron while Celtic had Kennaway, Hogg and Morrison; Geatons, McDonald and Paterson; Delaney, Buchan, McGrory, Crum and O'Donnell.

May 3 1986

A brave effort by Forfar to reach the Premier League finally came to an end at Recreation Ground, Alloa.

The Loons could only draw 2-2, thus finishing fourth and just short of second placed Falkirk. Arguably the damage was done against Morton last week, but there was still a chance today.

Forfar's loyal support turned out in strength to see a close fought game with Gordon Scott and Jim Liddle scoring for Forfar. It was a sign of just how far Forfar had come in recent years to see the pictures of sadness on the faces of disgruntled Forfarians, but as someone pointed out, this meant that they were the 14th best team in Scotland. For a club of limited resources, this was no mean feat; in recent weeks they had beaten Kilmarnock, Partick Thistle and Hamilton Academical.

On the same day as Forfar drew at Alloa, Hearts were blowing up at Dundee to two late Albert Kidd goals, and Celtic won the League title almost by default by winning 5-0 at St Mirren in the rain.

It would have been nice for Forfar to be in among the really big boys next season, but a few, more realistic, voices pointed out that the opposition would have been tough and that hammerings might have been the order of the day more often than not.

Forfar's team was Kennedy, Lorimer, McPhee, Smith, McKillop, Bell, Lyons, Brewster, Liddle, Scott and Clark with Murray and Ward as the substitutes.

May 4 1974

Forfar may have been (in fact no "may have been" about it – they were!) at a low ebb at the end of the 1974 season – only Brechin were between them and rock bottom.

In the Scottish Cup final of this year, Celtic beat Dundee United 3-0 at Hampden before a crowd of 75,959.

OK, I hear you ask, but what has this got to do with Forfar?

Well, only that three future Forfar Managers played in this game! Archie Knox and Doug Houston played for Dundee United and Stevie Murray (who was, after all, technically, a Manager of Forfar as well) played for Celtic – in fact he even scored a goal. The three Forfar Managers were only part of a star-studded cast list which included Danny McGrain, Jimmy Johnstone, Kenny Dalglish and Davie Hay on one side, and Walter Smith and Andy Gray on the other, with the Managers being the grim-faced scowlers of Jock Stein and Jim McLean, neither of whom were likely to crack a joke to each other at half-time.

1974 was a great year for Scottish football, for we were about to set out to West Germany to compete in the World Cup for the first time since 1958. There was much going on in the world, with Britain between General Elections in February and October, an American President about to be compelled to resign for telling lies, and inflation reaching silly levels – but for Forfar supporters the summer came as a relief from the weekly Saturday slaughter.

May 5 1928

Alec Troup

May 5 1928

Forfar's season was now over, and they had finished fifth in the Second Division – something that represented their best ever performance in the Scottish League.

But at Goodison Park, home of Everton, Alec Troup was collecting his English League medal, the first ever Forfarian (as far as can be established) to do so. Everton had won the League without kicking a ball earlier in the week as their rivals had slipped up. Today therefore the trophy was on show draped in blue and white ribbons, something for which the ever-present Wee Troupie was given his deserved credit.

Dixie Dean had scored the goals, but he was the first to admit that it was the diminutive Forfarian who had provided him with most of the ammunition.

Now on the last day of the English season, in the very last minute of the game, a piece of history was carved. Dean had scored twice that day and was now on 59 goals, equalling the record of George Camsell of Middlesbrough. Another goal would give him the record, and as luck would have it,

Everton were awarded a corner kick on the left. Totally aware of all that was at stake, Alec trotted over to take it. Dixie looked upwards to indicate that he wanted a high one. Remembering the corner kicks that he used to take for Forfar North End at the Market Muir (and indeed for Forfar Athletic at Station Park), Alec judged the wind, direction and weight perfectly for Dixie. The blue figure rose like a bird to head home a glorious goal. The League had already been won, the goal scoring record was now Dean's and Everton's as well, and the unpretentious, modest shy little Forfarian had been the "main man" in both.

May 6 1892

It was the clash of top v bottom today at Carolina Port, Dundee where Dundee East End (as distinct from Forfar East End who were a Junior team) played Forfar Athletic in a game that had been postponed early in the season because of bad weather.

Forfar had endured a dreadful season, and quite a few of their supporters were not sorry to see this season fizzle out. Interestingly, even at this early stage of their history, fans were going about the town saying that "it was better in the old days" – yet the club had only been in existence for seven or eight years! – but quite a few of them had travelled to see Muckersie; Stewart and Cable; A Shepherd, McFarlane and Mann; Bowman, Anderson, Ramsay, Milne and G Shepherd take on East End.

The crowd was a good one, for East End had quite a few supporters, particularly as they had enjoyed a good season. For a while the game was equally balanced with Tom Muckersie in Forfar's goal doing well – always a sign that the rest of the team were doing badly! In the second half the aspirants to the Northern League Championship stepped up a gear or two. The "whites" of Dundee East End scored twice, to put the game out of Forfar's reach, and to consign them to the bottom place, compelling them to seek re-election if they wanted to stay in the Northern League next season.

It was by no means one of Forfar's vintage seasons, but better days would come as well.

May 7 1915

Dreadful things were going on Europe and Gallipoli and the war now a major factor, if not the predominant one on everyone's lives. News had reached the town today of the sinking of the *Lusitania* off the coast of Ireland.

Forfar Athletic held their AGM at Jarman's Hotel under the Chairmanship of George Potter. Secretary Jim Black stressed the problems that had been caused by the war, particularly with some teams in both the Central and the Northern League being unable to fulfil all their fixtures through shortage of manpower or transport logistics, the latter factor exacerbated by the railway companies suspending their cheaper week-end fares.

In spite of all this, however, the club had done reasonably well. If both Central and Northern Leagues had been completed, Forfar would have been at least second in the Central League and would have won the Northern one.

The Treasurer, James Jamieson, reported however a working deficit of £122 9 shillings and 8 pence, but as the Forfar Games of July 1914 had made a profit of £51, the deficit was less than that.

The Committee were duly re-elected with some added members to replace the three men who were in the Army, but no decision could be taken about whether or not there was to be a Forfar Games this Year, nor indeed on the larger issue of whether Forfar would be able to play football next year, something that at the moment looked decidedly unlikely.

Conscription was not yet in force, but more and more young men were in the colours.

May 8 1946

There had been a season of sorts in 1945/46 with Forfar playing in a small competition called the Eastern League.

Now with soldiers, sailors and airmen trickling back from the War, all proudly wearing "demob" hats bestowed on them by a grateful Forfar Town Council, football was able to take itself a little more seriously, although most teams were still a quaint combination of grizzly veterans and fresh-faced youngsters.

Tonight, exactly a year since the end of hostilities, Forfar travelled to Dens Park to play Dundee "A", who contained goalkeeper Reuben Bennett, a young Doug Cowie and a great player whose best years had been lost to the War with the remarkable name of Kinnaird Auchterlonie.

Dundee "A" won 3-2, but Forfar put up a great fight, *The Courier* being impressed by the long throws of Forfar's right half Hugh Robertson who on one occasion compelled goalkeeper Bennet to tip a "shy" over the bar in the mistaken belief that it would have been a goal if the ball had gone in!

Frank Christie and Willie Cairns scored for Forfar who had real bad luck in not getting a draw. The team was Pattie, Jack and McWalter; Robertson, Smeaton and Fraser; Newman, Christie, Cairns, Steele and Linton.

Football would start officially next season with a Scottish Cup and a Scottish League which would contain Forfar Athletic in Division "C".

May 9 2009

Talk about finishing the season with a bang!

Although there had been fun and games in all three Cup competitions (and a big cheque from Sky Television for our 0-4 defeat by Rangers in February) the League season had failed to inspire.

Forfar finished 6th with inconsistent form which had new Manager Dick Campbell tearing out what little hair he had left.

Today however Forfar and Stenhousemuir rocked and thrilled Station Park with a 4-4 draw in which the initiative passed to first one team and then the other. Within the last ten minutes, Forfar went 4-2 up. We thought that that was that and that poor Stenny might not make the playoff places. But the chronic poor defending which had cost Forfar so dear throughout the season struck again and Stenhousemuir equalised to the delight of their fans in the minuscule 392 crowd.

It was a pity that more were not there, for it was a fine game. Stenhousemuir then capitalised on their opportunity, for they had now reached fourth spot and they duly reached Division Two by beating first Queen's Park, and then Cowdenbeath in a penalty shoot-out after two goalless draws! They clearly believed in making their fans sweat!

For Forfar, it was a disappointing season, and the jury was still out on Dick Campbell. Clearly a charismatic figure and a strong personality with a good and obvious rapport with the Forfar fans, he was nevertheless going to need some more time to build up a team.

May 10 2003

465 loyal souls turned up to Station Park to watch Forfar and Cowdenbeath bring down the curtain on the eventful 2002/03 season.

Forfar had done very well to finish fourth in the Second Division, and unfortunately this was before the days of play-offs, otherwise Forfar might just have squeezed in to the First Division.

For a spell Forfar had been going well, but bad weather in January had disrupted things and when the weather eased, a long line of depressing draws had been the order of the day. Even at that, there had been a late rally in which we beat Champions-elect Raith Rovers at Stark's Park, but it was Brechin City who earned the second spot. Poor Cowdenbeath, however, were to be relegated.

One has a little sympathy for the "Blue Brazil", for it is an area which does not have too much going for it, and which suffered dreadfully in the Thatcher years. Today's game was hardly a classic with Paul Tosh scoring Forfar's goal, but loads of effort went in to deny the "end of season" "nothing at stake" sort of nonsense that one heard rather too often.

The rest of the Scottish season had been a good one with Celtic reaching the final of the UEFA Cup beating two English teams in the process, but, if we hadn't realised it before, there was now quite clearly a major problem with the Scotland national team.

May 11 1921

Great news for Forfar!

They were admitted to be part of the new 20 team Scottish League Second Division at the Annual General Meeting in Glasgow, along with Arbroath, Dundee Hibs and other local teams like St Johnstone and several of the Fife teams.

There had been a Second Division before the Great War, but it had failed to restart until now, and in any case Forfar had never been part of it. This meant that Forfar's future was secured, for the trouble with the Northern League, the Central League and Eastern League, all of which Forfar had dabbled with, was that they were liable to implode through lack of numbers at any time.

Forfar's admission had of course followed some intense negotiation and lobbying by Jim Black, but he had made the reasonable point to influential men like his good friend Willie Maley of Celtic (who had subsequently taken up the cudgels on Forfar's behalf) that a Scottish League really must be representative of all parts of Scotland, and not just west central Scotland. His arguments had won the day, and he was well fêted in Arbroath for his efforts for them as well.

As yet, there was no sign of Brechin City or Montrose in any proposed League structure, but that could wait for the future. In the meantime, there was the priority to get together a good team to justify a place in the Scottish League, but the crafty Black, now enjoying the status of a hero in the town, was working on that as well.

May 12 1911

The Courier reported on Forfar's AGM held at the Masonic Hall last night.

It was a very peaceful and optimistic occasion – such things hadn't always been the case in the past – after a very successful season, distinguished by the giant-killing of Scottish League First Division opponents Falkirk last February, "bringing the club into greater prominence than ever before" and obviously strengthening their case for admission to the Scottish League Second Division at some time in the future.

But the really good news was the financial position whereby in spite of some heavy expenditure on ground improvements, the club had made a profit of £85 (an enormous sum in 1911). The Falkirk game had attracted a large crowd, and the resultant trip to Aberdeen, although unsuccessful in playing terms, had nevertheless been very profitable financially. The team had won more games than it had lost, and progress was already being made on signing up players for next season.

The main office bearers James Taylor (Chairman), James Black (Secretary) and James Jamieson (Treasurer) – the "three Jeemies" as they were known locally – were all re-elected for the following season, and everything looked quite happy.

The game in the town had never been more popular with a proliferation of teams at all levels, Junior, Juvenile and even primary schools, and even during the summer, games would be played in the daylight of the long evenings. The Junior teams were East End, North End, West End and Celtic – funnily enough there was never a South End. Forfar Athletic's season, however, would not start again until August.

May 13 2015

An excellent start to the Championship play-off with a 3-1 win in the first leg over Alloa at Station Park. The game was shown live on BBC Alba, something that the large Gaelic-speaking section of the Forfar support would surely have enjoyed!

We English speakers went to Station Park instead and saw a fine Forfar performance in which Omar Kader scored early, Chris Templeman scored with a fine header and then Michael Travis notched a third in the dying minutes. In between the second and the third goal, the Alloa loanee Kyle Benedictus (with the lovely name that sounds as if he should be leading the Prayers in a Monastery on Iona, or someplace!) scored for Alloa, but the 3-1 score line delighted the crowd of 1212 and put us in an optimistic mood for the trip to Alloa on Sunday.

But first it was home to see on catch-up TV the game in Gaelic. You always think that the commentator is saying "Ya hoor" or something like that, but we did make out the salient words like "Swankie" "Denholm" and "Templeman" and we enjoyed seeing the goals again.

Now, who else would be in next year's Championship? Our team was Douglas, Travis, Malcolm, Dods, Kennedy, Kader, Young, Fotheringham, Denholm, Templeman, Swankie with substitutes Dale, Malin and Smith.

May 14 2011

Forfar put up a good performance in their final game of the season, but it was all too late, the damage having been done on the previous Wednesday night.

This was the play-off semi-final for Division 1 (then the second tier in the Scottish League). Forfar had entertained Ayr United on the Wednesday but had appalled their fans by going down 4-1 to the "honest men".

Today they travelled to Somerset Park with a fair smattering of supporters among the 1198 crowd, but the deficit was too much to cope with and Forfar had to be content with a 3-3 draw which did at least satisfy the crowd with a pair of late penalties, one for each side, adding to the excitement. Forfar's scorers were Dale Hilson, Barry Sellars and Ross Campbell who converted Forfar's penalty.

It was a disappointment but Forfar were forgiven by their supporters. This was the end of a very long hard season during which – because of the heavy snow in December – Forfar had gone from November 20 2010 until January 25 2011 without kicking a ball.

The subsequent pile up of fixtures had taken its toll on the players, and of course was the catalyst for Forfar deciding to get for themselves an artificial pitch which would make for fewer postponements. Those of us who deplored "not playing on grass" were countered by the argument that Forfar were simply losing too much money in a bad winter, and the fans suffered likewise with a bad attack of boredom.

May 15 1963

A miserable season finished appropriately at a desolate Station Park as a crowd of less than 500 watched Forfar lose 2-3 to Morton in the last game of the season.

There was a semblance of a fight with goals from Campbell and Dick as against the Morton ones of McTurk, Turner and McGraw, but the atmosphere was dead with many spectators listening to the Scottish Cup final replay on that fairly new phenomenon, the transistor radio.

Forfar finished second bottom of the League, the only crumb of comfort being that bottom of the table were Brechin City, but serious questions were now being asked about how long the Scottish Second Division could last in its present form. (It would limp on for another 12 years, and Forfar would limp along with it more often than not).

This had been the season of the hard frost between January and March with very few games of football being played in Great Britain, and football had found it hard to recover from that. In addition Forfar had more than their fair share of boardroom squabbles and serious spectator unrest with letters appearing with distressing frequency in *The Forfar Dispatch* lambasting the team.

It was a distinct relief to see the cricket season in 1963, and to enjoy the sexual scandals enveloping the Conservative Government!

May 16 2010

Forfar gained promotion to the Second Division in the play-off by beating Arbroath 2-0 at Station Park before 2,207 supporters this Sunday.

This followed a goalless draw at Gayfield in midweek, and it was a glorious Sunday for Forfar who scored early through Martyn Fotheringham, then controlled the game in spite of the loss of Stephen Tulloch, sent off by referee Ian Brines for a second yellow card. Just at the end, Bryan Deasley scored the second and clinching goal.

It had not been the easiest of seasons for Forfar but a good run of form just at the vital time, namely in March and April when the postponed games were played off, brought Forfar back into contention.

This victory for Dick Campbell and his men was not only deserved in the context of how they had played, but a confirmation that, although Forfar will possibly never be one of the top teams in the land, nevertheless their organisation is such that they do not deserve to be one of bottom ones either. The applause at the end was totally justified, and the Arbroath men were dignified in their defeat as well. It was well summed up by a supporter in the vernacular "Bra', min!"

The team was McLean, McCulloch, Tulloch, Bishop, Tod, Sellars, Watson, Mowat, Gibson, Templeman, M Fotheringham. Substitutes K Fotheringham, Deasley and Gordon.

How appropriate it was that it was 125 years to the very day that Forfar Athletic played their first ever recorded game – beating Our Boys Rangers of Dundee 1-0 at Station Park!

May 17 2015

This was one of the more painful days of supporting Forfar!

Frankly, it was harder to take than the grim horrors of the mid 1970s when we hardly won at all. At least we could laugh then, but there was nothing vaguely funny about this one!

It was at the Indodrill Stadium, Alloa, although we knew it better as Recreation Park. It was a funny sort of spring day with bright sunshine one minute then heavy torrential rain the next, but for Forfar supporters, it was all gloom. Some light relief was provided by the repeated loudspeaker announcements relaying a message from the nearby supermarket complaining about Forfar supporters parking in their car park, and would we mind removing them? Such appeals were usually greeted by a reply in the vulgar vernacular!

The position at the start of this play-off was that Forfar were 3-1 up from the first leg at Station Park. All that we needed to do to reach the dizzy heights of the Championship was to "keep the heid" "nothing daft" "keep a grip".

Forfar were well represented in the 1,423 crowd, the supporters glad of a seat and a roof over our heads. For a while all went well, but then crucially on the stroke of half-time, we lost a goal, scored by Michael Chopra who had experienced English football. OK, a blow, but still advantage Forfar. Once more, we held out well, even missing the occasional opportunity ourselves, until, like Zeus in Olympus deciding that the Greeks were going to win on the windswept plains of Troy, Fate intervened and Alloa scored to level things. Actually it was nothing to do with Zeus or Fate, but more to do with crass defending. We all knew that Alloa would score again and win it from a corner kick.

No-one could grudge Alloa their triumph, but it was still a heartbreak, and perhaps the first indication of some sort of supporter rebellion against Manager Dick Campbell. Bravely Dick took the players to acknowledge the support.

Some supporters clapped; others like myself headed off in morose and angry silence to rescue my car from the car park of the supermarket whose irate manager I invited to do something that was biologically impossible.

May 18 1930

Frank "Tiger" Hill became the third Forfar man to win a cap for Scotland.

He did this in Paris, in one of Scotland's first ever trips to the continent of Europe, when Scotland beat France 2-0, both goals coming from the legendary Hughie Gallacher.

A few eyebrows were raised in Presbyterian Forfar about the game being played on a Sunday, but even as early as 1930, the Church had lost the control of things that they had maintained before the Great War, and the town of Forfar was all agog to hear about this game.

Hill was of course now playing for Aberdeen, a talented and creative left half. Those lucky and rich enough to own a "wireless" might have picked up the score in a late night news bulletin, but it was *The Courier* of the following day that broke the news, telling everyone in Forfar how well their hero had played with a special word also for the young Fife goalkeeper, John Thomson of Celtic, who was similarly making his international debut.

After the game, the Scottish players were given a week's holiday in Paris, a huge treat for those who, in the midst of the awful economic depression with the jute factories on "short-time", could only dream of the exoticism of the place.

Hill's career, a remarkable one involving, for example, allegations of bribery at Aberdeen and other things as well as a purple patch with Arsenal, was now about to move into top gear, but he never lost his humility when he returned to Forfar to spend his summers unpretentiously among his "en fowk". Latterly he moved to the USA where he died in 1993.

May 19 1980

Forfar Athletic went on tour to Canada!

Foreign tours used to be the prerogative of bigger team like Celtic and Rangers and were looked upon as a reward as much as any serious playing of football, and the thought of Forfar playing in the New World was looked upon as something fanciful.

They flew from Prestwick yesterday and had now arrived here to play a series of games mainly against a team called Guelph Oaks. This was all arranged by the energetic Chairman Sam Smith whose son Graham was now in Canada and had fixed up this series of games.

It was yet another example of how Forfar were forging ahead and adapting to the new age. Not all the players were available to travel because of their jobs, but those who did go would benefit from the camaraderie and the genuine welcome they received from the Canadians. Manager Archie Knox had flown out in advance to fine-tune arrangements.

Canada had never been a great footballing country, preferring sports like ice hockey, but there remained in the country a love for all things to do with Scotland, for Canada was built to a very large extent by Scottish people, including of course a fair smattering of Forfarians, some of whose descendants would make every effort to catch up with the Forfar party on their stay.

In the meantime, however, the Forfar players and officials had every opportunity to enjoy the lavish hospitality of their hosts before they played a few games of football!

May 20 1926

In some ways this was the most important day in the history of Forfar Athletic Football Club, for it was the day that Forfar were admitted (or perhaps re-admitted) to the Second Division of the Scottish Football League.

Forfar had finished third in the Third Division which had now imploded. Many games were being defaulted by teams who were going out of business. Being third in the Third Division did not guarantee acceptance in the Second Division but Forfar applied, knowing that there was hardly any place else for them to go otherwise.

The two clubs relegated from Division Two, Bathgate and Broxburn, also re-applied. Newspapers say blandly that Bathgate and Forfar were admitted, but this gives less than credit to the hard work of the indefatigable James Black and Tom Hanick for all their lobbying for Forfar's admission. In particular they had the ear of the immensely influential Willie Maley of Celtic, who had in the past been both Secretary and President of the Scottish League. Several visits were paid to the Bank Restaurant owned by Maley where nice things were presumably said about Celtic and the things that Maley held dear.

The fact that Tom Hanick, Forfar's Chairman, was a practising Roman Catholic was not a handicap either in Maley's eyes, and Maley would also frequently wax eloquent about "my friend Jim", when talking about Mr Black. Maley, ever genial and obliging, made sure that Forfar Athletic were elected. Cynics might sneer about "cronyism", but Forfar were in!

May 21 1994

Only twice in the 20th century did Dundee teams win the Scottish Cup and on each occasion, ex-Forfar men played a great part.

In 1910 when Dundee won the Scottish Cup, it was Geordie Langlands who scored the vital goal to earn Dundee a replay in the final when all seemed lost On this occasion some 84 years later, when Dundee United at last won the trophy after countless heartbreaks in previous finals, it was ex-Forfar's Craig Brewster who scored the only goal of the game.

Mind you, it was possibly the worst Scottish Cup final goal of all time, brought about when Rangers goalkeeper Ally Maxwell tried to clear and the ball rebounded off Christian Dailly who miskicked. The ball rolled across the goalmouth and hit the post. Then up ran Craig Brewster to score into an empty net!

By no means a candidate for goal of the season, but a valuable one for the Tannadice men whose long overdue triumph in the Scottish Cup was not undeserved, not least because it prevented Rangers from winning back to back trebles.

Craig had always been a favourite at Forfar where he had basically learned his trade, and for whom he played 191 times (more than he did for anyone else in his lengthy career) between 1985 and 1991. Future Forfar manager Gary Bollan was also involved on the margins of this game, for he was on the bench for Dundee United that day.

May 22 1898

1898 had been one of Forfar's better seasons in the opinion of the President Mr John Fenton at the Annual meeting in the Station Hotel.

The team had finished third in the Northern League (slightly disappointing for they had won the tournament in 1896) but they had won the Forfarshire League.

They were also the first ever winners of the Carry (sometimes spelt Carrie) Cup, a trophy that had done much to stimulate interest at the end of the season, beating Montrose, Arbroath Wanderers and Lochee United. It was especially created for clubs who had been knocked out of other tournaments at an early stage.

The office bearers were re-elected as before. Fenton, a huge man who was mine host of the Caledonian Bar (sometimes called, with a touch of Forfar hyperbole the "Station Hotel") was proud to show off the two trophies won that year and coined the slogan "If you want a demonstration, come to Fenton's at the Station" to entice customers into his bar.

The club were now well established in the town, and the game of football seemed to be going from strength to strength. Although professionalism was of dubious value according to some sources, Fenton was able to see that it presented a great opportunity for a boy from a poor home to make some money in the game, although like quite a lot of Victorians, Fenton retained a residual horror of someone actually making a living out of playing a sport.

May 23 1980

On the second match of Forfar's first ever Canadian Tour, Forfar defeated their hosts Guelph Oaks 3-0 in Guelph, Ontario.

The crowd was given as 2,000; this was Guelph's biggest crowd for many a long year and possibly a record attendance. The pre-match preliminaries were quite alien to Forfar, who occasionally had a pipe band or an instrumental band before a game back home.

This game was preceded by a live pop group and then an exhibition of model aircraft! The game was played in blistering heat this Friday night, and Forfar did well to win 3-0. The goals were scored by John Clark, then Ian McPhee with a powerful shot from a distance. Billy Gallacher finished the job. Archie Knox was apparently "not pleased" with his team, but one suspects this was all an act, for it was difficult to see anything in this performance to criticise. The team had all done well in demanding conditions and in front of a large crowd who appreciated them.

Perhaps, as some have suggested, Knox's displeasure came, perhaps, from one or two antics off the field, but then again, that sort of thing is hardly unusual when football clubs are on tour, and as the saying goes, "whatever happens on tour, stays on tour"! A footballer if asked the question if he ever misbehaved – "even on tour", would say "'on tour' doesn't count!"

May 24 1948

Self-congratulation was the theme of the Forfar Athletic AGM at the Masonic Rooms at the Little Causeway tonight.

Forfar Athletic had indeed done well and had recovered splendidly since the War. They had some success in local and Supplementary competitions; nevertheless the team were still in Division "C", something that would need to be addressed.

The AGM was not well attended, and unlike previous and future occasions, there was a total absence of heckling and criticism. Perhaps the writer in *The Forfar Dispatch* has his tongue in cheek when he says "It was intimated that in view of the consistent high standard of the team's play during the latter part of the season, the Committee had felt justified in re-signing all its members."

Maybe there is a play on words in "re-sign" rather than "resign", but anyway Mr Black had decided that the status quo on and off the park was to remain – and no-one argued with the grand old octogenarian, now happy to be called "Mr Forfar".

It was acknowledged however that but for the £700 raised by the Supporters Club from various events, the club might have been in financial difficulties. However, in tune with the fine sunny night and the general optimism of the post-war times, everyone seemed happy with the Forfar world, and of course, next season was destined to be a good one.

May 25 1967

In scenes reminiscent of the 1919 flu epidemic, the streets of Forfar were totally deserted for a couple of hours from 5.30 to 7.30 pm.

Not a soul was seen on the street, yet it was a fine bright evening, and apparently a cat walked all the way up the centre of East High Street wondering what had gone wrong with the world. Had a nuclear bomb killed all the people but left the buildings standing?

Then suddenly cries of triumph resounded, doors opened, people came out and shouted at each other with glee, hugging and kissing.

Celtic had won the European Cup, and the modern marvel of television had beamed it to everyone. There was no great obvious Forfar connection, but everyone was able to share in the triumph of Jock Stein and his men, with even known Rangers supporters shouting "Celtic! Celtic!" and some of the weaker among them renouncing their allegiance for next year.

In Forfar, a veteran supporter of both Celtic and Forfar had to hide in his Peffers Place shed, such was the tension of the last few desperate minutes. Another raised his arms to triumph to greet Gemmell's goal – and broke his mother's light shade. The great Davie McLean, a Celtic veteran of 60 years previously, watched the game and purred his pleasure at the triumph of the team he had played for.

Moments of joy in Scottish football are few and far between, but this was one of them! Football would never be the same again, and it was a perfect riposte to those who boasted rather too much about England winning the World Cup the previous year.

May 26 1949

Forfar supporters were sad to read in *The Courier* of the death of the Patrick Bowes-Lyon, Earl of Strathmore, at the age of 64, after suffering from poor health for some time.

He was the brother of the Queen. The wars of the early 20th century and the rise of the Labour Party had put the aristocracy under a little pressure of late; one did not have to be a passionate socialist to wonder why there was still so much wealth concentrated in the hands of so few. The Earl himself, a man of quiet disposition, did have a few saving graces, not least that he had been wounded in World War One "doing his bit" like everyone else.

But he was also an unashamed Forfar Athletic supporter and, like his father before him, attended quite a few of their home games. Sometimes he would attend officially, but other times, it was claimed that he would attend incognito wearing a hat or a scarf, fearing not so much any political demonstration against him as the grovelling sycophancy of some of the Forfar committee, whose Chairman was commonly believed to be angling for a knighthood!

The Earl was also not averse to having his coachman drive him into Forfar on a Saturday night for a quick half-hour in the West End Bar, it was said. He would have been glad to see Forfar win the "C" Division Championship a few months before he died, and he was also a lover of cricket and attended games at Lochside as well.

Patrick Bowes-Lyon,
uncle of Queen Elizabeth II,
and supporter of Forfar Athletic

May 27 1925

This was the day of the SFA summer meeting in Glasgow.

Forfar, relegated from Division Two of the Scottish League, now faced an uncertain future in the shaky Division Three which gave every indication of imminent collapse.

They were given a break at last when it was announced that they and the other relegated team Johnstone (of Renfrewshire and not to be confused with St Johnstone of Perth) were to be exempt from the Scottish Qualifying Cup and would be allowed to join the Scottish Cup in January.

This was a big thing for the club because so often in the past they had not managed to get through from the "Quallie" and therefore missed out on the chance of a big draw and some money. (In the event, they would have to travel to Douglas Water in January 1926, so it maybe was not the great triumph that it seemed to be at the time!).

Other matters at the SFA meeting included details of the proceeds of the Scotland v England game and the Scottish Cup final between Celtic and Dundee, and then various charges of misconduct were heard before the panel which included (there being no show without Punch!) Mr J Black of Forfar Athletic.

Fortunately no Forfar players were involved, but the panel had the disagreeable task of suspending Patsy Gallacher of Celtic (generally agreed to be the best player in the game at the moment) for 14 days following a sending-off in a game against St Mirren a month previously.

May 28 1937

You just could not keep this man out of the news, could you?

James Black again found himself named as one of the Scotland Selectors for the following year. He had done this job before, but had not been considered for it last year because of illness. Now he found himself reinstated and was in the distinguished company of Bill Struth of Rangers. The role of a Selector was, as the name suggests, to sit on a committee which chose the team for Scotland's game. This was, of course, long before the days of a full time professional Manager and it was a role which lent itself to usually ill-informed criticism.

In Black's case the question was asked "What does a man who runs a small team of part-timers know about International football?" But Black had always had a good eye for a football player, did not lack the energy to travel to all parts of Scotland and England to spot talent, and was also thick enough skinned not to allow himself to get upset by the cries of the ignorant. (He was not without his critics in Forfar itself either!)

More pertinent criticism could be applied to Struth, who, in spite of the naïve identification of Rangers with Scotland in those days, nevertheless did not shrink from making Rangers players unavailable to play for Scotland if Rangers had an important Cup tie the following week. Such criticism was hardly likely to apply to Forfar and Black!

May 29 1939

Nothing looked good this Monday night.

It was no secret that war was inevitable and possibly even imminent, as all the various preparations for blackouts etc were becoming obvious round the town.

Forfar Athletic were in dire straits, facing, according to Don John in *The Courier,* the biggest crisis they had faced in their 54 year history. It had been their proud boast that they had never had to appeal to the public, but this was precisely what was happening now. The reason was the basic one that expenditure was outpacing income by a considerable amount and the result of that was, according to Mr Micawber in David Copperfield, "misery".

It was by no means uncommon, of course, for football teams to go out of business – Bo'ness, Armadale, Broxburn and a few others would testify to that – but Forfar had always felt that the community would support them. A conference of interested people would be summoned to deal with the problem. Many people felt that this would be no bad thing, for it had often been felt that Forfar Athletic had been a "closed shop" and that Mr Black for all his good intentions and undeniable self-sacrificing for the club, had never been too good at appearing to want to "share" things.

But now circumstances were demanding a change, and the formation of a limited company did seem a possible way out of the problem. But did it all matter in any case, given the International situation?

May 30 1913

Following what was generally regarded as Forfar's poorest season to date, with poor results and even poorer attendances, Forfar had nevertheless had a good "close" season so far.

Today they announced the signings of two men from Brechin City, one being a centre half called "Lin" Bruce who was a Forfarian and had played for Forfar before at centre half, and another called John Walker, an accomplished inside forward.

This had followed hard on the heels of the return of Davie McLean from Sheffield Wednesday. McLean was of course a Scotland Internationalist by now, and there was a feeling that his presence in his home town might not last long and that he was using Forfar Athletic as a pawn in his dealings with Sheffield Wednesday, but he was welcome nevertheless.

Like many a thrawn Forfarian, McLean was not good at taking orders from dictators. He had similarly fallen out with Willie Maley at Celtic, and had moved on from there. But it suited him at the moment to be back in his home town, for he was getting married soon.

Things were, all in all, looking a great deal brighter for Forfar Athletic that they had been a month previously, when even the eternally optimistic Jim Black had wondered aloud whether Forfar had lost its appetite for senior football, such had been the alarming decline shown in every respect.

May 31 1967

In the same way as the streets of Forfar were deserted six days ago, a similar thing happened tonight, but this time the circumstances were different.

It was Rangers' big night in the European Cup Winners' Cup final. The kick-off was later than last week, but the feelings were just as intense with even Celtic supporters, secure in the knowledge that whatever happened they would be the Champions of Europe, feeling able to lend them some grudging support, for what a thing it would be if Scottish teams held both European trophies! Curtains were drawn in houses the better to watch the flickering black and white TV screen which still couldn't always be guaranteed to produce the picture and even wives and mothers joined in the general tension.

Alas, there was no joy tonight, for Bayern Munich, with the undeniable advantage of playing a final in Germany, scored late on to win the game. The fact that Celtic were the undeniable Champions of Europe did no favours to Rangers, and in a real sense, it was Celtic who beat them, psychologically if not physically.

Such were the implications of Glasgow football, something that even those Forfarians who supported one team or another did not really totally understand. But quite a few Forfar people were very upset tonight, and we could all understand their grief. After all, being a Forfar supporters gives you loads of practice in coping with grief!

June

The Forfar players and officials setting off for Canada in 1980

June 1 1980

Forfar Athletic arrived home from their tour of Canada, the first time that the club had undertaken such a venture.

It had been very successful with three victories out of three games played, but the main thing according to Manager Archie Knox had been the camaraderie and the benefits accrued by the players all being away together.

The whole party had consisted of 70 people and had contained wives and girlfriends. The hospitality had been first class and the only real problem had been the excessive heat throughout.

The first game had been played in London, Ontario against a team called "A Canadian Select" consisting mainly of German players and that had been won 5-2, then there had been a game against Guelph Oaks (won 3-0), before another game reduced, by mutual consent to 35 minutes per half because of the intense heat, against Ottawa Under-21s which Forfar had won 7-1.

In this game, the coach Kenny Dick had featured and had even scored a penalty, but the best player on the field had been Billy "Seagull" Gallacher who had finished the scoring with a long range header! There had been time for sight-seeing as well, with even some members of the party visiting the USA, and the whole exercise, it was felt, had done Scotland, Scottish football and Forfar Athletic a power of good.

The friendly relations between Forfar Athletic and Guelph Oaks would continue.

June 2 1893

A month had now elapsed since the SFA's historic decision to make professionalism legal, but the implications for teams like Forfar were taking a long time to sink in.

In actuality, there was really nothing new, for everyone was aware that it had been going on for some time, usually disguised as "travelling expenses" or "hospitality accounts", but now that it could be done openly, what was there to stop the big clubs of the country appearing at Station Park with large chequebooks and offering wages to men like "Jeck" Cable or Jamie Dundas to go to Glasgow to play? (Since 1886 it had been possible for English clubs to do just that).

The answer was of course, nothing, but the smaller club could ask for a fee. This might be the solution to the well-documented financial problems of certain clubs, said James Black, "including ane no' a' that far awa' fae here" to loud laughter at a public meeting to discuss the issue, but it was certain that football would never really be the same again.

Queen's Park would stay amateur – indeed they had fought tooth and nail against professionalism – but big city clubs like Hearts of Edinburgh and Celtic of Glasgow would no doubt generate the money to pay their players.

Someone else quoted the Biblical tag that "the love of money is the root of all evils", and there was general sage nodding of heads.

June 3 1978

Strathmore had beaten Mannofield by 61 runs at Lochside – a good win, but the important thing was that the cricket was over and done with long before we settled down to watch the really important event of the day, which was, of course Scotland playing Peru in the Argentina World Cup of 1978.

We had been told that Scotland were going to win the World Cup. Many of us believed it, including those who said afterwards that we didn't have a hope! Hindsight of course is what makes one always right! Even though we had lost to England in the build-up, what did that matter because we had qualified and they hadn't?

Besides miracles and the impossible do sometimes happen in football. Look at Forfar, we said. A bit of luck and we would have beaten Rangers! So of course Scotland would win the World Cup, we reckoned, as we settled with our Newcastle Brown Ales and McEwan's Export to watch.

And Scotland scored first!... But then, a couple of hours later, a Second World War veteran came home from the Salutation Hotel and said "The lest time I saw faces like that wis in 1943 fan we captured the Germans in Africa!"

Indeed the parallel was a striking one – people willing themselves to be conned by ruthless propaganda machines which nevertheless lacked the brake of reality. Then came the desolation of defeat. Those of us alive in 1978 were never the same again, and only those youngsters who love horror stories should look up books and videos to see what happened in Argentina in 1978.

June 4 1982

Not even the hardest hearted of Forfar Athletic fans could keep a tear from his eye as the train left Forfar Station that night, passing Station Park on the right on its last journey to Perth.

The line had, of course, been closed for many years now, but one of the many Railway Preservation Societies had organised what was positively the last trip to Forfar from Perth before the lines were to be lifted.

The day was roasting hot, a piper played "My Grandfather's Clock" and passengers were encouraged to wear Victorian dress as a tribute to all who had travelled to and from Forfar Station since its opening in 1839.

Station Park, of course, owed its name to the Station, and I am glad that no-one has ever tried to change "Station Park" to the name of some firm in a sycophantic and misguided attempt to take money by selling the soul of our club.

When one thought of the teams and the players who had travelled on that railway, getting off at the station, then the short walk up to the ground ... When one thought of the boys standing at the foot of the west terracing, then breaking off their concentration on the game to run up and have a look at the passing train ... When one thought of the away teams, referees and linesmen running across the field immediately after a game to catch a train back to Glasgow to save a wait for a couple of hours ... How could the tears NOT well up?

How I cursed those cynical politicians who took our railway away from us! I hope God can forgive them ... because I cannot.

June 5 1928

Three men with Forfar connections were selected to join the party arranged by "an Aberdeenshire select" team to tour Norway this summer.

This was of course a great honour and Davie Davidson, Frank Hill, and David McLean were the men chosen, as indeed was David "Napper" Thomson of Dundee. It would have to be admitted that the connections of the four men to Aberdeenshire were somewhat tenuous, to say the least, but Davidson was at least born in Aberdeen.

It was however a great feather in the cap of Forfar Athletic, and in the case of Frank "Tiger" Hill, it was a recognition of the talents of this fast developing and versatile young man, who would, of course sign for Aberdeen in due course later that summer, possibly because of the favourable impression gained of him on this tour.

Football in Norway was in its infancy and, as often happened in those days, Scottish teams would encounter difficulties there in the shape of referees who were enthusiastic amateurs rather than trained experts, and on pitches which were sub-standard, but the main thing was that it was a holiday – a footballing and a paid holiday – and allowed these young men to see a bit of the world. McLean of course by this time had enjoyed a long and varied career, but the big moments in the careers of Hill and Davidson were yet to come.

June 6 1908

The Northern League held its AGM in Dundee this sunny Saturday with James Phillip of Aberdeen in the Chair and James Black of Forfar acting as Secretary and Treasurer.

Mr Black reported a slight deficit over the past year, but there was a small working surplus of £14. Kirkcaldy United proposed that the annual subscription should be raised from £1 to £1 10 shillings, and Mr Black was voted an Honorarium of £10. Black was always keen to stress that he took "not a penny" from Forfar Athletic but he was clearly willing to take money from the Northern League for his indefatigable and energetic commitment to the institution.

Lochee United had to withdraw from the League because they had lost their ground to an Irish Junior team called the Harp. This was, in fact, an interesting social comment on how the village of Lochee had now been taken over by the Irish immigrants, and was well on its way to earning the nickname of "little Tipperary" or simply "little Tip".

A few other items of business were discussed and decided before the trophy, a new one, from last year's Championship was presented to the winners, Brechin City, a great triumph for the Brechin side which had only been in existence for a couple of years.

Forfar were of course very keen to be admitted to the Scottish League (which now had a Second Division) but it would take another 15 years and a World War before that was likely to happen. In the meantime, there were always rumours of teams leaving to join a Central League.

June 7 1930

It cannot be very often in sporting history that a Forfar Athletic man plays in the same cricket team as two Australian Test Match players, but this was precisely what happened here when Davie McLean was invited to join JM Barrie's Allahakbarries in a game to open officially the cricket pavilion on the Hill at Kirriemuir which JM Barrie had given to the club.

The day was scorchingly hot, and more or less all of Angus made their way to the Hill, in spite of the counter attraction of Brechin playing Arbroath in the Strathmore Union.

As this was the depth of the economic depression, and many of Forfar's factories were on "short-time", Forfarians, almost *en masse* decided to walk to Kirrie to save on the rail fare.

The two Australian cricketers were Arthur Mailey and Charles Macartney, and they were part of the 1930 Australian touring team who, having unearthed a new batting phenomenon by the name of Don Bradman, would win the Ashes later that summer, .

The First Test was due to start at Trent Bridge the following Friday. The Kirriemuir game was between Barrie's side against the West of Scotland, both sides being supplemented by "guests", and thus it was that when the great Charles Macartney reached his century, his partner was no less a man than Davie or "Dyke" McLean, the hero of Forfar and no mean cricketer for Strathmore, even though he was better known as a footballer. Macartney himself apparently was impressed and even flattered to hear that his partner was a Scottish international football player.

It was reckoned that over 5,000 watched that game.

June 8 1939

Forfar Athletic were saved!

Forfar's dire financial position had been well documented in the local press for some time, and there had been a certain fear that the club might just quietly fold. But Jim Black and the other officials, having swallowed a little humble pie, one feels, at a few meetings in the Jarman's Hotel for this very purpose, were able to put the minds of the supporters at rest.

The announcement was made that three men in particular were to guarantee Forfar's survival. They were Mr J H Melville, Secretary to Craiks Ltd and captain of Strathmore CC, Mr F M Thomson of Don Brothers, Buist and Company Ltd, and Mr Andrew Graham, partner in Waterston and Graham, Architects.

They were all genuine football men having either played the game in the past or shown support for the club. Melville, when captain of Strathmore was often described in not entirely unsympathetic terms as "the worst player, but the best captain" in the team, meaning that he was not athletically gifted, but could study the game of cricket. It was hoped that he could bring these skills to save Forfar. The other two had local Church connections, so maybe God had decided to save Forfar, but folk also said that "Blackie'll hae tae watch his language", for it was not unknown for Jim to let slip the odd oath. But, any way Forfar were now saved.

All that remained in 1939, now, was to deal "wi that Hitler led" in Germany.

June 9 1953

Forfar Athletic had to back down in their wage negotiations for the new season.

Players were paid £5 per week, and then £2 for a win and £1 for a draw. This system had worked reasonably well for a few years, but in an attempt to economise, Forfar had tried to worsen the conditions of the bonus by offering £1 for an away win and 10 shillings for a home win. Not surprisingly, this did not find favour with the players, so the new "offer" had to be withdrawn, and they reverted to the original.

Chairman William Callander, however, was a little unconvincing when he pleaded poverty and said "we are finding it increasingly difficult to carry on". He had been known to say the same sort of things to his workers at similar stages of wage negotiations.

Forfar had never been a rich club and probably never would be, but this was the 1950s when prosperity was slowly beginning to make an appearance. Recently for example, money had been splashed out all over the town to celebrate the Coronation of Queen Elizabeth II, and with housing schemes planned in several parts of the town, austerity seemed to have gone.

Forfar Athletic supporters, in any case, tended to see the amusing side of this and to wonder what all the fuss was about, because the way the team played, they were not likely to be coughing up too much in the way of bonus money anyway!

June 10 1938

It is now generally accepted that pubs will show live TV football matches, or they might find that their trade suffers.

In 1938, there was no TV as yet, at least not in Scotland, and only a very limited service in the London area, but the Salutation Hotel at the East Port pointed the way for hostelries in the future.

This Friday was the final of the Empire Exhibition Trophy between Celtic and Everton at Ibrox in Glasgow, and the second half of the match which was more or less the championship of Great Britain was to be broadcast on the BBC Home Service with commentary from Rex Kingsley, the football writer of *The Sunday Mail*.

Not everyone in 1938 owned a radio (or "wireless" as they were called then) and the Salutation Hotel rigged one up with loudspeakers in the bar so that the customers could hear the progress of the game.

The reception was not great with loads of "whistling" and "crackling" and sounds that reminded one of someone breaking wind, but the large crowd of punters were able to hear with delight that in extra time, Johnny Crum scored for Celtic to win the game, and then proceeded to do a sort of Highland Fling in front of his fans.

And the "Sally" as the hotel was lovingly called, did a roaring trade!

June 11 1892

Forfar may well have approached this AGM of the Northern League with bated breath, for there was no guarantee that they would be allowed to continue.

They had finished bottom, and under the terms of the constitution, they and St Johnstone (who had finished second bottom) were "stricken off the Roll" (as if they were a doctor or a lawyer in disgrace, or were being excommunicated from the Church) and then they had to apply for re-election.

Fortunately both clubs had good friends who voted them back in, on the grounds that they both attracted reasonable crowds. Not only that, but the authorities actually increased the size of the League from next year to include Aberdeen Victoria and Dundee Wanderers who would thus join Forfar, St Johnstone, Dundee Our Boys, Dundee East End, Lochee Harp, Arbroath, Montrose and Aberdeen to make a League of 10. The League Championship this year had to be shared with Our Boys and East End being declared joint winners.

In an unworthy display of meanness, the Northern League refused to commission a League flag for either team! Various other matters were discussed, but the one that was overshadowing everything was professionalism, something that was not yet legal in Scotland and wouldn't be for another year, but one would have to have been blind, deaf, dumb and astonishingly stupid not to realise that it had been going on for some time.

What would the effect of official legalisation have on a small League like the Northern one?

June 12 1967

This was the day that I met and talked at length to the great David Prophet McLean. A student, home on holiday, I was working at the Co-op Bakery at the East Port and was sent to pick up some rhubarb at the great man's house in Craig O' Loch Road.

I was in total awe of such a God, but he proved very sociable, and being a Forfar man, he knew immediately who I was (Forfar people do know each other!) and talked at length of his career particularly at the two clubs that he really loved, Forfar and Celtic. (It was just a couple of weeks after the great Celtic triumph in Lisbon).

Davie was known as the goal scoring machine by some people, and actually scored more goals than even Jimmy McGrory, although for snobby reasons, the fact that so many were scored for Forfar (for whom he actually signed four times) meant that they were not rated so highly. Modest, genial and sociable, he really was "just an ordinary man", and his wife was equally pleasant.

I could have stayed there all day talking to him, but the boss was needing the rhubarb for the tarts, so I couldn't stay too long. He told me to come back and talk to him some other time, but I never had to courage to knock again on the door of this footballing God. I had cause to regret my cowardice when the great man died the following December.

June 13 1945

The war had been over now for a month and the Scottish League met in Glasgow to arrange the Divisions of the Scottish League for the first peacetime season.

The Scottish League had suspended itself in 1939 and been replaced by regional Leagues. To the disappointment and astonishment of most people in Dundee and Angus, the First Division was to contain 16 teams from the west-central area of the country plus Aberdeen, whereas the Second Division would contain 14 teams including Dundee, Dundee United and Arbroath, but no Forfar, Montrose or Brechin!

There was no logic in this at all and Forfar's objection was based mainly on the fact that 16 teams in the Second Division would have made a lot more sense, and that if Arbroath and Dundee United were there, why not also Forfar and Montrose? The argument of the legislators was that, as the war in the Far East was still going on, this would be an unofficial season anyway with no Scottish Cup or official Internationals and it would make sense not to involve clubs in too much travel.

Why then ignore Forfar with a mainline station 100 yards away from the ground? Why also ask Aberdeen to travel to Queen of the South? It made no sense at all, and probably only happened because Jim Black, that indefatigable fighter for his beloved club, was now an old man!

Bitterly, Forfar people asked when the Scottish League refused to change its mind, if all the dictators were really dead after all?

June 14 1953

The death was announced in Maryfield Hospital, Dundee of George Henderson, one time of Forfar, Dundee and Rangers.

It is astonishing that this man is not better known nowadays, for he was one of the best players on his day, very unlucky not to win a Scottish "cap" while winning four Scottish League medals with Rangers. He was part of the immortal Ibrox forward line of Archibald, Cunningham, Henderson, Cairns and Morton, and scored 123 goals from 170 appearances for Rangers.

Born in Green Street, Forfar in 1897, he started off with Forfar Celtic (ironically enough in view of the team which he played for later!), then joined Forfar Athletic in the portentous year of 1914. He performed well until Forfar Athletic stopped playing for the duration of the war in 1915. On his return from the war where he served in Egypt, France and Salonika, Geordie joined Dundee but was soon signed by Rangers where in spite of his success, he was never totally loved by the Ibrox faithful, who were completely embittered by their side's failure to win the Scottish Cup when Henderson played for them. He played for a few other teams as well before become a publican in Dundee.

He was never a boastful man, and may even have been ashamed of his involvement with Rangers at a time when sectarian hatred was being actively fostered by his employers. Like Davie McLean (who of course was mainly identified with the other side) he never understood why terms like "Catholic" and "Protestant" were in any way significant in football. Yet a man who could hold his own among men like Tommy Cairns and Alan Morton is surely demanding of more credit and glory

June 15 1895

A meeting was held at the Central Coffeehouse in Arbroath concerning the construction (or perhaps the re-construction) of the Northern League. This institution had fallen on bad times. It had imploded on itself because of lack of teams after Dundee Our Boys and Dundee East End had amalgamated to form Dundee FC with a view to joining the Scottish League. (By an odd coincidence more or less exactly a hundred years later, a similar thing happened in Inverness!).

Clearly some dynamic leadership was required and the appointment of James Black of Forfar Athletic to the joint post of Secretary and Treasurer leaves the historian in no doubt as to who the "dynamic leadership" was.

But Black was shrewd enough to suggest Mr Smith of Montrose as President and Mr Russell of Aberdeen Orion as Vice President and appointing five other people from other clubs to be on the Committee. Lochee United were admitted, and from now on the Northern League would be a strong force in local football circles until the First World War.

There seemed to be no limits to what the indefatigable Black could do. He was already the man who ran Forfar Athletic, he was a referee, he sat on various other committees and he gained his prestige through his constant ability to do hard work, particularly in the jobs that no-one else wished to do, and also by his constant good nature and affability. He already had a few enemies in his home town, but then again that always happens to ambitious young men, and although Black was undeniably ambitious for himself, he did have a genuine love of Forfar Athletic and of football.

June 16 1936

Forfar Athletic were pleased to announce two pieces of good news.

One was that James Black had recovered from his recent illness and was resuming his duties at Station Park. His illness was not specified, but it was hardly surprising that a man of his age (he was now not far short of his 70th birthday) should be feeling the strain, given his energy and commitment to running the club that he had done so much to create.

He would often say, however, like so many Forfar people in other walks of life, that it was his love of the club that kept him going and that it some ways, he was afraid to "stop", and start feeling sorry for himself. Typical of the man was his announcement on the first day back from his illness that he had signed a full back, a local boy with the unusual name of Anson Keith, who played for Forfar West End juniors, and that most of the current squad had also been re-signed for next season.

"Ans" Keith, in later years an employee of the Gas Board, would actually prove to be one of Black's shrewder signings, and it was part of his policy to look for local boys. Sometimes, one got disappointments, of course, but it was certainly cheaper than bringing in players from Dundee. Black also fervently believed that local boys would put more effort in for their own club. 1936 had, arguably, been one of Forfar's better seasons and Black was hoping to make further improvements.

June 17 1955

After much discussion, the Scottish League decided to reform itself for next season.

Instead of two 16 club Divisions and then a "C" Division for the rest, it was decided to have an 18 team First Division and a 19 team Second Division. Ironically it was decided on the proposal of Berwick Rangers, a team who are based in England!

It was good news for Stirling Albion and Motherwell who would have been relegated from Division "A" but were now re-instated, and it meant that Berwick Rangers, Dumbarton, Montrose, East Stirlingshire and Stranraer would now join Forfar and the others in Division "B" which would now be called the Second Division.

For Forfar, this was not necessarily good news, and arguments raged throughout the town on this issue. On the one hand, Montrose would be a nice local derby, but Berwick Rangers and particularly Stranraer were a long way away. But the big disadvantage was that because there were 19 teams, there would be more fixtures, some of them in midweek, and there would be two days on which they were the odd team out. But it had been voted for by 25 to 12 with 0 abstentions, and that was that!

The same meeting put Forfar in the same section for the League Cup in August as Motherwell, Dundee United and Albion Rovers. Now that was something to look forward to!

June 18 1885

At the meeting tonight in the Lamb's Hotel, Dundee of the Forfarshire Football Association, it was announced that 13 teams had "qualified for membership" (which means, one presumes, that they had paid their fees!) and among them was "Forfar Athletics" (sic). This was a small but significant step towards the acceptance of the club in local footballing circles.

The origins of our club are complicated, but according to the superb "Centenary History" they broke away from a team called Angus Athletic (who also played in Forfar) and played their first game on May 16 of this year. According to *The Courier* in its report of this meeting, the 13 teams were Dundee East End, Dundee Our Boys, Dundee Strathmore, Harp, 3rd FRV (Forfarshire Reserve Volunteers), Dundee West End, Arbroath, Arbroath Strathmore, Forfar Athletics, Forfar Angus, Broughty Ferry, Monifieth and Brechin Dalhousie. (Interestingly only Forfar Athletic(s) and Arbroath have survived in that form from 1885 until 2017).

Mr Scott, Broughty Ferry, the Secretary of the Forfarshire Football Association, in his report is very upbeat about the future of this young sport of football, saying that "the public interest in the game was not only being kept up, but was steadily increasing" Indeed it was, and the "beautiful game" which was, admittedly, born in England was now fast becoming the national obsession of Scotland, not least because of Scotland's ability to beat England at it!

Dundee and Forfarshire were no exception to this national revolution.

June 19 1954

A new era in football watching started today when Scotland's match, playing against Uruguay in their first ever World Cup, was transmitted on live television from Switzerland.

Streets in Forfar were deserted at 4.45 pm when the transmission began. Those very few people who had televisions in Forfar suddenly found they had loads of "friends" who wanted to come to their houses to see the World Cup. Televisions were expensive, believed to be subversive as far as people's morals were concerned, and also very new.

TV had only started in Scotland in 1952. There had been games on TV before, notably the English Cup final between West Bromwich Albion and Preston North End earlier that summer, but this was Scotland playing!

The television screen was usually very small, about the size of a tablet, in the middle of a huge cabinet. There was only one channel and it took a long time to heat up. The picture was unreliable and could easily be disrupted by a motor bike going up the road, particularly if it were in North Street, for example, which was long and straight.

It was my privilege to watch this game in the house of the widow of James Black, the Forfar supremo who had died a couple of years previously and whose portrait gazed imperiously at the television. I wonder what on earth he would have made of it all, for Scotland managed to lose 0-7 to Uruguay! Me? A few tears, but a quick recovery, for I was only five and a half.

The word "Uruguay" scarred me for life, though!

June 20 1900

On a hot but showery day at Clepington Park, John Janes, the talented Forfar Athletic full back proved his sporting versatility by winning the "sack race" at the Sports organised by Dundee Wanderers.

This "sack race" was where you had to race with your feet and legs inside a bag made of jute (Naturally! It would have to be jute, or "jit", as it was called. This was Dundee in 1900!).

The race was limited to the players who played in the Five-A-Side football tournament, held earlier. The fair haired Janes, ever popular at Station Park, won this race by some distance for he mastered the art of jumping with his legs together.

It was some consolation for Forfar supporters who had seen their team lose in the semi-final of the football tournament to Arbroath by one goal and one corner to one goal. Wanderers themselves won the competition.

There were two political demonstrations outside the ground. A couple of ladies stood with a placard wanting "Votes For Women" – they were generally ignored or met with vulgar comments from men.

The other was about the South African War. A century later, any War would attract a demonstration *against* it. In 1900 this was *pro-*War with older men upbraiding younger ones for not joining up and for spending time at "sports conventions" rather than serving God and their Queen! Not everyone was convinced by them, though, for although the newspapers gave the impression that Britain was driving the Boers out of South Africa, the stories of wounded men returning to Dundee and Forfar gave an altogether different impression.

June 21 1918

Midsummer's day and the war had been going on for almost four years now. Forfar Athletic had folded for the duration in 1915, although there was still the very occasional game of junior football played.

Now at last, if the newspapers were to be believed there was some progress in sight, with the British advancing slowly.

But the newspapers had proved to be nothing other than propaganda in the past. In the meantime, conscription was in force and the "comb-out", as it was called, of previously "protected" jobs was going on, and James Black was heavily involved in the Tribunals to decide whether an application for an exemption or a deferment was in order.

Tonight, for example, in the Masonic Hall, Black was on the panel dealing with an agricultural worker, a baker, a blacksmith – all three of whom, one felt might have served the war effort a little better at their civilian job – but the panel had to make a decision. There was a certain amount of evidence that Black, basically a humane if somewhat officious man, made some attempt to "save" some of the applicants, but he was generally outvoted, and the man, even if a personal friend, had to go to what was left of the war.

Black was very aware that there were now very few men of military age left in the town.

June 22 1974

A friend of mine, who really should have known a lot better, decided to get married on this day, and my wife and I were duly invited to the wedding at the East Church and the Royal Hotel.

This might have seemed like good news, and it would have been on another day, but this was the day of Scotland playing Yugoslavia in the 1974 World Cup, the game which determined our qualification to the later stages. Hard though it might be for younger readers to believe this, Scotland actually had a good team in 1974, having come within a whisker of beating Brazil on the Wednesday night.

So, do you go to the wedding, or watch the game on TV? Repeated pleas to my friend to get him to change the date all failed on the weak grounds that the wedding had all been paid for etc., so we had to go to the wedding, because I suppose it was more important. No problem with the Church – the game hadn't kicked off yet – and the meal and the speeches at the reception finished with the score at 0-0 at half time – apparently, for this was long before texts and we had to rely on information supplied by sympathetic waiters. The one at our table was a useless nerd with no interest in football (yes, you get these guys!) but the one at the next table kept us informed.

Still 0-0, I stood up, talked politely to some folk, and then I cracked. Feigning necessity to go to the toilet I eventually found the TV that the waiters had been watching, and saw the last 10 minutes. An honourable draw, but Scotland were out on goal difference. Sad, very sad – and I had to pretend to be happy at the wedding reception!

June 23 1924

Ramsay MacDonald's minority Labour Government, dependent on the Liberals, was still continuing but the political situation was very uncertain.

Forfar Athletic however announced that preparations were being made for the start of the new season which was now less than two months away. Five players had been signed up, three familiar to the Station Park faithful and coincidentally the first three that would be read out over the loudspeaker, namely the goalkeeper Bruce and the full backs Gerrard and Braid, but there were also two new players from Brechin called Rae and Jeffrey.

Rae had also played for Dundee Hibs (or Dundee United as they had been called for the past year) and was a versatile midfielder, whereas Jeffrey was described as an inside left "of considerable promise". Brechin had been an easy target for the approaches of Black, for they had finished bottom of Division Three amidst considerable doubts about their ability to survive in the Scottish League.

Black was of course shrewd enough to realise that a good Brechin team would work to the advantage of Forfar, and tried very hard with all his friends at the Scottish League to include them, but that did not stop him from poaching a few of their players if he thought they could do a good job for Forfar.

It was expected that several other players of experience would be signed within the next few weeks, for "the officials are in contact with a number of men with senior experience" and the team would have a lot of new blood for next season.

June 24 2014

The death occurred of David Taylor, General Secretary of UEFA. He had had a similar post in the SFA before then, and he was an unashamed supporter of Forfar Athletic.

He suffered a heart attack in Turkey, was brought home but did not recover. He was only 60, and he still had a great deal left to give the game. He was born in Forfar in 1954, and his father was Alec Taylor who played for East End and had taught at Forfar North School for a spell.

David attended Dundee High School, but followed in his father's footsteps by playing for Forfar East End while he studied to become a lawyer. When he moved to the west of Scotland, he played for Westerlands AFC and won the Scottish Amateur Cup with them.

When Jim Farry was sacked from his job as Chief Executive of the SFA in 1999, Taylor got his job and was very active in his efforts to maintain all that was good in Scottish football, earning great plaudits for the organisation of the European Cup final of 2002 at Hampden, overseeing all arrangements including the hospitality offered to the King of Spain.

In 2007 he moved to UEFA. He never forgot his roots, though, and was frequently seen at Forfar's games particularly when they were playing in the west of Scotland, and doing a great deal to prove that an administrator need not be a faceless bureaucrat, but could be a grass roots fan as well.

June 25 1939

It has often been the perception in Forfar that Aberdonians are mean, torn-faced, moaning and cold people.

This is arrant nonsense, of course, and today Aberdeen FC drove another horse and cart through this belief by giving Forfar Athletic a substantial donation to help them through their current financial troubles.

The amount is not specified, and Jim Black said that he was only complying with the wishes of the Aberdeen Directors in not divulging such information. It remains of course not entirely outwith the bounds of possibility that there was a string or two attached, in that maybe Aberdeen would get first option on some promising Forfar youngster, but even if that were the case, it was a gift that was much appreciated by the people of Forfar.

There was of course a certain amount of affection at Pittodrie for Forfar, particularly those who recalled the excellent Frank Hill who had played for both clubs a decade previously, but there was also, perhaps, a realisation that the collapse of one football club was not good news for another and that they were all in this business together.

For whatever reason, the "black and golds" (they did not change to red until after the Second World War) had raised their profile in Forfar. Aberdeen of course were not a poor club, and had recently shared with Celtic the gate for the 1937 Scottish Cup final, for which the attendance remains a record to this day.

June 26 1902

An air of sadness, anxiety and anti-climax hung over Forfar today.

This was meant to be the day of the Coronation of King Edward VII, and the town had been well prepared for weeks with flags, bunting and general celebration with the football clubs all playing their part.

There had already been a Coronation Cup (sometimes called the British League Cup) between Sunderland, Everton, Rangers and Celtic and won by Celtic a week ago, and at a local level Forfar had taken part in a Five-A-Side tournament held at Clepington Park, the home of Dundee Wanderers, reaching the semi-final.

Sadly, two days before his Coronation, the King had "been teen bed" with perityphlitis, a form of intestinal infection akin to appendicitis, and surgery had been required to save his life. The King survived, and his Coronation was eventually held in August, but this did not lessen the disappointment of June. Station Park was going to be deployed for a sports festival, and a particular blow was struck to school children whose day's holiday was suddenly withdrawn by the vindictive School Board!

1902 had been a remarkable year for football, characterised by the horrific Ibrox Disaster on April 5, when 26 people had been killed while watching the Scotland v England game. Forfar had finished half way up the Northern League, neither a triumph nor a disaster, as the great poet Rudyard Kipling might have said.

June 27 1955

It is not very often that a Forfar Athletic player graduates from Edinburgh University, but inside left Wilfred J Allsop, 70 Nolt Loan Road, Arbroath did just that. Having previously passed an Ordinary MA, Wilf graduated with MA Second Class Honours in English.

He was currently playing inside forward for Forfar, and he was able to play inside right or inside left in a forward line which usually read Currie, Allsop, Dunn, Craig and Martin. He was a hard-working, fast running inside forward with very long legs as it always seemed to this six year old who idolised him.

He became a teacher of English, eventually becoming Assistant Head Teacher at Kirkcaldy High School, where he was well respected and loved by his pupils. He lived in Glenrothes. He was not only my boyhood hero for being a football player but in adult life I also idolised him for he was quite the best reciter of Burns poetry at Burns Supper that one was likely to meet, even reciting Tam O' Shanter at a stage of his life where arthritis made it difficult for him to stand straight for any length of time.

Although he also played for Arbroath and Hearts, he recalled with a great deal of affection the men he played with at Forfar with a particular fondness for trainer Davie Ogg, and he was a particular admirer of outside left Tommy Martin. His funeral was one of the best attended that anyone at Kirkcaldy Crematorium could recall.

June 28 1914

The weather was lovely this Sunday with most Churches opening their services with the hymn "Summer Suns Are Glowing". The traditional Forfar Sabbath was relaxed a little in the good weather with families going for a walk or a picnic. Young women revealed a little more flesh than normal in these allegedly sexually repressive times. Youngsters were looking forward to the summer holidays.

Everyone seemed happy, and Forfar Athletic, who had finished the season on a high, announced that they had captured two new players – Gordon Bannerman and David Scrymgeour – for the new season, for which training would be starting soon. These two new players were discussed and dissected on the traditional Forfar walk of "East the toon, Wast the toon, roond the Spoot and hame" as were the prospects for the wee prodigy called Alec Troup who had emerged this last season.

Cricket hadn't gone well yesterday, for both Strathmore and St John's (who played either in the Myrie or the Market Muir) had lost and it was general agreed that Geordie Langlands was a great football player but "nae cricketer".

In the outside world, the Irish Home Rule question was not proving easy to resolve, the Suffragettes were a perpetual nuisance, the Liberals were continuing their fight against the House of Lords ... and some Archduke or other was assassinated at a place called Sarajevo by some Serbian terrorist ... not that *that* was going to affect Forfar at all, was it?

June 29 2013

The artificial pitch at Station Park had been up and running for a season now.

There have been complaints and groans (there always would be, wouldn't there, given the propensity of the human race to become moaning gits now and again?). The general consensus was that it had been a success, although players did say that the pitch played a little better when it was wet.

My own personal feeling was that the longer the game went on, the quicker the ball flew off the pitch but my friend insisted that this was merely an illusion, and that the real reason was that the players were getting more tired!

However that may be, there is little doubt that the artificial pitch has saved Forfar from the financial costs incurred by the many postponements that used to happen in the winter, particularly horrible ones like 2010/11.

Today Forfar announced that they had a device to water the pitch. Many people questioned the necessity of it, and indeed one or two wondered whether today's date was April 1 rather than June 29, but the announcement was made of the Forfar Athletic Patented Artificial Pitch Automated Moisture Application Bowser system (no kidding!).

It was revealed with photographs of it on the website. It was envisaged that it would be used when there was a particularly long period of dry weather – something that was rare in Forfar.

June 30 any year

This is the day on which various things happen.

It is of course exactly half way through the year.

It is usually, give or take a day or two, the day when the schools break up for the summer holidays, and it is, officially, the end and start of the football season in the sense that contracts usually run until June 30, and various transfer windows throughout the world open or "slam shut" as Sky Sports likes to put it.

We are not necessarily all that involved in football at this time – cricket and other sports hold sway at least temporarily – but football is never far away.

Nowadays as the "close season" gets shorter and shorter, the players are usually back doing some training, and this is always said to be the hardest time of year for them, for they really have to prove themselves to be fit.

For a Forfar supporter, there is a passing interest, but nothing all that serious yet.

Some pre-season friendlies are in the offing, perhaps.

There is usually also for a Forfar fan a determination to put the horrors of the previous season behind us (there have been more horrors since 1884 than anything else, if we are to be truthful about it) and to look forward with renewed hope for the new season.

Pandora, in Classical mythology, released all the horrors on the world – defeats from Brechin, hammerings from Arbroath, standing in the teeming rain watching a 3-0 defeat at Stenhousemuir, 3-0 up at half-time against Dumbarton or Albion Rovers or someone and then blowing it – but she also released Hope.

Tickets for the 50/50 draw.

In These Years

Angus Athletic 1884-85. Many of the players in this photograph assisted with the formation of Forfar Athletic.. Back row (left to right) R. Hampton, A. Gordon, W. Cummings, A. Ogilvie, J. Ormond (Trainer). Middle row: D. Smith, J. Menzies, D. Stormonth, D. Christie, A. Lamont, James Black. Front row: W. Anderson, J. Samson.

Forfar Athletic 1890 wwith Forfarshire Charity Cup. Back row (left to right) J. Fyfe (Trainer), Craik, Stormonth, Boath, Forrest, Cable, O. McPherson (President) James Black (Secretary). Middle row: Bowman, Maxwell, Anderson, Lamont, Lyon, Mann. Front row: Dundas, Lindsay.

Northern League Champions 1895-96. Back row, left to right: W. Dalgety, D. Stormonth, J. Jamie, J. Janes, A. Easton, A. Scott, J. Counie, D. Piggot. Middle rows: C. Samson, W. Thomson, J. Cable, A. Black, J. Fenton, R. Boath, D. Fairweather, G. Shepherd, James Black. Front row: W. Anderson, D. McFarlane.

The men who rocked Scotland by their 2-0 win over Falkirk in the Scottish Cup of 1911. Back row (left to right): W. McKay, (Treasurer), C. Malcolm, D. Gibb, W. Paterson, J. Hannah, J. Bowman (Vice-President), J. Prophet. Middle row: J. Jamieson (Financial Secretary), J. Taylor (President), V. Lawrence, W. Chapman, L. Bruce, J. Ferguson, G. Shepherd (Trainer). Front row: P. Lavery, G. Low, A. Bowman (Captain), D. Easson, J. Petrie.

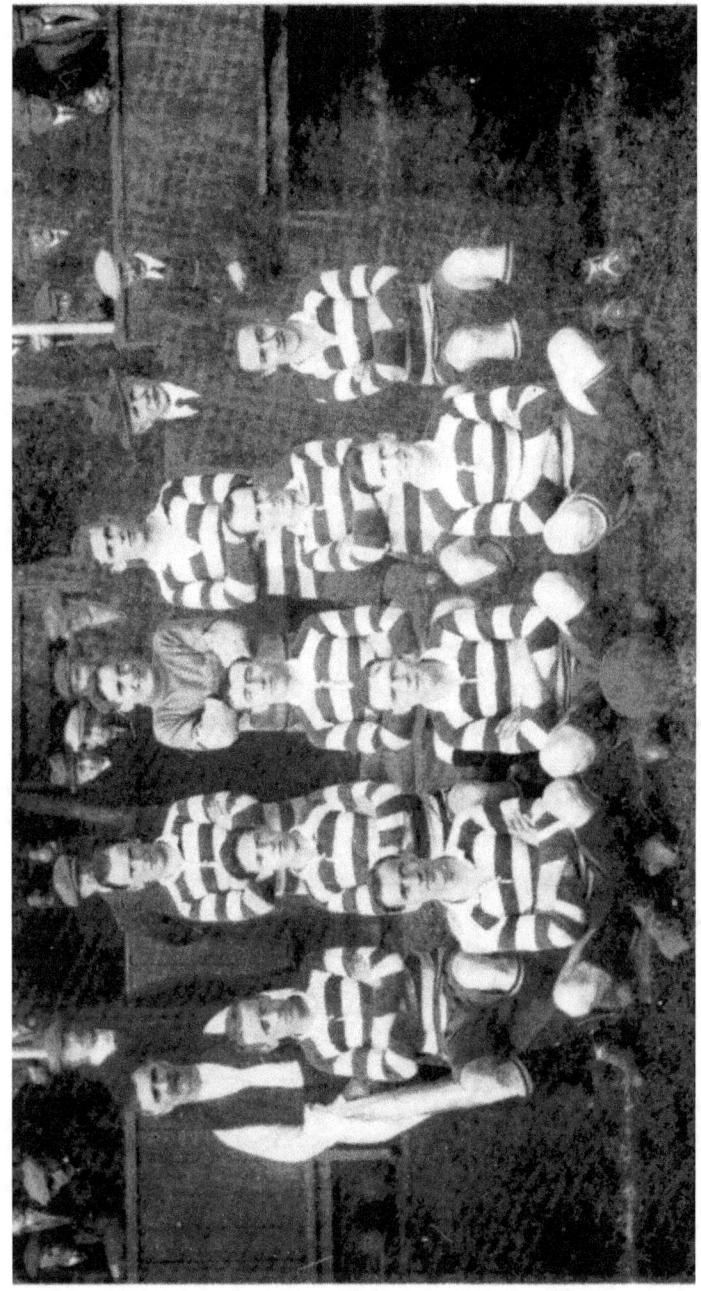

Forfar Athletic 1922-23.

Forfar Athletic 1935-36. Back row (left to right) John Mitchell, Willie McGregor, Newman, Dave McFarlane, Jimmy Morton, Bob Laird, Jimmy Gabriel. Front row: Willie Black, Johnny Bateman, Bob Black, George McLean, Tuck Gardiner

Forfar Athletic 1928 before a game at Stenhousemuir. James Black is half cut off at the back but in the front row are two Scotland Internationals in Frank Hill (second from left) and the unmistakeable bulk of Davie McLean next to him

Forfar Athletic 1928-29. Back row, left to right: W, Menzies, A. Braid, J. Bruce, A. Somers, J. Deuchar. Middle row: G. Shepherd, James Black, J. Mitchell, D. Smith, C. Cameron, A. Wilson, Tom Hanick - sometime Chairman of the club and Provost of the town - and J. Miller. Front row: Peter Craigmyle - from Aberdeen, who refereed many International games and Scottish Cup finals, A. Spence, D. Kilgour, D. McLean, A. Wilson, R. Geckie.

1932 Team. Back row: Smith, Smart, Orchison, Cabrelli, Ramsay, Collie, Ogilvie and Andrew "Skip" Soutar - a great administrator for the club after his playing days were over. Front Row: Allardyce, Lawie, Black, Preston and Duncan.

Forfar Athletic 1932. Front row (left to right): Linton, Wilson, Kilgour, Lowrie, Cabrelli, Black. Back row: Smith, Geddes, Sunter, Collie, Smart

Snow on the ground and body language indicates that January 26 1933 was a very cold day to watch Forfar lose 3-7 to Hibs in a Scottish Cup replay. Back row (left to right) A. Smith, Soutar, Harvey, Smart, Collie, Ogilvie. Front row: Linton, Lawie, R. Black, Cabrelli, Preston

Forfar Athletic 1935-36. Back row (left to right) John Mitchell, Willie McGregor, Newman, Dave McFarlane, Tommy Morton, Bob Laird, Jimmy Gabriel. Front row: Willie Black, Johnny Daleman, Bob Black, George McLean, Tuck Gardiner

1936 team. Back: (Players only) J. Morton, A. Keith, D. McFarlane, R. Laing, A. Lawson, W. Sturrock. Front: R. Black, G. McLean (Captain) W. Black, G. Preston, D. Laing

Presentation of portrait to James Black (on right of his portrait) at Hotel Seaforth, Arbroath in 1949 in token of his services to Scottish football

Forfar Athletic 1948-49. Back row (left to right) S. Liddle, A. Soutar, A. Gerrard, W. McLean. F. Liddle, (committee members). Centre row: D. Ogg (trainer), R. Boath (groundsman), F. Hunter (committee member), J. Rodger, W. Shaw, D. Reid, A. Anderson, J. Wotherspoon, J. Sunter, A. Gall, A. Strachan (committee member). Front row: R. Neil (secretary), W. Gerrard, C. Robbie, J. Massie (captain), James Black (chairman), William Callander (vice-chairman), J. Henderson, R. Cruickshank, G. Morrice, R. Battes (treasurer).

Forfar Athletic 1949. Reid, Anderson, Gall, Massie, Shaw, Crickshanks, Gerrard, Robbie, Rodger, Wotherspoon, Sunter.

Forfar Athletic 1949-50. Back row (left to right) Sam Smith -who would become a dynamic Chairman in 25 years' time, Stevenson, J. Smith, Garrie, Young, Wotherspoon. Front row: Adams, Unknown, Rodger, McLaren, Sunter.

Forfar Athletic players and officials. 1949-50

William F. Callander, Chairman 1951 - 1970

Forfar Athletic 1954 – back row Berrie, Allsop, Crawford, Smith, Stewart, Elder, Herron, Blyth, front row Currie, Trialist, Dunn, Craig and Martin

Forfar Athletic 1954-55. Back row (left to right): Berrie, Blyth, Rough, Stewart, Crawford, Elder. Front row: Currie, Craig, Dunn, Allsop, Martin.

The Loons at Berwick in 1957. Back row (left to right): Stewart. Cormack, Mowatt, Ogilvie, Berrie, Steen.. Front row: Malloy, Dudman, Craig, Weir, Martin.

Forfar Athletic in April 1958. Back row (left to right): Steen, Berrie, Mowatt, Johnston, Ogilvie, Buchan. Front row: Rodger, Russell, Craig, Brodie, Dick.

The Stands - 1: An excellent view of Station Park on February 15 1958 at the Scottish Cup tie between Forfar and Rangers

The Stands - 2: January 1959. The new stand is almost complete and work is in progress on the terracing.

The Stands - 3: The completed article

Forfar Athletic 1958. Back row (Left to right): Ian Steen, Doug Berrie, Jimmy Mowat, Jimmy Johnstone, Bill Ogilvie, Joe Buchan. Front Row: Ian Rodger, Jimmy Russell, Peter Craig, Eric Brodie, Dickie Ewen.

Forfar Athletic 1960-61. Back row (left to right): Doug Berrie, Knox, Mackay, Newman, Mann, Joe Buchan. Front row: Brett, Gray, Coburn, Brodie, Markie.

Forfar Athletic in civvies before a game at Cliftonhill, home of Albion Rovers, in the early 1960s

Forfar Athletic in August 1967. Back row (left to right): Archie Knox, Potter, Ritchie, Walker, Young, Wilson, Keddie, I. Campbell (Trainer). Front row: Wyles, Mathews, Carrie, Malcolm, May.

Forfar Athletic 1968-69, Back row (left to right): Carrie, Grimshaw, Philip, Fyfe, S. Dick, Wyles, Milne. Front row: Mackle, Knox, Young, K. Dick, Stewart.

David Callander, Chairman 1970 - 1976

Archie Knox. Player 1965 - 1970, Manager 1976 - 1980

Forfar Athletic August 1976. Back row (left to right): Murphy, Law, McHugh, Milne, Cairney, Brash, Ritchie. Front row: Clark, Whyte, Kinninmonth, Payne, Kyles, Arbuthnott, Spink.

Forfar Athletic, December 1977. Back row (left to right): Smith, Rankin, Brash, Nicholl, Brown, Gavine, Archie Knox, K. Dick (coach). Front row: Alex Rae, Gallacher, Henry Hall, Clark, Graham, Payne.

Forfar Athletic 1978.

Alex Rae. Manager 1980-1983

Forfar Athletic 1981. Back row (left to right): Alex Carswell (coach), Ian McPhee, Mark Alexander, Raymond Farningham, Rab Morris, Colin Craig, Gerry Burn (physiotherapist). Middle row: Ken Brown, Jim Allan, John Clark, Stewart Kennedy, Ian Boardley, Alex Brash, Neil Watt, Brian Rankin. Front row: Gordon Leitch, Steve Hancock, John Mitchell, Alex Rae (manager), Billy Bennett, Billy Gallacher, Tom O'Rourke, Tom Downie is missing from the photograph..

The Loons of 1982 celebrate their Quarter-final success in the Hampden bath

Forfar Athletic Directors in 1984. Back row (left to right): George Enston, Andrew Lowson, James Robertson, Brian Harlock, A. Smart. Front Row: David Potter, Andrew Gordon Webster, Sam Smith, David McGregor.

FORFAR ATHLETIC FOOTBALL CLUB — CENTENARY SEASON
Club Directory October 1984

Chairman: Sam Smith   Vice-Chairman: Gordon Webster
Match Secretary: David McGregor   Treasurer: David Potter
Directors: George Enston, Bryan Harlock, Gordon Lowson, James Robertson, Al Smart.
Company Secretary: Ian Fleming, c/o MacLean & Lowson.   Financial Adviser: John Seaton
Club Doctor: Dr Duncan Milne   Supporters Club Representative: David Leighton
Manager: Doug Houston   Assistant Manager: Henry Hall   Coach: Dave Nicoll
Physiotherapist: Andy Dickson   Assistant Physiotherapist: Bill McMillan   Groundsman: Will Watson
Kit Supervisor: Norman Knight   Programme Editor: David McGregor   Supporters Club President: David Leighton
Supporters Club Secretary: Mrs Yvonne Nicoll   Supporters Club Treasurer: David Strachan

PLAYING STAFF

	Date of Birth	Date of Signing		Date of Birth	Date of Signing
Archie Bell	12.4.65	1983	Raymond Lorimer	31.8.61	1982
Billy Bennett	5.7.55	1978	Jim Moffat	27.1.60	1983
Alex Brash	21.2.55	1974	Rab Morris	7.3.57	1980
Ken Brown	3.4.56	1977	Gary Murray	19.8.59	1984
John Clark	16.3.58	1978	Kenny McDonald	9.3.61	1982
Bobby Cormack	12.1.58	1982	Ian McPhee	31.1.61	1979
Raymond Farningham	10.4.61	1979	Philip Smith	28.8.60	1982
Billy Gallacher	3.5.58	1977	Ronnie Scott	15.5.61	1984
Stewart Kennedy	21.8.49	1980	Graeme Robb	5.2.65	1984
Gordon Leitch	6.3.60	1980	John Weir	25.2.52	1982
Jim Liddle	9.4.58	1983			

Centenary Season Club Directory

Gordon Webster, Director and Chairman, 1980s

Team with Division Two trophy 1984

Four Managers at Centenary Dance 1985 – Doug Houston, Archie Knox, Alex Rae and Alex Ferguson (then Manager of Aberdeen)

Forfar Athletic 1995-96. Back row (left to right): Bowes, Ross, Mann, Archibald, Glennie,. Middle row: Loney, Bingham, Donegan, Arthur, Craig, McKillop. Front row: Hannihan, Morgan, McPhee, Irvine, McVicar, Paterson.

Neil Wilson - sometime player, Director and Chairman of the club - and always a supporter

Forfar Athletic 1997–98. Back row (left to right): Ally Gray, Jim Peacock (physiotherapist), Donald Ritchie (youth team physio), Malcome Lowe (youth team coach), Raymond Lorimer (reserve team coach), Dougie Craig. Middle row: Andy Cargill, Jimmy Nairn, Ben Honeyman, Mark Bowes, Dean Robertson, Stuart Glennie, Graeme McCheyne, Jamie Loney, John Allison. Front row: Martin McLauchlan, Paul Hannigan, Sean Christie, Jim Hamilton, Ian McPhee (manager), Billy Bennett (assistant manager), Bobby Mann, Alan Morgan, Iain Lee, Paul Roberts.

Veterans of the great days of the late 1970s are re-united some 20 years later. Back row (left to right): Norrie Vannart, Gordon Smith, Ken Brown, Alex Brash, Dave Nicholl, Alex Rae, Kenny Dick. Front row: Billy Gallacher, Billy Gavine, Kenny Payne, Stevie Graham.

Forfar Athletic 1999–2000. Back row (left to right): Stuart Glennie, Jimmy Nairn, Alan Rattray, Stuart Garden, Graeme McCheyne, George Johnston. Middle row: Jim Peacock (physiotherapist), Alex Taylor, Graeme Ferguson, Ralph Brand, Barry McLean, Ross Kiddie, Steven Milne, Paul McLeavy, Innes Macdonald, Jim Moffat (coach). Front row: Craig Robertson, Stuart Ferguson, Euan Donaldson, Dougie Craig, Ian McPhee (manager), Andy Cargill, Gary McPhee, Sean Christie, Roberto Morris.

Dave McGregor welcomes Neil Cooper to the Manager's job in November 2000

Forfar Athletic 2001-02. Back row (left to right): Paul Tosh, Barry Sellars, Neal Ferrie, Barrie Moffat, Michael Brown, Craig Farnan, Kevin Byers. Middle row: Iain Good, Alan Rattray, Robbie Horn, David Williams, Sean Christie, Roberto Morris, Jim Henry, Willie Stewart, Mark Yardley, Kevin Milne. Front row: Brian McCloy, Scott Taylor, Paul Lunan, Dean Walker, Phil Bonnymann (assistant manager), Neil Cooper (manager), Ian Barrett (physiotherapist), Calum Bett, Euan Donaldson.

Ian Miller, Assistant Manager 2004

Forfar Athletic first team squad 2003-04. Back row (left to right): David Williams, Hugh Davidson, Colin Hodge, Paul Tosh, Barry Sellars, Scott Taylor, David McClune, George Shaw. Middle row: Donald Ritchie (assistant physio), Brian McNeill (physiotherapist), Simon Vella, Robbie Horn, Michael Brown, Neal Ferrie, Paul Shields, David Stewart, Darren Henderson, George Browning (goalkeeping coach). Front row: David Lowing, Steve Florence, Paul Lunan, Raymond Stewart (manager), Ian Miller (first team coach), Alan Rattray, Martin Maher, Kevin Byers.

Ray Farningham - player and Manager

*George Shaw, Manager
2006/07*

Forfar Athletic 2008-09. Back row (left to right): Stuart Ferguson, Stephen Tulloch, David Dunn, Andy Tod, Pat Keogh, Graham Gibson, Mark Allison, Ross Campbell. Middle row: Martyn Fotheringham, Sean Kilgannon, Craig Winter, John Gibson, Sandy Wood, Ally Brown, Elliot Smith, Kevin Gordon, Kevin McLeish. Front: Donald Ritchie (assistant sports physio), Johnny Russell, Darren Brady, Dick Campbell (manager), Derek Lilley (captain), Iain Campbell (assistant manager), Barry Donnachie, Stephen McNally, Scott Shepherd (sports therapist).

*Dick Campbell,
Manager 2008 - 2015*

Second Division Playoff Champions 2009-10

Forfar Athletic 2011-12

Odmar Faero - Forfar's Faroese Internationalist in 2013-2014

Forfarshire Cup Winners 2014-15

Forfar Athletic 2014-15

The irrepressible David McGregor who has done everything for them for the past 60 years, except play! A Forfar Athletic polymath. Quite simply, if it hadn't been for David McGregor, there would be no Forfar Athletic! He follows in the tradition of James Black of selfless devotion to the club he loves.

Index

Index

3rd FRV (Forfarshire Reserve Volunteers), 440

A

Aberdeen 215, 332, 464
Aberdeen Bon Accord F.C. 130
Aberdeen F.C 54, 63, 103, 118, 128, 171, 230, 232, 239, 240, 280, 294, 305, 306, 309, 316, 319, 322, 323, 332, 376, 377, 382, 399, 406, 427, 428, 435, 447, 500
   Pittodrie 43, 250, 294, 305, 332, 447
Aberdeen Orion F.C. 87, 437
Aberdeen Press and Journal, The 250, 305
Aberdeen Sunnybank F.C. 97
Aberdeen Victoria F.C. 433
Academy F.C. 17
Academy, Forfar 197, 202, 271, 370
Adam, Charlie 194
Adam, Grant 37, 317
Adam, Hugh 216
Adams, Tommy 57, 97, 98, 100, 105, 131, 158, 280, 294, 351, 473
Addison (Hearts) 290
Agnew (Falkirk) 288
Aird (Rangers) 43
Airdrie 4, 46, 66, 136, 206, 264, 335
Airdrieonians F.C. 66, 136, 175, 206, 264
Airdrie United F.C. 136, 206
   Shyberry Excelsior Stadium 206
Aitken (East Fife) 109
Albion Rovers F.C. 125, 185, 194, 216, 223, 233, 313, 335, 439, 452, 485
   Cliftonhill 223, 335, 485
Alexander, Mark 494
Alexander (Dumbarton) 294
Allan, Lewis 69, 325
Allan, James 119, 290, 369, 495
Allan, Raymond 258, 268
Allardyce, 1930s 465
Allen, (Newcastle United) 376
Allison, D (fruit farmer) 100
Allison, John 503
Allison, Mark 512
Alloa Athletic F.C. xi, 88, 94, 99, 117, 159, 187, 193, 194, 251, 291, 379, 380, 386, 389, 410, 405
   Recreation Park 94, 99, 159, 193, 251, 380, 405
   Indodrill Stadium 405
Allsop, Wilf 139, 140, 178, 187, 232, 449, 476, 477
Anderson, 1890s 287, 393
Anderson, 1920s 124, 138, 237, 250
Anderson, 1960s 182, 309
Andrews, Marvyn 43
Anfield 144
Annfield see Stirling Albion
Angus Athletic F.C. xiv, 440, 456
Annan Athletic F.C. xi, 327
Arbroath 2, 9, 14, 47, 63, 85, 91, 112, 134, 144, 164, 213, 232, 255, 267, 429, 437, 449, 471
Arbroath F.C. 16, 29, 33, 47, 61, 63, 70, 85, 88, 89, 91, 105, 106, 112, 123, 127, 130, 134, 158, 159, 164, 184, 208, 223, 224, 231, 232, 233, 236, 240, 253, 255, 267, 286, 298, 324, 325, 328, 341, 380, 398, 404, 410, 433, 435, 440, 442, 449, 452
   Gayfield 33, 105, 134, 164, 232, 233, 240, 255, 404
Arbroath Herald, The 85, 134, 164
Arbroath Wanderers F.C. 91, 410
Arbuthnott, Scott 490
Archibald, Eric 501
Archibald (Rangers) 436
Armadale F.C. 291, 376, 378, 417
Armistice Day 7, 167

Arnott, Jackie 182, 283, 309
Arthur, Gordon 367, 501
Arthurlie F.C. 354
   Dunterlie Park 354
Ayr Parkhouse F.C. 69
Ayr United F.C. 26, 83, 96, 143, 182, 185, 295, 342, 380, 402
   Somerset Park 69, 182, 402

B

Baillie, (Celtic) 96, 100, 268
Bain, Jamie 23, 26, 220; 1930s 133
Balaclava Rangers F.C. 81
Balderstone, (Queen of the South) 173
Balmashanner 8, 128
Balmoor 26
Bank Restaurant 31, 408
Bannerman, Gordon 201, 450
Bannon, Eamonn (Dundee United) 329
Barcelona F.C. 329, 340
Barclay, Moss 149, 240, 309, 383
Barclay, referee 283
Barkas, Sam 10
Barrett, Ian 507
Bateman, Johnny 234, 462
Bathgate 306, 376, 408
   Mill Park 306
Battes, Bob 471
Baxter Bridie 43
Bayview 78, 122, 161, 338
BBC Home Service 264, 432
Beat, 1890s 253
Beckenbauer, Franz (Germany) 7
Belgium 44, 62, 134
Bell, Archie 293, 347, 389
Bell (Arbroath) 61
Bellamy, (Dundee) 360
Benedictus 401
Bennett, Billy 59, 94, 119, 125, 281, 290, 323, 329, 331, 369, 395, 494, 503

Berrie, Doug 3, 29, 48, 106, 140, 144, 158, 178, 216, 232, 249, 273, 292, 294, 316, 366, 372, 476, 477, 478, 479, 483, 484
Berwick xiii, xiv, 64, 88, 167, 172, 184, 199, 207, 219, 279, 313, 383, 439, 478
Berwick Rangers F.C. xiii, 64, 167, 172, 184, 207, 279, 383, 439
   Shielfield Park 64, 184, 219
Bett, Callum 507
Bett (Rangers) xiii, 296, 357
Bevan (politician) 315
Bingham, David xiii, 159, 170, 203, 359, 367, 501
Binnie, (1920s) 138
Bishop, Jamie 404
Black, Bob v, 27, 155, 215, 224, 277, 306, 388, 462, 463, 468, 470
Black, James xiii, xiv, xvii, 3, 11, 12, 30, 31, 32, 56, 66, 69, 70, 85, 86, 101, 108, 111, 120, 121, 123, 135, 161, 222, 223, 248, 250, 253, 256, 265, 282, 301, 315, 328, 339, 344, 351, 362, 376, 377, 378, 388, 394, 398, 399, 408, 412, 415, 416, 417, 418, 424, 428, 430, 435, 437, 438, 441, 443, 445, 447, 456, 457, 459, 464, 465, 466, 467, 468, 469, 470, 471, 519
Black, Willie 65, 123, 127, 155, 197, 237, 306
Blackie, Billy 59
Blackley, John (Hibs) 265
Blind Jock 2
Blyth, Jim 178, 195, 324, 336, 476, 477
Boardley, Ian 36, 119, 494
Boath, Alan 143
Boath, Bill "Carr" 124, 138, 318
Boath, Bob (groundsman) 471
Boath, 1890s 84, 95, 253, 318, 457, 459
Boghead 141, 183, 272, 282, 326
Bollan, Gary 317, 325, 342, 409

Bo'ness F.C. 301, 417
Bonner, Pat (Celtic) 59, 258, 268
Bonnymann, Phil 507
Bonthrone, Jimmy 109, 158, 216
Borough Briggs *see* Elgin City
Bowes, Mark 501, 503
Bowes-Lyon, Patrick xiv, 123, 414
Bowman, 1890s 84, 130, 393, 457;
Bowman, 1910s 288, 460
Boyle, Paul 379
Boys Brigade vii, 1
Bradford Park Avenue F.C. 10
Bradman, Don (cricketer) 17, 429
Bradshaw (Sheffield United) 28
Brady, Darren 512
Braid, Andrew 101, 138, 445, 464
Bramall Lane *see* Sheffield United
Brand, Ralph 118, 292, 505
Brash, Alex xiii, 51, 88, 94, 119, 143, 148, 157, 173, 227, 281, 290, 293, 323, 347, 357, 369, 371, 379, 490, 491, 494, 504
Brazil, Ally 59, 258, 268
Brechin 14, 25, 58, 93, 111, 197, 240, 249, 256, 293, 319, 341, 346, 352, 383, 397, 398, 403, 418, 428, 429, 445
Brechin City xi, 1, 4, 11, 18, 47, 48, 58, 93, 106, 111, 112, 125, 127 163, 196, 232, 234, 240, 256, 293, 335, 352, 383, 390 397, 398, 403, 418, 428, 435, 445, 452
  Glebe Park 58
Brechin Dalhousie F.C. 440
Brechin Harp F.C. 93
Brechin Hearts F.C. 93
Brett, Chris 484
Brewster, Craig xiii, 59, 67, 194, 258, 268, 329, 389, 409
Bricklayers F.C. 17
Bridgeford, Frank 61, 306, 326
bridie 2, 21, 148, 210, 295
Bridie xiii, 21

Brines, (referee) 404
Bristol City F.C. 86
Brittle, (referee) 260
Broadwood 317
Brockville Park *see* Falkirk
Brodie, Eric 48, 142, 273, 321, 334, 365, 380, 479, 483, 484
Broughty Ferry 13, 440
Brown, Ally 47, 172;
Brown, Ken xiii, 35, 94, 119, 140, 143, 173, 200, 290, 293, 307, 323, 347, 357, 369, 371, 491, 494, 504
Brown, Michael 507, 509
Brown, Willie 200, 223
Browning, George 509
Browning, (Celtic) 299
Brownlee, Chic 97, 196
Brownlie (Hibs) 265
Brownlie (Third Lanark) 339
Broxburn 328, 408, 417
Bruce, Jock 124, 138, 250, 266, 301, 338, 445, 464
Bruce, 1900s 7, 131, 288, 299, 418, 460
Buchan, Joe 48, 273, 479, 483, 484
Buckley, (St Johnstone) 280
Burn, Gerry 494
Burns, (politician) 44
Burns, Robert (poet) 153, 253, 267, 449
Butcher, (Motherwell) 104
Byers, Kevin 199, 507, 509
Byrne, (Hearts) 290

C

Cable, "Jeck" 3, 81, 87, 95, 102, 130, 134, 253, 278, 287, 393, 424, 457, 459
Cabrelli, Peter 85, 465, 466, 467
Cairney, Mike 490
Cairns, Willie 395
Cairns (Rangers) 436
Caldow, Eric (Rangers) 273

Caledonian Bar 410
Caley Thistle 90
Callander, David xv, 52, 449
Callander, William, xiv, 189, 431, 471, 472, 476
Callanders F.C. 17
Cameron, Jimmy 155, 208, 215, 376, 388, 464
Campbell, Dick xv, 33, 41, 43, 69, 136, 204, 242, 341, 342, 367, 396, 404, 405, 512, 513
Campbell, Ian 284,486
Campbell, Ross 136, 142, 412, 512,
Campbell, Tommy 171, 341, 367
Camsell (Middlesbrough) 392
Canada xiv, 8, 407, 422, 423
Canadian Select 423
Cant (East Fife) 338
Capper (Dundee) 181
Cappielow *see* Greenock Morton
Cargill, Andy 118, 366, 503, 505
Cargill 1900s 93
Carnegie, Angus 379
Carnegie (capitalist) v, 65, 299, 363,
Carnoustie 248
Carolina Port 102, 160, 298, 393
Carrabine (Third Lanark) 147
Carrie (Ally) 129, 149, 176, 201, 219, 283, 352, 410, 486, 487
Carry (sometimes spelt Carrie) Cup 201, 352, 410
Carswell, Alec 286, 494
Caskie, Jimmy xiii, 98, 169
"C" Division 11, 18, 54, 169, 255, 414, 439
Celtic F.C. 17, 18, 22, 31, 42, 43, 52, 59, 63, 68, 70, 78, 83, 84, 85, 86, 96, 98, 99, 100, 102, 106, 108, 109, 118, 120, 131, 141, 144, 146, 147, 148, 155, 158, 160, 162, 167, 169, 173, 175, 176, 185, 195, 198, 200, 208, 214, 216, 219, 223, 232, 239, 258, 267, 268, 272, 278, 280, 282, 284, 287, 288, 289, 292, 294, 299, 305, 306, 318, 321, 323, 337, 354, 357, 360, 373, 377, 382, 388, 389, 390, 397, 398, 399, 406, 407, 408, 413, 415, 418, 419, 424, 432, 434, 436, 447, 448
Celtic Park 42, 43, 59, 63, 78, 83, 96, 148, 214, 357
Celtic "B" 17
Centenary Dance xv, 500
Central and the Northern League 394
Central League 12, 18, 62, 134, 231, 318, 328, 337, 378, 394, 398, 428
Central Park *see* Cowdenbeath
Chalali (Aberdeen) 239
Chamberlain (Prime Minister) 117
Chapman, 1910s 134, 231, 256, 288, 299, 337, 460
Chirnside United F.C. xiii, 107
Christie, D 1880s 278, 456
Christie, Frank 395
Christie, Sean 503, 505, 507
Churchill, Winston (Prime Minister) 88, 117, 269
Clackmannan F.C. 108
Clark, John 59, 67, 94, 119, 143, 153, 157, 173, 194, 227, 258, 268, 290, 307, 323, 329, 340, 347, 358, 364, 369 371, 389, 411, 490, 491, 494
Clepington Park (Tannadice) *see* Dundee United
Cliftonhill *see* Albion Rovers
Clinging, Iain 258
Cloy (Queen of the South) 153
Clyde F.C. vii, xi, 29, 101, 156, 157, 158, 180, 194, 220, 271, 289, 304, 309, 316, 317, 344, 360, 372
Shawfield 101, 157, 158, 271, 277, 289
Clydebank F.C. xi, 136, 252, 276, 281
Kilbowie Park 252
Coburn, Jackie 158, 216, 294, 316, 334, 381, 484

Collie, Jim 85, 155, 388, 465, 466, 467
Collier (Raith Rovers) 19, 188
Collington (Dundee United) 155
Collins (Celtic) 96, 268, 373
Commercial Hotel 105, 324
Connelly, Charlie 251
Connon, Jackie 108, 291, 306, 326
Consolation Cup 248, 328
Cook, Willie 101, 131
Cooper, Neil (Manager) xv, 506, 507
Cooper (Rangers) 307, 359, 379
Cord, John 292
Cormack, Bobby 103, 281, 293, 323, 329, 478
Cormie, Tommy 142, 273
Cornock, Matt 266
Coronation Cup 448
Counie J., 1890s 459
County Cup 253
Coupar Angus 53, 187
Couttie, 1890s 211, 298
Cowan (Manchester City) 10
Cowdenbeath F.C. xi, 1, 4, 49, 70, 71, 142, 152, 195, 197, 204, 225, 270, 315, 322, 330, 377, 396, 397
   Central Park 49, 142, 197
Cowie, 1890s 137, 322,
Cowie (Dundee) 395
Cowlairs F.C. 81
Cox, David 23, 220
Coyle, Frazer 55
Coyne (Celtic) 268
Craig, Albert 139, 140, 178, 187, 232, 264, 300, 336, 372, 373, 375, 449, 476, 477
Craig, Peter 48, 273, 292, 321, 478, 479, 483
Craig, Steven 342, 367, 501
Craiglockhart 269
Craigmyle (referee) 464
Craik, 1890s 457
Crawford, George 178, 336, 476, 477
Crichton, 1890s 343

Croall (Falkirk) 288
Crockatt, Bert 245
Crowe, Gilbert 232, 260
Cruickshank, Dick 57, 97, 169, 196, 471, 472
Cruickshanks, (Chairman) 324
Crum (Celtic) 388, 432
Cummings, 1880s 456
Cunningham, George 49, 96, 100, 200
Cunningham (Rangers) 436
Currie, Bill 178, 236, 449, 476, 477

D

Dailly, Christian (Dundee United) 409
Daleman, Johnny 468
Dalgety W. 1880s 459
Dalglish, Kenny (Scotland) 148, 390
Dall (John) 124
Dartford F.C. 19
Darvel Juniors F.C. 236
Davidson, David 108, 376, 427
Davidson, Hugh 206, 509
Davidson, Willie 108
Davin (Dumbarton) 326
Davis (Rangers) 273
Dawson William 124, 138
Dawson (Rangers) 307
Dean (Everton) 392
Deane (Sheffield United) 28
Dear, William 124, 138
Deasley, Bryan 404
Delaney (Celtic, Falkirk) 182, 200, 249, 309, 388
Denholm, Danny 41, 69, 317, 401
Dens Park see Dundee
Derry City F.C. 200
Deuchar, James 464
Devanney (Celtic) 100
Devine, Frankie xiii, xviii
Dick, Kenny 78, 149, 176, 182, 249, 271, 345, 356, 370, 403, 423, 487, 491, 504

Dick, Len 60, 232, 273, 292, 300, 479
Dingwall 38, 367, 383
Disraeli, Benjamin (Prime Minister) 13
Division B 336, 351
Division Two xv, 65, 90, 124, 184, 202, 213, 251, 316, 342, 396, 408, 415, 499
Docherty, 1900s 131
Dodds, (Celtic) 299
Dodds,(Rangers) 304
Dods, Darren 401
Doig (Arbroath) 106, 130
Don (Dundee Wanderers) 137
Donaldson, Euan 118 505, 507
Donaldson, W G (Minister)
Donegan, John 501
Donnachie, Barry 512
Doonhamers *see* Queen of the South
Dossing (Dundee United) 283
Dougan, 1960s 316
Douglas, Rab xiii, 57, 69, 204, 205, 401
Dougray (referee) 360
Downie, Ian 203
Downie, Tom 494
Doyle (Celtic) 148, 185
Draffen's 140
Drummond, Bob 124, 138
Ducat (England) 362
Dudman, Len 292, 478
Duff, Ian 97
Dumbarton F.C. 1, 9, 23, 34, 96, 118, 141, 165, 183, 272, 282, 294, 326, 364, 380, 439, 452
Dumfries 48, 153, 203, 222
Duncan, Bob 85, 326, 465
Duncan (Raith Rovers) 188
Dundas, Jamie 81, 130, 198, 424, 457
Dundee 9, 16, 19, 25, 34, 81, 84, 86, 87, 100, 120, 132, 137, 140, 148, 186, 208, 211, 271, 278, 282, 284, 286, 332, 375, 393, 428, 438, 440, 442, 446

Dundee "A" 25, 395
Dundee Courier, The 4, 9, 10, 16, 22, 25, 49, 60, 62, 70, 93, 100, 117,123, 134, 139, 161, 164, 186, 216, 234, 236, 287, 322, 333, 337, 344, 352, 362, 363, 376, 381, 395, 399, 406, 414, 417, 440
Dundee East End F.C. 393, 433, 437, 440
Dundee F.C. xiv, 6, 9, 11, 16, 18, 19, 25, 29, 34, 35, 36, 37, 38, 45, 47, 54, 55, 56, 60, 61, 62, 63, 67, 69, 70, 86,102, 103, 111, 112, 118, 123, 124, 155, 158, 160, 167, 181, 187, 214, 216, 231, 232, 236, 253, 260, 271, 280, 282, 287, 288, 293, 298, 305, 308, 313, 319, 333, 337, 340, 346, 360, 361, 362, 381, 382, 389, 395, 409, 415, 427, 435, 436, 437
  Dens Park 16, 25, 37, 47, 62, 102, 111, 118, 120, 158, 214, 271, 282, 305, 309, 324, 346, 363, 382, 395
Dundee Harp F.C. 93
Dundee Hibernian F.C. 60
Dundee Hibs F.C. 9, 70, 86, 132, 179, 398, 445
Dundee Our Boys F.C. 102, 433, 437, 440
Dundee Strathmore F.C. 440
Dundee United F.C. 11, 16, 19, 29, 34, 38, 55, 60, 67, 103, 112, 118, 132, 140, 155, 169, 171, 186, 208, 282, 283, 293, 323, 329, 334, 340, 390, 409, 435, 439, 445
  Tannadice Park 38, 43, 86, 132, 140, 155, 169, 179, 186, 282, 283, 329, 409, 442, 448
Dundee Violet F.C. 171
Dundee Wanderers F.C. 84, 137, 179, 201, 248, 433, 442, 448
Dunfermline, 363
Dunfermline Athletic F.C. 65, 110, 136, 170, 179, 202, 210, 216, 285, 328

Dunlop, Michael 69
Dunn, Willie 53, 106, 126, 139, 140, 144, 178, 232, 260, 336, 372, 375, 449, 476, 477, 512
Dunterlie Park see Arthurlie
Duthie, James 249, 283
Dykehead F.C. 266
  Parkside Park 266
Dziekanowski (Celtic) 258, 268

E

Eassie 17
Easson, Dave 288, 299, 378, 460
East End F.C. 22, 50, 102, 106, 108, 110, 195, 216, 278, 393, 399, 433, 437, 440, 446
Easter Road see Hibernian
Eastern League 12, 18, 70, 181, 362, 395, 398
Eastern Section 11
East Fife F.C. xi, 22, 48, 78, 109, 116, 122, 125, 161, 179, 206, 328, 338, 368, 381
  Methil 161
Easton, Allan 253, 298, 459
East Pilton Park *see* Edinburgh City
East Stirlingshire F.C. xi, 11, 18, 112, 125, 162, 165, 170, 172, 193, 221, 252, 312, 313, 325, 334, 344, 350, 359, 369, 383, 439
  Firs Park 313, 344, 369
Edgar (East Fife) 338
Edinburgh 60, 65, 100, 103, 138, 185, 202, 212, 265, 269, 369, 424, 449
Edinburgh City F.C. xi, 11, 18, 40, 112, 208, 245, 325, 368
  East Pilton Park 208, 245
Edinburgh University F.C. 202, 269, 449
Edward, 1900s 137, 164, 197, 201, 277, 448
Elder, Sandy 139, 178, 232, 372, 476, 477

Elgin City F.C. 165
  Borough Briggs 165
Ellacott, 1960s 294
Empire Exhibition Trophy 22, 432
English Premier League 28
Enston, George 496
Evans, (Celtic, Raith Rovers) 96, 100, 227
Evening Telegraph, The 27, 233
Evening Times, The 309, 331, 373
Everton F.C. vii, 111, 169, 236, 392, 432, 448
Ewen, Dickie 64, 86, 182, 309, 483
Ewen, Roy 365
Ewen, 1920s 86

F

FA Cup 376
Faero, Odmar xvi, 516
Fagan (Albion Rovers) 335
Fairweather, 1890s 201, 324, 333, 459
Falconer, Eddie xiii, 97, 255, 288, 289
Falkirk F.C. xi, xiv, 1, 9, 131, 168, 175, 200, 278, 281, 288, 293, 299, 305, 306, 313, 344, 364, 372, 389, 399, 460
  Brockwille Park 278
Fallon (Celtic) 100
Farnan, Craig 507
Farningham, Raymond xiii, xv, 35, 45, 51, 88, 110, 119, 125, 193, 210, 281, 290, 293, 295, 296, 323, 347, 364, 369, 371, 494, 510
Faroe Islands 83
Farry (SFA) 446
Fascism 197, 377
Fearn, Jack 100
Fenton, John 352, 360, 410, 459
Ferguson, Ernie 378
Ferguson, Graeme 505
Ferguson, Ian 366
Ferguson, Stuart 505, 512

Ferguson, Willie (referee) 270
Ferguson (Aberdeen) 500
Ferguson (Clyde) 220
Fergusons 62
Ferrie, Neal 507, 509
Finlay (referee) 155
Finnie (referee) 257
Fir Park *see* Motherwell
Firhill Park *see* Partick Thistle
Firs Park *see* East Stirlingshire
First Division 1, 51, 56, 67, 103, 109, 111, 158, 204, 212, 216, 252, 268, 281, 283, 288, 305, 313, 315, 318, 331, 341, 347, 369, 373, 380, 397, 399, 435, 439
Five-A-Side 16, 17, 442, 448
Fleming (East Fife) 109
Florence, Steve 509
Flucker (St. Bernard's) 368
Foo Lang Since 379
Forbes, David 256
Forfar Academy 197, 202, 271, 370
Forfar Angus F.C. 440
Forfar Athletic Handbook xvii
Forfar Athletic F.C. i, iii, v, vii, 1, 3, 13, 16, 17, 19, 21, 24, 25, 30, 31, 32, 35, 56, 63, 70, 91, 98, 107, 108, 112, 117, 120, 122, 144, 173, 178, 182, 198, 201, 208, 218, 219, 221, 223, 231, 245, 248, 253, 286, 301, 313, 322, 328, 329, 334, 339, 347, 351, 363, 376, 392, 393, 394, 395, 399, 404, 407, 408, 412, 414, 415, 417, 418, 423, 426, 427, 428, 429, 430, 431, 436, 437, 438, 440, 442, 443, 445, 446, 447, 449, 450, 451
Station Park xiii, 1, 2, 3, 7, 8, 14, 15, 17, 21, 23, 24, 28, 29, 34, 35, 43, 48, 49, 52, 54, 55, 57, 60, 61, 63, 65, 66, 68, 78, 81, 84, 87, 89, 91, 94, 96, 100, 102, 104, 107, 108, 109, 110, 117, 119, 123, 126, 127, 128, 129, 130, 137, 139, 141, 143, 147, 148, 160, 162, 165, 167, 170, 173, 178, 183, 184, 187, 188, 189, 194, 195, 199, 200, 201, 207, 210, 211, 213, 214, 215, 216, 220, 221, 233, 234, 236, 237, 239, 240, 242, 250, 251, 252, 256, 257, 258, 264, 266, 267, 268, 270, 271, 273, 278, 280, 281, 283, 285, 288, 291, 293, 294, 295, 297, 298, 299, 301, 308, 315, 316, 319, 321, 322, 329, 333, 343, 351, 356, 359, 364, 366, 368, 370, 372, 373, 379, 381, 383, 387, 392, 396, 397, 401, 403, 404, 405, 424, 426, 438, 442, 445, 448, 451, 480
Steele Park 8
Forfar Athletic Patented Artificial Pitch Automated Moisture Application Bowser system 451
Forfar Athletic Supporters' Club 24
Forfar Celtic F.C. 70, 106, 108, 195, 436
Forfar Dispatch, The 4, 8, 32, 46, 54, 57, 94, 105, 127, 133, 245, 255, 371, 377, 403, 412
Forfar East End F.C. 22, 106, 108, 393, 446
Forfar Games 24, 32, 394
Forfar Herald, The 62, 95, 102, 160, 161, 195, 211, 253, 287, 298
Forfar "Farfar" Holiday Week 30, 31, 32, 34, 35
Forfar Instrumental Band 24, 54, 324, 363
Forfar North End F.C. 195, 214, 231, 392, 399, 441
Forfar West End F.C. 399, 414, 438, 440
Forfarshire 34, 35, 86, 111, 112, 137, 198, 240, 253, 278, 298, 324, 333, 343, 363, 410, 440
Forfarshire Charity Cup xiv, 457
Forfarshire Cup xvi, 6, 34, 35, 111, 112, 240, 253, 298, 324, 333, 363, 517
Forres xi, xiii, 243, 244
Forres Mechanics F.C. xi, 244
Forrest, Eddie 47

Forrest, 1890s 457
Forrest (Aberdeen) 128
Forsyth (Rangers) 307
Forthbank *see* King's Park F.C.
Fotheringham, Martyn xiii, 41, 43, 69, 165, 166, 220, 317, 401, 404, 512
Fox, John 306, 326
Fraser, 1940s 43, 395
Fulton (Raith Rovers, Celtic) 215, 258, 268
Fyfe, John 122, 176, 284, 370, 457, 487

G

Gabriel, Jimmy 46, 155, 183, 344, 388, 462, 468
Gaffie 139, 245, 285
Gala Fairydean F.C. 265, 304
Gall, Andy 471, 472
Gallacher, Billy "Seagull" 51, 88, 94, 119, 125, 173, 185, 209, 281, 293, 307, 323, 329, 347, 358, 364, 369, 411, 423, 491, 494, 504
Gallacher (Airdrie) 136, 301, 406
Gallacher (Celtic) xiii, 298, 299, 306, 415
Gallagher (Dumbarton) 272
Galloway (Celtic) 258
Gallowshade Fruit Farm 100, 128
Garden, Stewart 118, 505
Gardiner, Tuck 462, 468
Garrie, 1940s 473
Gavine, Billy 143, 173, 185, 307, 491, 504
Gayfield *see* Arbroath
Gayle (Sheffield United) 28
Geatons (Celtic) 388
Geddes, 1930s 85, 466
Geekie, Bob 256, 464
Gemmell (Celtic) 413
Germany 7, 45, 127, 200, 277, 365, 390, 419, 430
Gerrard, Eck 132, 196, 445, 471, 472
Gibb, Dickie 86, 131, 137, 288, 352, 363, 460

Gibson, Billy 308
Gibson, Graham 512
Gibson, John 512
Gie *(sic)* Gordons Broadcasting Band 24
Gilbert, John 62, 133, 260
Gilfeather, Doris 24
Gilhaney (Stenhousemuir) 342
Gillespie, Alex (Headmaster) vii, 271
Gilligan, Sam 86
Gilzean (Dundee) 35, 37, 271
Glasgow vii, 11, 31, 41, 51, 103, 138, 147, 153, 157, 158, 173, 184, 196, 206, 234, 260, 267, 299, 308, 316, 318, 319, 329, 331, 335, 351, 360, 366, 372, 398, 415, 419, 424, 426, 432, 435
Glasgow Rangers F.C. *see* Rangers F.C.
Glebe Park *see* Brechin City F.C.
Glennie, Bobby 194, 367, 501, 503, 505
Glenrothes v, 232, 379, 449
Glidden (Hearts) 294
Godfrey, Tom 306, 326
Good, Adam 236, 289
Good, Iain 507
Gordon, Kevin 512
Gowans, "Chappie" 25, 131, 363
Graham, Stevie 143, 173, 307, 407, 491, 504
Grainger, John 101
Grant Mr. (Vice Chairman) 324
Grant (Celtic) 258
Grant (St.Bernard's) 368 v, 37, 258, 317, 324, 368
Gray, Ally 503
Gray, Frank 138, 484
Gray, Jim 149, 182, 269, 309
Great War 9, 12, 70, 86, 120, 133, 134, 167, 181, 183, 222, 339, 398, 406
Greenock Morton F.C. xi, 9, 46, 47, 49, 155, 178, 194, 224, 300, 306, 309, 330, 344, 388, 389, 403, 436, 462, 468, 469
  Cappielow 178, 194, 300, 309
Greig (Rangers) 284, 307, 340

Gretna F.C. 136, 218, 251
  Raydale Park 218
Gribben, Darren 55, 218
Grimmond, Alec 379
Grimshaw, George 487
Guelph Oaks 407, 411, 423
Guernica 377
Guild, Alan 122, 370
Guthrie, Charlie 221

H

Haddock (Clyde) 157, 158, 220, 372
Haffey (Celtic) 36
Haig, Douglas (General) 7, 167, 369
Haimes, Andrew 372
Hall, Henry xiii, 15, 59, 143, 171, 173, 209, 307, 491
Hamill, Alec v, 59, 170, 258, 268, 315, 329
Hamilton, Alex 100, 200, 345
Hamilton, Jim 503
Hamilton (Dundee) 49, 271,
Hampden Park *see* Queen's Park F.C.
Hampton, 1880s 456
Hancock, Steve 88, 119, 290, 319, 369, 494
Hanick, Tom (Provost) 31, 98, 111, 388, 408, 464
Hannan, 1910s 288, 460
Hannigan, Paul 367, 503
Harlock, Brian (Director) 496
Harp F.C. 93, 428, 433, 440
Harper, Eric 97, 200
Harper (Aberdeen) 128
Harris, Gordon 149
Harrison (Leith) 212
Harrow, George 292
Hartley (Dundee) 37
Harvey, 1900s 131
Harvey, 1930s 467
Haugh Works 27
Hay, Kerr 69
Hay (Celtic) 131, 339, 390

Hazel, Nigel (cricketer) 14
Heart of Midlothian (Hearts) F.C. 1, 18, 93, 103, 138, 140, 142, 173, 218, 232, 249, 286, 288, 290, 293, 318, 319, 332, 368, 369, 373, 375, 389, 424, 449
  Tynecastle 103, 286, 290, 294, 375
Hearts of Beath F.C, 332
Heddle, Ian 90, 170, 203
Hegarty, Paul 268, 329
Helensburgh F.C. 354
Henderson, Darren 104, 509
Henderson, George 124, 181, 436
Henderson, James 245, 255, 471
Henderson, Sandy 249, 283, 309
Henry, Jim 507
Herbert (Montrose) 127
Hermiston (Aberdeen) 128
Heron, James 237, 250
Herron, 1950s 476
Hibernian (Hibs) F.C. 9, 18, 60, 69, 70, 86, 103, 132, 138, 169, 179, 212, 232, 265, 272, 325, 368, 398, 445, 467
  Easter Road 265
Highland League 165, 199, 383
Hill, Darren 41
Hill, Frank 61, 233, 266, 291, 306, 326, 376, 406, 427, 429, 447, 463
Hillsborough, Sheffield 362
Hilson, Dale 136, 402
Hinshelwood (Morton) 178
Hitler, Adolph 197
HMRC 20
Hodge, Colin 69, 509
Hogg (Celtic) 388
Holiday Week *see* Forfar Holiday Week
Holley (England) 339
Holt, John 268,
Holt (Dundee United) 340
Honeyman, Ben 503
Hood (Queen of the South) 173
Hopcroft, Bobby 379
Hope, Kenny (referee) 353, 452

Horn, Robbie 507, 509
Houston, Doug xiii, 15, 110, 135, 358, 364, 390, 500
Hubbard (Rangers) 182, 292
Huddersfield Town F.C. 10, 155
Hughes, Pat 283
Hunter, Ferg (committee member) 471
Hunter (East Fife) 161
Hunter (Dundee) 360
Huntly F.C. 199
Husband, Bob 306,
Husband, Jackie (Partick Thistle) 366
Hutcheson, 1900s 131
Hutton, Guy 250, 258

I

Ibrox *see* Rangers
Indodrill Stadium *see* Alloa Athletic
Ingram, John 100, 200, 223
Inverleithen 209
Inverness 18, 90, 199, 437
Inverness Caledonian Thistle F.C. 90
 Telford Street 90
Ireland 70, 139, 301, 306, 343, 345, 394
Irvine, Andy 346, 501

J

Jack, David 87, 112, 134, 202, 376, 395
Jackson (Queen of the South) 176
Jackson (Rangers) 307
James (Raith Rovers) 188, 215
Jamieson, James (Treasurer) 394, 399, 460
Janes, John 84, 137, 253, 343, 442, 459
Jardine (Dumbarton) 294
Jarman's Hotel 105, 377, 394, 430
Jeffrey, David 101, 445
Joe Anderson's XI 86

Johnston, George 505
Johnston, James 479
Johnston (referee) 352
Johnstone, Alec 86, 97
Johnstone, 1920s 181
Johnstone (Celtic) 299
Joyner, Francis 308
Junior (usually a pseudonym for a triallist) 70, 93, 176, 224, 242, 309, 316, 379, 381, 393, 399, 428

K

Kader, Omar 43, 401
Kay (Dundee United) 155
Keddie Dave 89, 486
Keith, Anson 438, 469
Keith (Brechin City 234
Kelly, James 85, 249
Kennaway (Celtic) 388
Kennedy, Dennis 182, 249, 309
Kennedy, Michael 401
Kennedy, Stewart iv, xiii, 34, 36, 51, 58, 59, 94, 95, 125, 157, 202, 290, 307, 329, 347, 364, 369, 389, 494
Keogh, Pat 512
Kerr, Jerry (Manager) 313
Kichenbrand, Don 249
Kidd (Hearts) 290
Kidd (Dundee) 389
Kiddie, Ross 505
Kilbowie Park *see* Clydebank
Kilgannon, Sean 33, 165, 213, 512
Kilgannon (Dumbarton) 294
Kilgour, Davie 3, 19, 111, 162, 222, 256, 301, 376, 464, 466
Killacky, John 42
Kilmarnock F.C. 1, 53, 54, 69, 96, 139, 158, 233, 281, 364, 372, 382, 389
King, David 47
King's Park F.C. 11, 224, 237, 256
Kinnaird (Dundee United) 329
Kinninmonth, Alec 490

Kirkcaldy 19, 45, 188, 208, 215, 227, 283, 362, 370, 449
Kirkcaldy United F.C. 328, 428
Kirkwood, (Dundee United) 329
Kirriemuir 81, 129, 270, 298, 301, 429
Kirrie Thistle F.C. 270
Kivlichan (Celtic) 131
Knox, Archie xv, 8, 63, 135, 143, 173, 176, 209, 216, 219, 221, 239, 284, 307, 345, 356, 371, 382, 390, 407, 411, 423, 484, 486, 487, 489, 491, 500
Knox, Bill 158, 167, 294, 316
Kopel, Scott 203
Kruzycki (East Fife) 78
Kyles, Jimmy 379, 490

L

Laing, David 256, 277, 344, 469
Laird, Bob 46, 133, 155, 215, 344, 462, 468
Lamb (Baillie) 363, 440
Lambie, John (Partick Thistle) 366
Lamont, Alec "Wappie" 81, 198, 278, 456, 457
Langlands, Geordie "Purkie" xiv, 44, 86, 93, 101, 124, 131, 132, 134, 138, 161, 231, 237, 299, 324, 333, 337, 360, 361, 362, 363, 409, 450
Larkhall Royal Albert F.C. 198
Lasley (Motherwell) 104
Lavery, 1910s 288, 460
Law, Mark 221, 490
Lawie, Charlie 85, 162, 188, 465, 467
Lawrence, John 100, 200, 223, 236, 288, 460
Lawrence, Valentine 9, 288, 460
Lawson, Alf 133, 377, 469
League Challenge Cup 33, 41, 45, 47, 55, 83, 118
League Cup 41, 43, 47, 48, 49, 50, 53, 57, 59, 60, 64, 67, 68, 78, 83, 88, 96, 100, 103, 104, 109, 118, 119, 136, 140, 141, 142, 143, 144, 146, 147, 173, 185, 202, 214, 223, 227, 239, 249, 272, 289, 292, 307, 309, 439, 448
Lee, Iain 503
Lee, Jennie (politician) 315
Lee, Walter 14
Legge, Robert 158, 167
Leighton, 1910s 134, 299
Leishman (Dunfermline) 210
Leitch, Gordon 119, 125, 290, 319, 369, 494
Leith Athletic F.C. 11, 18, 112, 137, 212, 265, 326, 368
   Marine Gardens 212
   Meadowbank 212
Leslie, Alan 258
Letham xiv, 17, 130, 355
Liddle, Jim xiv, 51, 110, 125, 202, 281, 293, 323, 347, 358, 359, 389, 471
Lilley, Derek 172, 512
Lindertis 81, 129
Lindsay, Peter 457
Links Park see Montrose
Linlithgow Rose F. C. xi, 241, 242, 257
   Prestonfield 242
Linton, William 85, 395, 466, 467
Linwood (Morton) 178
Lister, Jim 23, 220, 317, 325
Livingston F.C. xi, 263, 314, 369
Lochee village 428
Lochee Harp F.C. 433
Lochee United F.C. 211, 237, 322, 410, 428, 437
Lochgelly 315
Lochgelly United F.C. 179, 328, 333
Lochgilphead F.C. 81
Logan (Raith Rovers) 188
Logan (Falkirk) 288
Logie Green see St Bernard's
Lombardi, Michele 295
London, Ontario 423
Loney, Jamie 501, 503
Loney (Celtic) 131
Longworth (England) 362

Lorimer, Raymond 51, 67, 177, 258, 268, 281, 323, 329, 347, 364, 389, 503
Lossiemouth 132
Love Street see St Mirren
Low, Geordie 288, 460
Lowe, Malcolm 379, 503
Lowing, David 47, 295, 509
Lowrie, 1930s 466
Lowson, Albert 496
Lumsden, Craig 45
Lunan, Paul 47, 507, 509
Lynch, Mary 24
Lyon 1890s 457
Lyons 364, 389

Mac/Mc

Macartney (cricketer) 429
McAtee (Celtic) 299
McCabe, Neil 24, 43
McCafferty, Thomas 258, 364
McCahill (Celtic) 258
McCheyne, Graeme 118, 503, 505
McCloy, Brian 507
McClune, David 47, 509
McCluskey, James 100, 200
McCluskey, Jamie 136
McCoist (Rangers) 43
McColl (Celtic) xiii, 298, 299
McColl (Rangers) 292
McConnell, 1900s 93
McConville (Kilmarnock) 364
McCormick, Steven 159, 341, 367
McCorquodale (Dumbarton) 294
McCoy (Hearts) 290
McCulloch, Mark 43, 364, 404
MacDonald, Innes 38, 118, 505
MacDonald, Kenny 51, 58, 59, 125, 202, 281, 293, 297, 329, 340
MacDonald, Ramsay (Prime Minister) 44, 85, 132, 162, 338, 445
McEwan (Dumbarton) 294, 425
McFarlane, David 42, 46, 84, 87, 127, 131, 155, 186, 253, 298, 344, 388, 393, 459, 462, 468, 469
McGillivray (referee) 367
McGivern (Kilmarnock) 364
McGrain (Celtic) xiii, 148, 390
McGraw (Morton) 194, 309, 403
McGregor, David v, vii, xv, xvi, xvii, 3, 19, 122, 133, 135, 183, 186, 299, 344, 388, 462, 468, 496, 506, 519
McGrillen (Partick Thistle) 366
McGrory, Frank 321, 380
McGrory (Celtic) 214, 321, 388, 434
McHugh, John 490
McIleavy, Paul 505
McIlravey, Paul 118
McInally, 1900s 179
McInally (Dundee United) 329, 340
McIntosh (Dundee) 56
McIntyre (Dumbarton) 294
McIvor, Arthur 48
McKay, Donald 48, 142, 158, 216, 273, 283, 334, 365, 460, 484
McKenna (Kilmarnock) 364
McKenzie, Derek 97, 100, 200, 280
McKenzie, John 284, 345
McKiddie, Gavin (cricketer) 14
McKillop, Alan 364, 367, 389, 501
McLaren, Malcolm 169, 473
MacLaren (Hearts) 290
McLauchlan, Martin 503
McLaughlan (referee) 326
McLaughlin, Brian 316, 367
McLean, Barry 505
McLean, Davie 3, 21, 29, 31, 61, 85, 96, 111, 124, 131, 162, 188, 214, 233, 256, 288, 301, 306, 318, 332, 339, 360, 413, 418, 427, 429, 434, 436, 463, 464
McLean, Geordie 10, 117, 127, 155, 212, 234, 318, 344, 462, 468, 469
McLean, Stuart 97, 100, 200
McLean (Dundee United) 34, 390
McLeish, Kevin 33, 172, 512
MacLeod (Kilmarnock) 147, 364
McManus, William 379

McManus (Montrose) 331
McMenamin, Colin 342
McMenemy (Celtic) 214, 299, 352, 388
McMillan (Airdrie, Rangers) 264, 273
McMillan (Dumbarton) 294
McMillan (Prime Minister) 64, 142
McMurdo, Eddie 182, 269, 271, 283, 309, 370
McNab (Kilmarnock) 123, 364
McNair (Celtic) 339
McNally, Stephen 268, 512
McNaught (Raith Rovers) 227
McNeill, Brian 509
McNeill, John 219
McNeill (Celtic) 59, 148, 219, 313
McNellis, John 100, 200
McPhail (Airdrie) 136
McPhail (Celtic) 100,, 289
McPhee, Ian xiv, 51, 118, 125, 148, 159, 170, 281, 290, 293, 323, 329, 341, 346, 347, 355, 358, 364, 367, 369, 371, 389, 411, 494, 501, 503, 505
McPherson, 1890s 457
McQuarrie (Albion Rovers) 216
McQueen (Kilmarnock) 364
McStay (Celtic) 258, 268
McTurk (Morton) 403
McVicar, Donald 367, 501
McWalter, Robert 395

M

Mackle, Tommy 141, 149, 219, 252, 283, 284, 345, 383, 487
Maher, Martin 509
Mailer, Angus 26
Mailey, Arthur (cricketer) 429
Malcolm, C. 1880s 460
Malcolm, Gordon 176, 486
Malcolm, Richard 86
Malcolm, Stuart 43, 401
Maley (Celtic) 31, 42, 98, 120, 131, 388, 398, 408, 418

Malin, Gavin 43, 69, 401
Mallan (Celtic) 100
Malloy, James 478
Malpas, Maurice (Motherwell) 104, (Dundee United) 329
Manchester City F.C. 9, 10
Manchester United F.C. 128, 200, 285, 292
Mann, Bobby 367, 393, 501, 503
Mann, 1890s 95, 253, 393, 457
Mann, 1960s 484
Marine Gardens see Leith Athletic
Marinello, Peter (Hibs) 290
Markie, John 484
Marr, Bill 219
Martin, Tommy 36, 60, 68, 106, 128, 139, 166, 178, 187, 199, 264, 372, 375, 449, 476, 477, 478, 503, 509
Mason (Third Lanark) 147, 233
Massie, Gordon 245
Massie, Jock 471, 472
Mathews, Ian 486
Mathie (Celtic) 258
Maxwell, 1890s 457
Maxwell (Rangers) 409
May, John 245, 284
Meadowbank see Leith Athletic
Meadowbank Thistle F.C. 94, 103, 369, 371
Mechan, James 100
Megginson, (Aberdeen) 239
Melville, JH (cricketer) 430
Melvin, 1900s 201, 324, 333
Mennie, Vince 175
Menzies, J 1880s 456
Menzies, William 306, 326, 464
Methil see East Fife
Mid Annadale F.C. 354
Millar (Rangers) 273, 317
Millburn Park see Vale of Leven
Miller, Ian xv, 508, 509
Miller, George 101, 124, 318, 354
Miller, (Celtic) 258, 268
Miller, (St. Mirren) 67

Mill Park *see* Bathgate
Millsop (Celtic) 100
Milne, Jim 158, 249, 284, 313, 345, 379
Milne, Lewis 23, 270
Milne, Steven 118, 505, 507
Mitchell, John 193, 280, 495
Mitchell, 1900s 7, 131, 231, 232, 333, 337
Moffat, Jim 165, 202, 281, 293, 323, 331, 505, 507
Moir, David 86
Monifieth 440
Montrose 44, 133, 324, 437
Montrose F.C. xi, 11, 14, 18, 63, 82, 87, 95, 112, 119, 127, 133, 145, 179, 189, 226, 232, 277, 287, 321, 322, 331, 341, 343, 346, 359, 363, 369, 382, 387, 398, 410, 433, 435, 439
   Links Park 63, 82, 95, 133, 287, 324, 341, 346, 382
Morgan, Alan 367, 501, 503
Morley John (M.P.) 44
Morrice, Jimmy 196, 245, 255, 471
Morris, Rab 51, 59, 119, 268, 281, 290, 293, 329, 364
Morris, Roberto 118, 496, 505, 507
Morrison, 1920s 24, 124, 388
Morton F.C. *see* Greenock Morton
Motherwell F.C. 1, 53, 104, 140, 218, 323, 335, 366, 439
   Fir Park 104, 323
Mowat, David 404
Mowatt, Jimmy 144, 232, 292, 372, 478, 479, 483
Muckersie, Tom 287, 393
Muirhead, Doug 232, 292, 372
Muirhead (Kilmarnock) 54
Muirton Park *see* St Johnstone
Munro, Andy 23, 26
Murphy, 1920s 212
Murphy, Kenny 490
Murray, Gary 51, 103, 293, 324, 331, 364
Murray, Steve 63, 369, 390
Murray 1900s 201, 324

Mutch, Cyril 365
Myles, George 14

N

Nairn, Jimmy 503, 505
Nairn County F.C. 207
Narey, David (Dundee United) 34, 329
Neave, 1890s 137
Neeson (Dumbarton) 294
Neil, Ralph (Secretary) 471
Neilson (Dundee United) 283, 370
Newcastle 425
Newcastle United F.C. 9, 69, 337, 376
Newlands, Doug 219, 252
Newman 61, 176, 200, 219, 237, 291, 294, 381, 388, 395, 462, 468, 484
Newton, Watt 48, 373
Nichol, Dave 143, 173, 307, 491, 504
Nichol, Dyken 161, 181, 266
Nichol, Ralph 368
Niven, George (Rangers) 273
Northern League xiv, 84, 93, 95, 102, 137, 160, 164, 179, 195, 201, 211, 287, 322, 328, 332, 333, 343, 393, 394, 398, 410, 428, 433, 437, 448, 459
North Street 2, 3, 106, 120, 216, 271, 324, 441
Norway 88, 427
Nursery Park 93, 352

O

O'Brien, Tam 41, 270
O'Donnell (Celtic) 388
Ochilview *see* Stenhousemuir
Ogg, Davie 300, 333, 449, 471
Ogilvie, Bill 1930s 85, 465, 467
Ogilvie, Bill "Peerl" 1950s 48, 273, 372, 380, 478, 479, 483
Ogilvie, 1880s 456
Oldham Athletic F.C. 9
Oram (Brechin City) 111
Orchison, Jimmy 133, 301, 465

Ormond, 1880s 456
Orphant (East Fife) 381
Orr, 1900s 93, 131
Osborne, John 306
Ottawa 423
Our Boys Rangers F.C. 404

P

Palmerston Park *see* Queen of the South
Panther (Raith Rovers) 188
Park, John 252
Parkside Park *see* Dykehead
Parlane, Derek (Rangers) xiv, 306, 307
Partick Thistle F.C. xi, 45, 51, 92, 142, 144, 280, 281, 318, 366, 389
   Firhill Park 158, 280, 318
Paterson, Bill 65, 288, 351, 388, 460, 501
Paton, Paul 268
Pattie, 1940s 395
Pattillo (St Johnstone) 260
Pavilion Cinema 285
Payne, Kenny 143, 173, 307, 490, 491, 504
Peacock, Jim 503, 505
Peacock (Celtic) 96, 100
Pearson (Motherwell) 104
Peffermill 269
Peffers Place 413
Penman (Raith Rovers) 227
Pennington (West Bromwich Albion) 214, 339
Perrie, Dave 97
Perth 18, 93, 126, 144, 208, 215, 280, 381, 415, 426
Perth Craigie F.C. 93
Perthshire 14, 86, 160
Peterhead F.C. 26
Peter Reid Rock 13, 254
Peters, Josh 23, 270
Petrie, "Jummer" 62, 134, 161, 288, 299, 305, 324, 337, 352, 460
Petrie, Stewart 28, 170, 268
Pettigrew (Hearts) 290
Philip, Dave 284, 345, 487
Phillips (referee) 187, 334
Piggot, D 1880s 459
Pittodrie *see* Aberdeen F.C.
Poors House 2, 358
Porter, Stewart 353, 369
Potter, Angus (poet) 27
Potter, David 496
Potter, George 176, 219, 283, 486
Potter, George (Chairman) iii, iv, vii, 4, 27, 176, 219, 283, 394, 486, 496
Premier League 20, 28, 33, 34, 37, 55, 67, 69, 104, 143, 218, 258, 281, 290, 297, 323, 331, 341, 364, 389
Preston, George 127, 315, 344, 465, 467, 469
Prestonfield *see* Linlithgow Rose
Prophet, 1910s 14, 214, 434, 460
Pryde, Ian 28
"Purkie" *see* George Langlands

Q

Queen of the South F.C. xi, 48, 113, 143, 153, 154, 173, 176, 184, 185, 203, 222, 293, 356, 435
   Palmerston Park 48, 153, 176, 222
Queen's Park F.C. xi, 41, 52, 84, 97, 139, 167, 187, 196, 204, 267, 287, 308, 319, 320, 321, 336, 351, 365, 373, 396, 424
Queen's Park Strollers F.C. 196
Quinn (Celtic) 131, 214, 299, 339, 352

R

Rae, Alec xv,, 119, 135, 143, 173, 185, 193, 290, 307, 353, 491, 493, 494, 500, 504
Raeburn (Raith Rovers) 19

Raith Rovers F.C. 19, 45, 188, 199, 215, 227, 308, 354, 362, 370, 379, 397
Ramsay, Davie 155, 215, 244, 388, 465
Rangers F.C. xi, xiii, xiv, 1, 18, 20, 34, 36, 43, 54, 59, 64, 68, 81, 99, 103, 104, 124, 128, 135, 136, 141, 146, 147, 158, 167, 169, 171, 172, 173, 175, 182, 184, 185, 207, 214, 216, 220, 227, 232, 239, 249, 258, 264, 272, 273, 279, 284, 285, 287, 288, 289, 292, 293, 294, 297, 302, 304, 305, 306, 307, 319, 344, 346, 353, 357, 364, 365, 375, 382, 383, 396, 404, 407, 409, 413, 416, 419, 425, 436, 439, 448, 480
   Ibrox 36, 85, 104, 127, 146, 167, 200, 297, 304, 343, 360, 432, 436, 448
Rankin, Brian 88, 143, 173, 307, 491, 494
Rattray, Alan xiii, 45, 47, 55, 118, 171, 505, 507, 509
Raydale Park *see* Gretna
Recreation Park *see* Alloa Athletic
Redford (Rangers) 329
Reid, Bruce 182, 216, 249, 294, 316
Reid, Peter (confectioner) xiii, 13, 253
Renton F.C. 17
Ring (Clyde) 29, 157, 220, 289, 372
Riordan (Edinburgh City) 325
Ritchie, Donald 503, 509
Ritchie, Norrie 176, 486
Ritchie, Mark 490
Ritchie 1900s 324, 313 176, 486, 490, 503, 509, 512
Robb, Ronnie 34, 128
Robbie, Chick 54, 196, 267, 471, 472
Roberts, Paul 503
Robertson, Archie 158, 216, 316
Robertson, Bobby 131
Robertson, Jim 3, 496
Robson (Aberdeen) 118
Rodger, Ian xiii, 54, 57, 105, 196, 201, 255, 273, 282, 471, 472, 473, 479, 483

Roger, 1890s 324
Rollo (Celtic) 100
Ross County F.C. 38, 90, 199, 203, 359, 367, 383
   Victoria Park 38, 209, 367
Rough, Andy 106, 178, 477
Russell, Jimmy 109, 142, 479, 483
Russell, Johnny 512
Rutherford, Gordon 197

S

Salutation Hotel 425, 432
Samson, Bob 117, 456, 459
Scotland iv, xiv, 10, 14, 22, 28, 29, 34, 36, 43, 50, 52, 64, 68, 83, 85, 88, 89, 99, 111, 120, 123, 127, 128, 130, 136, 139, 158, 178, 193, 198, 200, 202, 204, 206, 209, 211, 213, 218, 219, 236, 239, 248, 250, 253, 266, 267, 282, 285, 288, 290, 293, 301, 306, 315, 316, 319, 336, 339, 343, 347, 351, 352, 354, 362, 365, 372, 382, 387, 389, 397, 398, 406, 407, 415, 416, 418, 423, 425, 429, 432, 433, 440, 441, 444, 446, 448, 460, 463
Scott, Ashy 216, 294, 316
Scott, Gordon 51, 59, 67, 281, 323, 364
Scott, Ronnie 358
Scott, 1910s 7, 134, 161, 181, 231, 299
Scottish Alliance League 12, 318
Scottish Brewers Trophy 34
Scottish Cup xiv, 1, 8, 22, 50, 53, 67, 81, 84, 99, 118, 119, 124, 129, 130, 131, 136, 137, 138, 139, 140, 147, 157, 165, 169, 171, 175, 199, 200, 202, 203, 204, 206, 207, 209, 210, 216, 218, 231, 233, 239, 240, 242, 249, 250, 256, 257, 258, 265, 266, 267, 268, 269, 271, 272, 273, 278, 280, 281, 282, 283, 284, 287, 288, 289, 290, 292, 293, 294, 296, 297, 304, 305, 309, 318, 319, 323, 328, 329, 333,

335, 336, 340, 344, 346, 353, 354, 357, 359, 360, 368, 369, 372, 373, 375, 377, 382, 383, 387, 390, 395, 403, 409, 415, 435, 436, 447, 460, 464, 467, 480
Scottish Football Association (SFA) 18, 21, 50, 120, 269, 305, 415, 424, 446
Scottish Football League 20, 408
Scottish League 1, 11, 18, 23, 36, 38, 41, 43, 47, 53, 55, 56, 59, 60, 64, 65, 67, 68, 83, 86, 90, 100, 101, 102, 103, 104, 108, 109, 110, 112, 118, 119, 124, 128, 132, 135, 136, 138, 139, 140, 141, 142, 143, 144, 146, 147, 158, 165, 173, 175, 199, 202, 203, 214, 222, 227, 239, 245, 249, 256, 260, 267, 272, 280, 282, 287, 288, 289, 292, 301, 306, 307, 309, 313, 318, 325, 353, 358, 360, 364, 367, 369, 372, 375, 381, 392, 395, 398, 399, 402, 408, 415, 428, 435, 436, 437, 439, 445
Scottish League Cup 41, 43, 47, 53, 59, 60, 64, 67, 68, 83, 100, 103, 104, 109, 118, 119, 136, 140, 141, 142, 143, 144, 146, 147, 173, 214, 227, 239, 249, 272, 289, 292, 307, 309
Scottish Premier League 20, 218, 341
Scottish Qualifying Cup 86, 91, 107, 137, 161, 248, 415
Scrymgeour, David 87, 102, 132, 450
Second Division xiv, xvi, 22, 24, 47, 48, 52, 53, 55, 58, 60, 61, 82, 101, 104, 110, 119, 122, 123, 128, 132, 135, 138, 139, 142, 148, 185, 204, 207, 210, 214, 220, 270, 273, 291, 306, 309, 315, 317, 318, 334, 341, 345, 355, 358, 365, 366, 379, 382, 383, 392, 397, 398, 399, 403, 404, 408, 428, 435, 439, 514
Second Division Trophy xiv, 355
Sellars, Barry 47, 50, 206, 402, 404, 507, 509

Semple (Celtic) 131
Shand, 1900s 324, 333
Shaw, George xv, 38, 45, 471, 509, 511
Shaw, John 190, 474
Shaw, 1940s 196, 472
Shaw (Celtic) 162, 299
Shawfield see Clyde
Shearer (Hamilton) 68, 273
Sheffield 362
Sheffield United F.C. 28
    Bramall Lane 28
Sheffield Wednesday F.C. 214, 339, 418
Shepherd, George 30, 211, 253, 287, 298, 393, 459, 460, 464, 512
Shield (Hearts) 290
Shields, Paul 47, 104, 509
Shielfield Park see Berwick Rangers
Shirra (Stenhousemuir) 213
Shotts F.C. 266
"Shup" see George Shepherd
Shyberry Excelsior Stadium see Airdrie United
Sime, John 284
Simpson, George (musician) 54
Simpson (Rangers) 292
Skene, 1910s 352
Smart, Allan 85, 101, 124, 132, 138, 237, 306, 465, 466, 467, 496
Smeaton, Robert 395
Smith, Gordon xiii, 114, 143, 504
Smith, John 308, 336
Smith, Sam xiii, 3, 15, 221, 351, 358, 407, 49
Soccer Star 141
Solway Star F.C. 354
Somers, A. 1920 464
Somerset Park see Ayr United
Somme, Battle of 7, 70
Soutar, Andrew "Skip" 29, 181, 224, 284, 465, 467, 471
Soutar, Doug 269, 283
Southern League of England 19

Spartans F. C. 202
Spence, Andrew 464
Spiders 187, 267, 308
Spink, Jimmy 490
Sporting Post, The 85
Stair Park *see* Stranraer
Stanton, Pat (Hibs) 265
Stark (Celtic) 59
Station Hotel 18, 208, 410
Station Park *see* Forfar Athletic
St Bernard's F.C. 11, 18, 65 112, 138, 368
  Logie Green 138
Steel (Clyde) 316
Steele, 1940's 395
Steele Park *see* Forfar Athletic
Steen, Ian 48, 273, 292, 478, 479, 483
Stein, Jay , 63, 110, 148, 176, 216, 219, 284, 335, 373, 390, 413
Stein, Jock 47
Stenhousemuir xi, 1, 52, 57, 106, 125, 129, 174, 177, 202, 213, 236, 286, 313, 337, 342, 347, 376, 396, 452, 463
  Ochilview 177, 337, 342, 347
Stevenson, John 273, 473
Stewart, Ian 106, 129, 176,178, 232, 260, 264, 284, 300, 372, 476, 477, 478,
Stewart, Willie 184, 393, 504
Stirling Albion F.C. xi, 11, 18, 144, 158, 192, 224, 316, 370, 439
  Annfield 144, 244
  Forthbank 224
Stirlingshire 11, 18, 112, 125, 162, 165, 170, 172, 193, 221, 252, 278, 313, 325, 334, 344, 359, 369, 383, 439
St John's 450
St Johnstone F.C. xiii, 11, 18, 68, 126, 259, 260, 280, 281, 328, 381, 398, 415, 433
  Muirton Park 126, 260, 280, 381
St Mirren F.C. 1, 19, 44, 50, 67, 86, 119, 202, 214, 282, 319, 389, 415
  Love Street 50, 67
Stockbridge, Edinburgh 138, 368

Stormonth, 1880s 456, 457, 459
Strachan (Morton) 309
Strachan (committee member) 471
Stranraer xi, xiv, 45, 80, 119, 136, 139, 149, 217, 345, 358, 359, 439
  Stair Park 149
Strathmore, Earl of 3, 32, 61, 123, 233, 414
Strathmore Cricket 14, 25, 425, 429, 430, 450
Struth, Bill (Rangers) 416
Sturrock, Willie 133, 469
Sturrock, Paul (Dundee United) 329
Sunday Post, The 97, 101, 138, 326, 351
Sunderland F.C. 130, 337, 448
Sunter, Charlie 85, 111, 162, 466,
Sunter, James 105, 196, 471, 472, 473
Forfar Supporters Club 412
Swankie, Gavin 23, 43, 55, 220, 242, 401
Sweeney, David 158, 216, 294, 316

T

Tannadice Park *see* Dundee United
Taylor, Alec 505
Taylor, David 50, 446
Taylor, James (Chairman) 399
Taylor, Scott 507,509
Telfer (Rangers) 232
Telford, Harry 273
Telford Street *see* Inverness Caledonian Thistle
Temperance Abstainers 81
Templeman, Chris 43, 69, 401, 404
Templeton (Scotland) 339
Third Division 38, 61, 98, 108, 159, 266, 291, 326, 359, 367, 408
Third Lanark F.C. 147, 158, 214, 256, 278, 344
Thom, 1890s 95
Thoms, Jackie 147

Thomson, Fred 370
Thomson, "Napper" 427
Thomson, Peter 264
Thomson, Sandy 342
Thomson, W. 1890s 253, 343, 459
Thomson, (Celtic) 85, 406
Thorpe, Margaret 128
Tod, Andy 172, 404, 512
Tosh, Paul 47, 50, 104, 206, 397, 507, 509
Travis, Michael 69, 242, 401
Trialist, 131, 476
Troup, Alec "Troupie" vii, xiii, xiv, 3, 29, 44, 56, 62, 86, 111, 124, 134, 181, 231, 235, 236, 299, 332, 337, 362, 363, 378, 391, 392, 450
Tulloch, Stephen 404, 512
Tully (Celtic) 96, 100
Turner (Morton) 194, 403
Tynecastle *see* Heart of Midlothian
Tyneside 9, 376

U

UEFA 50, 329, 397, 446
Ure (Dundee) 35, 37, 313
Uruguay 441

V

Vale of Atholl F.C. 160
Vale of Leithen F.C. 209
Vale of Leven F.C. 124
  Millburn Park 124
Vale of Lunan F.C. 17
Vannart, Norrie 307, 504
Vella, Simon 509
Verdun 70
Vernon (Aberdeen) 239
Victoria Park *see* Ross County
Victoria United F.C. 322
Victory International 200

W

Waddell, Harry 52, 284
Walker, Dean 507
Walker, James 176, 486
Walker, John 134, 299, 337, 339, 418
Wallace (Hearts) 249
Walsh (Celtic) 96, 100
Wann, Willie 215, 388
Ward, Kenny 59, 329, 364, 389
Ward, Tommy 272
Watson, Paul 404
Watt, Hamish 78
Watt, Neil 94, 119, 494
Wattie, John 133
Wdowczyk, (Celtic) 258, 268
Webster, Gordon (Chairman) xv, 135, 496, 498
Weir, Donald 99, 250, 292, 372, 478
Weir, John 51, 347
Wembley 22, 29, 36, 37, 58, 59, 364, 372, 376
West Bromwich Albion F.C. 214, 441
Westerlands A.F.C. 446
Wharton, Tom "Tiny" (referee) 78
White, Sandy 221
Whitelaw, 1930s 224
Whitton, 1900s 179
Whyte, Gary 258, 268, 490
Wick Academy F.C. 242
Williams, David 507, 509
Willoughby (Rangers) 128
Wilson, Andy 256, 464, 466
Wilson, Neil xv, 502
Wilson, Willie 2, 126, 358
Wilson, 1940s 196
Wilson (Rangers) 272
Wilson (Scotland) 339
Wimbury, Michael 53, 60
Winter, Gordon 258, 268, 332, 512
Wishaw 187, 198, 335
Wi Wan Eence 189, 379
Wood, Sandy 512

World Cup 37, 45, 52, 88, 219, 387, 390, 413, 425, 441, 444
Wotherspoon, Jimmy 54, 97, 196, 351, 471, 472, 473
Wrexham 22
Wyles, Ian 122, 129, 284, 345, 486, 487
Wylie, 1910s 7

Y

Yardley, Mark 507
Yeaman (referee) 21
Young, Derek 41, 69, 401
Young, Jake 129, 284, 309, 345, 356, 486
Young, Jim 122, 129, 271, 345, 382, 487
Young, Neil 68, 473
Young (Celtic) 299
Young (Hearts) 375

www.ingramcontent.com/pod-product-compliance
Lightning Source LLC
Chambersburg PA
CBHW052040220426
43663CB00012B/2382